FAR EASTERN WAR

1937–1941

WORLD PEACE FOUNDATION

40 Mt. Vernon Street, Boston, Massachusetts

Founded in 1910

The World Peace Foundation is a non-profit organization which was founded in 1910 by Edwin Ginn, the educational publisher, for the purpose of promoting peace, justice and good-will among nations. For many years the Foundation has sought to increase public understanding of international problems by an objective presentation of the facts of international relations. This purpose is accomplished principally through its publications and by the maintenance of a Reference Service which furnishes on request information on current international problems. Recently increased attention has been focused on American foreign relations by study groups organized for the consideration of actual problems of policy.

FAR EASTERN WAR

1937–1941

BY

HARORD S. QUIGLEY

Professor of Political Science
University of Minnesota

WORLD PEACE FOUNDATION
BOSTON
1942

Woodcut by Yeh-fu of the China Institute in America on jacket and paper cover used with the permission of *FREE WORLD, INC.*, New York City.

PRINTED IN THE UNITED STATES OF AMERICA

TO MY WIFE

PREFACE

FAR EASTERN WAR begins with Lukouchiao and ends with Pearl Harbor. It essays to examine the circumstances bearing upon the outbreak of a conflict for which historians will find a title more impressive than "Incident," to provide a concise account of hostilities, to describe political and economic repercussions in China, Japan and Western states, and to analyze the policies and trace the diplomatic, economic and strategic maneuvers of the major powers in relation to the war and to Japan's program for a "New Order" in Eastern Asia and Oceania. I appreciate that no study of war that is written *inter arma* may claim to be definitive, but I have sought to deal objectively with available materials.

Without involving others in responsibility for what appears in the following pages, I feel constrained to express my obligations to the several scholarly volumes published by the Institute of Pacific Relations in its valuable Inquiry Series. I have relied also upon the Institute's quarterly *Pacific Affairs* and its bi-weekly *Far Eastern Survey*. The intelligent and timely *Reports* of the Foreign Policy Association have been similarly helpful. For the Chinese point of view Dr. Shuhsi Hsü's *Political and Economic Studies* may be recommended. For Japanese interpretations of events *Contemporary Japan* (Tokyo) is authoritative. The American-edited *China Weekly Review* and the (until recently) British-edited *Japan Weekly Chronicle* have furnished factual and editorial materials of considerable value. No treatment of contemporary affairs would be possible without the unrivalled news coverage of the *New York Times*. Documents have been drawn from several sources but principally from the comprehensive *Documents on American Foreign Relations* edited by Dr. S. Shepard Jones and Denys P. Myers, and published by the World Peace Foundation. Footnotes acknowledge debts owed to other sources too numerous to be mentioned here, but my obligations to friends in governmental and academic life who have given generously of their time and thought to my advantage are beyond acknowledgment.

To Dr. S. Shepard Jones, Director of the World Peace Foundation, to Mr. Denys P. Myers, Research Director and to Miss Marie J. Carroll, Chief of the Reference Service, I am especially indebted for courteous editorial assistance and scholarly suggestions for improvement of the text. The editorial staff of the Foundation has provided the index and maps.

HAROLD S. QUIGLEY

Minneapolis, Minnesota
Christmas, 1941

CONTENTS

PREFACE vii

CHAPTER

I. Progress and Poverty in China 1

II. Militarism and Industrialism in Japan . . . 17

III. China's International Position 32

IV. Major Issues in Controversy 51

V. The Renewal of War 65

VI. "Free China" Carries On 85

VII. The "New Order" in Occupied China 114

VIII. Foreign Residential Areas in Jeopardy . . . 134

IX. The "New National Structure" in Japan . . 149

X. Japan and the Axis 166

XI. "Co-Prosperity in Greater East Asia" . . . 181

XII. American Leadership in Resistance 194

XIII. Britain's Secondary Role 228

XIV. Soviet Russia's Dilemma 252

XV. United Front in the Pacific 263

EPILOG 277

APPENDICES

I. Statement by Premier Konoye, December 22, 1938 283

II. Statement by General Chiang K'ai-shek, December 26, 1938 285

III. The Three-Power Pact between Germany, Italy and Japan, signed at Berlin, September 27, 1940 294

IV. Neutrality Pact between Japan and the Union of Soviet Socialist Republics, signed at Moscow, April 13, 1941 296
Frontier Declaration on "Manchoukuo" and on the Mongolian People's Republic . . . 297

V. Summary of Past Policy of the United States in the Pacific. Message of the President to the Congress, December 15, 1941 (Excerpt) . 298

VI. Japanese Action respecting Strategic Islands
1. Paracels Islands—Statement of the Foreign Office Spokesman regarding the Question of French Occupation of Sisha Islands, July 7, 1938 306
2. Hainan Island
a. The Foreign Office Spokesman's Statement regarding the Occupation of Hainan Island, February 10, 1939 306
b. Statement of the Foreign Office regarding the Occupation of Hainan Island, February 13, 1939 308
3. Spratley Islands
a. The Foreign Office's Statement concerning the Administrative Jurisdiction over Shinnan Gunto (Spratley Islands), March 31, 1939 . . . 308
b. The Foreign Office Spokesman's Statement on the French Protest regarding the Same, April 7, 1939 . . 309

VII. Japanese-Netherlands Arbitration Treaty—Statement of the Japanese Foreign Office Spokesman, February 12, 1940 310

VIII. Protocol between Japan and France regarding the Joint Defense of French Indo-China, Vichy, July 29, 1941 311

IX. Final Documents of the Japanese-United States Negotiations
1. United States Note to Japan, November 26, 1941, handed by the Secretary of State (Hull) to the Japanese Ambassador (Nomura) 312

2. Memorandum of the Japanese Government, presented by the Japanese Ambassador (Nomura) to the Secretary of State (Hull), 2:20 p.m., E.S.T., December 7, 1941 . . 317

X. ACTION TAKEN BY THE LEAGUE OF NATIONS

1. Resolution of the Assembly of the League of Nations adopted October 6, 1937 . . 325
2. Resolution of the Council of the League of Nations adopted February 2, 1938 . . 326
3. Resolution of the Council of the League of Nations adopted May 14, 1938 . . . 326
4. Invitation from the President of the Council of the League of Nations to the Government of Japan, September 19, 1938 . . 327
5. Reply Telegram, dated September 22, 1938, from the Japanese Government to the Secretary General of the League of Nations (Avenol) 328
6. Statement of the Japanese Foreign Office Spokesman concerning The Application of Article 16 of the League of Nations Covenant, October 3, 1938 328
7. Resolution of the Council of the League of Nations adopted January 20, 1939 . . 329

XI. STATEMENT OF THE JAPANESE GOVERNMENT REGARDING THE CHINESE MARITIME CUSTOMS QUESTION, MAY 3, 1938 331

BIBLIOGRAPHY 333

INDEX 343

MAPS

PACIFIC AREA

EASTERN ASIA AND NEIGHBORING ISLANDS

I

PROGRESS AND POVERTY IN CHINA

NATIONAL policies are born in the minds of men. But men are controlled by their environments, and their policies are prompted and conditioned by circumstances. The precise relationship between economic and political conditions prevailing within countries and the development of controversy and conflict between them is a problem too difficult for solution. All that may be hoped for is that out of a survey of prewar conditions some generally acceptable conclusions may be drawn as to the causes of the breakdown of peace. Amid controversy contemporary with war no one but a seer would pretend to feel assurance even on this restricted ground. In this chapter and the next an attempt will be made to describe briefly the prewar situation of the governments, of the masses of the people, and of industry and foreign trade, in China and Japan.

National policies are, however, in part determined by external influences. The relationship existing between two states is a matter of importance to other states, particularly when the states are neighbors and one of the neighbors is politically ill-organized and militarily weak. Conversely, the relationship between the weaker state and third states is bound to be of primary concern to the stronger neighbor. Opinions will differ upon the relative importance of internal and external factors in the march of events toward war. But it will be agreed that both sets of circumstances play a part. To restate briefly the international background of the Far Eastern war is the task of the third chapter.

Essential also to a survey of the war is an examination of issues as they are put forward by the contending parties. Chapter four undertakes to describe the issues as they are seen in China and in Japan. Against the background of available facts it should be possible for the conscientious reader to reach his own conclusions upon Japan's theses in justification and China's rebuttal. Let it be granted that such conclusions may have to be revised in the fuller light of other facts. It is the author's conviction that an objective judgment now is unlikely to undergo fundamental modification. But whether this be true or not we who live today are concerned in a more practical sense than any who come after us can be to find the meanings of great events.

China in Revolution

The most obvious fact is often the least considered. That China, after 2200 years of absolute monarchy, has been, since the Revolution of 1911–12 which overthrew the Manchu dynasty, attempting to adapt itself to republican principles, is the dominating fact in contemporary Chinese politics. It explains not only the recurrent civil warfare but also, to a large degree, the international rivalry which added an external stimulus to Chinese nationalism. It accounts, on the one hand, for the independence movement and, on the other, for the failure of China to equip itself militarily and in other ways for the struggle against Japan. Economic and social revolution has, inevitably, accompanied political revolution. In circumstances which might be likened to those of a sick Gulliver in a death grapple with a vigorous and armored Lilliputian, China's continued existence is proof of that innate strength which has rescued it from past periods of disturbance.

For fifteen years, from 1912 to 1927, the Chinese liberals tried to establish a democratic political order similar to the representative systems of Europe and the United States. In this effort they were defeated by the politico-militarist provincial governors who disrupted the Republic and corrupted a majority of the original supporters of the revolution. Ragged provincial armies fought one another for an opportunity to control local government and to pillage the treasuries. Cliques of regional satraps rose to power, one after another, at Peking. The country appeared to be doomed to a breakup into a number of weak and contending states.

An end to this trend was brought about by the new national revolution headed by Chiang K'ai-shek. Revived and reorganized in 1924 at Canton, the National Party or Kuomintang dropped its earlier pursuit of parliamentarism and took the political system of the Soviet Union as its model. With the invaluable aid of Russian advisers, notable among them Michael Borodin and General Galens (Blücher), a new economic program was advanced to win popular support and a new army was trained and inspired with zeal to rid the country of the warlords. Beginning a campaign in 1926, the combined armies of propagandists of reform and Nationalist troops won their way rapidly to the Yangtze River. Checked there and in Shantung for a year, they moved northward again in 1928 and took Peking, which the Kuomintang renamed Peiping to signalize the transfer of the national capital to Nanking. Those of the *tuchün* (provincial military leaders) who refused to accommodate themselves to the new regime were forced into retirement in all but a few far western provinces. The National Government was established at Nanking.[1]

China was not unified but it was closer to unity than it had been since 1916. The Government was controlled by the Kuomintang, which was supported by a strong, partially modernized army led by a determined, shrewd and con-

[1] Holcombe, Arthur N., *The Chinese Revolution,* Cambridge, Mass., 1930; MacNair, Harley F., *China in Revolution,* Chicago, 1931.

medicine rather than in liberal arts. This was essential, since the latter had developed disproportionately. Scarcity of funds kept educational appropriations to a pitifully low figure.[7] On the social side, however, the Government's attitude, if the "New Life Movement" is a criterion, was conservative and superficial. This movement neglected popular education, substituting instruction in the classical virtues: etiquette, justice, integrity, and conscientiousness.[8] The people were to "work harder and spend less"—as if that were possible for the Chinese masses. Confucianism, which recognizes the authority of the head of the family, a useful principle in a time of social revolt, was dusted off and included in the ideology of the "New Life." General Chiang K'ai-shek, who inaugurated this program, was the author of the complementary "People's Economic Reconstruction Movement," designed to increase production. Conscription of labor for public works was permitted by this "People's" movement.[9] In fairness it must be said that with preparation for war the pressing task, reversion to these ideas was a natural reaction from the educational policies of the earlier years of the Republic.[10]

The orientation of the National Government toward the business world is indicated by the measures above described. In 1927 it had broken with its Russian advisers and expelled the Chinese Communists from the Kuomintang. What this meant to the peasants and urban laborers is discussed below. It may be stated here that the alliance between the Kuomin-

[7] "Chinese Higher Education," *China Institute Bulletin*, October 1939 (New York).

[8] Taylor, George E., "The Reconstruction Movement in China," *Problems of the Pacific*, New York, 1936, p. 397–8.

[9] *Ibid.*, 403–5.

[10] For an extremely critical examination of foreign, particularly American, influence upon Chinese education, see *The Reorganization of Education in China*, League of Nations' Institute of Intellectual Cooperation (Paris, 1932). This report of a mission of European scholars is discussed by Stephen Duggan, Bulletin No. 1, 14th Series, Institute of International Education, January 9, 1933; also by William F. Russell, *Teachers College Record*, March 1933.

tang and the Third International was a marriage of convenience, not a meeting of minds. When it became apparent to the conservatives who controlled the former that they could not win the financial support of the great Chinese bankers, protected as the latter were in the foreign concessions, unless they repudiated the Russian alliance, they quickly decided upon a return to bourgeois economic doctrines, though retaining the Soviet type of government.

Chinese Industry and Commerce

Public ownership and management of industrial and business enterprises were alien to Chinese political tradition. Scarcity of national revenues made departure from tradition doubly difficult. Necessity, however, induced the Government to plan the establishment of heavy industries and to make a start upon the execution of the plan. Private enterprise was to receive public support for new undertakings, while going concerns, such as cotton factories and silk filatures, were aided by higher tariffs and reduced taxes, and by scientific investigation to improve cultivation, processing, and testing.[11]

Chinese industry has developed mainly through private initiative and in the face of severe competition from foreign factories in the port cities. The latter have been favored by freedom from Chinese taxation under extraterritoriality, by greater experience in joint stock financing and by connections with foreign concerns with access to large amounts of capital. Japanese spinning and weaving mills in the textile industry in China outdistanced Chinese so rapidly after 1919 that the industry appeared likely to be absorbed by the Japanese.[12] Foreign activities were important also in tobacco

[11] Hubbard, G. E., *Eastern Industrialization and Its Effect on the West,* London, 1935, p. 198–205.

[12] *Chinese Year Book, 1935–36,* Shanghai, p. 1115.

processing and the manufacture of rugs. Smaller factories, numbering more than 2000 in 1931, were Chinese, producing silk, woolen and knitted articles, flour, leather goods, paper, matches, brick, tile, etc.

Industry in China is advantaged by the quantity and variety of raw materials locally available. Coal, iron, tin, antimony, tungsten, and manganese exist in amounts relatively large in proportion to industrial development. Cotton, wool, silk, tobacco, vegetable oils, and other products supplement the minerals.[13] It is now recognized, however, that China's own resources are not sufficient for the development of a great industrial state.

Between 1919 and 1929 China's foreign trade increased steadily, more than doubling during the decade.[14] But the depression in Europe and America reversed the favorable trend. After the prosperous year 1931 trade declined rapidly. From an index number of 106.27% (of 1930) in 1931, the total foreign trade fell to 43.53% in 1935.[15] (These figures in part reflect the loss of the Manchurian provinces.) In 1936 it rose slightly, to 47.96%.[16] Silver was exported in ever-increasing amounts to redress the balance of payments. The only favorable feature of the period was a considerable decline in import surpluses.

The Distress of the Chinese Peasantry

The farmers of China are suffering from a landlordism which has no parallel outside of Asia. Their history is a series of cycles each of which "begins with a revolt against intolerable rents and taxes, followed by a period of adjustment that leads into a new depression caused by overpopulation,

[13] Cressey, George B., *China's Geographic Foundations,* New York, 1934.
[14] *China Year Book, 1931,* p. 270.
[15] *Chinese Year Book, 1935–36,* cited, p. 1076.
[16] *Ibid., 1937,* p. 648.

and thence again to revolt."[17] What is called communism today in China is, for the rural masses, the latest in a long series of peasant revolts. Land has been and is today a near-monopoly of the landlord-banker-merchant class. This class controls the local government and includes the district and village officials. It determines the amount and incidence of rents and taxes, the great bulk of which are paid by the farmers. Within the last decade these burdens have been greatly increased to obtain funds and workers for the building of new roads essential for military transport. The farmers have been forced deeply into debt, bankruptcy, and the loss of their lands.[18]

No people is more tenacious of its place on the soil than the Chinese. It follows that no people is less susceptible to communism than they. The Chinese are accustomed to communal landholding but this system is a form of private property, an integral element of the family or clan order of life. The Chinese peasants, like the Russians, welcomed the opportunity afforded them by the civil war of 1926–27, between the Nationalist armies and those of their oppressors, the *tuchün,* to destroy title deeds and distribute the land. But this treatment of their superiors was an act of desperation induced by extreme poverty, famine, and unemployment. An authoritative Chinese student of the Chinese farm problem recently wrote: [19]

> The peasants who constitute the bulk of the 450,000,000 people of China are now undergoing a life and death struggle. The choice for them is either continued collapse of their economy or a complete alteration of the usury-merchant-landlord system.

[17] Quigley, Harold S., "Free China," *International Conciliation,* No. 359 (April 1940), New York, p. 151; reprinted in part as Chapter VI, below.

[18] Chen, Han-seng, *Landlord and Peasant in China,* New York, 1936, p. viii–x.

[19] Wu, Leonard T. K., "Merchant Capital and Usury Capital in Rural China," *Far Eastern Survey,* March 25, 1936, p. 68.

Paradoxical is the combination of a landless peasantry and peasantless lands. Landowning farmers are being forced by bankruptcy to abandon their lands and to swell the percentage of tenants and farm-laborers. Idle land is increasing for lack of cultivators and of proper fertilization and reclamation. The size of peasant-owned farms is decreasing. These changes spell the decline of production and consequent higher costs of food grains. Wu states that only 22% of the 1,500,000 square *li* (a *li* is one-third of a mile) of cultivable land in China was under cultivation in 1936.[20]

The desperate situation of the great mass of China's population was aggravated by the world depression. A deep decline in the prices of agricultural products was one feature of the depression. Another was the appreciation of silver, caused principally by the silver purchasing policy of the United States, which drained the Chinese rural areas of their medium of exchange, already heavily concentrated in the port cities. A third factor was the raising of the embargo on the export of rice and wheat, in 1933, which enabled foreign purchasers, principally the Japanese, to reap the advantages of low prices on Chinese products.[21]

It is apparent that the Chinese peasants had little reason to regard the National Government as more concerned than its predecessors with their welfare. Madam Sun Yat-sen criticized the party's inconsistency of program and action in 1927: [22]

> . . . today the lot of the Chinese peasant is even more wretched than in those days when Dr. Sun was driven by his great sense of human wrongs into a life of revolution. And today men who pro-

[20] Wu, Leonard T. K., "Rural Bankruptcy in China," *Far Eastern Survey*, October 8, 1936, p. 212. Cressey accepts estimates of nearly 4,000,000 square *li* for cultivable land and of nearly 3,000,000 square *li* as under cultivation in average years (cited, p. 96).

[21] *Far Eastern Survey*, November 18, 1936, p. 249.

[22] Woo, T. C., *The Kuomintang and the Future of the Chinese Revolution*, London, 1928, p. 271–2.

fess to follow his banner talk of classes and think in terms of a revolution that would virtually disregard the sufferings of those millions of poverty-stricken peasants of China.

Worse rather than better conditions followed Madam Sun's repudiation of the National Party. As the forces of General Chiang K'ai-shek gradually drove the Communist armies westward, the dispossessed landlords were restored to their lands. Many thousands of peasants were killed in anti-revolutionary pogroms, and greater numbers were forced to flee from their lands.[23] Military requisitions and *corvées* (unpaid labor) reduced the incomes of the survivors. While Japanese armies occupied Manchuria and Hopei the Chinese peasantry was sinking to lower depths of distress and resentment.[24]

Proletarianism in China

The Chinese urban laborer, who does the work of both men and animals, is normally as depressed as the peasant. The lowest class of these workers, the coolies, live as precariously as the poorest of the farm population. Labor unions appeared in China after the World War, 1914–18, but it was not until 1924, when the Kuomintang admitted the Chinese Communist Party to its fold, that the labor movement began to show effectiveness. In 1927 there were more than 3,000,000 members in Chinese unions.[25] At that date the rising Nationalist movement was outwardly cordial to labor organizations, which aided it against the *tuchün*.[26] This attitude gave way to opposition and finally to intolerance when General Chiang K'ai-shek broke with the Communists. The radical element among the workers was crushed

[23] Wu, Leonard T. K., "Rural Bankruptcy in China," cited, p. 210.

[24] Isaacs, Harold, *The Tragedy of the Chinese Revolution,* London, 1938.

[25] Condliffe, J. B., *China Today: Economic,* Boston, World Peace Foundation, 1932, p. 109.

[26] Malraux, André, *Man's Fate,* New York, 1934.

and the whole labor movement was greatly weakened. Unions remained, however, and there were many strikes, with some resulting improvement in wages and conditions of work.[27]

The year 1936 and the first half of 1937 were comparatively prosperous periods. Factories worked double shifts, new factories were opened, unemployment disappeared among skilled workers. Conditions improved in handicraft industries.[28] On the whole, however, the depressed situation of labor, an existence of incredible poverty, continued.

It was natural under prevailing conditions that a Communist movement should develop in China. In 1920 two professors at Peking National University, Ch'en Tu-Hsiu and Li Ta-chao, organized a society for the study of Marxism. In the following year the Chinese Communist Party was inaugurated. In 1923 Dr. Sun Yat-sen and Alexander Joffe, a Bolshevik envoy, held a conversation of which the upshot was the appearance at Canton of Michael Borodin, General Galens, and other Bolshevik collaborators with the revived Nationalist movement. It was their influence which opened the Kuomintang to the Communists. From a society of intellectuals the party expanded rapidly after 1924, but its principal strength lay in the labor and peasant unions affiliated with it. After the repudiation of the Communist alliance by the Kuomintang in 1927, the movement wavered for two years but took on new life in the south-central rural areas controlled by the Communist-led armies of Mao Tse-tung, Chu Teh, and P'eng Teh-huai.[29] The struggle of these

[27] Hubbard, G. E., cited, p. 205–11; Lowe, Chuan-Hua, *Facing Labor Issues in China,* Shanghai, 1934.

[28] *China Year Book, 1938,* p. 322; *1939,* p. 484.

[29] Snow, Edgar, *Red Star Over China,* New York, 1938. This is a remarkable first-hand study, as interesting as *Man's Fate* and more understandable. T. A. Bisson's "The Communist Movement in China," *Foreign Policy Reports,* April 26, 1933, is a good brief account. The best treatment from the Communist point of view is that of Harold Isaacs, *The Tragedy of the Chinese Revolution,* cited.

forces to maintain themselves against the superior equipment but lower morale of the government armies, and their subsequent part in China's fight for independence is an epic of proletarian history.

A central government of Chinese soviets was set up at Juichin, in the hills of southern Kiangsi, in November 1931. But the capital of Communism was captured by the government forces three years later. The Communist Party line in that period was an "attempt to carry out an agrarian transformation on the basis of bourgeois property relations." [30] This proved illusory, as the richer peasants, through whom the poorer did their trading with markets outside Communist-controlled areas, resorted to the old tactics of the landlords. The bulk of the farm population, finding itself still in conditions of serfdom, lost confidence in the Communist leaders and deserted in large numbers from the Communist armies, thereby aiding in the recovery of South China by General Chiang K'ai-shek. The armies themselves were able to retreat westward and ultimately, in December 1936, to set up a new capital at Yenan, Shensi.

For several years an agrarian revolt had been under way in Shensi, provoked by conditions similar to those in central China. Mao Tse-tung and his colleagues thus found a haven and took possession. Their influence spread into the neighboring provinces—Kansu, Ninghsia, Shansi, Suiyuan, and Hopei. Since these are essentially farming areas the political economy of the Yenan regime was directed toward improvement of the peasants' lot. Political organization was modelled upon the Russian soviet in a hierarchy of five stages—village, sub-district, district, provincial, and central soviets.[31] All of the representatives who sat in these five grades of assemblies were elected in the villages. Numerous committees worked

[30] Isaacs, Harold, cited, p. 415.

[31] Snow, Edgar, "Soviet Society in Northwest China," *Pacific Affairs*, X, September 1937, p. 266–74.

upon problems of community life and defense. Instruction was given in cultivation of the soil and diversification of crops.

The people found that the new order actually was devoted to their interests, and they gave it in return their confidence and support. They could not but be impressed by remission of taxes, the distribution of land and livestock expropriated from their oppressors, the richer landlords, reduced interest rates for loans, and the provision of implements and seed grain. They appreciated the beginnings of a system of free education. With something tangible to fight for, the peasants became an auxiliary factor of vital significance in the program of resistance.

Communism in China was an imported percussion cap fitting loosely on a native high explosive shell. Whether the consequences of the explosion would develop according to Russian precedents or along lines determined by Chinese conditions remained to be seen. Proletarianism as a factor in the war against Japan is left for later consideration.[32] Important in 1937 was the fact that the Chinese peasantry welcomed a regime antagonistic to the National Government because it offered them a decent place in society and a hope of something better than blueprints of social reform.

The program of internal reforms announced by the Kuomintang in 1924 was admirable.[33] Paraphrasing Dr. Sun Yat-sen's Principle of the People's Livelihood, it declared:

> *This principle of the Kuomintang contains two fundamental aspects. The first is the equalization of land, and the second is the control of capital.* Inasmuch as the greatest cause of inequality of economic organization lies in the fact that the right of land is controlled by the few, the Kuomintang proposes that the State shall prescribe the law of land, the law for the utilization of land, the law of the taxation of land, and the law for the taxation

[32] See below, Chapters IV–VII.

[33] Woo, T. C., cited, p. 265–6; italics the author's.

of the value of land. Private landowners shall declare its value to the Government, which shall tax it according to the value so declared with the option of buying it at that price in case of necessity. This is the essence of the equalization of land.

Private industries, whether of the Chinese or of foreign nationals, which are either of a monopolistic nature or are beyond the capacity of private individuals to develop, such as banking, railways, and navigation, shall be undertaken by the State, so that private-owned capital shall not control the economic life of the people. This is the essence of the control of capital. These two things will provide a good foundation for the principle of the people's livelihood.

But a word must be added for the peasants. *China is an agricultural country, and the peasants are the class that has suffered most.* The Kuomintang stands for the policy that those peasants that have no land and consequently have fallen into the status of mere tenants should be given land by the State for their cultivation. The State shall also undertake the work of irrigation and of opening up the waste land so as to increase the power of production of the land. Those of the peasants who have no capital and are compelled to borrow at high rates of interest and are in debt for life should be supplied by the State with credit by the establishment of rural banks. Only then will the peasants be able to enjoy the happiness of life.

In addition we must say a word to the laborers. *The livelihood of the laborers of China has no guarantee at all.* The policy of the Kuomintang is that the State shall find remedies for unemployment. And what is most necessary is the establishment of a labor law to improve the livelihood of the laborers. Other measures which affect the support of the aged, the bringing up of the young, the succor of the sick and the disabled, the spreading of education, and complementary services, shall be pushed until they are realized. All these are within the compass of the principle of the people's livelihood.

Obviously this was a counsel of perfection, not a program for immediate or early accomplishment. But instead of moving in the direction of implementation, the Kuomintang contented itself with reasserting its devotion to the Three Principles of the People. Conservative elements in the party regained control, aided by fears that radicalism was likely to involve the country in foreign intervention, and by the need for the funds controlled by the merchant-bankers of the great port cities, to whom the proletarian movement was anathema. Out of this reversal of attitude developed the civil warfare which ended only with the compromise between Chiang K'ai-shek and Mao Tse-tung early in 1937. Chiang and his military entourage were not arrested by the Communists, but the terms of release were settled in consultation with them.[34] Although these terms were directed mainly toward obtaining a united front against Japan they included provision for a return to Dr. Sun's "Three Principles," most important of which was that of the "People's Livelihood."

Only in the Communist-controlled portions of northwest China were public policies of a fundamental character, grounded in respect for the dignity of human beings, adopted. In the rest of the country reform measures were scattered, half-hearted and of slight effect. Improvement of seed and livestock by scientific research is an excellent line of effort. Rural credit banking is another. Model districts and health centers to suggest standards of local administration and individual conduct are valuable. Irrigation, flood-control, and afforestation projects are essential items in a long-time program. Both private and governmental efforts were exerted in these and other directions in the decade of Kuomintang government that preceded the war.[35] But the immediate gains to the people at large were microscopic, while their losses from civil warfare were prodigious.

[34] Snow, Edgar, *Red Star Over China,* cited, p. 405–29.

[35] Hsü, Leonard S., "Rural Reconstruction in China," *Pacific Affairs,* X, September 1937, p. 249–65.

II

MILITARISM AND INDUSTRIALISM IN JAPAN

JAPAN is a feudal wineskin bursting with the new wine of the industrial revolution. The feudal system was abolished only 70 years ago. Inevitably, ideas nurtured for a thousand years have lived on after the institutions they inspired and reflected disappeared. Naturally enough, since feudalism is a military order of politics, the heirs of the *samurai* were the officers of the modern army and navy. Naturally, also, the people placed their trust in the descendants of their overlords, now in command of the national military forces. Feudal principles owed their continuance chiefly to the controlling position of the supreme command in the Restoration state.[1]

The position of the military oligarchy was challenged even before the Restoration by the Mitsui and other rice merchants who controlled the supply of money during the transition from a rice to a money economy.[2] The challenge was not, however, directed toward destruction of the power of the landed aristocracy but rather toward obtaining from it recognition of the importance of the bourgeoisie. It was

1 The term "Restoration" is applied to the change produced in 1867 and thereafter by the overthrow of the feudal shogunate and the establishment of a centralized government under the Emperor.

2 Honjo, Eijiro, *The Social and Economic History of Japan*, Kyoto, 1935; Norman, E. H., *Japan's Emergence as a Modern State*, New York, 1940, p. 50–70; Russell, O. D., *The House of Mitsui*, Boston, 1939; Ahlers, John, "The House of Mitsui Reorganizes," *China Weekly Review*, April 13, 1940, p. 222–3; "Empire of the Mitsuis," *ibid.*, April 20, 1940, p. 253–4; "The Mitsuis in Politics," *ibid.*, April 27, 1940, p. 291–2.

an attempt by the merchant class to raise itself in the social scale, not to establish itself politically as the dominant element. The latter program was impossible because of the dependence of the merchants upon the nobility for markets for loans and goods. Despite the contempt of the *samurai* for the money-lenders, necessity forced the mortgaging of land to them and even the adoption of their sons, or their acceptance as sons-in-law of the *samurai*. Young *samurai* married into merchant families and themselves became men of business. Eventually it was by this alliance between the clans and the merchants that the shogunate was overthrown.

After the Restoration this alliance was maintained. The Government, constituted of the *samurai* of the greater clans which had ousted the greatest of them all, the Tokugawa, from the shogunate, subsidized the new power-driven factories and provided *entrepreneurs* with foreign advisers. Mercantile houses engaged in great industrial enterprises under such encouragement. Their interest in an aggressive foreign policy coincided with that of the military leaders in the Government. Both desired to free Japan from the unequal treaties and to obtain assured markets and raw materials on the Asiatic mainland and in the south seas. As Japan's economic power grew stronger its foreign policy increased in vigor: [8]

> As the compromise agreed upon with the feudal lords did not permit the Japanese bourgeoisie to destroy the medieval structure of husbandry (as a matter of fact, the bourgeoisie itself soon became territorialized, i.e., connected with the feudal landownership), it continued to *adapt* itself to this structure and found a means, in new colonial seizures, of reducing the sharpness of the contradictions between the rapidly growing large-scale industry and the preservation of feudal relics in the whole national economy of the country.

[8] Tanin, O., and Yohan, E., *Militarism and Fascism in Japan*, London, 1934, p. 39.

Constitutionalism on Trial

The constitution, promulgated in 1889, was borrowed from Prussia and other German states.[4] It purported to embody an age-old tradition of imperial autocracy. Although it provided for a Diet of two chambers it gave that body so little power that the executive agencies were in fact able to control national policy. Among these agencies there was a dispersion of authority which made it impossible to identify the responsible agency in particular circumstances. What could be said was that a comparatively small number of the nobility, the majority of them high officers in the army and navy, held the positions of power. They composed an oligarchy locking together the great offices of state. The cabinet was their mouthpiece in the Diet.

Within the Diet the House of Representatives was composed of men elected under the auspices of political parties by voters who, until 1925, were required to be taxpayers. Among the members of the House there were genuine liberals, but the great majority were henchmen of their leaders with little concern for anything but the fruits of office. They were forced, moreover, into alliances with the oligarchy if they were to have any share in those fruits. This opportunism, with its accompaniment of corruption, prevented the development of popular confidence in liberal institutions.

The decade that followed the Treaty of Versailles was, relative to the previous twenty years, a period of political liberalism in Japan. Not all, but a number of, cabinets were composed mainly of leaders from the majority party in the House of Representatives. The principle that a government which failed to keep the support of a majority in that House should resign came to be recognized. A manhood suffrage law

[4] Quigley, Harold S., *Japanese Government and Politics*, New York, 1932; Reischauer, R. K., *Japan: Government-Politics*, New York, 1939; Colegrove, Kenneth W., *Militarism in Japan*, Boston, World Peace Foundation, 1936.

was passed. The enfranchisement of women was seriously debated. The army was considerably reduced in numbers, if not in strength, and a ratio of naval power was agreed upon with other states. Cooperation with other governments in the revision of the treaty regime in China was undertaken. The program of expansion in Manchuria and eastern Siberia was throttled down.

Industrial-commercial trusts, such as the Mitsui, Mitsubishi, Sumitomo, Yasuda, and Suzuki families (called the *Zaibatsu*) had built, were asserting themselves even in opposition to the military oligarchs during this decade. Their representatives were found in the *genro* (elder statesmen, who advised the Government on important matters), the imperial household ministry, the House of Peers, the cabinet and the civil service. Their financial support was given generously to the political parties—bread upon the waters which returned in favorable legislation. They viewed the Diet as a dam against a rising tide of radicalism, and a prominent element among them considered it also an ally in their attempt to substitute financial and commercial methods for military action in relations with China. This influential group also wanted friendly relations with Europe and America as the basis for commerce. They were opposed, however, by an equally strong group of capitalists and manufacturers who maintained liaison with the supreme military command, supported chauvinistic patriotism, and continually sought to check the liberal movement.

The lessened influence of the military men during this period was due to a number of factors. One was the loss of prestige suffered through the failure of the expensive intervention in Siberia. Another was the absence of the aggressive leadership of Marshal Yamagata, the Choshu clansman who had dominated the political life of Japan for a generation. A third was the defeat of Germany, which left Great Britain and the United States in a dominant position navally and diplomatically. A fourth was the prosperity brought by the war trade, which raised the mercantile interests in the eyes of the people. (Between 1913 and 1919 industrial production increased from a value of 1,300,000,000 to 6,500,000,000 yen. Foreign trade rose from 1,300,000,000 to 4,172,000,000 yen.) It may well be, also, that the army and navy leaders were willing to leave to the politicians the first essays at dealing with the rising labor movement.

The older political parties, the Seiyukai and the Minseito, and their predecessors, made the mistake—if we regard them as proponents of democracy—of fighting one another more ardently than they fought the militarist-chauvinist alliance. They made the same mistake in their relations with the new labor unions and labor parties that attained ponderable influence during the 1920's. What they gave in friendly legislation they took back in repressive administration and in such acts as the "peace preservation law," which imposed the severest penalties upon individuals and organizations that sought fundamental political and social reforms. Thereby they prevented the fusion of middle class and proletarian-peasant opposition to obscurantist government. They paid the penalty for this blunder in the loss of political leadership. When economic conditions deteriorated in the later 'twenties the businessmen were forced back to their former secondary position, and the political heir of Yamagata, General Tanaka, became premier. Inept, corrupt, and reckless in both domestic and foreign policy, Tanaka failed ignobly and was replaced by the liberal Minseito politician, Hamaguchi. He was extremely popular, courageously opposing militarist budgetary demands, and risking his life for a program of international equilibrium. By assassination and the provocation of war in China his efforts were nullified. With the death of Hamaguchi in April 1931, constitutionalism went into eclipse. The murder of Premier Inukai in May 1932 brought the liberal era to an end.

Agrarian Distress

Japan's farmers are suffering under circumstances and governmental neglect similar to those in China. It is apparent that the masses of these countries are fighting one another when they should be making common cause against oppressive conditions. Approximately a million absentee landlords in Japan rent some 7,000,000 acres to 4,000,000 tenant and part-tenant farmers who cultivate 45% of the arable land.[5] High rents and interest charges, extremely small holdings, a high proportion of tenancy, and disproportionately high tax rates are characteristic of Japanese agriculture.[6] Under these conditions farm debt rose to 6,000,000,000 yen in 1936, an amount nearly three-fourths as great as the national public debt at that date. The productivity of land is decreasing due to deficiency of higher-priced fertilizers, farms are being abandoned, farmers are more than ever dependent upon sericulture and home industries for a cash income.[7]

Although industry has progressed rapidly in Japan the expansion of population has outpaced industrial growth, and the farm population continues to press upon the means of subsistence. There are too many farmers for the cultivable land under existing methods of cultivation. Farm wages are lower than those paid in the factories. Farmers' daughters in some parts of the country are sold into industrial peonage or prostitution to keep their parents and brothers alive. The rapid increase of tenant-farmer unions and of disputes between tenants and landlords (5800 in 1934) are further testimony to the seriousness of the situation.[8] Japanese agri-

[5] Farley, Miriam S., "Japan's Unsolved Tenancy Problem," *Far Eastern Survey*, VI, July 7, 1937, p. 155.

[6] Holland, W. L., "The Plight of Japanese Agriculture," *Far Eastern Survey*, V, January 1, 1936, p. 1–5.

[7] Crocker, W. R., *The Japanese Population Problem*, New York, 1931, p. 64–9.

[8] Utley, Freda, *Japan's Feet of Clay*, New York, 1937, p. 141–6, 162–72; also Fisher, G. M., "The Landlord-Peasant Struggle in Japan," *Far Eastern Survey*, VI, September 1, 1937, p. 201–6.

culture felt the effects of the great depression. Not only did the prices of rice and other grains fall but the decreased American demand for silk reduced the farmers' incomes by several hundred million yen.[9] Tenancy increased as small owners were forced to sacrifice mortgaged land. In the northeastern prefectures the people were close to starvation. Appropriations of the Diet for farm relief were too small to be effective.

Population pressure was recognized as a problem of Japan fully a generation ago. It was then believed that industrialization and immigration would solve the problem.[10] But emigration was soon found to be a very limited recourse and the importance of industrialism was correspondingly emphasized. Labor was drawn into the factories from the rural areas and there was no urban unemployment until the depression reached Japan. By installing up-to-date machinery, eliminating marginal concerns and "rationalizing" generally, industrial organization was brought to a higher degree of efficiency. In this process some injury was caused to workers in the small handicraft shops where hours were already long and wages extremely low.[11] And since the new machinery required less attendance, the number of unemployed increased while wages were reduced as labor was drugging the market. Industrialization had failed to cope with the problem of population pressure.

The peasantry of Japan, like that of China, is notably tolerant of hardship. But it feels the same dependence upon the soil that stirs the emotions of the Chinese. Only one who studies Japanese publications is competent to describe the violence of the peasants' reaction to the conditions of the last decade.[12] Attacks occurred upon local government offices

[9] Lockwood, William W., "Japanese Silk and the American Market," *ibid.*, V, February 12, 1936, p. 31–6.

[10] Ishii, R., *Population Pressure and Economic Life in Japan*, London, 1937, p. 39–40.

[11] Hubbard, G. E., cited, p. 127.

[12] Utley, Freda, cited, p. 146–56. Miss Utley makes use of reputable Japanese and foreign newspapers and periodicals.

and upon owners of mines from which refuse poisoned irrigation waters. Unions increased rapidly in numbers and membership but those of radical inclinations were suppressed. Thus the Government managed to confine rebellion to disunited local efforts.

Proletarianism in Japan

Neither in China nor in Japan is it realistic to attempt to separate the problem of the urban laborer from that of the workers on the land. In both countries it is the great reservoir of rural labor existing at the brink of starvation that keeps the wages of the handicraftsman and the factory operative extremely low. In the textile factories and silk filatures, where the strength of women and girls is sufficient for the work, comparatively few men are employed, another factor in low labor costs. Poverty-stricken peasants contract with the factories for their daughters' services over a term of years, the girls having no word in the transaction. Or they employ them in home industry on contracts with manufacturers who furnish materials and take the finished product. Domestic industry undermines the factory worker by restricting his bargaining power.

The rise of heavy industries in Japan in recent years has brought about an increase in the numbers of male factory workers, which today are larger than those of female labor. While wages in the filatures and textile mills have fallen in the past decade, those in the heavy industries have risen appreciably,[13] reflecting the urgent interest of the Government in armaments and shipbuilding. Even so, the costs of living have risen so rapidly that the better-paid workers are still badly housed, clothed and nourished. A high percentage of illness and mortality is an inevitable consequence of such conditions.

[13] Utley, Freda, cited, p. 174.

Japanese labor is unionized to a negligible extent. On occasion strikes have been successful in raising wages and reducing hours of work. But the restrictive laws and the enormous power of the Government, through ordinances, to penalize exhibitions of recalcitrance have stultified the labor movement. Labor parties with more than the most moderate and vague programs of reform have been dissolved by executive decree.[14] Liberal statesmen and editors have been intimidated. In the face of these tactics the election of 36 members to the House of Representatives by the largest labor party in 1937 is the best possible evidence of social unrest.

Communism has attempted to raise its head in Japan but has met with crushing repression from the Government. Nevertheless it has continued as an underground movement which the authorities admit to be expanding rather than dying out. Flashes from the latent embers burst forth in such unexpected places as the school for peeresses, the judiciary, and the army. Communist literature enjoyed the position of best seller in the decade of the 'twenties. By repressing the liberal labor organizations the Government has placed in Communist hands the leadership of the movement against living conditions no less bitterly resented than those of China. Communism has not, as yet, become a people's movement in Japan, in part because of the ingrained respect for authority inherited from the feudal age, in part because there has not occurred the division in the military ranks which enabled the Chinese proletariat to venture upon forceful action.

Sympathy for the hard lot of the masses has been expressed by younger military officers, sons of well-to-do peasants and small landowners, who are closer than the men of the high command to the rank and file of the army, largely drawn

[14] Quigley, H. S., cited, p. 236–46; Tanin, O., and Yohan, E., cited, p. 228–48; Colegrove, Kenneth W., "Labor Parties in Japan," *American Political Science Review,* XXIII, May 1929, p. 329–63.

from the rural population. The younger officers undoubtedly desire the improvement of conditions among the peasantry. However, their objective is not primarily social reform but the continuance of military control over the state. They see the danger of acute agrarian distress to the present regime. Their purpose is to make the existing order more tolerable, not to advance the political position of the people. It is in this opposition to internal reform that the imperialist program of recent years finds one of its principal incentives.

Japan's Economic Position

In 1914 Japan was a debtor state. The World War of 1914–18 altered that situation by stimulating a great expansion of exports. By 1920 Japan's gold reserves had risen from 130,000,000 yen to 700,000,000 yen plus war credits of 660,000,000 yen; meanwhile foreign balances of Japanese merchants had reached the enormous total of 1,355,000,000 yen.[15] The country was full of newly-rich businessmen and their expensive but amorphous Eurasian houses.

The earthquake of 1923 cost the nation 3,000,000,000 yen. Reserves were reduced further by the continuance of government subsidies to industry and by the decline of exports caused by the Government's policy of maintaining high prices and exchange rates while prices abroad were falling. This policy was abandoned in 1924 with favorable results. In 1925 foreign trade stood at 4,879,000,000 yen, which was considerably higher than in 1919. Fearful of inflation and anxious to balance its budget, the Government returned too soon to a program of higher taxes and interest rates. In consequence the year 1927 was a period of business failures and bank closures of panic proportions, though there was

[15] Allen, G. C., *Japanese Industry: Its Recent Development and Present Condition,* New York, 1940, p. 81.

no panic because the Government advanced large sums to protect depositors.[16]

The results of retrenchment measures appearing to justify a return to the gold standard, this was undertaken in 1929 on the eve of the world-wide depression. The step proved to be inopportune; Japan's foreign trade dropped sharply, reaching low point in 1931 at 2,383,000,000 yen.[17] The country again left the gold standard at the end of 1931, adopting the measures of rationalization referred to previously. Foreign trade began to climb and by 1935 had reached nearly 5,000,000,000 yen, with a favorable balance of 27,000,000 yen. The Government borrowed heavily in an effort to stimulate industrial recovery. By 1937 the national debt had risen to 10,500,000,000 yen. In part this increase was due to expenditures in "Manchoukuo" and the military and naval outlays.

Between 1925 and 1936, inclusive, Japanese imports exceeded exports in every year but one, 1935. Although Japanese exports to both China and "Manchoukuo" remained a stable proportion of the total, those to China proper dropped from 16.9% of China's imports in 1929 to 6% in 1935. Prior even to the intervention in Manchuria in 1931 Japanese exports to China were declining while those of the United States and Germany were increasing. Exports to all Asia and to Europe were greater in 1935 than in 1925, but to the United States they were cut nearly in half during the decade.[18] It must be remembered that the exports of the United States and of European states were in general decreasing during this period, while those of Japan were increasing; also that Japanese tariffs were highly protective,

[16] Schumpeter, Elizabeth B., ed., *The Industrialization of Japan and Manchukuo, 1930–1940*, New York, 1940, p. 873–95.

[17] *Recent Developments in the Foreign Trade of Japan,* U. S. Tariff Commission, Report No. 105, Second Series, 1936, p. 3.

[18] *Expansion of Japan's Foreign Trade and Industry,* U. S. Department of Commerce, Trade Information Bulletin No. 836, 1937, p. 5, 69; *cf.* Uyeda, T., *The Recent Development of Japanese Foreign Trade,* Tokyo, 1936, p. 7–72.

over a hundred commodities bearing duties of 100%.

It is often argued that Japan was at a disadvantage because it was dependent on foreign states for raw materials. Actually, under depression conditions an important factor in Japan's commercial prosperity was the embarrassment of foreign producers with surplus raw materials which caused them to dump large amounts abroad at low prices. It has been pointed out, e.g., that Japan's steel industry suffered a maximum depression of but 12% while that of the United States dropped 75%. Japan's great raw material, silk, suffered a drop in export value of 23.3% between 1929 and 1934 while her cotton textile exports, dependent upon foreign sources of supply, boomed.[19] Thus at the beginning of large-scale warfare in 1937, Japanese trade was, relative to that of other more industrialized states, quite favorably placed. Its national debt had increased greatly but, again, not disproportionately to economic conditions or national wealth. Its trade, under the revised policies influenced by the military services as well as by the new conditions in international economic relations, had become more diversified and less dependent upon the markets of the United States and China. But its working population had not profited from a prosperity stimulated by low wages, and it had suffered from the adjustments necessitated by the process of industrial reorganization. Moreover, the policy of developing heavy industry in competition with the great steel manufacturers of the West, in order that Japan might arm itself to the teeth, was obviously uneconomic as a long-time program.[20]

It is well known that after 1931 the tariff rates of many states were raised against Japanese goods.[21] The practice of

[19] Wallace, B. B., "Fallacies of Economic Nationalism," in *Peace or War*, ed. by Harold S. Quigley (University of Minnesota, Day and Hour Series, Nos. 17–18, June 1937), p. 52–5.

[20] Allen, G. C., cited, p. 15–24.

[21] Dietrich, Ethel B., "Closing Doors Against Japan," *Far Eastern Survey*, August 10, 1935, p. 181–6.

making quota agreements also worked against Japan, since exports from that state exceeded imports to many countries while imports exceeded exports with but few. Self-restriction was practiced by the Japanese in a number of commodities to fend off the imposition of higher tariffs. Foreign barriers were easily explainable in view of the serious conditions of foreign trade generally. But they were hardly necessary, since in 1935 Japan's export trade in gold dollar value was but 3.3% of the world's total, compared with 12% for the United Kingdom, 11.7% for the United States, 8.8% for Germany, 5.2% for France, and 3.8% for Canada. It will hardly be disputed either that of all these states Japan was most dependent upon foreign trade.

It is also well known that Japan is poverty-stricken in raw materials.[22] Its supply of coal is appreciable but it is difficult to mine, and poor in coking quality. In 1932 Japan's output of petroleum "equalled for the entire 12 months only about 70% of the yield of the petroleum fields of the United States for a single day." [23] Iron ore occurs in quantities almost negligible industrially. Copper is more adequate but is difficult to extract. Cotton could be grown but the land is needed for food grains. Wool-growing is restricted by the lack of pasturage. In silk alone is Japan abundantly supplied. How, the Japanese were entitled to ask, can we industrialize if we cannot sell abroad to buy the raw materials of industry?

"Patriotism" and Kodo

Militarism and industrialism have not been seriously antagonistic to each other in Japan, though they have had their differences. Liberalism was unfortunate in having to meet

[22] Porter, Catherine, "Mineral Deficiency versus Self-Sufficiency in Japan," *Far Eastern Survey,* January 15, 1936, p. 9–14.

[23] Orchard, J. E., "The Japanese Dilemma," in Barnes, Joseph, ed., *Empire in the East,* New York, 1934, p. 49.

2447

the depression before it had accumulated enough political power to save itself from criticism and repudiation. Political consciousness among the masses remains feudal. There is no effective check upon the militarist-industrial oligarchy which rules in the name of the Tenno or Emperor.

Japanese believe that Westerners are incapable of understanding their political system. Westerners wonder whether the Japanese do not manage it without understanding it. Avowed devotion to the Tenno, who is termed father as well as ruler of his people, appears to disguise the actuality of oligarchy. The disguise may be necessary to assure obedience or it may be an expression of loyalty, or it may be both. In any case it has the desired effect of holding the people bound within the medieval swaddling clothes of emperor-worship while their actual rulers determine policy.

Undoubtedly the feeble evidences of interest in democracy which have appeared since the abolition of feudalism have prompted an effort by the bureaucracy to impress the people with the doctrine that they are members of an unique society, a family state, which must be preserved by unquestioning loyalty to an emperor descended from the gods and himself a god. This doctrine is espoused by conservative scholars, and opposing doctrines now are banned. Dr. Tatsukichi Minobe, professor of public law at Tokyo Imperial University, was charged with *lèse majesté* and forced to resign from the House of Peers in 1935 for writings which had been taught freely for twenty-five years.[24] He was a liberal who did not fear the militarists and who held that in a constitutional government the Emperor was not the state but an organ thereof and that the civil power was superior to the military.

Kodo is the doctrine of the "way of the Tenno," i.e. of government in accordance with that "way." The most recent Japanese scholarly treatise on the constitution reaffirms the

[24] Young, A. Morgan, *Imperial Japan, 1926–1938,* New York, 1938, p. 270–3.

doctrine of the divine origin of emperor and people.[25] Japanese are encouraged to regard themselves as distinguishable from all other peoples by virtue of their divine descent and as bound thereby to the imperial family—highest in the hierarchy of ancestor-gods—in a peculiar loyalty surpassing that of any other people for their rulers. Without disparaging the idealism and reality of this, the Japanese form of nationalism, it may be observed that like other forms it has been perverted to serve the ends of ruling cliques.

The multitude of so-called patriotic societies provides a radical dynamic for nationalist and imperialist policies at Tokyo.[26] They may be relied upon to whip up public sentiment, and to frighten, or if necessary to assassinate, any who may question the program of a dominant faction. Acts of terrorism are seldom penalized in the courts, which feel the compulsion of popular willingness to extenuate a "patriot's" crime. These societies are increasing in number and are entering into federations. They vary in the degree of their opposition to liberalism and internationalism and in their methods for the destruction of these tendencies, but they agree in their principal objectives. In fact if not in name they form an influential bloc, of fascistic ideals. They abet and incite extremism, supporting the militarist-industrialist oligarchy.

[25] Fujii, S., *The Essentials of Japanese Constitutional Law,* Tokyo, 1940, p. 47–53.

[26] Colegrove, K., *Militarism in Japan,* cited, p. 27–41; Tanin, O., and Yohan, E., cited, p. 69–127, 173–227.

III

CHINA'S INTERNATIONAL POSITION

IN his scholarly treatise, *The International Relations of the Chinese Empire,* Hosea B. Morse epitomizes the period 1834–60 as "The Period of Conflict," that from 1861–95 as "The Period of Submission," that from 1896–1911 as "The Period of Subjection." A younger scholar, Dr. Robert T. Pollard, called the years after 1917 "The Period of Recovery." [1] These terms admirably suggest that during the fifty-odd years after the compelled treaty settlements of 1858 and 1860 China was the object of policies which reduced its sovereignty to a fiction, but that its position improved thereafter until, in 1931, Japan began an attack, the outcome of which remains to be seen. Not only to aid in an appraisal of the Japanese attitude but also to suggest inferences bearing upon a peace settlement it seems important to give brief attention to the earlier struggle between the greater states for territory and influence in China.

Three methods have been employed in this struggle. One method is that of outright seizure of territory. A variant of this method is the establishment of a leased area or a sphere of influence, with the purpose of strengthening the stronger state strategically or of obtaining priorities or monopolies for trade and investment. A second method takes an essentially economic guise, making use of foreign capital either in direct investments or in loans to the government, in the expectation that the latter will accept the advice of the government and the financial and industrial concerns of the former in the expenditure of the borrowed funds.

[1] Pollard, Robert T., *China's Foreign Relations, 1917–1931,* New York, 1933.

Finally, there is the ideological method which seeks to create political and social ideals and institutions similar to those of the foreign state.

Territorial Conquests and Spheres

The relations of China with the great powers of the nineteenth century—Great Britain, France, Germany, and Russia—exhibit a combination of methods. Great Britain took Hong Kong in 1842 and a portion of nearby Kowloon in 1860. In 1898 the same state secured 99-year leases over a larger portion of Kowloon, and over Weihaiwei in Shantung. Tibet, Burma, Sikkim and Bhutan, all vassal-states of China, fell wholly or partly under British influence before the Manchu dynasty fell in 1911. Great Britain obtained numerous areas in Chinese cities for residential settlements or concessions, within which either British or international administrations exercised exclusive jurisdiction. The enormous Yangtze River basin was recognized by China, against its will, as a British sphere of influence, into which great sums of British capital were poured for investment purposes and within which British trade and river shipping predominated. From 1854 to 1938 a British inspector-general controlled the administration of the Chinese Maritime Customs. The extensive reach of British and other Occidental influence led Dr. Sun Yat-sen to term his native state a "quasi-colony."

France absorbed the several states, all vassals of China, which were combined within the great colony of French Indo-China. The same state secured many settlement areas and obtained, by war, Chinese acquiescence in a French sphere in the provinces of Kwangtung, Kwangsi, Kweichow and Yunnan. The leased area of Kwangchowwan, near Hong Kong, became the French naval base for the protection of this extensive sphere. Germany held Kiaochow as a lease from 1898 to 1915, and Shantung and adjacent territory was the German sphere. Russia took the Maritime Province of Siberia in 1860 and a lease in South Manchuria in 1898; all China north of the Great Wall was a Russian sphere of influence after 1896 until, in 1904–5, Japan defeated Russia in war, forced the cession of the lease to itself, and took a large portion of Manchuria for its sphere. Ten years earlier Japan had defeated China in war and taken Korea, Formosa and the Pescadores Islands as fair spoils.

Generally speaking, up to the enunciation of the "Open Door" doctrine by Secretary Hay in 1899 and 1900, it may be said that the policy of the powers in China was to annex outlying, loosely-held territories or islands, and to divide China proper into spheres of control which might, if China completely collapsed, be added outright to the empires of the competing states. The United States took a very minor part in this disintegrating process. Interested only in trade, it had insisted upon sharing any general treaty rights obtained by other states but had not demanded territory or spheres of influence.[2] Japan was too fully occupied until the 'nineties with its own reorganization to enter into the game extensively. But it was observing the players' methods and sharpening its sword for the opportune moment.

Treaty Limitations

China's quasi-colonial position resulted not only from the establishment of spheres but also from the general treaty rights enjoyed by a large number of states. Extraterritoriality was the most comprehensive of these rights, enabling nineteen foreign systems of justice to be extended into China. Treaty limitation of China's tariffs, with precise lists of duties applicable to specified commodities, was a form of

[2] Secretary Hay did not press his request for a naval base in Fukien. See Griswold, A. Whitney, *The Far Eastern Policy of the United States,* New York, 1938, p. 83–4.

foreign control inconsistent with sovereignty. Rights to engage in coastal and river navigation, to station garrisons of troops, to set up postal systems, etc., were assured by treaty. The United States shared in all of these restrictions upon China's freedom of action. It should not be overlooked that the freedom from Chinese taxation and from legal and administrative controls, resulting from extraterritoriality, was a stimulant to foreign business interests to enter China. These interests enjoyed advantages in competition with Chinese concerns, a situation directly opposite to that usually occurring under the laws of sovereign states.

The interest of a large number of states in the privileges secured by the unequal treaties was, however, a deterrent to the partitioning process. It held China together while exploiting the country's resources and people. The United States was the principal protagonist of China's integrity, and Great Britain was too greatly concerned with trade to promote partitionism, though determined to have its share if worse came to worst. International forms of control were preferable to those of individual states, since they preserved the fiction of sovereignty until the reality could be restored.

"Dollar Diplomacy"

Between 1899 and 1931 a second type of activity which has been called "dollar diplomacy" [3] – displaced the territorial expansionism of the previous cycle of Cathay. The United States was aroused to the danger that its growing trade with China might be cut off by the partition of the country. The doctrine of the "Open Door," latent in the most-favored-nation clauses of the commercial treaties, was strengthened by being restated affirmatively as a positive interest of this country and was buttressed by our complementary declara-

[3] Nearing, Scott, and Freeman, J., *Dollar Diplomacy: A Study in American Imperialism,* New York, 1925.

tion of respect for China's territorial and administrative integrity. In treaty after treaty these two ideas were reaffirmed until in 1922 they received definitive expression in the Nine-Power Treaty. Not the United States only but all the great states gave support to the principle of equality of opportunity in relation to an independent China.

American policy aimed to implement this doctrine by inserting our influence, exercised through private participation in large loans to China and in direct business investments, into the complicated design of the older fabric of relationships. This program proved to be difficult to realize against the vested interests of other states. The indifference of American businessmen and financiers, and our tradition of avoidance of foreign entanglements, were obstacles which placed the Department of State under the necessity of stimulating public sentiment to support this new departure into world affairs. In the upshot this country became little more than a brake upon the more aggressive states. Our investments remained comparatively small.[4] In 1931 British investors held 36% of China's foreign loans, Japanese 38%, French 16½%, American 7%. Between 1914 and 1931 British holdings increased very slightly, French decreased considerably, while Japanese increased 23 times and American six times.[5] Most notable is the fact that the comparatively impecunious Japanese outdistanced the well-established British investors as the result of the activities of Mr. Nishihara, supported by his Government. American diplomatic efforts rather than the extent of our investments aroused the suspicion of Japan that our policy was designed to frustrate its expansion into Eastern Asia.

[4] Lockwood, W. W., "America's Stake in the Far East, II: Investments," *Far Eastern Survey,* August 12, 1936, p. 176–85.

[5] Remer, C. F., *Foreign Investments in China,* New York, 1933, p. 138.

American Private Loans Insignificant

American efforts to share in the Hukuang railway enterprise and in the internationalizing of Manchurian railways early in the present century were unsuccessful. Japan and Russia cooperated against the latter project. A few years later, in 1913, President Wilson brought his predecessor's program of joining in the large Reorganization Loan to naught because he disapproved of the stringent controls it involved over Chinese administration. The major expression of dollar diplomacy was, however, initiated by President Wilson. This was the second financial Consortium, organized between 1918 and 1920 by the Governments and leading banks of the United States, Great Britain, France and Japan.[6] Its purpose was to restrain China from borrowing in the cheapest market by an agreement of the foreign bankers to cooperate in all loans to Chinese governmental agencies. It was a direct challenge to the war-time financing of China by unsecured Japanese loans granted in return for extensive concessions for exploitation of Chinese resources. Japan found it expedient to enter the Consortium but only after obtaining guaranties that assured it economic predominance in Manchuria and Eastern Inner Mongolia.

The terms upon which the Reorganization Loan was made illustrate the point that political influence was a feature of the arrangement.[7] The Chinese Government was required to establish a Central Salt Administration, analogous to the Maritime Customs Administration. Security for the loan was the revenue from these two sources. Over both of them the control of administration was in foreign hands. It was further required that all salt revenues were to be deposited in

[6] *Treaties and Agreements with and concerning China, 1919–1929,* Washington, 1929 (Carnegie Endowment for International Peace, Division of International Law), p. 32–6.

[7] MacMurray, J. V. A., ed., *Treaties and Agreements with and concerning China, 1894–1919,* II, New York, 1921, p. 1007–17.

the foreign banks participating in the loan. The signature of a foreign inspector was required for the withdrawal of any funds from the salt account, or for the sale of any salt. The loan funds were deposited in foreign banks and paid out only upon requisitions approved by foreign officials of the banks and the Chinese bureau of foreign loans. An option was obtained by the banking group upon any subsequent loans secured on the salt revenue or designed for such purposes as those of the Reorganization Loan.

This loan was made during the struggle between General Yuan Shih-k'ai, then provisional president of China, and the newly organized National Assembly for control of the Republican Government.[8] It ensured the victory of Yuan and the destruction of the influence of the Assembly, which opposed the loan and passed a resolution condemning the contract as unconstitutional. The American Government withdrew its support for the loan, stating that: [9]

The conditions of the loan seem to us to touch very nearly the administrative independence of China itself, and this Administration does not feel that it ought, even by implication, to be a party to those conditions. The responsibility on its part which would be implied in requesting the bankers to undertake the loan might conceivably go the length in some unhappy contingency of forcible interference in the financial, and even the political, affairs of that great Oriental state, just now awakening to a consciousness of its power and of its obligation to its people. The conditions include not only the pledging of particular taxes, some of them antiquated and burdensome, to secure the loan but also the administration of those taxes by foreign agents. The responsibility on the part of our Government implied in the encouragement of a loan thus secured and administered is plain enough and is obnoxious to the principles upon which the Government of our people rests.

[8] Farjenel, F., *Through the Chinese Revolution,* New York, 1916, p. 289–309.

[9] MacMurray, cited, p. 1025.

Withdrawal of the American bankers consequent upon their Government's action did not deter the other members of the Consortium from continuing with the Reorganization Loan. "Dollar diplomacy" was neither invented by the United States nor as strenuously pursued by it as by European states and Japan at this period. But for the World War, 1914–18, it cannot be doubted that railway-building and other enterprises would have been financed on a considerable scale by European funds. Japanese loans amounting to $100,000,000 U. S. were made during the war period. The Siems-Carey Company, an American concern, obtained contracts to build and finance 1100 miles of railway but was obliged to surrender them when China was reminded by France, Great Britain and Russia that the proposed railways would infringe upon their spheres of interest.[10]

Between 1913 and 1917 the Wilson administration remained aloof from international projects for the financing of China. In 1917, however, Secretary of State Robert Lansing informed American bankers and foreign governments that the United States desired to join in the creation of a new Consortium on a broader basis of bank membership and upon conditions that would not impair China's sovereignty.[11] The reason for this reversal of attitude was the apprehension for the "Open Door" policy aroused by the observation of the reckless borrowing of the Chinese Government from Japanese banks. But the Chinese Government of the day and its successors refrained from dealings with the new Consortium. No official statement of reasons for this attitude was issued but it was made clear unofficially that the Chinese regarded the plan as monopolistic, derogatory to the dignity of an independent state, and likely to involve unacceptable restrictions upon China's administration. Con-

[10] MacMurray, J. V. A., "Problems of Foreign Capital in China," *Foreign Affairs,* III, 1925, p. 411–22.

[11] Field, Frederick V., *American Participation in the China Consortiums,* Chicago, 1931, p. 142–65, 173–85.

sequently no loans were made by the second Consortium.

It is not to be supposed that the United States Government favored international over national loans. The expansion of investment by American citizens was very rapid after 1914. It rose from $2,500,000,000 in that year to more than $16,000,000,000 in 1930.[12] Less than $200,000,000, exclusive of missionary, medical and educational enterprises, was invested in China. Only $40,000,000 of this total was in the form of loans. Nearly $450,000,000 had gone to Japan. It is apparent that in China the priorities of European states and the uncertainty of profits deterred Americans from extensive investment. Secretary Lansing preferred to support separate American loans but was opposed in this by the bankers, who insisted upon an international pooling program.[13]

Foreign Business Investments

Whether or not a private concern operating an electric tramway, a bank or a cotton factory is to be regarded as a political instrument depends upon the relationship between the concern and a foreign government in connection with activities affecting the domestic or foreign policy of the weaker state within which it is located. Four fifths of American investments in China in 1930 were in business concerns —banks, public utilities, shipping, tobacco companies, oil stations, newspapers, small factories, etc. While it would seem that an approximate total investment of $160,000,000 in these enterprises would exert a negligible leverage upon American policy it must be presumed that our insistent reaffirmation of the "Open Door" doctrine is directly related

[12] Gayer, A. D., and Schmidt, C. T., *American Economic Foreign Policy*, New York, 1939, p. 19; also Remer, C. F., *Foreign Investments in China;* Field, F. V., "Battle of the Bankers," in Barnes, Joseph, ed., *Empire in the East*, p. 151–2, 167.

[13] Field, Frederick V., "American Participation in the China Consortiums," cited, p. 143–5.

to these interests. In themselves and in their importance to trade they compose a considerable stake requiring protection from local and outside infringement.

Business investments take on additional significance when they contribute to the military power of a state. Whether or not they are endorsed by a foreign state as a device to strengthen a weaker friend against anticipated attack they have that character and will be viewed as political instrumentalities by other states. In 1933 the Central Aircraft and Manufacturing Company, an American corporation, built a factory in Chekiang under a contract to build planes for the Chinese Government. Pan-American Airways owns 45% of the stock in the principal Chinese commercial air line, the China National Aviation Corporation.[14] The latter investment is held by a company subsidized by the United States Government to develop airways and carry mail across the Pacific. Such enterprises aroused the antagonism of Japan because they challenged its program of Sino-Japanese "cooperation" by assisting in the emancipation of China from external controls. The Japanese Government professed to view them as disguises for occidental financial imperialism. Their significance becomes clearer when it is recognized that very few states possess great financial power and that the larger the surplus capital within a state the greater is the urgency that new outlets be found for investment. The greater the investment, also, the greater becomes the foreign state's responsibility for its protection.

British business investments in China were six and a half times as great as American holdings in 1931. They amounted to nearly a billion dollars (U. S.), 39% of all foreign business investments in all China. Japanese investments were 37% of the total, Russian 11%, American slightly over 6%.[15] The total of foreign business investments was nearly

[14] Lockwood, "America's Stake in the Far East," cited, p. 178.
[15] Remer, cited, p. 99.

three and a half times the amount invested in governmental obligations. Between 1914 and 1931 British holdings increased nearly two and a half times, though their proportion to the total remained approximately the same. Japanese investments quadrupled, mainly due to Japan's controlling position in Manchuria. American interests rose more than three and a half times during the period. The relative significance of portfolio and direct investments is clearly shown in the totals for each as of 1914 and 1931. In 1914 the former were $496,000,000 (U. S.), the latter $1,084,000,000; in 1931 the former had risen to but $587,000,000 while the latter reached $2,474,000,000. It is apparent that the focus of foreign policy in such circumstances must be the direct investor rather than the holder of government bonds.

The record of foreign intervention in China for the protection of private interests remains to be written, but the so-called "gunboat policy" was a byword in that country during the half-century that preceded the Washington Conference (1921–22). The treaties themselves provided for patrol of China's coasts and of certain rivers by foreign naval craft. Land garrisons were posted at strategic points. Diplomatic table-pounding was supported by threats. Governmental prestige was undermined by the insistent evidence of foreign influence.

The "Twenty-One Demands"

The most unexpected change in the balance of influence in China during this period was marked by the dramatic move of Japan in 1915, designed to reduce all China to subservience.[16] By treaties and exchanges of notes imposed by ultimatum the Japanese Government forced China to accede to sweeping territorial and political demands, thereby throwing away an opportunity to establish a Far Eastern "front"

[16] MacMurray, *Treaties and Agreements,* etc., II, cited, p. 1215–37.

on a genuinely cooperative basis. In secret negotiations with Russia, Great Britain, France and Italy, Japan obtained approval in advance for its succession to German rights in Shantung.[17] The objection of the United States to Japan's purposes was obviated by the Lansing-Ishii Agreement of 1917. At the Paris Peace Conference in 1919 Japan reaped the reward of sharp diplomacy. Although Japan's gains were whittled down at the Washington Conference the fundamental principle of special interest in contiguous territory was not surrendered.[18]

The Diplomatic Revolution

The Washington Conference did not produce a *volte face* by the great states but it may be called the beginning of a gradual turning movement which continued through the decade 1921–31. New motives had been at work long before the Conference, represented chiefly by the twin doctrines of the "Open Door" and the "Integrity of China." The revolution in Russia had modified, though it had not destroyed, the Far Eastern policy of the Soviet Union. The World War, 1914–18, had removed Germany from the common front of European concession-hunters. Internationalism and the doctrine of national self-determination were deeply felt among Western peoples at the end of the war. Chinese nationalism became a positive and vigorous force in its own behalf. The combination of these and perhaps other factors reduced the current of foreign interference and induced a new charge of neighborly support for China's recovery.

The Nine-Power Treaty, signed at the Washington Conference and ratified or later adhered to by fourteen states (four British Dominions and India included as separate members of the British Empire), raised the "Open Door"

[17] La Fargue, T. E., *China and the World War,* Stanford University, 1937, p. 95–8.

[18] Willoughby, W. W., *China at the Conference,* Baltimore, 1922; Ichihashi, Y., *The Washington Conference and After,* Stanford University, 1928.

and "Integrity" doctrines to the status of a multilateral treaty and enlarged their scope by a provision for the cessation of all types of effort designed to create spheres of influence. The signatory powers, not content with a negative policy of self-restraint, agreed: [19]

> To provide the fullest and most unembarrassed opportunity to China to develop and maintain for herself an effective and stable government.

It will be hardly questioned that China's collateral agreement not to discriminate in economic relations between foreign countries, "whether parties to the present Treaty or not," was a provision in China's interest rather than a vestige of foreign interference.

First steps toward relieving China of foreign control over customs tariffs and of foreign jurisdiction (extraterritoriality) were taken at the Washington Conference. In 1928 eleven states, led by the United States, took the final step in relinquishing the former control by signing new treaties.[20] With Japan's accession to the group in 1930 China became again a free nation in this important sphere. Extraterritoriality continued to exist, in all probability because of interruption of negotiations for gradual abolition which were under way when Japanese intervention began in 1931.[21] The mixed courts in Shanghai were abolished in 1930.

In addition to these improvements in its treaty position, China also gained ground through the retrocession of leased territories—Kiaochow and Weihaiwei—and of several areas of foreign residence.[22] Three of the former and fifteen of the latter (including the settlements at Shanghai and Amoy), remain in foreign hands. Retrocession of a number of such

[19] *Conference on the Limitation of Armament,* Washington, 1922, p. 1624–28.

[20] Quigley and Blakeslee, cited, p. 123–33.

[21] *Ibid.,* p. 135–50.

[22] *Ibid.,* p. 155–69.

areas has the effect of demonstrating that in legal principle they are temporary holdings and not, as a number of authorities formerly asserted, disguised cessions.[23] Regrettably it cannot be stated that the foreign rights to patrol Chinese waters and to maintain garrisons have been relinquished.

Brief mention is needed of the position of foreign missionaries. Their rights remain intact under the treaties but the interventionism that formerly weakened their standing among the Chinese people was discontinued during the decade after the World War, 1914–18. Proof of this statement is the restraint shown by foreign governments during the great exodus of missionaries from the interior provinces during the Nationalist campaigns of 1926–28. Their societies accepted the restrictive regulations of the new National Government in a cooperative spirit and their work was energetically continued. Apparently they were willing to accept the consequences of their own teachings of democracy and national independence.

Communist Influence

A third form of foreign expansionism has already been referred to as ideological.[24] The classic example of this type of effort is the propaganda of the Third International, not because it is unique but because it takes ideas rather than military force or finance as its principal instrument, whereas other states had, in the main, left the propagation of national doctrines—democracy, Christianity, etc., to their citizens' private efforts. The Bolsheviki have not, however, refrained

[23] Norem, Ralph A., *Kiaochow Leased Territory,* University of California, 1936, p. 57–61.

[24] N. Bukharin asserted in 1936 that it is "senseless . . . to talk about the 'imperialism' of the U.S.S.R. . . ." While admitting that Communism believed in the "world triumph of socialism," he held that the U.S.S.R. would not "pursue a world policy of conquest," because to do so would be "stupidity." Bukharin's error is in confusing war with imperialism. ("Imperialism and Communism," *Foreign Affairs,* XIV, p. 563–77.)

from using both force and finance as auxiliary weapons.

Russian overtures to China after the Bolshevist Revolution of 1917 fell on receptive ears.[25] No other state had offered to give up its treaty rights. The vitriolic attacks of M. Karakhan, the Soviet Ambassador, upon the "imperialist powers" sounded reasonable on the morrow after the Treaty of Versailles, in which Japan's succession to German rights in Shantung was recognized. At Canton the reorganized Kuomintang, under the tutelage of the very capable Michael Borodin, admitted Chinese Communists into its membership. A proletarian-peasant movement got under way. There were serious riots at Shanghai, Canton and Hankow, directed principally against British interests. Under the protection of the new Nationalist army trained by the Russian General Galens (Blücher), the peasants of Kiangsi and Hunan drove out landlords and appropriated their lands. But the Kuomintang leaders repudiated these tactics in 1927, expelled the Communists, killed great numbers of radicals, and broke off relations with the Third International.[26]

Two considerations prompted the breach. One of these was the apprehension of Chiang K'ai-shek and his supporters in the Kuomintang that the Communists planned to dominate Party policies.[27] The other was the necessity of cooperation with the merchant-bankers of the port cities in order to obtain the large loans that enabled the National armies to sweep the country and to set up a new central government. The desire for the recognition of democratic states was also a factor. Although diplomatic relations with the Soviet Union were re-established in 1932, the National Government, despite the similarity of its structure to that of the Union of

[25] Weale, Putnam, *Why China Sees Red,* New York, 1925; Wang Ch'ing-wei, *China and the Nations,* New York, 1927, p. 120–6.

[26] See above, Chapter I.

[27] Trotsky criticizes Stalin for failing to espouse such a plan and for suggesting instead a program of "revolution by stages." See his *Problems of the Chinese Revolution,* London, 1932, p. 23–82.

Soviet Socialist Republics, kept clear of Communist influence.

After the collapse of the alliance between the Comintern (the Third International of Moscow) and the Kuomintang, the former altered its program to one of support for the Chinese Communists who organized peasant armies to struggle for the radical reorganization of China's economic order which the Kuomintang was repudiating. It issued precise instructions on political strategy to the Chinese Communist Party. It advised remaining within the Kuomintang while "continuing the struggle to bring to a finish the bourgeois-democratic revolution through 'plebeian' ways, i.e., by a revolutionary advance of the bloc of workmen, peasants and paupers of the cities under the hegemony of the proletariat."[28] This is the method of "boring from within" so widely practiced under the tutelage of Moscow.

Soviet influence, however, continued principally in the revolutionary local juntas and their armies and peasant followings which were the aftermath of the breach within the Kuomintang.[29] Apparently, although the Chinese Communist leaders took their basic ideas from the Comintern, they developed their own program and often were in advance of the cautious suggestions of the Kremlin. Neither arms nor funds in sizable quantities were obtained in this period from the U.S.S.R. The Chinese rebels found the advice and encouragement of the Russians sustaining to their morale and believed themselves to be part of a world movement to liberate the oppressed. They emulated the unifying discipline of the Bolshevists, substituting the principle of "one for all" for the traditional emphasis upon family loyalty. They adopted and

[28] Resolution of the Third International, printed in Yakhontoff, V. A., *Russia and the Soviet Union in the Far East,* London, 1932, p. 410–17.

[29] Snow, Edgar, *Red Star Over China,* cited, p. 369–85; Snow points out that both money and military aid were supplied to Chiang K'ai-shek, by foreign governments, to destroy the Communists, in vastly greater amounts than the latter received from the Soviet Union.

adapted Russian military and political agencies and methods. Nothing remotely resembling a "puppet" relationship to the U.S.S.R. developed. But an influence based upon acceptance of ideas may be stronger and more permanent than one imposed by force or purchase.

Soviet Protectorates in China

The Soviet Union failed to live up to the standards of international conduct which it prescribed for other states. With cynical realism it not only maintained the Russian hold upon northern Manchuria but it also established a system of control over Outer Mongolia far more complete than the Tsars had enjoyed and extended its influence in a decisive degree over Sinkiang.[30] Together these areas comprise one and one-third million square miles, nearly a third of the Chinese Empire. In Outer Mongolia the Soviets assisted in setting up a revolutionary government of "Young Mongols" along Communist lines. With the U.S.S.R. alone has the Mongolian People's Republic had diplomatic relations and it has been called an all but avowed member of the Soviet Union. Soviet penetration of Sinkiang is essentially economic in character, but has been pursued through political arrangements with the provincial government. Chinese government and trade in Sinkiang exist only on sufferance.[31]

The Way Ahead

There were inconsistencies in China's international position in 1930–31. Clearly the country's treaty status had im-

[30] Karl Radek, in his article, "The Bases of Soviet Foreign Policy," in *Foreign Affairs*, XII, p. 193–206, omits all reference to these areas, while stating that: "The Soviet Union takes no part in the struggle for the redistribution of the world."

[31] Lattimore, Owen, "Sinkiang," in *China Year Book, 1939*, cited, p. 463–5; Conolly, Violet, *Soviet Economic Policy in the East*, London, 1933.

proved. Territory had been regained. In all departments of government—legislative, executive, judicial—national action was less restricted. On the other hand, many features of foreign control embarrassingly remained. And foreign business investments had more than doubled at a time when the Chinese Government was refusing to have any dealings with the second Consortium which frankly planned to monopolize the market for public loans until China learned how and where to borrow economically. It appeared to be true that China's politics was still subject to foreign—particularly financial—influence. The second Consortium, whose strength was far greater than any banking combination hitherto dealt with by China, could be relatively unconcerned whether China borrowed on its terms or not since the alternative door—that of business investment—was open to its members. It must be kept in mind that Japan was a reluctant member of the Consortium and regarded it as an agency to frustrate the expansion of Japanese loans.

Communist influence had played a notable part in the reorganization and unification of the country but had failed to hold the support of Chiang K'ai-shek, with the result that its net effects were divisive and promotive of disastrous civil strife. It had disseminated suspicion of Occidental motives while the Soviet Government maintained Tsarist policies of territorial expansion. Its doctrines of social regeneration were permeating the Chinese masses, unsettling their loyalties but arousing a self-consciousness likely to have profound influence upon the country's ultimate destiny.

Finally, the attempt of Japan to assume the role of self-appointed supervisor of China's political and economic development, previously carried by European states, was a portent fully borne out during the last decade. In assessing the Japanese charges of foreign influence in China which are outlined in the next chapter it will not be overlooked that Japan's position in 1931 was already very strong. The facts given above show that in control of territory, in trade and in finance, Japan's relationship to China was one of special advantage. In view of the relaxation of European vigilance, and of the general antagonism to the spread of Communism, there was good reason to believe that Japanese participation in the development of a prosperous, independent China would be cordially welcomed.

IV

MAJOR ISSUES IN CONTROVERSY

A SMOULDERING antagonism kept the governments and peoples of China and Japan on edge after the Tangku truce of May 25, 1933.[1] Diplomatic relations were severely strained and local incidents were of frequent occurrence.[2] On July 7, 1937, one such incident in which shots were exchanged by Chinese and Japanese troops at Lukouchiao, near Peiping, proved to be the opening skirmish of the tremendous military struggle which has continued to this day. The full import of the struggle cannot be perceived *inter arma.* The emphasis that history will place upon one or another action or event or line of policy in its assessment of responsibility is beyond reckoning today. It is, however, possible to discern certain major issues out of which the *de facto* war arose.

The difficulty of distinguishing between wheat and chaff in the allegations of states in controversy with one another is recognized. This is increased by the necessity of gleaning the relevant data from a considerable number of statements, official, semi-official and non-official, since no comprehensive and definitive official declarations have been published by either China or Japan. It is impossible to say to what extent Japan's purposes as of 1941 were regarded as practicable in 1937. An attempt will be made to deal objectively in this chapter with the evidence applicable to the outbreak of large-scale warfare. Japan's "New Order in East Asia" is left to later consideration since this doctrine was not enunciated until 1938,[3]

[1] Quigley and Blakeslee, cited, p. 81, 284; Amau statement, p. 285.
[2] *Ibid.,* p. 80–102.
[3] See below, Chapters VII, XI.

though it was foreshadowed by the Amau statement of April 18, 1934.

Viscount Ishii wrote in January 1933, that the "permanent basis" of Japanese foreign policy was the attainment of "equality" and "security."[4] Equality was sought for the Japanese as a people or race; "security" was a many-sided objective. It is significant that while Ishii gave no intimation of a planned program of continental hegemony, his interpretation was broad enough to include any measures deemed necessary to Japan's strategic and economic security:

> Japan is an island nation. But her distance from the continent of Asia is so small that she cannot be indifferent to what happens in Korea, Manchuria, China and Siberia, any more than England can keep aloof from developments in the Low Countries across the Channel and along the North Sea.

"Security" is a comprehensive term under which any desired specific objective can be brought. It cannot be challenged *per se* but there may be wide difference of opinion upon the means of its attainment as well as upon the reality or degree of insecurity.

Communism as an Issue

Viscount Ishii attributes Japanese fears of insecurity in part to "misgivings as to the activities of the Third International" which was believed to be sponsored by the Soviet Union. References to the menace of communism appear in many official statements. In his first speech as foreign minister before the two houses of the Diet, on January 23, 1934,

[4] Ishii, Viscount Kikujiro, "The Permanent Bases of Japanese Foreign Policy," *Foreign Affairs,* XI (1932–33), p. 220–9; *cf.* Miyaoka, Tsunejiro, "The Foreign Policy of Japan," *International Conciliation,* No. 307, February 1935, p. 31–42. For a concise, well-reasoned analysis and rebuttal of Japan's position see Willoughby, W. W., *Japan's Case Examined,* Baltimore, 1940.

Mr. Koki Hirota expressed regret that "the Soviet Union should now take to broadcasting at home and abroad through press and other channels unwarranted criticisms directed against Japan. . . ."[5] A year later Mr. Hirota said that relations had improved but in 1936 he told the Diet that:[6]

> The greatest of all difficulties confronting China today is, I believe, communism, which has found a ready soil for propagation in the unsettled conditions of East Asia, and which has affected China most seriously, endangering not only her border regions but her internal social order itself. The rampancy of communism in China seems to surpass all our knowledge. . . . The suppression of the communist activities in our part of the globe and the liberation of China from the Red menace is, therefore, a matter of vital importance not only for China but for the stabilization of East Asia and of the world . . . It is the desire of the Japanese Government to cooperate with China in various ways for the eradication of communism.

During the period between 1933 and 1937 Japanese diplomacy was exerted unsuccessfully toward obtaining an agreement for Sino-Japanese cooperation against communism. On November 25, 1936, the German-Japanese convention against the Communist International was signed.[7] Mr. Hachiro Arita, then foreign minister, explained Japan's entrance into this much-criticized pact mainly on grounds of Soviet activities in China, particularly the organization of the "Anti-Japanese People's Front."[8] The Japanese Foreign Office, in its statement of October 28, 1937, explaining the refusal of Japan to attend the Brussels Conference,[9] declared that, "as compared with the time when the [Nine-Power] treaty was concluded, the situation in East Asia has been rendered totally

[5] *Contemporary Japan,* II, 1933–34, p. 765.
[6] *Ibid.,* IV, 1936, p. 638.
[7] Quigley and Blakeslee, cited, p. 304.
[8] *Contemporary Japan,* V, 1937, p. 710–11.
[9] Quigley and Blakeslee, cited, p. 121–2.

different, owing to the infiltration of communist influences and the changes of internal conditions prevailing in China." [10]

Turning to China's attitude on this issue we find, not cordiality toward communism but equally impressive statements of antagonism to that doctrine. On April 25, 1934, an official repudiation of certain implications of the Amau statement included a declaration that: [11] ". . . China at the present moment is concentrating all her efforts on the eradication of communism and [on] productive rehabilitation." (For seven years Chinese armies and police had been conducting bitter and costly anti-communist campaigns.) A year later the Government forbade the formation of any organization which might be detrimental to international relations.[12] General Chang Chun, Chinese Foreign Minister, spoke considerately of Japan's attitude on May 25, 1935: [13]

> Japan has frequently professed her concern over communist disturbances in certain parts of this country; and such concern is well understood by us, insomuch as the effects of internal agitations in one country are bound to be felt by the neighbors, due to the close interdependence of modern nations. During the last few years the Chinese Government has waged a relentless struggle against the Red menace, and the situation has been pacified to such an extent that we are confident of the early liquidation of the whole trouble. In whatever circumstances China is determined not to relinquish, even temporarily, her firm stand against the communists. . . .

The Central Executive Committee of the Kuomintang, China's National Party, at its session in February 1937, which followed the dramatic kidnapping of Chiang K'ai-shek at

[10] *The Conference of Brussels,* November 3–24, 1937, convened in virtue of Article 7 of the Nine-Power Treaty of Washington of 1922, Department of State, Washington, 1938, Pub. 1232, p. 14.

[11] *China Year Book, 1934,* cited, p. 727.

[12] *Ibid., 1936,* p. 176.

[13] *Ibid.,* p. 178.

Sian, in the province of Shensi,[14] passed a resolution of severe censure upon the communist leaders. The resolution laid down four conditions for reconciliation with them: [15] (1) abolition of the Red army as such and its incorporation into the national forces; (2) dissolution of the Chinese Soviet Republic; (3) cessation of propaganda; and (4) discontinuance of the class struggle. The eradication of communism was declared to be the cardinal policy of the Government.

It is clear that communism was anathema to both the Japanese and the Chinese theories of society. The issue between them was not doctrinal but practical. To the Japanese the paramount fact was that communism was a potent force in China in spite of Chiang's efforts to stamp it out. To the Chinese the Government's policy appeared to be succeeding and the danger to a neighbor state was negligible. To them, furthermore, there was danger to China's independence in Japan's proposal of joint action against communism.

Western Capital in China

Japan's antagonism to communism in China was matched by its opposition to occidental capitalism, which was regarded as a political wolf in the clothing of an economic sheep. Foreign investment in China was opposed because of the fear that out of it would develop *imperia in imperio* which would lead to the breakup of China. According to Viscount Ishii [16] this process had gone far before Japan was strong enough to stop it. By that time China "had already become so helpless in the face of foreign aggression that Japan, from sheer motives of self-preservation, was constrained to entrench herself in some of the regions from which she had ejected the aggressor."

[14] Chiang K'ai-shek and Mei-ling, *Sian, a Coup d'État,* Shanghai, 1938.
[15] *China Year Book, 1938,* cited, p. 532.
[16] Viscount Ishii, cited, p. 10–11.

Mr. Amau's statement [17] made it clear that Japan would interpret "any joint operations undertaken by foreign powers [with China] even in the name of technical or financial assistance . . . as bound to acquire political significance." Japan would oppose "any attempt on the part of China to avail herself of the influence of any other country in order to resist Japan." Mr. Amau left free only such commercial or financial transactions as would, in the judgment of Japan, benefit China and conduce to peace.

Mr. Yosuke Matsuoka, who was appointed foreign minister of Japan in the summer of 1940, gave a colorful interview to the Associated Press in October 1937. He was reported to have said, *inter alia:* [18]

> A historic fact dominates Asian scenes like Fuji, namely that without Japan there can be no China. Suppose Japan had chosen to play safe and crawled into her shell on her own tight little islands in the spring of 1904. Suppose again that Japan had gone down before the tidal-wave sweep of Russian adventure for her own Far Eastern empire on the plains of Manchuria in the autumn of 1905. There would have been no Manchuria, for which the Chinese patriots froth at the mouth and the League of Nations denounced Japan as an international robber. And in place of the proud Republic of China one would have seen a crazy quilt of European colonies after the fond fancies of the author of *The Break-up of China.*

Mr. Matsuoka finds the explanation of the present struggle in the continued threat of imperialism and Bolshevism:

> For what, then, is Japan fighting? She is fighting simply for her conception of her mission in Asia. There is the whole answer. She is fighting to keep Asia from becoming another Africa and, in particular, to save China from the death grip of the Comintern, just that. Billions of yen, thousands of her young men's lives—all are offerings on the altar of her own conviction and

[17] Quigley and Blakeslee, cited, p. 285–8.

[18] *Japan Weekly Chronicle,* October 21, 1937, p. 548–9.

aspirations. She is simply footing the bill which the leadership of Asian races calls for. No treasure trove is in her eyes—only sacrifice upon sacrifice. No one realizes this more than she does. But her very life depends on it as do those of her neighbors as well.

A younger but influential diplomat, Toshio Shiratori, more recently wrote with unusual and bitter frankness: [19]

From the very beginning of the China Affair it was said that Japan was fighting the hostile powers in the background of China rather than China herself. . . . The Japanese Government has hitherto studiously refrained from making a bold statement of this fact, of which it has always been aware. . . . In the present China Affair, Japan has not frankly stated her true mind to the world as yet. . . . If she had boldly proclaimed that her sole desire was to clear China of improper white influences and that she herself was absolutely free from any ambitious designs on China, the Affair would have been settled in a short time.

Chinese apprehension concerning the importation of Western capital has been strongly in evidence since President Yuan Shi-k'ai suppressed the liberal leadership of the Kuomintang with the help of the Reorganization Loan.[20] The Government declined to deal with the New Consortium [21] for a number of reasons, among them the fear that the foreign banks would demand controls over revenues which would prolong indefinitely the country's status of inequality in international relations. Since 1920 the former type of loan contracts has been discontinued.

China's need of foreign capital was, however, urgent, and the most favorable money markets were New York and London. The Chinese Government could not but regard

[19] *Ibid.*, April 10, 1941, p. 442–3.

[20] Willoughby, W. W., *Foreign Rights and Interests in China,* Baltimore, 1920, II, p. 992–9.

[21] Field, F. V., *American Participation in the China Consortiums,* cited, p. 178–85.

the Amau statement as an open challenge to China's independence in financial matters: [22]

> Japan pretends to be apprehensive of the possibility that the powers and the League of Nations might adopt an attitude of joint control toward China. Leaving aside the point that the powers and the League do not harbor any such design, the fact that China is an independent state should at once dispel the fear that she would tolerate for a moment to be bound by any form of joint control. China's opposition to any form of international control is just as strong as her aversion to domination by any one country.

The issue of capitalism between China and Japan came down, as did the issue of communism, to the fact that capitalist countries continued to have large interests in China, as in other countries. Japan regarded the influence of those states as inimical to it on two counts: (1) that it threatened China's territorial integrity and internal order; (2) that it enabled China more successfully to oppose Japan. That these ideas were inconsistent with one another is apparent. The Chinese denied the first count and repudiated the second, on the ground that China was an independent state.

"Cooperation"

The converse of Japan's opposition to the influence of other states in China was its determination that China should "cooperate" with Japan. This demand had been foreshadowed since the Russo-Japanese War and had been advanced, with shrewd reference to American policy, as a "Monroe Doctrine for the Far East." [23] The "Twenty-One Demands" of 1915 were the most complete revelation of the scope and po-

[22] *China Year Book, 1934,* cited, p. 726.

[23] Professor George H. Blakeslee's article, "The Japanese Monroe Doctrine," *Foreign Affairs,* XI, July 1932, p. 671–81, is the best brief discussion of this formula for Japanese policy.

litical implications of this overworked parallel. It was neatly phrased in the Lansing-Ishii Agreement of 1917 (abrogated in 1923):

> The Governments of the United States and Japan recognize that territorial propinquity creates special relations between countries, and, consequently, the Government of the United States recognizes that Japan has special interests in China, particularly in the part to which her possessions are contiguous.

The transition from the doctrine of "special interests" to that of "cooperation"—in the sense of Chinese acceptance of Japanese leadership—is found in the statement of Koki Hirota, Japan's Foreign Minister, before the Diet on January 23, 1934:

> . . . Our Government sincerely hope for the political and economic rehabilitation of China. They hope that she will be enabled to unite with Japan in performing the obvious mission of both Japan and China to contribute through mutual aid and cooperation to the peaceful development of their part of the globe.

In speech after speech Japanese premiers and foreign ministers have returned to the theme of cooperation.[24] Cooperation against communism and through commercial and financial channels was insisted upon, at times with patience toward China's handicaps, at others with contemptuous denunciation. Mr. Matsuoka has given vivid expression to the latter attitude: [25]

> One thing is clear even to a donkey running along an Asian highway: constant and hearty cooperation between the peoples of Japan and of China . . . alone can work out the destiny of Asia. . . . China and Japan are two brothers who have inherited a great mansion called Eastern Asia. Adversity sent them both down to the depths of poverty. The ne'er-do-well elder brother

[24] Quigley and Blakeslee, cited, p. 90–102.
[25] *Japan Weekly Chronicle,* October 21, 1937, p. 548.

turned a dope fiend and a rogue, but the younger, lean but rugged, and ambitious, ever dreamed of bringing back past glories to the old house. He sold newspapers at a street corner and worked hard to support the house. The elder flimflammed the younger out of his meager savings and sold him out to their common enemy. The younger in a towering rage beat up the elder—trying to beat into him some sense of shame and awaken some pride in the noble traditions of the great house. After many scraps the younger finally made up his mind to stage a show-down fight.

The Chinese Government was not opposed to cooperation, as was shown by the lowering of tariffs on imports from Japan, restraint of anti-Japanism, and other measures. But China's problem was to cooperate without losing its identity as a state. Mr. Matsuoka's bland assumption that there are no boundary lines in Eastern Asia, that the area forms a single "house" jointly inherited by China and Japan, sharply summarizes that problem. China insisted upon treatment as an independent state and asked of Japan the respect for its territorial integrity which is due from one state to another. It could not accept Japan's interpretation of cooperation. Japanese writers are disturbed over Western "misunderstanding" of Japanese explanations of such matters as Sino-Japanese "cooperation." Apparently the subjection of China to Japan is, according to Japanese ideas, "cooperation." The dullness of Western intelligence is extenuated, however, by the inability of the Chinese, culturally much nearer to the Japanese than ourselves, to follow the subtleties of Japanese psychology.

Anti-Japanism

Undoubtedly the most difficult task laid upon the Chinese Government by Japan was the extermination of anti-Japanese feeling among the people. On the morrow of the founding of "Manchoukuo" out of territory which the Japanese Government previously had recognized to be part of China, Mr. Hirota [26] told the Diet that "much to our regret, there are at this moment student agitations in China which contravene the very spirit of our program" but that "it is expected that the present situation will soon be rectified by the Chinese authorities. . . ." Clearly the Chinese Government had no power to alter popular feeling but it attempted to prevent the exhibition of that feeling in ways harmful to normal relations with Japan.[27] Violators of laws and ordinances protective of international amity were penalized, in some cases severely. Nevertheless a number of attacks upon Japanese subjects in China occurred at widely scattered points during 1936.[28] These were branded as "organized terrorism" in the statement of the Japanese Foreign Office issued on October 28, 1937.[29]

The importance attached to anti-Japanese feeling as an issue in Sino-Japanese relations is indicated by the lengthy consideration it received in the above-mentioned statement, which explains the outbreaks at Lukouchiao and Shanghai from the Japanese point of view. This document is a masterpiece in the editing of history. It mentions only the incidents and injuries caused by Chinese anti-foreignism, omitting all reference to foreign acts provocative of Chinese resentment, and picturing Japan's attitude as generous and benign. A few excerpts may be permitted: [30]

> . . . Japan has always striven to promote friendship and cooperation among the nations of East Asia, in the firm conviction that therein lies the key to the stability of that region. Japan wel-

[26] *Contemporary Japan,* IV, 1936, p. 639.

[27] See, *e.g.,* the "good will mandate" of June 10, 1935, *China Year Book, 1936,* cited, p. 176.

[28] Quigley and Blakeslee, cited, p. 96–7.

[29] Jones, S. Shepard, and Myers, Denys P., *Documents on American Foreign Relations, January 1938–June 1939,* I, World Peace Foundation, 1939, p. 167.

[30] *Ibid.,* p. 167–8.

comed the deepening of Chinese national consciousness which followed upon the revolution, believing that it would conduce to intimate Sino-Japanese collaboration, and she adopted the policy of meeting the legitimate national aspirations of China to the utmost possible extent.

. . . The Nanking Government [Author's note: the Chinese resented the use of the word "Nanking," carrying an inference of temporary or regional importance.] employed anti-Japanism as a convenient tool in domestic politics . . . and resorted to the unheard-of tactics of making it the foundation of moral education in the army and in the schools. . . .

A belligerent spirit toward Japan came to prevail throughout the land. . . . Japan's cautious attitude and her policy of local settlement were both doomed to utter failure.

Political Disorder

The Japanese contention that China was not an organized state was brought forward belatedly at Geneva, during the consideration of the Manchurian controversy.[31] "China," said the Japanese representative, "has for more than ten years been in a state of civil war, in a condition of complete chaos and incredible anarchy." This situation, he contended, made it impossible to settle controversial issues by pacific and normal methods and compelled Japan to take into its own hands the protection of the lives and rights of its nationals. The Chinese reply to this charge was in part a declaration that "chaos" and "anarchy" were libellous terms, in part a *tu quoque* grounded upon Japan's dual diplomacy and barbarous methods of warfare, in part an assertion that Japan was largely responsible for such disorder as existed. The Chinese delegate declared that Japan had intrigued to prevent the development of a strong and united China.

[31] League of Nations, *Official Journal,* XIII, 1932, p. 384; Willoughby, W. W., *The Sino-Japanese Controversy and the League of Nations,* Baltimore, 1935, p. 245–8.

"Manchoukuo"

The last issue to be dealt with here is that created by the establishment of "Manchoukuo."[32] The Japanese Government took the position that this new state, though aided into existence and subsequently protected by Japan, was an international person deserving of recognition by all states, including China. Japanese diplomacy was exerted to this end most persistently but without offers of compensation. No easing of the pressure for "cooperation" throughout all China was suggested by the Japanese as *quid pro quo.* It is unlikely, however, that the Chinese Government would have bargained for peace on such terms since the Manchurian provinces and Jehol were regarded as integral parts of China.

A Struggle for Existence?

China and Japan consider themselves to be fighting for the same thing: national existence. Each believes, correctly or mistakenly, that the other is a menace to its vital interests. The several issues discussed above are significant aspects of this fundamental issue. China's present position is proof enough of the insecurity of that state. Why the Japanese are apprehensive is less understandable. The more frank among the Japanese statesmen admit that Japan is carrying the battle to China but they affirm with their more taciturn colleagues that it is doing so in self-defense. They foresee, rightly or wrongly, Japan's involvement with communistic or capitalistic armies, or the loss of lives and wealth in a recalcitrant China. What they fail to admit, publicly, is their fear of a unified China. Possibly this fear is the most driving incentive in their effort to reduce China to vassalage.

When we speak of "national existence" today we have

[32] Quigley and Blakeslee, cited, p. 49–65, 90–102.

in mind not merely a large population of generally homogeneous culture within a compact area but also the possession by this people of a government of sovereign powers, constituting the area an independent state. The Chinese are not content with the "love" which the Japanese profess toward them, since they are expected to accept with it Japan's sense of a "mission" to control their political destiny. They wish to continue to live not only as a *civilization* but as a *state*. They wish to *govern* themselves.

Thus a settlement of the conflict that will satisfy both parties must leave China not only the appearance of independence but its reality. And it must establish conditions within China that will assure Japan of the safety of its legitimate interests. It must bring into Far Eastern relationships a mutual confidence that will enable Japan and China to see in one another's prosperity and strength not danger but security for both.

V

THE RENEWAL OF WAR

INTERNATIONAL law regards war as "a legal condition of affairs dealt with as such and so described both by participants and non-participants." [1] While war is "a condition of armed hostility between states," [2] such a condition may exist in the absence of war. To the layman this fact must appear absurd, particularly if acts of war on an extensive scale are described (as they were by the Japanese Government in the controversy with China), as an "incident" or an "affair." From one point of view it may be considered that states have deliberately refrained from declarations of war in order to evade obligations under treaties, such as the Covenant of the League of Nations or the Pact of Paris. From another point of view it can be shown that both participants and non-participants derive advantages from non-declaration of war. For example, one participant may not blockade the ports of another in the absence of a recognized state of war.[3] Nor may a participant government under these conditions capture the goods of non-participants as contraband. The fact that the legal responsibilities of a participant for damages and injuries to non-participants are more onerous than those of a belligerent works advantage to the latter but may involve an attacked participant in claims that lack moral justification.[4]

[1] Hyde, Charles Cheney, *International Law, Chiefly as Interpreted and Applied by the United States,* II, Boston, 1922, p. 189.

[2] *Ibid.;* for an opposing view see Lester H. Woolsey, "Peaceful War in China," *American Journal of International Law,* XXXII (1938), p. 314–9.

[3] Pacific blockade may be used only to shut off ports to the vessels of belligerents.

[4] Fenwick, C. G., "War without a Declaration," *American Journal of International Law,* XXXI (1937), p. 694–6.

The conflict between China and Japan had not been termed "war" by either state prior to December 9, 1941, when China declared war upon Japan. No third state had termed it "war." [5] Technically, therefore, it must be regarded as military intervention on a scale hitherto unknown in modern times. It is believed, however, that realities will be better served in this survey if "war" is used in the general sense of large-scale physical combat. While keeping in mind the legal position of belligerents and neutrals—technically to be identified as participants and non-participants—we shall avoid rather than invite confusion by calling this holocaust war.

Lukouchiao and Peiping

The great conflict is reckoned as having begun on the night of July 7, 1937, when an exchange of shots occurred between a Japanese force conducting maneuvers at the small district city of Wanping—which stands at the eastern end of Lukouchiao (the famous Marco Polo bridge),—and Chinese troops in garrison in that area. At this point a short railway from Fengt'ai connects the Peiping-Tientsin line with the Peiping-Hankow railway, making possible the transfer of trains between the lines without entrance into Peiping. Wanping was thus a highly important strategic position. Fengt'ai had been garrisoned by Japanese troops since May 1936, although no right under treaty existed for this loca-

[5] The Assembly of the League of Nations adopted a report of a subcommittee of its Far East Advisory Committee on October 6, 1937, in which Japan's military operations were declared to be "in contravention of . . . the Pact of Paris of April 27, 1928." On the same date Secretary Hull issued a public statement that "the Government of the United States has been forced to the conclusion that the action of Japan in China is . . . contrary to the provisions . . . of the Kellogg-Briand Pact of August 27, 1938." (Jones and Myers, *Documents,* I, p. 158, 163.) It does not appear that these statements were regarded by the Assembly or the United States as the recognition of a state of war.

tion of their forces.[6] The Lukouchiao area[7] was available to foreign commanders for drilling their men, but the Chinese troops in the area were suspicious of the Japanese because of the unusually large-scale maneuvers and their duration.[8] Both Chinese and Japanese were anticipating hostilities as the outcome of the diplomatic struggle over relationships in North China which had filled the period since the signing of the Tangku truce.[9]

In the absence of trustworthy evidence by which to test the divergent accusations of either side that the other started the shooting it is impossible to advance beyond speculation upon that point.[10] Of greater importance is the obvious fact that the Lukouchiao incident was in itself of slight importance and might readily have been settled as a local issue. It was not settled as such because the underlying attitude of the parties was that war was inevitable, while the commanders of the opposing forces on the ground were willing to try conclusions without further delay.

There appeared to be a prospect of local settlement when on July 9 agreement was reached at Peiping for withdrawal

[6] *China Year Book, 1936,* cited, p. 434; Feng'tai was not one of the localities listed in Article IX of the Boxer Protocol as agreed points for occupation by foreign troops. However, British troops garrisoned Feng'tai from 1912 to 1926; see *China Year Book, 1913,* p. 293–4; *1914,* p. 330; *1921,* p. 537; *1923,* p. 603; *1924,* p. 962; *1925,* p. 1205; *1926,* p. 1087. Feng'tai was an important junction on the Peiping-Mukden railway, which was built with British and Chinese capital and was operated with a British chief engineer. British occupation followed a resolution of the Diplomatic Body at Peking issued during the Republican Revolution. Article I of the resolution provided: "That troops should be placed at important stations, bridges, etc., along the line of the railway." (MacMurray, J. V. A., *Treaties and Agreements,* cited, I, p. 318.)

[7] The Chinese Government had authorized such use of the area on November 15, 1913. (Hanson, Haldore E., *"Humane Endeavor," The Story of the China War,* New York, 1939, p. 42, n. 4.

[8] Hsü, Shuhsi, *How the Far Eastern War Was Begun,* Shanghai, 1938, p. 6. One feature of the maneuvers, especially provocative at night, was a sham attack upon the city of Wanping.

[9] Quigley and Blakeslee, cited, p. 80–102; also see Chap. IV, above.

[10] The Japanese explanation is found in the statement of the Foreign Office, July 9, 1937 (*Contemporary Japan,* VI, 1937, p. 351–2); that of China in the statement of July 11, 1937 (*China Year Book, 1938,* cited, p. 353–5).

of the troops of both countries from Lukouchiao. This agreement was not carried out and further skirmishing occurred, but on July 11 the withdrawal of Chinese forces was agreed to, also the punishment of Chinese officers found to be responsible for the incident, and the suppression of anti-Japanese organizations. None of these locally-arranged terms actually was executed, however. For this failure the explanation appears to be that the Japanese sent heavy reinforcements into North China, causing the National Government to oppose the withdrawal of the Chinese troops.[11] The latter dispatched large additional forces of its own into Hopei.[12] One cannot overemphasize the real issue revealed by the great concern on both sides—the political control of North China.

General Sung Cheh-yuan, chairman of the Hopei-Chahar Political Council, with his seat of government at Peiping, tried to reach a local settlement that would be acceptable to both sides. He failed therefore to satisfy either side, which led to the Japanese encirclement of Peiping, the flight of General Sung, and the surrender of the city on July 27. At Tungchow and Tientsin Chinese troops attacked Japanese garrisons successfully until the Japanese brought bombing planes into action. The National army at Paotingfu did not take part in these engagements, which brought the Peiping-Tientsin area into Japanese hands.

The Drive into Inner Mongolia

At the end of July a Japanese division moved north from Peiping toward Nankow pass, the nearest entrance into Inner Mongolia. General Chiang K'ai-shek's 89th division held the pass for three weeks but was outflanked and forced to flee

[11] Japanese declaration of July 11, 1937, *Contemporary Japan,* VI, 1937, p. 352–3.

[12] Chiang K'ai-shek's statement of July 17, 1937, *China Year Book, 1938,* cited, p. 355; Chinese statement of August 15, 1937, *ibid.,* p. 356–7.

into the mountains. The Japanese army advanced rapidly along the railway through Kalgan in southern Chahar and on into Suiyuan. By occupying Kalgan they placed themselves astride the caravan route running through Outer Mongolia into Siberia, thereby cutting China's principal trade route to the Soviet Union. This route is the most available one for offensive or defensive action against the Soviets. Although Mr. Hirota made no mention of an anti-Soviet objective but confined his explanation of the purposes of this campaign [13] to the necessity of driving large Chinese forces out of Chahar, it may be assumed that the isolation of Outer Mongolia was a major interest in the occupation of the Inner Mongolian corridor.

After entering the province of Suiyuan Japanese forces were divided, one army pressing westward toward Kweihua, capital of Suiyuan, the other turning south toward Shansi. The former, greatly re-enforced and including "Manchoukuoan" and Mongol levies, captured Kweihua [14] on October 14, and Paotow, terminus of the Peiping-Suiyuan railway on October 17.

The invasion of Shansi province was designed as a blow at the Chinese Communists in that province and in neighboring Shensi, and also to cut the long route from Sian to the Turkestan-Siberian railway which maintained a back door into West China. Japanese forces moving south into Shansi were met at P'inghsing pass by a Chinese division from the Communist army of north Shansi, seasoned veterans of the civil war. The Japanese were badly defeated by the guerrilla tactics of the poorly armed peasant troops, who, with the aid of National troops sent in from central China in large numbers, drove the enemy out of twenty-six counties within two months. Taiyuan, capital of Shansi, fell to the Japanese on

[13] *Contemporary Japan,* VI, 1937, p. 563.

[14] *China Weekly Review,* October 23, 1937, p. 170; November 27, 1937, p. 305.

November 9, 1937, after a second army, driving along the railway from the east, had endangered the Chinese from the rear and forced their withdrawal. Losses were extremely heavy and the results of slight importance since the Chinese kept their hold on the province and completely frustrated Japanese designs on the Shensi-Turkestan road.[15] The success of the Eighth Route Army, as the Communist force was renamed upon incorporation with the National armies in August 1937, was profoundly significant in its effect upon the national morale as well as in its lesson for commanders on other fronts where defeat had disrupted armies far better equipped and where casualties were counted in the hundreds of thousands.

Severe fighting went on in Shansi as the Japanese continued efforts to occupy the entire province. They extended their occupation toward the south but failed to conquer the western districts. The rugged terrain of this area was well suited to guerrilla warfare. The Generalissimo sent strong forces to aid the Eighth Route Army, forces which are entitled to greater credit than they have received for holding back the Japanese. Employing at times as many as 140,000 men, the latter launched many attacks during the years that followed their invasion of the province, all to no avail. Not only was the province held but Chinese detachments were able to slip through the Japanese lines to disrupt rail and telegraphic communications between Shansi and the coast. Recruits swelled the defending armies from 70,000 to 500,000 men.[16] At the end of 1941 the Japanese were no further into Shansi than they had been in 1938.

Second Battle of Shanghai

Apprehension that the ill-feeling between the peoples would lead to mob attacks caused the Japanese Government

[15] Snow, Edgar, *Red Star Over China,* cited, p. 462–6.
[16] *New York Times,* December 2, 1941.

to evacuate civilians from the cities along the Yangtze in July and early August 1937. Japanese consulates at Chungking, Ichang, and other Yangtze cities were closed. A regiment of Japanese marines left Hankow and the Japanese concession there was taken over by the Chinese municipality.[17] Japanese warships appeared in larger numbers along China's coast-line and Japanese aeroplanes reconnoitered at will over central China. But there was no dispatch of additional troops or warships to Shanghai prior to August 11, two days after the occurrence of an incident at Hungjao aerodrome in which a Chinese sentry, a Japanese sub-lieutenant and a Japanese seaman were killed.[18] At that time the Japanese garrison in Hongkew, the northern section of the Settlement, numbered 5000 men. The reinforcements brought the total to 9000, all bluejackets and marines. Four cruisers and seven destroyers augmented the large Japanese naval force already lying in the Whangpoo river off the Settlement.[19]

The Chinese Government did not deny the Japanese charge that it greatly increased the gendarmerie at Shanghai and constructed defense works between Shanghai and Woosung, but those actions were not contrary to the letter of the Sino-Japanese armistice agreement of May 5, 1932.[20] Not until after the reinforcement of the Japanese garrison were troops of the regular army rushed into Chapei and Kiangwan.[21] In the forenoon of the following day, August 13, fighting began between the Chinese and Japanese forces. It would appear that whereas after the Lukouchiao incident the Japanese forced the issue to the point of war, at Shang-

[17] *China Weekly Review,* August 14, 1937, p. 398.

[18] *Ibid.,* p. 410; *Japan Weekly Chronicle,* August 19, 1937, p. 262–3. The Japanese sought to enter the grounds of the aerodrome, were refused admission, and the shooting followed. Hungjao is within the environs of Shanghai.

[19] *Ibid.,* September 11, 1937, p. 23.

[20] *China Year Book, 1931–32,* cited, p. 678–81; *1938,* cited, p. 368–73.

[21] This took place on August 12, 1937. (*China Weekly Review,* September 11, 1937, p. 23; Hsü, Shuhsi, *Japan and Shanghai,* Shanghai, 1938, p. 19.)

hai it was the Chinese who, by throwing immensely superior numbers into the danger zone, precipitated the extension of the fighting into central China, where their best troops were located, with the object of relieving the pressure in North China. Had the Japanese been free to devote their full energies to the conquest of the North, the provinces of Hopei, Shantung, Chahar, and Suiyuan, and probably Shansi and Shensi as well, would have fallen as completely into their power as did Manchuria and Jehol, though less quickly.[22] There can be little doubt that such was Japan's purpose. As it turned out the campaign in central China became the major focus of Japan's efforts and the northern provinces remained largely unoccupied and a significant factor in the program of resistance.

The blood of both sides was up and there was no further effort by either side toward conciliation. For three months the fighting at Shanghai was extremely severe. The Chinese used 300,000 of their best troops, the Japanese 90,000.[23] The guns of the Japanese warships were employed effectively and Japanese equipment was greatly superior to the Chinese. Although Chinese air pilots were inexpert at the beginning—on August 14 they dropped some twenty bombs in the business district of the International Settlement which killed 1200 and wounded 1400 non-combatants [24]—they improved rapidly and were able to maintain their attacks on the enemy's troops and warships throughout the struggle for Shanghai. As in 1932 the Chinese eventually were defeated by a turning movement, this time on their right flank, made possible by the failure of forces at Hangchow to hold their lines.

[22] That the Chinese moved to create a division of Japan's forces is the view of impartial observers; see Haldore Hanson, *"Humane Endeavor,"* cited, p. 127; Frank Oliver, *Special Undeclared War,* London, 1939, p. 136–7; H. G. Woodhead, "Sino-Japanese Hostilities: A Frank British Opinion," *Contemporary Japan,* VI, 1937, p. 411–12.

[23] Carlson, Evans F., *The Chinese Army,* cited, p. 69.

[24] *China Weekly Review,* August 21, 1937, p. 423–4; Oliver, Frank, cited, p. 137–8.

Warfare on all sides of the International Settlement and the French Concession brought danger and death to foreigners and disastrous losses to their personal, industrial, commercial, and cultural interests. Bombs and shells burst within the foreign areas on several occasions. An attempt [25] was made to prevail upon the opposing commanders to recognize a neutral zone around Shanghai, a proposal incapable of execution unless both sides withdrew from their positions. Foreign garrisons were reinforced and the foreign municipalities were ringed about with their troops and the locally organized Volunteer Corps of the Settlement. Naval contingents also were increased.

Japanese air attacks upon lower Yangtze cities, railway trains, roads and river traffic began soon after the outbreak of hostilities at Shanghai. Retirement of the Chinese from Shanghai began on November 9. Their intense military effort left them exhausted and drained away the best trained divisions of the army.[26] Inexperienced officers failed to organize the retreat from Shanghai, while the Japanese sent fresh troops to pursue the defeated enemy westward. Nanking was not seriously defended and it was taken by the Japanese on December 12–13, 1937. On November 20, the National Government had been transferred to Chungking, Szechwan.[27] Actually the Government moved temporarily to Hankow and remained there for nearly a year. In a statement issued on November 20 the Government reviewed the course of events and said: [28]

The enemy has, however, failed to realize that since the day when the policy of resistance and war was decided upon, we have been convinced of the fact that the ultimate crisis has arrived.

[25] *China Weekly Review,* September 18, 1937, p. 39.

[26] Major Carlson states that Japanese casualties at Shanghai were about 40,000 men, Chinese "well over" 100,000. (*The Chinese Army,* cited, p. 70.)

[27] *China Year Book, 1939,* cited, p. 410.

[28] *Ibid.*

For the sake of our national existence, of the status of our race, of international justice and of world peace, China finds no ground for submission. All those who have blood and breath in them must feel that they wish to be broken as jade rather than remain whole as tile.

Space is not available here for treatment of the effects of the warfare upon the lives and ways of living of the Chinese masses.[29] Some mention must be made, however, of the sack of Nanking. From an account by an eye-witness known to the author as a man of the most scrupulous integrity, the unpleasant, even incredible, fact must be accepted that the officers of Japan's army permitted the slaughter of thousands of disarmed soldiers and civilians, the rape of many hundreds of women, the looting and burning not only of the shops and homes of the wealthy but those of the poorest coolies, and the abuse of foreigners, including an American consul, who sought to intercede for the people. The wanton burning of splendid new government buildings and the bestial manner of the attacks on men and women expressed a contempt and rage beyond control. The Japanese embassy staff did its best to assist foreigners seeking to protect the Chinese but it was helpless.[30]

It can hardly be doubted that the sinking of the American gunboat *Panay*[31] and the attacks upon the British gunboats *Ladybird, Bee, Scarab* and *Cricket*[32] by Japanese airbombers and shore batteries—all of which occurred during the battle for Nanking—were manifestations of the same disregard of world opinion and the same war psychology that made pos-

[29] Timperley, H. J., *What War Means: the Japanese Terror in China,* London, 1938.

[30] For a careful survey of the results of violence after the surrender of Nanking see Smythe, Dr. Lewis S. C., *War Damage in the Nanking Area.* The findings of this sociologist were published by the Nanking International Relief Committee, which did heroic work on behalf of the people of Nanking during the whole period of excesses.

[31] See p. 212.

[32] See p. 233.

sible the orgy of hate and destruction at Nanking. All of these vessels were well-known to the Japanese, all were well-marked with their respective national flags. It would appear that certain local commanders rather than General Iwane Matsui, commander-in-chief of the Japanese army on the Yangtze front, or the Japanese Government, were responsible for these gross departures from legal and moral standards. From Tokyo instructions to maintain discipline were carried to China by an officer of high rank and there was no later repetition of the degree of ruthless barbarism exhibited at Nanking.[33]

The Fall of Hankow and Canton

Early in September 1937, the Japanese added to their costly undertakings in Inner Mongolia and at Shanghai by the inauguration of campaigns along and between the Peiping-Hankow and Tientsin-Pukow railways, the two main lines from North China to the Yangtze valley. In these thrusts they were opposed to comparatively untrained and very poorly equipped provincial troops unacquainted with guerrilla methods. Although, under the instructions of German military advisers, lines of concrete pill-boxes and trenches had been prepared, the troops were unable to make effective use of them in the face of Japanese tanks, heavy guns and aeroplanes. Unity of command also was lacking in the Chinese armies of the North, which fought desperately when well led.

After the capture of Shanghai, a Japanese army was sent north from Pukow to attempt a junction of forces with the army advancing along the Tientsin-Pukow railway from the north. Governor Han Fu-chu of Shantung failed to offer serious resistance and was court-martialed at Hankow and

[33] Oliver, Frank, cited, p. 186.

shot. Japanese cotton mills and other properties at Tsingtao valued at 300,000,000 yen were dynamited and burned by the Chinese.[34] Chinese strategy improved and determination increased after the removal of Han. At Taierhchwang, junction point of the Grand Canal and the Tientsin-Pukow line, General Ch'ih Feng-ch'eng out-maneuvered and severely defeated a Japanese division, forcing it to retreat some twenty miles. The Japanese were forced to assemble an army of 200,000 men to capture Hsüchow, where the east-west Lunghai railway crosses the Tsinpu line. This was accomplished on May 19, 1938.

The campaign then turned westward, with Hankow as the objective. Troops and naval craft were also moving up the Yangtze toward that city. The Chinese mustered a million men in central China to defend this important industrial and commercial center. They cut the Yellow River dikes, flooding a vast area. Not until October 25 were the invaders able to enter Hankow. The Chinese forces were not surrounded but were able to withdraw to the west. It is noteworthy that the Japanese army advancing down the Peiping-Hankow railway did not take part in the capture of Hankow. A section of the railway from a point north of Chengchow southward to Sinyang remained in Chinese hands when the southern terminus fell.

Canton, the great capital of Kwangtung province, was taken by the Japanese on October 21, 1938, after a sudden descent upon Bias Bay, north of Hong Kong. The Chinese forces in that area were too widely distributed and made no appreciable resistance. Probably the proximity of Hong Kong had given the Chinese at Canton a false sense of security. It is difficult nevertheless to understand the failure to provide first-rate troops and defenses at Canton since that port was China's main reliance for the importation of military supplies.

[34] *Japan's War in China,* II, p. 10 (published by *China Weekly Review*).

Stalemate in Central China

General Chiang K'ai-shek withdrew from Hankow to strong positions in the hills of western Hunan, Hupeh and Honan. The Japanese did not attempt to attack these positions but dug in around the Wuhan cities—Hankow, Hanyang and Wuchang. They extended their lines to Yochow, on the Wuchang-Hankow railway in November 1938, and took Nanchang, capital of Kiangsi, in March 1939, thereby cutting the railways connecting Hangchow with the Wuchang-Canton line. A huge Chinese force released by the fall of Hankow circled the Japanese lines and took up guerrilla tactics behind their main armies. A Japanese thrust toward Sian in May 1939 was frustrated. The bombing of western cities, including Chungking, was destructive but ineffectual as a means of compelling China's capitulation.

Occupation of Pakhoi and Nanning

The only considerable extension of Japan's occupation after the fall of Hankow was accomplished in November 1939, when a large force was landed at Pakhoi in southern Kwangtung. Penetrating northward approximately a hundred miles, this army captured Nanning in Kwangsi, a strategic crossroads for transportation to and from French Indo-China. Attempts to push further into the interior were unsuccessful.[35]

That the Chinese general staff was alert and competent was demonstrated in October 1939, when a Japanese army drove from Yochow toward Changsha, capital of Hunan province and an important rail and road center. The Japanese were caught between Chinese forces east and west of the Canton-Wuchang railway down which they were advancing. They

[35] *China Weekly Review,* November 25, 1939, p. 461–2; December 2, 1939, p. 17–18.

reached the outskirts of Changsha where they were surrounded and forced to retreat under continuous fire to Yochow.[36] This victory, though won at heavy cost in casualties, was inspiriting to the Chinese people.

The Japanese won important advantages in June 1940, when they captured Ichang, on the Yangtze river at the eastern entrance to the gorges. This success gave them a point of departure for the bombing of Chungking. Ichang is but 240 miles by air from the latter city. But they refrained from attempting to push further by land and river. In October they retired from Nanning, Kwangsi, explaining that their occupation of northern Indo-China made the city strategically unimportant. Subsequently they evacuated all of Kwangsi and southwestern Kwangtung. Nearly a year elapsed before any new extension of their lines was attempted. In October 1941, they advanced from Yochow, Hunan, upon Changsha but evacuated the city after a few days of looting. In that month also a Japanese force, after three years of unsuccessful effort, finally succeeded in crossing the Yellow River and capturing Chengchow, railway junction of the Peiping-Hankow and Lunghai railways in Honan province. This success brought them within 275 miles of Sian, an important station on the long route into Free China from Russian Turkestan. At the same time Chinese forces recaptured a part of the Yangtze port city of Ichang but failed to hold it in the face of Japanese artillery and air attacks. Failing to overcome Chinese resistance west of Chengchow, the Japanese evacuated the city, returning to their base across the Yellow River.

Frustrated in the north, center and south, the Japanese resorted to widespread bombing from the air. Chungking, Kunming and the Burma road were frequently attacked. Between January 15, 1938, and September 1, 1941, Chungking was bombed 142 times. Thousands of civilians were

[36] *Ibid.*, October 14, 1939, p. 253.

slaughtered and enormous damage was done to property. The planes flew too high to be reached by anti-aircraft guns and the Chinese had no planes capable of resistance. Not until August 1941 were a few Chinese fighters, in Russian planes, seen in the skies above Chungking. Military results of the bombing were slight. Breaks in the Burma road were repaired quickly, and Chinese morale grew stronger, not weaker.

Naval Activities

During the struggle for Shanghai, Japanese naval squadrons went into action along the coast of China. On September 5, 1937, an order was issued by fleet commanders for the blockade of all ports except Tsingtao and those in foreign leased areas or settlements against Chinese shipping.[37] Tsingtao was exempted in the beginning because of an agreement by Governor Han Fu-chu of Shantung[38] to protect Japanese properties there, but was subsequently blockaded. Amoy, an important port near the southern boundary of Fukien, was bombarded from the sea; Swatow, a neighboring city in Kwangtung, received the same treatment, as did a number of smaller cities on the coast and on Hainan Island. Chinese forts and aeroplanes replied to these attacks. The bombing of Canton, metropolis of South China, began in September. Although the Japanese asserted that these attacks were aimed at military objectives, the losses of civilian lives were disproportionately heavy.

Aside from blockade and troop transport the major accomplishment of the Japanese navy was the support it provided for the army in the battle of Shanghai and subsequent operations in the Yangtze valley culminating in the occupation of Hankow. Japan's complete command of the maritime

[37] *Ibid.*, October 2, 1937, p. 87.
[38] Hanson, Haldore, cited, p. 110.

approaches to China enabled it to ferry troops back and forth across the Yellow Sea at will. Except for occasional attacks from the air and some resistance from coastal batteries, the Japanese navy met little opposition since China's naval craft were either obsolete or too small to venture against even the over-age vessels employed by Japan. The blockade was tightened by degrees until the entire Chinese coast was sealed to Chinese vessels and only professional smugglers, including many Japanese, were able to continue trading.

In the second year of the conflict the navy found an opportunity to participate in the expansion of Japan's area of occupation. It took part in the seizure of the island of Hainan on February 10, 1939. Since Hainan lay within the former French sphere of influence this action may be deemed the first sign of Japan's readiness to repudiate its commitments under the Franco-Japanese entente of 1907. The Japanese Government denied that its action was a violation of the agreement of 1907, asserting, contrary to its thesis of Chinese disorder, that since 1907 conditions in China had "undergone a complete change" and that "the unrest and disturbances have steadily decreased!" (See below p. 307.) It was followed in March by the seizure of the Spratley Islands, small coral isles 700 miles south of the southernmost point of China, 130 miles from the southeastern coast of Indo-China and about the same distance from Palawan, the nearest island of the Philippine archipelago. The Japanese claimed the islands on the basis of commercial activities of Japanese subjects there. France had indicated prior rights in 1933.[39]

Small as it was, the Chinese navy participated in hostilities on the Yangtze with some success. By blocking first the Whangpoo River and later the Yangtze, at Kiangyin below Nanking, it impeded Japanese naval support of land forces and aided substantially in prolonging the defense of Shang-

[39] *China Weekly Review,* April 8, 1939, p. 164.

hai and Nanking. Subsequently it repeated this blocking maneuver below and above Hankow with similar effect. It also made use of fixed and floating mines with considerable success, sinking warships, transports and merchant craft. During the 13 months from January 1940 to February 1941, 12 warships, 45 transports, 6 merchant ships and 66 other vessels were sunk by this method.[40]

Overtures for Peace

On January 2, 1938, following the capture of Nanking, the Government of Japan made overtures for peace through Dr. Oscar Trautmann, the German ambassador to China. Four proposals were made: [41]

1. That China abandon attitudes favorable to communism and unfavorable to Japan; that China collaborate with Japan and "Manchoukuo" against communism.
2. That China agree to the establishment of certain demilitarized zones and accept a "special" (i.e. a Japanese-controlled) regime for such areas.
3. That an economic bloc be formed between China, Japan and "Manchoukuo."
4. That China pay "necessary" indemnities to Japan.

It is obvious that these terms embody the principal issues which engendered the conflict, plus the imposition of indemnities. There was in fact no basis for a settlement in them that would permit China to remain an independent nation. Apparently the Chinese Government did not, however, reject them outright,[42] but gave them some consideration.

[40] Wang, Shih-fu, "Naval Strategy in the Sino-Japanese War," *U. S. Naval Institute Proceedings,* LXVII, 1941, p. 991–8.

[41] Address of Foreign Minister Hirota, *Contemporary Japan,* VI, 1938, p. 785.

[42] Lin, P. S., "Aide Defends Peace Drive," *China Weekly Review,* October 21, 1939, p. 285. Mr. Lin, a supporter of Wang Ch'ing-wei, stated that Chiang K'ai-shek submitted the terms to Stalin.

Failing to receive a "sincere" reply, Premier Konoye, on January 16, 1938, issued a declaration that:[43]

> . . . the Japanese Government will cease from henceforward to deal with that [the Chinese National] Government, and they look forward to the establishment and growth of a new Chinese regime, harmonious coordination with which can really be counted upon.

Apparently contacts were made in secret between Chinese and Japanese emissaries at Hong Kong and at Shanghai after an emergency congress of the Kuomintang in April 1938 had reaffirmed basic principles—sovereignty, administrative independence and economic equality—upon which China would make peace.[44] At the time of the congress General Chiang K'ai-shek took it upon himself to seek the "reasonable solution of the question of the four northeastern provinces" (i.e. "Manchoukuo"), for which the manifesto of the congress had expressed China's hope. Wang Ch'ing-wei, a former President of the Executive *Yuan* and later head of the Japanophile government at Nanking, has stated that General Chiang agreed to shoulder this grave responsibility on condition that Japan would guarantee to refrain "from further encroachment upon Chinese territory and sovereignty."[45] Presumably the conversations above mentioned dealt unsuccessfully with this peace gesture.

The fall of Hankow was the signal for another Japanese move for a settlement. Premier Konoye issued a brief statement on December 22, 1938 which demanded that China "do away with the folly of anti-Japanism," "enter of her own will into complete diplomatic relations with Manchoukuo," conclude with Japan "an anti-Comintern agreement," agree to the stationing of Japanese troops "at specified points,"

[43] *China Year Book, 1939,* cited, p. 426.

[44] Lin, P. S., cited; *China Year Book, 1939,* cited, p. 413.

[45] Manifesto of the so-called sixth Kuomintang Congress, August 28–30, 1939, reprinted in *International Conciliation,* No. 359, April 1940, p. 175.

designate the Inner Mongolian region "as a special anti-Communist area," recognize "freedom of residence and trade for Japanese subjects in the interior of China," and "extend to Japan facilities for the development of China's natural resources." [46]

This statement maintained the position taken by Japan on January 16, 1938, declaring that the "Japanese Government are resolved . . . to carry on the military operations for the complete extermination of the anti-Japanese Kuomintang Government . . ." It went beyond the demands submitted through Dr. Trautmann in requiring recognition of "Manchoukuo." In one respect it retreated from the earlier terms, i.e. in withdrawing the requirement of an indemnity. Presumably this leniency was due to the anticipation of Wang Ch'ing-wei's willingness to attempt the realization of the "new order in East Asia." [47] Japan offered also to consider the abolition of extraterritoriality and foreign residential areas.

General Chiang K'ai-shek's statement of December 26, 1938, was a strong and well-argued repudiation of Prince Konoye's demands.[48] He made it clear that the Chinese people understood Japan's purpose to be not cooperation but subjugation. "The aim of the Japanese," he said, "is to control China militarily under the pretext of anti-communism, to eliminate Chinese culture under the cloak of protection of Oriental culture, and to expel European and American influences from the Far East under the pretext of breaking down economic walls." He reviewed the plans and agencies already created in China for the purpose of economic conquest. He pointed out that Japan was asking more of China than of itself in resistance to communism. Japan does not ask indemnities because the absorption of China would in-

[46] Appendix, p. 283.
[47] For Wang Ch'ing-wei's movement see Chapter VII.
[48] Appendix, p. 285.

clude its wealth. While condemning Japan's militarists as seekers of world dominance, he assured the Japanese people of China's continued friendship.

Wang Ch'ing-wei, whose relations with the Japanese are dealt with in a later chapter,[49] became the principal Chinese agent of a settlement. It is believed that the Japanese Government did not allow its pledges to Wang Ch'ing-wei to interfere with further overtures to Chiang K'ai-shek. With the outbreak of war in Europe and the quick successes of Germany, Japanese ambitions for empire in the South Pacific prompted vigorous efforts to end the conflict in China. Wang failed to win support from his countrymen. Chiang had gained rather than lost popular respect through Wang's defection. Maneuvers to reach a settlement with him cannot now be documented. Apparently German would-be mediators offered to use their influence to obtain a peace on the basis of gradual evacuation of China proper, dominion status for "Manchoukuo" within the Japanese empire, and special economic privileges for Japan. Presumably such intercession would have Japanese approval.[50] But where there was no confidence there could be no settlement. On December 7, 1941, China's future became a problem of world settlement.

[49] See Chapter VII.
[50] *New York Times,* November 29, 1941.

VI

FREE CHINA CARRIES ON *

"FREE CHINA" is the area within the borders of the former Chinese empire over which no European or Asiatic state has extended its military or political control. It does not include Tibet and Outer Mongolia. These immense but lightly peopled lands are semi-autonomous, under the influence, respectively, of Great Britain and the Union of Soviet Socialist Republics, though still acknowledged, in treaties between those states and China, to be Chinese territories. However, Chinese influence has recently increased in Tibet, which accepted Chinese auspices in the enthronement of the Dalai Lama in 1940.[1] Whether Free China includes the western two-thirds of Inner Tibet, or the province of Sinkiang is doubtful, in view of the slight influence exerted by the National Government in those areas. The eight provinces that may now be regarded as wholly within Free China are Yunnan, Szechwan, Shensi, Kansu, Sikang, Ch'inghai, Ninghsia and Kweichow. Large sections of ten other provinces: Honan, Shansi, Suiyuan, Kiangsi, Hunan, Hupeh, Fukien, Chekiang, Kwangsi and Kwangtung also should be included. Obviously the territorial extent of the National Government's actual jurisdiction may be only roughly estimated.

The area of the eight completely free provinces is 1,018,218

* Acknowledgment is due to the Division of Intercourse and Education of the Carnegie Endowment for International Peace for permission to reproduce here a considerable portion of *International Conciliation*, No. 359, April 1940 (New York, Carnegie Endowment for International Peace).

[1] *Chinese Year Book, 1940–1941*, p. 99.

square miles;[2] that of the unoccupied portions of the other named provinces may fairly be estimated at 500,000 square miles; the total area of Free China, therefore, is approximately 1,500,000 square miles, which is comparable with the 1,800,000 square miles of India, including Burma. It is more than three fourths of all China, exclusive of Manchuria, Outer Mongolia, Sinkiang and Tibet. The eight free provinces had a population of approximately 88,000,000 prior to the exodus westward caused by the recent warfare. If there be added to this number two thirds of the 192,000,000 people in the partly-occupied provinces, the total free population approximates 216,000,000.[3] Migration from occupied territory probably has increased this number by many millions.[4]

These estimates would leave 520,000 square miles within Japanese lines of occupation, in addition to "Manchoukuo." But in fact, within this area, the most densely populated and wealthy portion of China, a large proportion of rural territory is unoccupied by enemy forces. The great majority of rural counties or *hsien* in so-called occupied China are still administered by district magistrates loyal to the National Government and uncontrolled by the occupying soldiery. Between the railway lines the larger part of occupied China is in fact still part of Free China, a source of supplies, of conscripts, and of danger to enemy garrisons. To maintain its hold on strategic and commercial centers, the Japanese general staff must keep large numbers of men practically immobilized in garrisons.

The transfer of the National Government to Chungking, Szechwan, from Nanking, in November 1937, was accompanied by an official declaration that "those who have blood and breath in them must feel that they wish to be broken

[2] Cressey, Geo. B., *China's Geographic Foundations,* cited, p. 55.
[3] *Chinese Year Book, 1938–1939,* p. 32–5.
[4] *Far Eastern Survey,* April 6, 1938, p. 82.

as jade rather than remain whole as tile," wherefore a protracted war of resistance would be carried on.[5] Szechwan, a province without railways, with but a few hundred miles of motor roads, had been practically autonomous in administration under the Republic. The governor of Szechwan, General Liu Hsiang, who had inherited his position from an uncle, and who was naturally disinclined to his own eclipse by a national luminary and opposed the establishment of the Government in his province, died, perhaps providentially, at Hankow in January 1938. His place was filled by the appointment of General Chang Ch'un, a native of Szechwan, who had the confidence of General Chiang K'ai-shek and who had been mayor of Shanghai and foreign minister. The national offices were not moved to Chengtu, capital of Szechwan, but to Chungking, a smaller city southeast of Chengtu. In October 1939, Generalissimo Chiang K'ai-shek found it necessary to assume the governorship himself, as local jealousies were still hampering the national administration.

At the time of the transfer of the capital, the province of Yunnan was if anything more independent of the central government than Szechwan had been. Governor Lung Yün also was opposed to the influx from the east and has been far from cordial toward the Chungking regime. Only the fear of invasion by loyalist troops has held him in line.[6] Moreover, Yunnan and Kweichow were extremely backward in economic organization, subsisting upon primitive agriculture, domestic industry and small-scale mining. The only railway in the whole region was the French-owned line from Indo-China to Kunming, capital of Yunnan. In the territories still further west, political and social life was even more primitive. The measures which have been taken to transform

[5] *China Year Book, 1939,* cited, p. 410–11.

[6] *China Weekly Review,* March 4, 1939, p. 13; *Japan Weekly Chronicle,* Nov. 16, 1939, p. 539.

western China into a center of commerce, industry, education and military reorganization are sufficient proof of the Chinese will to live as an independent nation.

The Party and the Government

Since 1927, as is well known, the Government of China has been a one-party government, modelled in part upon that of the Soviet Union, in part upon older Chinese institutions. The Kuomintang or National Party exercises control through a Congress, a Central Executive Committee, and a Central Supervisory Committee. The Congress meets irregularly at the call of the Central Executive Committee, which largely controls the choice of delegates, though they are supposed to be, and to a considerable extent are, representative of local branches of the Party, elected by the rank and file. Although the Congress is dominated by the C.E.C., its sessions afford an opportunity for discussion of general policies, and provide publicity for the decisions of the principal committees. In the absence of a national legislature, the Party Congress is something of a substitute, since the policies of the Kuomintang are, in the main, not Party but national policies.

In general, the system and functioning of administration in war times have been maintained on the prewar basis. The Central Political Council, which operated as a bridge between the Central Executive Committee of the Party and the five governmental departments (*yuan*),—formulating policy for them in accordance with the decisions of the C.E.C. and supervising their execution of policy—has surrendered its powers temporarily to a new body—the Supreme National Defense Council. General Chiang K'ai-shek is Chairman of this Council, in which governmental control now centers. It is composed of the superior officers of the Party and the Government, with other members designated by the chairman.[7] In the recently created position of *tsung-tsai* (director-general) of the Kuomintang, Chiang has the powers of the dead *tsungli* (leader), Sun Yat-sen. As *tsung-tsai,* he is chairman of the National Congress, of the Central Executive Committee, and of its standing committee.[8] He is recognized as supreme in Party affairs and, since the Party decides public policy, Chiang now has the powers of a dictator.[9] His headship of the Party was paralleled in the Government when, on November 20, 1939, Chiang was chosen chairman of the Executive *Yuan,* a post equivalent to the premiership and the actually dominant executive office.

Sun Yat-sen was never a dictator because Sun, with all his trying, was never able, after resigning the presidency early in 1912, to lead the Party to power in the state. Chiang would hardly have become dictator without the aid of the Japanese invasion. The distaste of the Party leaders for one-man control was demonstrated in 1931—after the invasion had begun—when a new constitution reduced the powers of the President of the National Government and forbade the President to hold any other post concurrently. At that time Chiang K'ai-shek was both president and premier. Too much weight should not be attached to formal legal change, since Chiang's influence was firmly founded upon the army. It is important, however, to note the opposition in the Party to the growth of dictatorship, indicating as it does the probability of a return to more liberal trends if and when the crisis is resolved. Retention of the Central Supervisory Committee, which is the auditing board and censorate of the Kuomintang, during the dictatorial regime, is additional evidence of the Chinese antipathy to barefaced autocracy.

[7] *Chinese Year Book, 1938–1939,* cited, p. 356–60; *People's Tribune,* Feb. 1939, p. 137–40.

[8] *China Year Book, 1939,* cited, p. 229.

[9] *People's Tribune,* Feb. 1939, p. 142; the best description of the National Government is given by Paul M. A. Linebarger, *The China of Chiang K'ai-shek,* cited, *passim;* see especially charts on structure of Government and Kuomintang organization.

The National Government is a complicated organization. Three parallel sets of organs are embodied within it: the Government proper, the Kuomintang, and the Military Affairs Commission. There are several Party ministries as well as large committees, the functions of which are essentially governmental in view of the Kuomintang's monopoly of political authority.[10] The Military Affairs Commission, originally inferior to a ministry, has expanded into a sixth *yuan*, embodying a dozen agencies of varied title but of ministerial rank.[11] Propaganda, the organization of societies of youth and of women, military education, etc., as well as strictly military functions, are undertaken by the agencies of the Commission which, like all other important organs, is headed by Chiang K'ai-shek.

People's Political Council

During the Republic's earlier years, when its models were the democratic governments of America and Europe, China had a parliament. The prevailing militarism and political inexperience of that period reduced a promising experiment to impotence. When the Nationalists came to power in 1928, they dispensed with parliament and the war period has not yet produced a national lawmaking body upon a democratic basis.

However, an important check upon Party dictatorship is being attempted through the establishment of the People's Political Council. This assembly, which has been enlarged from an original 200 to 240 delegates, is undoubtedly an expression of the Government's realization that it must provide a forum for discussion, as well as of its desire to maintain the approval of Occidental democracies. Although some sort of

[10] Linebarger, *The China of Chiang K'ai-shek,* cited, p. 124–58.
[11] *Ibid.,* p. 60–5.

citizens' assembly was rendered more obviously essential by the demands of the Chinese Communists, and followed the agreement for a united front with them, it should be remembered that the new constitution of 1936, adoption of which was prevented by the war, provided for a People's Congress, to be elected by "universal, equal and direct suffrage" with power to elect the superior officers of the Government, to recall them, to pass laws and to amend the constitution.[12] No such powers are enjoyed by the present Council, which may, however, consider measures of policy, demand reports from executive agencies and offer suggestions to the Government.

The People's Political Council was first convened on July 6, 1938 at Hankow, attended by 162 of the 200 members nominated by various national, provincial and local bodies and appointed by the Central Executive Committee from all provinces and territories and from Chinese residents abroad. They were teachers, college administrators, editors, businessmen, officials and former officials, military officers and priests, representative samples of the influential elements in Chinese society, including Communists and others outside the Kuomintang. The session lasted for ten days and there was controversial debate on governmental proposals.[13] The second session met at Chungking in October 1938, and showed considerable courage in criticism of the Government, particularly regarding the system of censorship of news.[14] The third session met in February 1939, under the chairmanship of Chiang, the fourth in September 1939, and the fifth in April 1940. A new Council, composed of 240 members, was elected during the latter months of 1940 and held its first session at Chungking early in March 1941. That a

[12] *China Year Book, 1939,* cited, p. 219. Linebarger, *The China of Chiang K'ai-shek,* cited, p. 21–40.

[13] *Chinese Year Book, 1938–1939,* cited, p. 346–55.

[14] *China Year Book, 1939,* cited, p. 232–7.

liberal atmosphere prevailed was indicated by the beginnings of party groups outside the Kuomintang.[15]

Chiang K'ai-shek

Generalissimo and *Tsung-tsai* Chiang K'ai-shek is credited even by his enemies and political opponents not only with preserving a large part of China as independent territory but also with arousing a national will to survive in the politically inert populace of China. Chiang is a native of Chekiang. He is 55 years old. His father was a wine merchant. At the age of twenty, Chiang entered a military academy in north China. His military training was completed in Japan, where he met Sun Yat-sen and joined the revolutionary society which later became the Kuomintang. He participated in the revolution which overthrew the Manchus but turned to non-political activities after his patron, Dr. Sun, was forced out of the presidency of the still-born Republic by Yuan Shih-k'ai. He returned to politics in 1920 and in 1924 became head of the new Whampoa Military Academy, the training-ground of a modern army. After leading the Nationalist troops throughout a successful three-year campaign against the provincial militarists who had stultified the Republic, he set up at Nanking a National Government which received the recognition of foreign states in 1928. He has dominated the political life of China ever since.

Chiang's rise to dictatorship was brought about by his personal command of the best-equipped, best-trained and best-paid divisions of the army, by the wealth of the bourgeois banker-landlords who liked his conservative views, by his personal qualities and his association with the wealthy and brilliant Soong family, and by the recognition and backing of Great Britain and the United States. In 1927, after mak-

[15] Linebarger, *The China of Chiang K'ai-shek,* cited, p. 69–79; Bisson, T. A., "China's National Front," *Foreign Policy Reports,* July 15, 1941, p. 109–10.

ing such use of the support of the Communist International as seemed to him opportune, he drove the Russian advisers out of China and authorized a wholesale purge of Chinese Communists and sympathizers with Communism. For nearly ten years he fought the Chinese Communist forces as well as reactionaries of pre-Nationalist antecedents. Not even the Japanese invasion of Manchuria and North China deterred him from relentless pursuit of his policy of anti-communism until in December 1936, he was made captive in the far western city of Sian by two of his own exasperated generals. The kidnapping brought an end to the long fratricidal war. The Chinese Communist generals accepted Chiang as their commander-in-chief. They modified their economic program and placed their knowledge of guerrilla tactics at Chiang's service. Thus the breach between dictator and revolutionary peasant was repaired, effecting an essential but precarious unity.

Chiang is slender, wiry, keen-eyed; he has limitless physical vigor, is abstemious, courageous and soldierly. While insensitive to social problems and ruthless in repression of his opponents, he admires courage and character and is loyal to those who serve him loyally. He is not a great strategist, but his patience and caution have aided him in avoiding reckless measures and in extricating his forces from untenable positions. Though lacking in fire and eloquence, he has poise, assurance and a quiet decisiveness that wins confidence.[16] He is thoroughly Chinese yet receptive to Occidental ideas.

Other Nationalist Leaders

Beside Chiang K'ai-shek, as in other dictatorships, all public figures look insignificant. Free China, however, has a number of able statesmen and generals, and a host of well-

[16] Snow, Edgar, "China's Fighting Generalissimo," *Foreign Affairs,* XVI, 1938, p. 612–25; Linebarger, *The China of Chiang K'ai-shek,* cited, p. 254–72; Tong, H. K., *Chiang K'ai-shek, Soldier and Statesman,* Shanghai, 1937.

educated younger men, to staff its government, economic and scientific enterprises, and army. In T. V. Soong, Chiang's brother-in-law, a graduate of Harvard, it has a financier of the first rank, who had, prior to the Japanese invasion, reorganized the fiscal system and won the confidence of the capitalists of his own country, enabling the Government to raise unheard-of sums by borrowing at home. To him goes much of the credit for the establishment of a managed paper currency in 1935 and the consequent calling into the Government's hands of the bulk of the silver holdings of the country prior to the outbreak of war. With this silver, transported to Hong Kong, London and New York, the credit of the Government was maintained during a critical period.

Another statesman of distinction is Wang Ch'ung-hui, foreign minister from 1937 to 1941. Yale D.C.L., barrister of the Middle Temple, translator of the German civil code, former judge of the Permanent Court of International Justice and life-time member of the Kuomintang, Dr. Wang has a brilliant mind and long experience in Chinese politics. Among the military officers, General Pai Ch'ung-hsi of Kwangsi is rated above Chiang himself as a strategist, and the two Communist leaders Mao Tse-tung and Chu Teh are probably the most experienced and successful leaders of guerrilla forces in the world.

Not the least valuable of Chiang's colleagues is his wife, Mei-ling Soong, sister of the financier. Madam Chiang is a graduate of Wellesley and has an excellent knowledge of English. She delivers eloquent speeches in both Chinese and English, writes articles for foreign periodicals, reads the English-language press and reports to Chiang upon foreign opinion. She is Chiang's interpreter and his counsel in handling foreign correspondents. Her courage was shown when she flew to Sian to intercede with the kidnappers for her husband's release.

Sun Fo, son of Sun Yat-sen, H. H. Kung, Minister of

Finance, T'ai Chih-t'ao, Chairman of the Examination *Yuan,* Ch'en Li-fu, Minister of Education, W. H. Wong, Minister of Economic Affairs, Chou En-lai, Communist member of the Military Affairs Commission, and many others of exceptional abilities, support what is sometimes called the "Soong dynasty." Hu Shih, China's most distinguished philosopher and a leader of the renaissance in literature and critical scholarship, a graduate of Cornell University, is Ambassador to the United States. Spread throughout the civil service at home and abroad are hundreds of able younger men, educated for their work and sincerely devoted to an ideal of a "new order" in China that shall not be "made in Japan." These younger men are the "Young China" of twenty years ago, who took the lead in the struggle against militarism and imperialism. Liberal still, but more mature and experienced, they are coming into their own today in all branches of the Government service.

The Program of Resistance

From the beginning of the intensive fighting in 1937, the strategy of the National Government has been based upon the expectation of retreat into western China and the necessity of building up a whole political, economic and social community of resistance that would be as nearly inaccessible as possible to the invading armies. General Chiang said on October 31, 1938, that "the defense of Hankow [in central China] had for its principal object the protection of works of reconstruction in the West . . . so that . . . communications could be developed in Western China, armaments could be concentrated and all Chinese industries in central and southeast China could be moved to the northwest and southwest." [17] The task of the Nationalists was to render the western provinces self-sustaining in order that Japan's con-

[17] *The People's Tribune,* November 1938, p. 161–2.

quest of the seaboard, the industrial cities and the principal lines of transportation, should not produce economic paralysis, enabling it to dispense with further military occupation.

Public Finance and Currency

The problem of constructing a new economic and military base appeared to be insuperable in the presence of a disorganized fiscal system and a correspondingly impoverished treasury. The National Government drew its revenues principally from the maritime customs, the salt monopoly, excise taxes on tobacco, alcoholic drinks, cotton yarn, cement, matches and other manufactures, and stamp taxes on checks and receipts. Japanese capture of all important ports deprived the Government of the bulk of the customs receipts, which in 1937 amounted to nearly $343,000,000 (Chinese currency). The more lucrative salt-producing centers and the larger factories are within the Japanese-occupied zone, which means that the excise returns on their products are being absorbed by the various puppet governments. What the residual amounts available to the Chungking administration may be has not been revealed.[18] Such innovations as income, inheritance and excess profits taxes are being tried, but with slight success.[19] The decreased area under Nationalist control has, of course, reduced the Government's requirements, but this reduction is many times smaller than the increased needs due to the costs of war and reconstruction. The announced budget for the fiscal year January 1–December 31, 1939, was $2,850,000,000, an amount nearly three times that of 1936.[20] The bulk of this great sum could be raised only by borrowing; the total revenues of the Gov-

[18] In 1938 the percentage of total imports that entered China through the land ports along the southern and southwestern boundary was but 1.5%.

[19] *Far Eastern Survey,* May 24, 1939, p. 133–4.

[20] *China Weekly Review,* April 22, 1939, p. 246; the announced budget for 1937 was $2,100,000,000; for 1938, $2,400,000,000.

ernment from taxes, government enterprises, etc., are estimated variously to be from $200,000,000 to $1,200,000,000.

The National Government has obtained very considerable sums through domestic loans. Bond issues totalling $3,980,-000,000 (Chinese) face value were floated during the first three years of intensive warfare.[21] The amount realized from these issues has not been published, but presumably they were absorbed by the four Government banks. The drain upon the revenue for payments of principal and interest is heavy. More than a half billion dollars was paid out on foreign and domestic obligations between July 1937 and April 1939.[22] Gifts of money from Chinese resident in the United States, the Philippines, Malaya, the Dutch East Indies and other countries have been considerable.[23] Individual donations by foreigners for relief and education also have been large, but the various types of credits extended by the United States, the United Kingdom and the Soviet Union have been of crucial importance.[24]

The task of maintaining the national currency at an exchange rate that would permit purchases of foreign commodities on a tolerable basis has been one of great difficulty. The National Government, though deprived of its principal trade outlets and revenues, has been obliged to consider the problems of currency and exchange on a national scale. Its difficulties have been multiplied by the Japanese policy of attack upon the currency, marked by the establishment of central banks issuing fiat currency and by efforts to supplant the national currency with various types of Japanese and Japanese-sponsored notes.[25]

The integrity of the national currency has been in part assured by the action taken in 1935 whereby a managed paper

[21] *Chinese Year Book, 1940–1941,* cited, p. 495.
[22] *China Weekly Review,* April 15, 1939, p. 204.
[23] *Ibid.,* May 13, 1939, p. 343.
[24] See Chapters XII, XIII, and XIV.
[25] Chapter VII.

currency upon a flexible gold exchange basis was established and the banks and other owners of the precious metals were required to turn coins and bullion into the Treasury. An estimated silver reserve of $1,200,000,000 was accumulated by this procedure. The silver was shipped to Hong Kong, London and New York, where it has been available for the purchase of war supplies, the payment of loan obligations and other necessities of foreign exchange, and as security for foreign credits.[26] An exchange equalization fund also has been employed. Early in 1939 the British Government lent £5,000,000 to support this fund, and an Anglo-Chinese committee of bankers was appointed to manage it.[27] This fund was effectively used until July 1939, when it neared the end of its resources and its functioning was suspended; in consequence the Chinese dollar dropped to 6 cents (U. S.). In May 1941, the fund was re-established through credits of $50,000,000 and £5,000,000 extended by the American and British Governments respectively. To administer the fund the Chinese Government appointed a Stabilization Board of 5 members, 3 of whom were Chinese, 1 an American recommended by the Secretary of the Treasury, and 1 a British subject recommended by the British Treasury.[28]

Free China's foreign exchange reserves have been conserved by the export of silver, newly-mined gold and commodities—notably tung oil, tea, mineral ores and bristles,—by suspension of payments on foreign loan obligations incurred before 1933, by control over remittances from Chinese living abroad and by credits granted by foreign governments to cover purchases of war supplies. The effort has been remarkably successful so far and it is now clear that additional assistance will be made available. Inflation has been un-

[26] *Far Eastern Survey,* May 18, 1938, p. 111–15.

[27] *China Weekly Review,* March 25, 1939, p. 96; *Far Eastern Survey,* March 29, 1939, p. 81.

[28] *New York Times,* May 26, 1941; Jones and Myers, *Documents,* III, p. 243–5.

avoidable, the outstanding issues of the four National Government banks standing at $2,627,000,000 at the end of June 1939, as compared with $1,407,000,000 on the corresponding date of 1937. Domestic prices have risen enormously with consequent distress among the people.[29]

The Ministry of Finance at Chungking on June 30, 1939, released information which warrants an estimate of the national indebtedness as of that date at $8,100,000,000. Of this total, $5,600,000,000 was in domestic, $2,500,000,000 in foreign debt, the latter equivalent to $735,000,000 U. S. These figures represented an increase of 80% in total debt, of 107% in domestic, and of 39% in foreign obligations since June 30, 1937. It may be estimated, roughly, that the total of domestic debt one year later had risen to $7,400,000,000, less payments on principal, and that foreign obligations had increased by some $50,000,000, less repayments. Because of the suspension of the debt service, Chinese bond prices in July 1939, were from 60% to 90% below their prewar levels in foreign markets.

Natural Resources

The free area contains very large deposits of coal and the bulk of China's reserves of manganese, copper, lead, zinc, tungsten, antimony and tin; also some gold, silver and precious stones. Tin is the most valuable export mineral, mined in southern Yunnan by primitive methods. Shensi, western Shansi and Kansu contain the bulk of the whole area's coal reserves, which are ample for its own industrial development but are not yet under modern methods of exploitation. Szechwan, Yunnan and Kweichow have adequate coal reserves for a considerable industrial life. There are, however, only small deposits of iron in the whole of Free

29 *Far Eastern Survey,* July 3, 1940, p. 165–6; Bloch, K., "Far Eastern War Inflation," *Pacific Affairs,* XIII, p. 320–43.

China. For industrialism on a large scale, therefore, it will be necessary that the iron and cheap transportation of the Yangtze River provinces, now largely under Japanese occupation, be combined with the coal and other resources of the western and southwestern provinces of Free China.[30] For the present emergency the iron mines of eastern Szechwan are being intensively worked. Copper reserves in all China are small, the largest deposits located in Yunnan. The salt wells of Szechwan are numerous and highly productive. No petroleum wells of commercial importance have been discovered; the findings so far are within Free China, in Shensi, Kansu and Szechwan.

Professor Cressey recently has recalled that "agriculture forms the foundation of the social and economic structure of the nation, and only as the rural districts prosper can China advance." [31] Among the unoccupied provinces of Free China on which statistics are available, the percentage of the total area devoted to farming varies from 2.6% in Kweichow to 22% in Kwangsi. Szechwan is the largest of the older provinces but has only 2.5% of its land, exclusive of gardens and orchards, under cultivation. This large variance from the figure of 15% for twenty-six of the provinces is due to the high percentage of hilly and mountainous country which characterizes the southwestern plateau.

The National Government has made the planning and execution of measures for increased production of agricultural commodities one of its primary objectives. In this it has been greatly aided by the migration of the country's best scientists to the southwest. Many of these men were engaged on such problems as the improvement of cotton seed and silk-worm eggs, the development of superior varieties of rice, wheat and various kinds of fruit, the breeding of cattle, the modernization of tea culture and the extraction of tung

[30] Cressey, cited, p. 107–32.
[31] *Ibid.*, p. 81.

oil. They are now engaged in applying their findings to the necessitous task of increasing the production of foodstuffs and other natural resources. Fields formerly sown to opium and tobacco are now growing cereals. In areas within the orbit of Japanese foraging parties the same tactics are employed to restrict the production of cotton and hemp and to prevent the sale of cotton, silk cocoons and other staples to the Japanese. To provide for the new industries in Yunnan, Kweichow and Szechwan, cotton-growing is being encouraged and improved varieties are under development. Already the distribution of improved seed, aided by Government loans, is showing results in increased yields of a large number of products. Silk culture in Szechwan is being subsidized and the farmers are being instructed in the various processes involved. The same may be said of tea culture in the unoccupied portions of several central and eastern provinces. Tung and other vegetable oils are receiving similar attention.[32]

Industry and Transport

Industry in Free China must for the present be mainly small and decentralized; it takes time to organize the "heavier" industries and Japanese bombers are capable of destroying large factories unless they are well concealed.[33]

The cooperative principle has been applied to this problem with remarkable results, though there is insufficient capital available, and trained engineers are scarce. With machinery moved from cities near the zones of Japanese occupation and with labor recruited among refugee artisans, coolies and peasants, village factories have been started in Shensi, Hunan, Kiangsi, Kansu and other provinces for the production of iron implements, stockings, soap, candles, flour, leather goods,

[32] *Chinese Year Book, 1938–1939,* cited, p. 462–82.

[33] Wales, Nym, "China's New Line of Industrial Defense," *Pacific Affairs,* XII, p. 286.

textiles of cotton and wool, paper, glass, etc., etc. Light machine-guns in large numbers are now being turned out by the cooperatives. The members of the cooperatives carry on the work and are content with small returns. They manage the industries through directors chosen by themselves. The hope of this movement is that supplies can be provided for the troops, civilian necessities furnished—thus limiting dependence upon Japanese goods—the people kept busy and contented, and a market afforded for the raw materials which would otherwise be sold or confiscated by the Japanese. The cooperatives are in operation within occupied territory as well as in Free China.[34]

Imports of machinery for coal and iron mining and for manufacture of munitions have, in recent months, been in quantities that indicate the development of industry on a larger scale. Arsenals capable of turning out rifles, machine-guns and small field-guns are in operation. A considerable tonnage of mining and metallurgical machinery was moved from eastern cities to Hunan and Szechwan and re-established there. Machine tools, electrical supplies, chemicals, paper, textiles, chinaware and other essentials are being manufactured with Government assistance and direction.

Transportation facilities have been the most urgent necessity, as they are the means of importing munitions, trucks, fuel oil, aeroplanes and other military materials; also for the movement of troops and guns, the distribution of provisions and locally manufactured equipment, and the export of products available for foreign trade. Efforts in this field have been made and are continuing to be well-conceived and executed. Several thousand miles of motor highways have been opened or reconstructed, and railway-building, which has not

[34] Alley, Rewi, "The Chinese Industrial Cooperatives," Chungking Pamphlets, No. 4, 1940; *Chinese Year Book, 1940–1941,* cited, p. 767–78; Linebarger, *The China of Chiang K'ai-shek,* cited, p. 223–34; Barnett, R. W., "China's Industrial Cooperatives on Trial," *Far Eastern Survey,* February 28. 1940, p. 51–6.

yet gone beyond a few hundred miles in the southwest, is being pushed ahead as rapidly as rails can be obtained. The rebuilt highway from Kunming in Yunnan to Lashio, Burma, branch terminus of a British line to the port of Rangoon, is under traffic. This road is only 700 miles long, but it was built too rapidly, is narrow and poorly protected, gradients are steep and most of the roadbed is unsurfaced. Much of the route is through mountains, at an elevation of 8000 feet. Heavy rains fall in this region from May to October. There are many difficulties to overcome in the use of the road, but these are inconsequential in view of available manpower and building material. The construction of a railway partially paralleling this route is under way. Munitions and other goods are moving into Yunnan and thence along the new network of highways into Szechwan, Kweichow and Kwangsi.[35] Entirely apart from its military value, the significance of this road for the future of British commercial and investment interests in China aroused speculative discussion in Threadneedle Street.[36]

A motor road to the northwest, connecting Szechwan with Sinkiang and running through that province to the Turkestan-Siberian railway, is under construction. This route is 2500 miles long from the national capital, Chungking, to the nearest point on the Soviet line. From Chungking via Chengtu to Sian, the road is well-built, having been in use for some years. Thence to Lanchow, capital of Kansu, and westward, there are hundreds of miles that resemble trails rather than roads.[37] There are passes on this route that are 10,000 feet above sea-level. Nevertheless, this road is carrying a growing

[35] *China Weekly Review,* October 22, 1938, p. 257–8; December 17, 1938, p. 71; January 7, 1939, p. 177; *Far Eastern Survey,* June 21, 1939, p. 155–6; January 17, 1940, p. 23–4; April 24, 1940, p. 105–6; September 25, 1940, p. 227–8.

[36] The cession of a border section of Yunnan west of the Lu River to Burma was reported in May 1939. (*China Weekly Review,* May 13, 1939, p. 341.)

[37] *Far Eastern Survey,* November 9, 1938, p. 258–60; "Highways in China," Council of International Affairs, Nanking, November 21, 1936.

trade in munitions, wool, tea, fur, hides and camel's hair. Camels, mules and motor trucks cooperate in this epic enterprise.

A railway and a motor road now connect nationalist territory with French Indo-China. The railway runs from Haiphong to Kunming, capital of Yunnan. A newer line, a branch of the former within Indo-China, runs to the border town of Chennankwan, whence it is to be extended via Nanning to Liuchow and Kweilin, Kwangsi; the latter are now connected by rail with each other and with Changsha, Hunan. A motor highway runs from Chennankwan via Kweilin, Kwangsi and Kweiyang, Kweichow, to Chungking.[38] All of these routes from Indo-China are within easy reach of Japanese air bases on Chinese and Indo-Chinese soil. The Nanning route was cut by the capture of that city in November 1939; the Yunnan railway was closed by the Japanese invasion of Indo-China in September 1940. In March 1941, the National Government sent engineers to survey a possible new route, a thousand miles long, from Ningyuan, Szechwan, to Sadiya (in the northeast corner of India), which is connected by rail with the Indian port of Chittagong.[39]

Higher Education

The National Government has endeavored to maintain Chinese traditions of scholarship and to preserve the national reservoir of educated men and women by encouraging and subsidizing the transfer of universities and colleges to western and southwestern provinces. The faculties and students of institutions destroyed or otherwise rendered incapable of independent operation by the invasion have, in a majority of cases, moved to centers relatively undisturbed, though en-

[38] *Far Eastern Survey,* November 9, 1938, p. 259–60; *Chinese Year Book, 1938–1939,* cited, p. 562–6; *China Weekly Review,* December 23, 1939, p. 146.
[39] *New York Times,* March 19, 1941.

dangered by bombing squadrons. Other schools have found refuge in foreign concessions and at Hong Kong. Thus a surprising amount of higher educational work has been carried on in spite of the warfare.

Seventeen universities and colleges had moved to Yunnan, Kweichow and Kwangsi by October 1939, seventeen had moved to Hunan and Szechwan, and five to Shensi and Kansu. Facilities have been combined and several new technical and normal colleges have been founded by the Government. The superior applicants for admission are selected by means of qualifying examinations. They are distributed among the several types of colleges on bases of preference, interest and available facilities. In 1938, 9081 men and 2038 women were successful. Curricula are being revised for war-time needs, and physical education and military training are required of all students.[40]

What has been the attitude of China's students—most of them members of the landowning, merchant and official families—toward the struggle for independence? Are they willing to sacrifice themselves for this cause?

From the beginnings of the student movement, aroused by Japan's "Twenty-One Demands" of 1915 and intensified by the Shantung clauses of the Treaty of Versailles, to the present time, nationalist feeling has run more violently in the universities than in any other circles. In the fall of 1931 bands of students marched to Nanking or held up railway traffic until granted free passage to the capital, demanding immediate resistance to Japan. The Government was embarrassed by their denunciations of the enemy and of its own cautious program. Subsequently, when resistance began, the

[40] *China Institute Bulletin,* October 1939; Freyn, Hubert, *Chinese Education in the War,* Political and Economic Studies, No. 9, auspices Council of International Affairs, Chungking, 1940; *Chinese Year Book, 1940–1941,* cited, p. 698–710. The Annual Report of the Associated Boards for Christian Colleges in China, dated June 30, 1941, stated that apparently there were 115 institutions of higher learning in China as compared to 108 in 1936–37.

trek to the back country was evidence that the students preferred hardship and scanty equipment to academic malnutrition in the occupied cities.

On the other hand, while many students have entered the armies, the great majority have accepted the Government's view that with manpower so plentiful, the educated few should be kept out of the fighting and their talents applied in such essential services as railway and road engineering, instruction of the farmers in methods of improving soils and varying crops, construction and operation of arsenals, industries and transport systems, propaganda for resistance, Red Cross work, etc. In these activities, they are developing a hitherto unknown appreciation of the "ignorant people without virtue." The admission of their dependence upon the people for succor will be difficult for the literate Chinese. In this common cause may be born a perception of democracy that will save the nation.

This policy of transferring China's men of learning and its enthusiastic youth from the older educational centers to provinces hardly touched by the scientific spirit is not moved solely by the determination to preserve the *literati*. There is also the desire to hurry the pace of political and economic reorientation among the people of the hinterland. Universities at their doors; newspapers, periodicals and books more plentiful; discussion of the whole country's problems at the teahouses; conferences with scholars upon methods of farming; observation of power-driven vehicles and factories; these experiences are the texture of a more modern civilization for the frontier people.

The Border Governments

Military resistance since the fall of Hankow in October 1938 has involved extensive use of guerrilla forces and armed peasants. The tactics of mobility rather than of position have been basic since that time. This embodies a tripartite program in which regular troops move against the enemy when circumstances are favorable, guerrillas and regulars harass them from behind their lines, and armed peasants who are half-time guerrillas assist by hampering them in all available ways, and by provisioning the guerrillas and obtaining information for them.[41] These tactics were inherited from the Communist armies which maintained for ten years, with weapons of small caliber, most of which were captured from the regular armies, a war of attack and retreat that baffled the best generals of China and their German advisers as well. The methods are in some respects similar to those of the Boers, the Partisans in Siberia, and the Spanish loyalists. They are the only means by which armies with inferior weapons and poor facilities of transport can resist modernized forces. The guerrillas make life miserable for the small Japanese garrisons along the railways, roads, canals and rivers of the occupied provinces. The Japanese do not dare to move out of their fortified barracks except in considerable force, and even while in barracks they must be constantly alert. When conditions are favorable, raiding parties attack and wipe out these garrisons. They remove sections of railway and telegraph lines, loot munition and food stores, and destroy trucks and airplanes.

The consequences of this mass resistance may be profound. The peasants have been accustomed to local self-defense against robbers but not to the responsibility of military service in national defense. Like their betters the merchant landlords they have despised and hated the soldier. Better, they thought, a national tradition of defeat than a people in arms. With this view the landlords were in hearty agreement. It insured their profitable relationship with a feudal

[41] Rosinger, L. K., "Politics and Strategy of China's Mobile War," *Pacific Affairs,* XII, 1939, p. 263–77; Hanson, H., "The People Behind the Chinese Guerrillas," *ibid.,* XI, 1938, p. 285–98; Carlson, Major E. F., *The Chinese Army,* cited; *Twin Stars of China,* New York, 1940.

tenantry, and a condition of serfdom that has characterized the Chinese social order for 2000 years. They have resisted the arming of the peasantry in the current fighting whenever they were able to make their influence felt.[42]

The area of largest opportunity for the Chinese peasant since the reconciliation of 1937 between the Kuomintang and the Communist leaders has been the so-called border region of the northwest. By the agreement worked out in 1937 and as yet unpublished in full, the Communist-led army became the Eighth Route Army (later renamed the Eighteenth Group Army), within the national military organization.[43] The available documents do not reveal what understandings were reached regarding the area, if any, over which the Eighth Route Army was to exercise political authority under the National Government. In point of fact the Army had carved out for itself a district of considerable size which included border sections of three provinces—Shensi, Kansu and Ninghsia. It had established a capital at Yenan, Shensi, in which an elected congress of soviets ruled.[44] Tacitly, apparently, it was permitted to retain its hold upon this area. This clearly was an unstable arrangement since it recognized an *imperium in imperio,* the latter being the three provincial governments, which continued to exercise as complete authority over their respective provinces as their military power and the political exigencies of the moment permitted. In this they were abetted by Chungking, which continued to dislike and fear the Communists.

With the invasion of the Japanese armies, the Communist forces moved into Shansi to meet them. How they dealt with the Japanese is described in the previous chapter. From

[42] Isaacs, H. R., *The Tragedy of the Chinese Revolution,* London, 1938, p. 425–57; Utley, Freda, *China at War,* Shanghai, 1939.

[43] *Chinese Year Book, 1938–1939,* cited, p. 339–40.

[44] Snow, Edgar, "Soviet Society in Northwest China, *Pacific Affairs,* X, 1937, p. 266–75; Norins, M. R., "Agrarian Democracy in Northwest China," *ibid.,* XIII, 1940, p. 413–22.

Shansi the Communist armies moved into Hopei, Chahar and Shantung, setting up a number of guerrilla bases and auxiliary governments. The most effectively organized of these was the Hopei-Shansi-Chahar border area, in which a "united front" government assumed jurisdiction, with the approval of Chungking, over portions of the three named provinces.[45] In March 1938, this government set up its capital at Wut'ai in northern Shansi. Twenty-eight organizations sent delegates to the conference in January 1938, at which it was planned. Among them were farmers' and laborers' associations, army units, patriotic societies, etc. In the absence of effective resistance to the invaders on the part of the provincial governors some other method of resistance was essential. In this necessity for union all patriotic Chinese could join, whatever their political leanings. A committee of nine men was elected as a temporary government. Two of these were Communists, four were members of a conservative group, one represented the Kuomintang, and two, one of whom was chairman, belonged to no party.

Without more complete data from independent investigators one cannot affirm confidently that these border governments are peasant governments. It is remarkable, however, that the fragmentary reports of non-Communists as well as Communists who have visited the areas agree that both men and women of all economic classes participate in elections, that they enjoy great freedom of discussion, that taxes are levied upon a regular basis, that rents and interest rates have been reduced and land confiscated from "traitors" distributed among the landless, and that education has been provided for those unable to pay for it. Since the protection of these benefits depends upon the Communist-led armies it must be assumed that their leaders also enjoy an important influence in the governments, which are described as "united

[45] Taylor, George E., *The Struggle for North China*, New York, 1940, p. 34-40, 96-117.

front" organizations. On the other hand leaders must have armies and as the original Eighth Route forces have been reduced by the long conflict it has been necessary to replace them with peasant youth. Clearly these would not have joined the armies by the hundreds of thousands, as they have done, were it not that they believe in the cause: [46]

That the Eighth Route Army leaders not only restored but also reconstructed Chinese government and administration in the Border Government area during six short months bears witness not only to organizing genius, but also to the urgency and the necessity, given the situation, of their program. For it must be borne in mind that the speed of reform could never be much faster than the pace at which the peasantry of North China could be persuaded to move. . . . The principles and policies of the Border Government illustrate one of the finest historical examples of the approximation of political means to political ends.

Kuomintang-Communist Friction

If these measures were successful in welding the North China peasantry into a formidable army of attack as well as resistance they were also highly disturbing to the conservative element in the higher councils of the Kuomintang. It is not surprising that these men feared that peasant nationalism eventually would disinherit them, or that many of them questioned whether compromise with a Japanese overlord would not be less disruptive to their way of life than the reckoning they foresaw with a victorious *jacquerie*. Although the expropriation of landlords was discontinued by the Communists after 1937 the program of reform was far too liberal for the dominant clique at Chungking. They cannot be greatly censured for their fears, in the light of the Russian

[46] *Ibid.*, p. 97–8.

Revolution. But it may be doubted that those fears were justified or that the methods of the men who entertained them were wise. Sun Yat-sen believed that so moderate a people as the Chinese could be trusted to apply democratic processes if these processes were employed to right the wrongs under which they had suffered for centuries.

The distrust of the National Government was manifested by the extremely limited allocations of money and ammunition to the Eighth Route Army, the failure to supply rifles, machine-guns or field-guns, and the erection of concentric crescents of blockhouses around the western and southern borders of the area allotted to that army. These were manned by a force of 200,000 men, so stationed as to form a blockade around part of the area. Several districts within the area were entered by these troops, forcing the Eighth Route to evacuate or fight. Blame may perhaps attach to Yenan as well as to Chungking for numerous clashes between units of their respective forces.[47] These clashes led up to a more serious collision between the Communist-led New Fourth Army and another National Government force at Maolin, Anhui, on the Yangtze River. The former was composed originally of remnants which stayed in the lower Yangtze valley when the main Communist army was driven westward in the early thirties by Chiang K'ai-shek. Reorganized after the reconciliation of 1937, it was assigned by the National Defense Council at Chungking to harass the Japanese in the Shanghai-Hangchow zone. It received funds from Chungking but was, like its compatriot organization in the northwest, most penuriously treated. Nonetheless it was successful and its numbers grew rapidly, arousing at the national capital an apprehension that it would influence the peasants against the Kuomintang.

Agreement is lacking on the point of responsibility

[47] Strong, Anna L., "The Kuomintang-Communist Crisis in China," *Amerasia,* V, 1941, p. 11–23.

for the battle at Maolin. It occurred early in January 1941, as the Fourth Army rear guard was crossing the Yangtze in obedience to General Chiang's order that it move north of the river. Many lesser skirmishes had occurred in central China during the previous year. The Fourth Army believed that its rivals were determined to destroy it while the latter published declarations that they were continually subject to attack by the Fourth Army.[48] At Maolin the Fourth Army's small force was attacked by 80,000 Chinese troops, with a resulting loss of 2000 killed, and 4000 wounded or captured. Shortly thereafter General Chiang ordered the Fourth Army to disband. This stern action against a force that had fought valiantly for three years against the invader was repudiated by the Communist leaders who reorganized the army and charged that pro-Nazi elements in the National Government were plotting with the Japanese to wipe out both the Eighth and the Fourth Armies, to turn over North China to Japan, and to join the Axis. Regardless of the truth of these charges, the fact that they were made and that great armies, each a half-million strong, faced each other in combative mood was an ill omen for China's nationhood.

Free China will not fully merit the title it has properly assumed until its people are free. On that issue the border governments hold a convincing brief for their existence. On the other hand, freedom will be unattainable unless China survives. General Chiang K'ai-shek's contention that no subordinate unit should be allowed to undermine the National Government is sound. So long as China's Communists take orders from Moscow the dangers of civil war will remain. There is ground for a compromise between the protagonists of freedom for the individual and those who demand a highly centralized system of authority. China's masses are not Communists. Their desires for a decent way of life can be met by

[48] Strong, cited; Bisson, cited; *China Weekly Review,* January 25, 1941, p. 276–8.

returning to the earlier (1924) platform of the Kuomintang. It should be possible for Chungking and Yenan to stand together on that platform. Failure to find common ground will retard the winning of national independence and provoke civil war and regionalism after independence is won.

VII

THE "NEW ORDER" IN OCCUPIED CHINA

THE Japanese Government issued a general statement [1] on November 3, 1938, after the fall of Hankow and Canton. The second paragraph of the statement read:

> What Japan seeks is the establishment of a new order which will insure the permanent stability of East Asia. In this lies the ultimate purpose of our present military campaign. The new order has for its foundation a tripartite relationship of mutual aid and coordination between Japan, Manchoukuo and China in political, economic, cultural and other fields. Its object is to secure international justice, to perfect the joint defense against Communism and to create a new culture and realize a close economic cohesion throughout East Asia.

It will be noted that the new order did not contemplate the disappearance of China as a state. "What Japan desires of China," the statement read, "is that that country will share in the task of bringing about this new order in East Asia." Even the Kuomintang Government was offered an opportunity to participate, on condition that it repudiate its policy and alter its personnel.

Hachiro Arita, Japan's Foreign Minister, emphasized the benevolent aspect of the new order in an address [2] before the Diet on December 19, 1938, in which he said:

> It is not only of benefit to the Chinese themselves but to the whole of East Asia to lift China from its present semi-colonial state to the position of a modern state. The establishment of

[1] Jones and Myers, *Documents,* I, p. 229–30.
[2] *Ibid.,* p. 232–6.

the new order, that is, of a relationship of mutual aid and coordination, between Japan, Manchoukuo and China, simply signifies the creation of solidarity between these three countries for the common purpose of preserving the integrity of East Asia and enabling each nation to maintain its independence and . . . develop its individuality.

Mr. Arita dwelt mainly upon the economic phase of the new order. A "certain degree" of coordination would be necessary, in fact "the formation of a single economic unit" out of the three states. However, the "bloc" would not involve "the exclusion of all interests other than those of the powers concerned." The intention was that "Japan, poor in natural resources and without a large domestic market, and China, still economically weak, should work together in order to ensure their independence as regards vital supplies as well as their increase in times of emergency." Japan, said Mr. Arita, was a supporter in principle of the doctrine of equality of commercial opportunity. But this doctrine must be applied under certain restrictions "demanded by the requirements of national defense and economic security."

Government in Occupied China

The first national government set up in China under Japanese auspices was the Provisional Government of the Chinese Republic, established at Peking on December 14, 1937.[3] The leading members had served in the Hopei-Chahar Political Council which was formed at Peking in 1935. Although affiliated with the National Government at Nanking this Council was composed of men outside the Kuomintang who were acceptable to the Japanese. These men were survivors of the former Peking regime, elderly, well-educated and

[3] Taylor, George E., cited, p. 20. Under occupation the old name "Peking," which the Chinese pronounce *Bayjing,* replaced "Peiping" (*Bayping*). Taylor gives brief biographies of several members of the Provisional Government, p. 22–5.

competent, trained partly in Japan. They represented the ideals of the old imperial mandarinate which the Republican revolution of 1911 destroyed. They had no place in the Kuomintang system and were resentful toward the younger element which had displaced them. The best-known among them were Wang Keh-min, T'ang Erh-ho, Tung K'ang, Wang Yi-tang and Kao Ling-wei. Remnants of a discarded order, they could not do more than stop the gap until the "new order" could be adequately staffed.

The principal organs of the Provisional Government were three committees: the Administrative Committee, the Deliberative Committee and the Judicial Committee.[4] Actual political powers were monopolized by the Administrative Committee. This Committee had six members, each of whom was director or assistant director of an administrative department.[5] It was authorized to present various types of matters to the Deliberative Committee and to supervise the administrative departments.

The Deliberative Committee, composed of six regular members and an indefinite number of others, some of whom were also members of the Administrative Committee, had the quasi-legislative function of the Legislative *Yuan* of the National Government. It was advisory rather than legislative in character. The Judicial Committee, also of six members, was given a variety of functions. Within it were the Supreme Court and the Administrative Court. It might appoint judicial officials of the lower ranks. It was the highest authority for legal interpretation and might submit proposals on legal reform to the Deliberative Committee. There was a rough similarity between this organization and that of the National Government of China.

[4] *Japan Year Book, 1939–1940,* Tokyo, p. 1076–7; *China Year Book, 1939,* cited, p. 601–3.

[5] Actually ten members were listed, including the chairman; the titles of the listed departments do not correspond entirely with those named in the text of the ordinance.

Behind the imposing "front" of elderly mandarins on these committees were the Japanese advisers, three of whom composed the actual policy-forming executive under the Japanese military officers in North China. These three were the general advisers on political, economic and military affairs. Under them were other Japanese attached to all governmental agencies and assisted by spies. While Chinese astuteness and knowledge of local conditions assured the native officials a certain degree of influence, they were subject in all final decisions to the will of the Japanese. They were appointed by them and had no security of tenure. Provincial and local government was left intact save for the restoration of the *tao* (dow, like how), a pre-Republican unit between the provincial and district governments. Numerous Japanese, some as advisers, others as bureau chiefs, clerks, etc., were given employment.

To instill in the people the ideals of the new order a propaganda agency called the *Hsin Min Hui* (New People's Association) was organized. A body of doctrine designed to supplant the Three People's Principles (*San Min Chu I*) of Sun Yat-sen was supplied to the association. These instrumentalities attacked democracy and communism with equal ardor and offered, to replace them, the ancient moral and political teachings of Confucius and Mencius. (It is of interest to observe the similarity between this propaganda and the New Life Movement fostered by Chiang K'ai-shek). The *Hsin Min Hui* was the right-hand man of the Provisional Government, its *alter ego* in the same way as the hated Comintern served the purposes of the U.S.S.R. It has remained, however, comparatively small in membership.[6]

Upon the establishment of the "Reorganized National Government of China" at Nanking on March 30, 1940, the Provisional Government at Peking was renamed the "Political Council of North China." In theory the northern regime

[6] Taylor, cited, p. 70–6.

became a subordinate unit of a new national system but in fact it remained autonomous, a reflection of the policy and influence of Japan's North China army, which was contending for a sphere of control with its Kwantung army on the north and its Central China army on the south.

The "Reorganized National Government" (Nanking)

The first war-time government with pretensions to a large area of jurisdiction in central China was the "Reformed Government of the Chinese Republic," inaugurated at Nanking on March 28, 1938. The titles of the Nanking and Peking regimes were contradictory—both indicating national rather than regional claims. With the purpose of reconciling the opposing factions in the Japanese army—whose interests were in prestige and profit—the "United Council of China" was created on September 22, 1938. Composed of members from the rival governments, this Council was merely a "liaison committee" through which conferences might be conducted and statements made on matters of general concern.[7] It disappeared with the establishment of the "Reorganized National Government of China" on March 30, 1940.

The structure of the "Reformed Government" was similar to that of "Provisional Government," constituted of three boards (*yuan*): executive, legislative and judicial. The personnel were of the same political stripe but somewhat younger and less distinguished than the Peking junta.[8] It was hastily organized to maintain appearances until a more permanent plan could be devised. There was strenuous argument upon the problems of the form, location and headship of the greatly desired national government. Quite naturally, both military cliques favored General Wu Pei-fu, a retired *tuchün*

[7] *Ibid.*, p. 177.

[8] *China Year Book, 1939,* cited, p. 603–4; *Japan Year Book, 1939–1940,* cited, p. 1082–3.

of comparatively high standing throughout the country. Wu, however, although not disinterested, refused to take office while Japanese troops remained in China.[9] Second choice was Wang Ch'ing-wei, after Chiang K'ai-shek himself the most highly placed member of the Kuomintang and of the National Government of Free China until 1938.

Wang Ch'ing-wei's acceptance of the presidency of the so-called Reorganized Government was an act difficult to reconcile with his record. He had been a loyal and aggressive member of the Kuomintang and of its predecessor the Tungminghui, and had taken a courageous part in the Revolution of 1911. That Dr. Sun Yat-sen regarded him as his spiritual successor may be judged from Wang's part in the drafting of his will. He was chairman of the Executive *Yuan,* a post equivalent to premiership, from 1932 to 1935, and subsequently, at Chungking, held the positions of chairman of the Central Political Council and of the newly established People's Political Council. His attitude toward the Japanese, at first conciliatory because he doubted China's capacity to resist attack, later became as belligerent as that of Chiang K'ai-shek.[10] As late as August 8, 1938, he wrote: [11]

> Whatever else may happen, our course is clear—we must renew our faith and continue to display endless courage, patience and endurance so that our war of resistance may be won and the reconstruction of our country resumed.

Wang explained his desertion of his colleagues and collaboration with the invader on grounds of practical statesmanship. China, he said, could not resist indefinitely and it was preferable to accept Japan's terms for economic cooperation, since Japan had no desire to destroy the state.[12]

[9] The death of General Wu in 1939 aroused suspicion that his recalcitrance had provoked an act of vengeance. No proof of assassination has been revealed.

[10] *China's Leaders and Their Policies,* China United Press, 1935, p. 17–18.

[11] *The People's Tribune,* August 1938, p. 100.

[12] Quigley, H. S., "Free China," cited, p. 157–9.

For several months he bargained with the Japanese on the terms of his acceptance of the "Presidency," seeking to obtain a degree of power that would appear to justify his stand. He asked, *inter alia,* that the funds collected by the Maritime Customs Administration be turned over to his government, and that taxes and salt revenues be paid into the new treasury. He wished also to reopen the Yangtze River between Shanghai and Nanking and to exercise certain police powers.[13] His requests were met with fair promises so indefinitely worded and so conditioned as to cause Wang to falter in his course.[14] However, he had become so deeply involved that escape may have been impossible had he desired it. Without Japanese guards Wang was apprehensive of assassination, with them he was a prisoner.

The solemn farce of the "return" of the national government to Nanking was enacted on March 30, 1940. Wang made it appear that the Kuomintang had elected him to the presidency by setting up a rump party, the "orthodox Kuomintang." That an appreciable number of party members had followed Wang was proved by the edict issued by the National Government for the arrest of 105 persons. In the list appeared such well-known names as Chu Min-yi, Chou Fu-hai, Chen Kung-po, Wen Tsung-yao, and Kiang Kang-hu.[15] It is of interest that the Japanese permitted use of Kuomintang ideology at Nanking while espousing obscurantism at Peking. Wang Ch'ing-wei insisted that he could not represent himself as a loyal, liberal Chinese unless he stood on the platform of Sun Yat-sen, somewhat revamped to distinguish his ideas from those of his late colleagues at Chungking.

The "Reorganized Government" was modelled upon the National Government which it was seeking to replace.[16] It op-

[13] *Chinese Year Book, 1940–1941,* cited, p. 256–7.
[14] *Ibid.,* p. 257–65.
[15] *China Weekly Review,* April 6, 1940, p. 199–200.
[16] See Chapter VI.

erates through the five *yuan* or boards: executive, legislative, judicial, supervisory and examination. Reproduction of the entire governmental structure, even to minor details, is entirely logical in view of Wang's assumption that his government is the former government restored and in its right mind. The Chinese officials are less closely supervised by their Japanese advisers than those at Peking, but the larger freedom is of no use to them since the military organization of Japan parallels their paper regime.[17]

On November 30, 1940, the Japanese and the Reorganized Governments entered into a treaty; in translation this document names the Wang regime the "National Government of the Republic of China." [18] The first article of this treaty admirably sums up the cynical "double talk" of indirect rule:

> The Governments of the two countries shall, in order to maintain permanently good neighborly and amicable relations between the two countries, mutually respect their sovereignty and territories *and at the same time take mutually helpful and friendly measures, political, economic and cultural.* (Italics the author's)

Provisions for "joint defense" against communistic movements, complementary economic development, special facilities for Japan in extraction of natural resources, a monopoly of "necessary assistance" to China's industrial and commercial progress, and other arrangements fully reflected Japan's position. In the treaty Japan was permitted to keep troops in North China and Inner Mongolia as a defense against communistic activities. Withdrawal of troops from other parts of China appears to be contemplated when there shall be "general peace" but is not definitely assured in the accompanying protocol. Vague promises to "make adjustments" regarding taxation, and to "take necessary measures"

[17] Linebarger, Paul M. A., *The China of Chiang K'ai-shek,* cited, p. 203–8.
[18] *Contemporary Japan,* X, 1941, p. 131–8.

to restore requisitioned properties leave actual disposition of such issues to Japanese discretion. The only concession made to China is the promise to relinquish extraterritoriality and residential concessions. A "Joint Declaration by Japan, Manchoukuo and China" (note the order of names), also signed on November 30, 1940, guarantees respect for each other's sovereignty and cooperation in every field. Thereby Japan secured "Chinese" recognition of "Manchoukuo." Not until July 1, 1941, was the Wang government recognized by another state. On that date Germany, Italy, Spain, Rumania, "Slovakia" and "Croatia" announced recognition.

Mengchiang (Mongolian Marches)

Under the auspices of the Kwantung Army three regional governments—those of North Shansi, Inner Mongolia and South Chahar—were brought together in November 1937, under the caption "Mengchiang."[19] This government is referred to as the Federation of Autonomous Governments of Mongolian Provinces. The province of Suiyuan was included within its jurisdiction, which left Hopei, Shantung, part of Shansi and part of Honan for the Peking wards of the North China Army. Of the federation one member, Inner Mongolia, is a Mongol community; the other two are Chinese. The seat of government of the federation is Kalgan, in Suiyuan. A "Federal Council" of Mongols and Chinese, with the Mongol Teh Wang as chairman and closely "advised" by the Japanese, is the supreme governmental authority.[20] As in the case of the Peking government, the autonomy of Mengchiang was carefully safeguarded when the "National Government" at Nanking was given titular authority over it.[21]

[19] *Japan Year Book, 1939–1940,* p. 1085–7.

[20] "Japan's Puppets on the Chinese Stage," American Information Committee, Shanghai, January 18, 1940.

[21] *Chinese Year Book, 1940–1941,* p. 264–5.

Local Government

Notice has been taken of the failure of the Japanese armies to bring the greater part of rural China lying within their lines of occupation under their effective control. In general it may be said that district magistrates were not removed from their posts and that the *hsien* and village system was not disturbed. In the urban centers, where Japanese control could be firmly applied, puppet regimes were appointed, their Chinese members a mask for the Japanese behind them, who paid themselves fat salaries, battened upon the sale of concessions, legitimate and otherwise, and subjected the Chinese officials and people to humiliating treatment.[22] Shanghai, Tientsin, Canton, Hankow, Tsinan and a host of other cities became milch cows for racketeers, both Japanese and Chinese.

The China Affairs Board

To correlate the supervisory relations of various Japanese Government departments with the political, economic and cultural institutions and activities under Japan's sponsorship in China, the China Affairs Board was set up in Tokyo on December 16, 1938.[23] This was placed under the Cabinet as a whole rather than a single ministry. General Ugaki, when Foreign Minister, opposed the transfer of administrative functions from the Foreign Office to this Board, but was over-ruled by the Army.[24] The premier is chairman of the Board and the ministers of foreign affairs, finance, war and the navy are vice-presidents. Chief responsibility for effective

[22] "Japan's Puppets," cited, p. 24–9.

[23] *Japan Year Book, 1939–1940,* cited, p. 1081, 1098–9; Fahs, C. B., *Government in Japan: Recent Trends in Its Scope and Operation,* New York, 1941, p. 66–70.

[24] Borton, Hugh, *Japan Since 1931: Its Political and Social Developments,* New York, 1941, p. 119–20.

operation rests upon the Board's director-general, who is an army officer of high rank. A large staff of military and civilian officers and clerks is necessitated by the broad sweep of the Board's work. In addition to its supervisory functions, the Board has responsibility for the recommendation of policy to the Cabinet. No representatives from China or "Manchoukuo" are on the Board. However, the Sino-Japanese Economic Council, liaison body between the Board and economic agencies in China, is of mixed membership.

The "New Order" in Economic Relations

Prior to the establishment of the China Affairs Board, the Japanese Board of Planning published a "Program for the Economic Development of China." [25] The objectives were stated to be the development of natural resources, the increase of Chinese purchasing power, the provision of iron, coal, cotton and other necessities for Japan, and the construction of transportation and communications facilities, electrical works and harbors. The statement was frank:

> Sufficient supply of necessary materials from a country within the yen bloc will, to a considerable extent, decrease Japan's overseas payments, while the coordinated adjustment of industries within the three countries of Japan, Manchoukuo and China, eliminating unnecessary competition and friction between them, will work greatly toward the adjustment of supply and demand of materials and the balancing of international payments.

The establishment of the North China Development Company and the Central China Promotion Company was announced in the statement. These had been set up on November 7, 1938, the former capitalized at 350,000,000 yen, the latter at 100,000,000 yen. In each case the Japanese Government provided half the capital. Each company was authorized to sell bonds up to five times the amount of its paid-up

[25] *Tokyo Gazette,* No. 18, 1938, p. 1-6; No. 19, 1939, p. 15-24.

capital. The Government undertook, for a period of five years, to guarantee principal and interest to private owners of shares and bonds. On the other hand, it held the companies under the strictest regulation as to policy, disposal of profits, raising of loans, etc. They are, in fact, agencies of the Japanese Government, established to monopolize every form of large-scale business enterprise. Neither company had any Chinese directors.

The function of the companies is to provide capital and to supervise business corporations interested in such enterprises as transportation, harbor-works, communications, electrical works, mining, fisheries and banking.[26] They are essentially holding companies but the Central China Company is permitted to engage directly in business undertakings. Reconstruction of war-damaged industries was the principal task of the Central China Company while the North China Company was established to develop new enterprises in order to exploit the great natural resources of that area. It may be assumed that the organization of two companies rather than one reflects political rather than economic considerations.

A more comprehensive "Program for Economic Construction Embracing Japan, Manchoukuo and China" was published by the Cabinet Information Bureau at Tokyo in November 1940.[27] By that date the Three-Power Pact between Japan, Germany, and Italy had been signed and the concept of a "New Order in East Asia" had been expanded to envisage a "Greater East Asia Co-Prosperity Sphere," which was to be part of a new world order. The revised program contemplated relating Japan, "Manchoukuo" and China to the other areas within the "Co-Prosperity Sphere." It was contrived on the theory that free trade was an obsolete system and that "impregnable economic strength able to meet any situation must be maintained by keeping the extent to which Japanese

[26] *Japan Year Book, 1939–1940,* cited, p. 1101. The law which authorized these companies was promulgated on April 30, 1938.

[27] *Tokyo Gazette,* December 1940, p. 213–22.

economy is dependent upon other countries to a minimum." It aimed at establishing "a new East Asiatic economic order under Japanese leadership within about ten years." That this doctrine of regional autarky is out of harmony with Japan's declared spirit of *hakko ichiu* (the world as one family) appears to have been overlooked.

The program does not prescribe for either "Manchoukuo" or China the simple role of providing raw materials and markets for Japanese industry. On the contrary, it suggests spheres of industrial activity suited to their conditions and phases of economic development. The "highest type of precision industry" is reserved for Japan. For "Manchoukuo" mining, heavy industry and chemical and electrical enterprises are suggested, for China the same, plus salt production and light industry. Transfer of rayon and other light industries from Japan to China is proposed. "Manchoukuo" is viewed as a great potential source of foodstuffs for export. Production of cotton in China can be greatly increased. Planned agriculture, involving distribution of crops, maintenance of the soil, improvement of seed, etc., also similarly organized forestry and fisheries, are contemplated. Technical training must be provided to increase productivity. Foreign trade is to be based upon the "principle of productive trade, which enables each country, region and economic sphere to supply to others goods required by them in exchange for the goods necessary for its own planned production." In view of this principle and of the scarcity of capital, the statement that "capital required for the three countries must of course be supplied by their own accumulation" seems inconsistent with the desire for rapid development.

Economic Controls in Operation

Exhaustive treatment of this topic is impossible here but examples may be taken from the fields of industry, trade, finance and transportation.[28] As provided for in the programs of the Planning Board, the North China Development Company and the Central China Promotion Company either confiscated or took over at a fraction of their value many prosperous concerns and organized new companies to manage them. Chinese owners willing to "cooperate" were required to contribute existing plants and equipment while the Japanese partners provided capital and management. Majority control always was reserved to the Japanese. There was no alternative to "cooperation" but expropriation. Coal and iron mines, railways and bus companies, gas and electrical works, telegraph and telephone lines, cotton and woolen mills, silk filatures, dockyards, shipping companies, banks—a complete list would cover the panorama of China's economic life—were handed over to these subsidiaries or to other Japanese corporations. Wherever a mandate of one of the new regional governments was found useful to provide a semblance of legality it was easily obtained.[29]

Japan's great need for iron and coking-coal made the exploitation of China's deposits its first concern. The rich iron deposits of Chahar province, estimated to contain 100,000,000 tons of ore, and those of Hupeh, Anhwei and Shantung, were taken over and the operating mines began at once to ship ore to Japan. The larger Chinese coal mines of North China were also appropriated and in 1939 Japan obtained two and a half times as much coal from that area as in 1936. The salt fields of Shantung and Hopei were placed under a subsidiary, the North China Salt Manufacturing Company,

[28] No comprehensive *ex parte* study of this process is yet available. Professor J. E. Orchard's article, "Japan's Economic Invasion of China" (*Foreign Affairs,* XVIII, p. 464–76), is excellent but necessarily brief; expressing the point of view of Free China are two useful monographs: *Japan Closing the Open Door in China,* by John Ahlers, Shanghai, 1939 (a summary of which appears in the *Chinese Year Book, 1940–1941,* cited, p. 202–32), and *Japan's Economic Offensive in China,* by Lowe Chuan-hua, London, 1939.

[29] Michael, F., "The Significance of Puppet Governments," *Pacific Affairs,* XII, p. 400–12.

enabling the export of greatly increased quantities of salt to Japan. Electric power for all purposes in North China was brought under the monopoly of another subsidiary, the North China Electric Power Industry.

Except for factories located in European concessions China's cotton mills have been absorbed by the Japanese, to be managed only by members of the Japanese Cotton Mill Owners' Association. Fifty-two mills, operating 1,540,000 spindles were taken over prior to May 1, 1939. In the Yangtze valley farmers are required to sell all silk cocoons to Japanese interests and the monopoly of silk filatures is in the hands of the Central China Silk-Reeling Company.[30] Electric power and water supply in the Yangtze valley, except for the American-owned light and power company in the International Settlement, is monopolized by the Central China Water and Electric Power Supply Company. Complementary to the seizure of Chinese properties has been the establishment of new Japanese and Sino-Japanese concerns and the exclusion of all new foreign enterprises from occupied China.

The most obvious effects of the "New Order" are observed in the fields of transportation and communication. This was to be expected since most of the railways and telecommunications lines were owned by the Chinese Government. The North China railways were placed under the management of a new agency, the North China Traffic Company, in which the South Manchuria Railway Company was the principal stockholder. Another body, the Central China Railways Company, took over lines south of the Yellow River. Thousands of employees were removed to make places for Japanese subjects. Although occidental bond-holders hold nearly $150,000,000 (U. S.) worth of the debentures of these lines, no consideration was given to their interests. Foreign shippers

[30] *Tokyo Gazette,* November 1940, p. 202; also *Economic Review of Foreign Countries, 1939 and Early 1940,* U. S. Department of Commerce, 1941, p. 321.

cannot use the railways without the assistance, at a price, of Japanese forwarding companies. The execution of ambitious plans for new railways has been impeded by guerrilla warfare and scarcity of funds but a line from Tehchow on the Tientsin-Pukow Railway crossing Hopei province to Shihchiachuang, where the branch from the Peking-Hankow line starts toward Shansi, was completed in November 1940. This line, 125 miles long, is a military and economic asset, shortening the distance from the seaboard for the transport of troops inward and of coal outward.

Seizure of all Chinese coastal and river shipping, also docks and warehouses, has accompanied monopolization of rail and road transport. Closure of the lower and middle Yangtze River to non-Japanese foreign shipping, which exceeded the Japanese in tonnage prior to the war, was decreed as a war measure which has not been revoked. This measure affords Japanese companies a highly profitable monopoly of passenger and freight service on the busiest sections of the Yangtze.[31] Various restrictions and preferential regulations favor Japanese shipping in the occupied coastal ports. Chinese docks and godowns were distributed among Japanese dockyard companies. Canal transport also has been absorbed. The airlines of occupied China are another Japanese monopoly.[32]

The most complicated field of "New Order" economics is that of finance and currency. On the institutional side, the creation of the Federal Reserve Bank of China at Peking, the Bank of Mongolia at Kalgan, and the Central Reserve Bank at Shanghai was a series of acts designed to consolidate the financial systems of the three new governments and to bring about the ultimate liquidation of National Government currency. Each of the new central banks was created ostensibly by mandate of a Chinese government and is managed

31 *Far Eastern Survey,* January 19, 1939, p. 20–2.
32 *Ibid.,* May 24, 1939, p. 132–3; *Chinese Year Book, 1940–1941,* cited, p. 214.

by Chinese with Japanese advisers. The Federal Reserve Bank began operations on March 10, 1938, the Mongolian Bank on December 1, 1938, and the Central Bank on January 20, 1941.[33] Capital was provided in part by confiscation of existing national and provincial banks, in part by contributions from current tax and customs revenues, in part by subscription of private bankers, in part by Japanese loans. Each of the new banks issues currency which is pegged to the Japanese yen, the whole group forming, with the Bank of Japan and the Bank of "Manchoukuo," the so-called "yen bloc." Their notes were issued at par with Chinese National currency but in North China and Inner Mongolia the circulation of the latter was prohibited subsequently, since it maintained itself at a premium and was preferred to the new currencies. The latter were inadequately secured, had a low value in foreign exchange, and were symbols of Japanese dominaton.[34] Issued in large amounts and forced upon the people they had an inflationary effect and prices rose accordingly.[35]

The principal obstacle to the success of the new currency was its unacceptability for the purchase of foreign exchange. To remedy this deficiency official control was established over foreign exchange in North China. Exporters were forced to accept F.R.B. currency at official rates in payment for exchange, which entailed heavy losses, and importers were restricted in the purchase of bills. Again the legal cover for these regulations was furnished by the Peking government while the enforcing agency was the Yokohama Specie Bank.[36] Similar measures were taken in Inner Mongolia and presum-

[33] *Japan Year Book, 1939–1940,* p. 1080–1, 1087; *New York Times,* January 21, 1941.

[34] Ahlers, John, cited, p. 84–98; *Far Eastern Survey,* February 16, 1938, p. 43–4; Lieu, D. K., "The Sino-Japanese Currency War," *Pacific Affairs,* XII, p. 413–26.

[35] Estimated Japanese and Japanese-sponsored currency in China at the end of 1939 was 1,400,000,000 *yuan. Economic Review of Foreign Countries,* cited, p. 326.

[36] *Far Eastern Survey,* May 24, 1939, p. 128–9.

ably will be taken in Shanghai, Canton and other commercial centers if and when they seem opportune.

In addition to establishing controls over banking and currency the Japanese took over the Maritime Customs funds in the occupied ports and the administration of the customs offices therein.[37] Funds were thus made available for the use of the sponsored governments and for other purposes. Although an agreement between Great Britain and Japan specified that a proportion of customs collections would be set aside for the servicing of foreign loans secured upon them, no monies actually were remitted. Tariff schedules were revised in favor of Japanese goods and extensive smuggling was not only permitted but protected.

The "New Order" in Education

Japan's educational program in China is designed to substitute Japanese for English as the second language of literate Chinese, to re-establish the Confucian ethical tenets of pre-Republican China, to destroy respect for Western political and social ideals, to undermine the National Government, and to inculcate a doctrine of "Asia for Asiatics" under Japanese leadership. Among measures taken is the revision of textbooks to eliminate unfavorable references to Japan, the doctrines of the Kuomintang and other liberal ideas, and to restore materials from the ancient classical writings. Vocational studies and physical hygiene are encouraged, the social sciences diluted to moral indoctrination.[38]

The hostilities played havoc with the buildings and equipment of China's universities, most of which were in the north and east, and drove the faculties and student bodies to the southwest. Revival of higher education was hampered by

[37] *Ibid.*, June 1, 1938, p. 130–1.

[38] Taylor, G. E., cited, p. 88–98; Professor Taylor thinks it possible that educational control may succeed in stultifying thought and intimidating the youth into acceptance of subjection.

lack of able teachers as well as by inadequate facilities due to destruction and by uncertainty as to curricula. Not until the summer of 1938 was Peking University reopened. Normal colleges for men and women were reopened in Peking somewhat earlier, to re-educate teachers along acceptable lines. Japanese teachers are mingled with Chinese and the regimented life of Japanese students is being enforced in occupied China.

Adult "education" is not neglected. The organization of societies and the holding of public meetings require police approval. There are no independent newspapers. Press and radio are agencies of Japanese propaganda. Posters and pictures on walls and sign-boards exalt the "Kingly Way" and provide such slogans as: "To love Japanese soldiers is to love our own life and property"; "Chiang has ruined the country and impoverished the people"; "Find jobs and food under Wang Ch'ing-wei." Societies are organized to receive the teachings of the *Hsin Min Hui* and are appealed to by gifts of money, seeds and entertainments. The temples of the ancient religions, including Mohammedanism, are being rehabilitated and their precepts revived. Intimidation by police and terrorist gangs is employed against recalcitrants.[39]

In this attempt to reverse the direction of Chinese social and political thought, the Japanese are repeating King Canute's futile order to the tide. Their resentment against Western influence in Asia has not blinded them to the universal applicability of the natural sciences but apparently they regard the social sciences as limitable by political boundaries. It may be suggested that they are as cosmopolitan as the natural sciences, although their diffusion is slower because it depends upon a wider literacy and consequent popular demand. In Japan their pressure has been strongly felt. It will be more powerful in China because of scholarly tradition

[39] "Japan's Cultural Aggression in China," American Information Committee, April 3, 1940.

and the absence of entrenched military conservatism. Historically China was the hub of the Asian universe, the mother culture and suzerain of all the states from Malaya to the Amur, including Japan. During the past fifty years liberalism has more deeply penetrated the minds of Chinese youth. Add to these factors the extreme emotional resistance to indoctrination induced by the brutalities of the war, and the inertia against it becomes impregnable.

"New Order" a Misnomer

It will now be apparent that there is nothing new in the "New Order" unless it be the extreme callousness of its application. The "New Order" is the most intensive and all-embracing imperialism, reviving the aims of European imperialism of the eighteenth century and the methods of the Dark Ages. That this should be possible in the relations of one people noted for grace of manner, courtesy and artistic temperament, with another of great dignity, ancient but living culture, and self-esteem, is a paradox. Taken at face value, the ideals voiced by the Japanese are outmoded. They contemplate a compartmented world, intellectually as well as economically and politically regionalized in a day of radio and aeroplane. But Japanese practice of these ideals has already proved that they cannot be taken at face value.

VIII

FOREIGN RESIDENTIAL AREAS IN JEOPARDY

FOREIGN nationals enjoyed a privileged position under treaties and other agreements with China.[1] In the ports of Shanghai, Tientsin, Canton, Amoy, Hankow and other cities the rights of residence and of conducting the normal activities of civilization were supplemented by that of residence in settlements and concessions governed by tax payers who possessed property within such areas.[2] The effects of the Japanese invasion upon the areas and the bearing of these effects upon the attitude of foreign governments toward that invasion require some consideration.

In 1935 the International Settlement at Shanghai had a population of approximately 1,160,000, of whom 39,000 were of foreign nationality. Among the foreign population the Japanese were most numerous—some 20,000. British residents numbered 6500, Russians 3000, Americans 2000. The population of the so-called French Concession—which is technically a settlement—in 1936 was about 480,000, of whom 24,000 were foreigners. Nearly 12,000 of the latter were Russians, 2700 British, 2400 French and 1800 Americans. Thus the two areas, which are separated only by streets, composed an urban district with a population of approximately 1,650,000,

[1] Quigley and Blakeslee, cited, Chapters X–XIII.

[2] *Ibid.*, p. 158–65; gives a brief description of government and an account of Chinese and Japanese criticisms of Settlement administration.

of whom 63,000 were foreigners.[3] Ringing them about was the Greater Municipality of Shanghai, with a population of 2,000,000, under Chinese administration. Shanghai was among the first ten ports of the world in value of trade and shipping. In 1935 more than half of China's foreign trade was handled at Shanghai.[4]

The International Settlement was essentially a British-controlled city. Approximately three fourths of British investments in China, which totalled above U. S. $1,000,000,000, were located there. The important administrative jobs, which paid high salaries and retiring allowances, were held by British subjects. On the Municipal Council there were five British, two Americans, two Japanese, and five Chinese. The Japanese wanted three seats but they lacked sufficient tax-paying voters, in spite of their large proportion of the foreign population, to win a third place.

Several states maintained garrisons at Shanghai. In 1937 the American force was the largest—150 officers and 2600 men; the British, having troops nearby at Hong Kong, had 90 officers and 2500 men at Shanghai; the French had 50 officers and 2000 men, the Italians 20 officers and 750 men. The Settlement maintained a Volunteer Corps, officered by the British.[5] After the armistice in 1932 the Japanese built a large fortified barracks in Hongkew, a section of the Settlement, in which they maintained a picked force of 1800 men. From time to time maneuvers, with tanks and artillery, were conducted by these troops along the Bund and on the principal streets of the Settlement. Hongkew became essentially a separate Japanese area uncontrolled by the Municipal Council.

[3] *China Year Book, 1939,* cited, p. 539.

[4] For a vivid, sardonic description of Shanghai, see Ernest O. Hauser, *Shanghai: City for Sale,* New York, 1940; William C. Johnstone's study, *The Shanghai Problem,* Stanford University, 1937, is a more conventional history; war-time Shanghai is described by Robert W. Barnett, *Economic Shanghai: Hostage to Politics,* New York, 1941.

[5] *China Year Book, 1938,* cited, p. 417–8.

Effects of Hostilities

Upon the outbreak of hostilities at Shanghai, on August 13, 1937, the Council of the International Settlement did not, as it had in 1932, declare a state of emergency, which would have authorized Japanese troops to take positions in Chinese territory bordering the Settlement.[6] Foreign troops and the Volunteer Corps manned the boundaries of the Settlement and the French Concession, Hongkew and Yangtzepoo being left, perforce, to the Japanese. The British Government requested both Japan and China to withdraw their forces from Shanghai. The latter was willing to do so but Japan declined.[7] Consequently the foreign areas were subjected to the dangers and financial losses incidental to intensive fighting around and above them. Extensive casualties resulted from misdirected bombing and cannonading; the damage to factories, looting and loss of income caused by the flight of workmen and stoppage of factories was considerable.

Inevitably acts of terrorism were to occur. The police of the areas were placed in a difficult position by such acts. On January 1, 1938, the Municipal Council issued a proclamation to the effect that persons committing offenses against armed forces would be liable to be handed over to the armed forces concerned.[8] In spite of this action the Japanese command threatened to send troops to search out culprits and demanded larger representation on the police force and in the administrative organization of the Settlement. It further insisted that the Council exercise rigid control over anti-Japanese newspapers, both Chinese and foreign. The Council, after receiving the advice of the British and the American embassies, agreed to the inclusion of additional Japanese in the police force, in return for which it requested that its

[6] *China Weekly Review,* August 21, 1937, p. 428.
[7] Hsü, Shuhsi, *Japan and Shanghai,* Shanghai, 1938, p. 24–8.
[8] *Ibid.,* p. 86–8.

authority in portions of the Settlement occupied during hostilities be no longer interfered with.[9] The Japanese, however, ignored this request.

In attempting to cope with the Chinese and Korean terrorists who served the national cause against the various juntas affiliated with the Japanese, and the Chinese and Japanese who operated in the same fashion against the supporters of Free China, the governments of the foreign areas faced an insoluble problem. In both China and Japan banditry for hire has long been a profession. Its operatives are Capone thugs raised to the *nth* power. Added to their numbers were the patriotic youngsters who shot from shadowed doorways or invaded an official's home in gangs. They were no respecters of persons. Dr. Herman Liu, President of Shanghai University and an ardent Nationalist, was killed on one of the principal streets. Anti-Japanese newspaper offices were bombed and journalists were assassinated. During the first two months of 1939 there were 18 murders or attempted murders in Shanghai of persons believed to be in league with the Japanese. Mayor Fu Hsiao-en of the Chinese Municipality, a satellite of Wang Ch'ing-wei, was butchered in his bed. His residence was in Hongkew, the Japanese-controlled section of the Settlement. The penalties prescribed by the Council appeared to be unheeded. Only in rare instances was an assassin apprehended. In February 1939, a new set of demands was made upon the Council by Japanese military and consular authorities.[10] Neither the Japanese communication nor the Council's reply was made public but the latter was accepted as satisfactory in principle.[11]

The area to the west of the Settlement, known as the Western Extra-Settlement Roads, jurisdiction over which was shared by the Council with the Chinese Municipality,

[9] *China Weekly Review,* April 2, 1938, p. 138; Hsü, Shuhsi, *Japan and The Third Powers,* Shanghai, p. 66–71.

[10] *China Weekly Review,* February 25, 1939, p. 389.

[11] *Contemporary Japan,* VIII, 1939, p. 435.

had been the most exclusive residential section of Shanghai. Under the stress of war conditions the Council was unable to prevent the development there of a situation which gave to this section the unpleasing title, "The Badlands." Various forms of vice found it a desirable location because of inadequate policing. The Japanese-controlled government of the Chinese Municipality, which exercised authority between the Roads, saw in the encouragement of these nuisances not only a source of revenue but the means of driving Settlement control entirely out of the section. Japanese military officers made large incomes from a share of license fees for gambling and opium dens and houses of prostitution. Violence and murder accompanied these invaders of the area.

Another development opposed by the residents along the Western Roads but encouraged by the Municipal Council of the Settlement was the establishment of industries. Chinese owners of factories destroyed, closed or confiscated in other parts of Shanghai sought and obtained permits to build new plants of various types in this hitherto exclusive section.[12] Between June 1 and October 31, 1938, the Building Surveyor of the Municipal Council approved some 200 applications for factory building permits. Silk filatures, enamel-ware plants, glassware factories, tanneries and other enterprises were brought into operation. The unsightly huts of workmen were crowded alongside, raising fears of unhealthful living conditions and increased fire hazards.

Demand for Governmental Reorganization

In May 1939, the Japanese Foreign Office complained to the British and American Governments that the Land Regulations, which constitute a sort of organic law or charter for the Settlement, were obsolete. It referred to the undemocratic system of elections, the near-monopoly of the British

[12] *China Weekly Review,* December 24, 1938, p. 121.

over official posts, the excessive cost of administration, and the unfair distribution of funds for such purposes as education.[13] The communication held it to be "imperative" that Japanese representation in the Council and administrative organization should be increased. It also insisted upon closer cooperation between the Settlement authorities and the new Chinese regimes at Shanghai and Nanking. It stated that "special consideration should be given to the position of the Chinese Court of Justice existing within the Settlement," and that "the question of restitution of the old City Government's Land Registers, held in custody by the Municipal Council, must be speedily settled."

The American reply stated that [14]

> The Government of the United States would be ready, as it has been in the past, to become a party to friendly and orderly negotiations properly instituted and conducted regarding any needed revision in the Land Regulations . . . [it] is constrained to point out, however, that conditions in the Shanghai area are, from its viewpoint, so far from normal at the present time that there is totally lacking a basis for a discussion looking toward an orderly settlement of the complicated problems involved which would be reasonably fair to all concerned.

The reply pointed out that the status of the Chinese courts was governed by a multilateral agreement which could not be satisfactorily revised under the prevailing abnormal conditions. It ignored the Japanese plea for a more democratic suffrage but argued that the existing system was not discriminatory and that under it, because of the low tax qualification, "the Japanese community enjoys . . . a vote . . . far greater in proportion to the total vote than the proportion which the general municipal rates and land taxes paid by the Japanese community bear to the total of the municipal rates and taxes paid in the International Settlement."

[13] Jones and Myers, *Documents,* I, p. 257–9.
[14] *Ibid.,* p. 259–61.

The American aide-mémoire then made certain suggestions bearing upon Japanese responsibility for the prevailing conditions. "In the absence of the duly constituted and recognized government . . . [the Settlement] authorities are entitled to expect every consideration from Japanese civil and military agencies." The traditional and essential practice of the Settlement had been to avoid involvement in outside controversies; no one interested government "should take advantage of developments which have their origin elsewhere to prejudice the international character of the Settlement." The faithful efforts of the Settlement to hold lawlessness to a minimum had been prejudiced by Japanese retention of control over the areas north of Soochow Creek. These areas should be returned. The aide-mémoire concluded upon a friendly note, the assurance that the Settlement authorities, as in the past, were prepared to meet reasonable requests for adjustments in administrative practices.

An amazingly frank and sweeping statement was issued on May 24 by the spokesman of the Japanese Foreign Office.[15] After asserting the obvious fact that the foreign settlements and concessions were not foreign territory, he said:

> Japan just now is taking actions in China with its national destiny at stake under conditions tantamount to war. The object of these actions is to place the sovereignty of China under Japanese control. In the light of this circumstance, Japan should be regarded as placing the entire territory of China under its control . . . It is only natural and proper . . . that Japan should take it upon itself to send armed forces to such concessions to clear them of . . . enemy elements . . . There is no reason whatsoever to hesitate to improve the structure of the International Settlement simply because of the China affair.

What appeared to be a sop thrown to Cerberus was a so-called *modus vivendi* or provisional agreement between the Municipal Council and the Chinese Municipality signed on

[15] *Ibid.*, p. 262.

February 16, 1940.[16] Under this arrangement, to quote the editor of the *China Weekly Review,* "the S. M. C. has relinquished authority over the outside roads in the Western district by agreeing to delegate it to a new police organization over which the S. M. C. will exercise no real control." The first sentence of the agreement bore out this view:

> The City Government of Greater Shanghai, after consultation with the Shanghai Municipal Council, has decided to establish a Special Police Force in the West Shanghai (Outside Roads) Area.

The share of police administration left to the Settlement authorities was slight. They were to be consulted regarding "the numbers and general structure of the new force; to recommend a number of principal and minor officers for required appointment by the Chinese municipality; to appoint liaison officers; and to participate in the settlement of disagreements between officers of different nationalities. The foreign police officers were to handle all cases involving foreigners.

Another agreement of a like character but dealing with the portion of the Settlement north of Soochow Creek was signed on March 1, 1939. Although it appeared to assure resumption of the Council's control of Hongkew and adjacent sections, its actual effect was to perpetuate Japanese control. It provided that Japanese police officers would be appointed divisional officer, i.e. chief, of one of the three police divisions north of Soochow Creek and associate divisional officer in the other two divisions. It also enlarged Japanese influence over the entire police force of the Settlement by establishing the office of special deputy commissioner, to be held by a Japanese, ranking next after the commissioner.[17]

[16] *China Weekly Review,* February 24, 1940, p. 435.

[17] *Ibid.,* March 9, 1940, p. 53; Mr. C. Akagi, first appointee to the post, was murdered on June 17, 1941.

The Council elections of 1940 offered an opportunity to obtain additional Japanese representation. Five Japanese candidates were presented; the British had six candidates, the Americans two. Each voter was entitled to cast one ballot for each of as many candidates as there were seats (nine foreign) in the Council. When the Japanese list of electors, which the British and Americans believed to be heavily "padded" but which could not be checked, was found to contain over 5000 names—contrasting with approximately 900 in 1936—the British and American landholders—who had listed some 1300 and 400 names respectively in 1936—not only used every effort to solicit the votes of other white nationals but greatly lengthened their own electoral lists by splitting up large properties and registering them separately, a device resulting in plural voting.[18] The result was that the white voters mustered about 8000 votes which they cast for the British and American slates. The new Council was composed of the customary five British, two Americans, and two Japanese.

Early in 1941 the Japanese formed a Ratepayers Association to work for larger representation. At that time the Association announced that 80,000 Japanese were residents of the Settlement and appurtenant areas.[19] The intensity of feeling among them was exhibited at a special meeting of Settlement ratepayers on January 23, 1941.[20] In the course of a heated discussion the chairman of the Japanese Ratepayers Association drew a revolver and slightly wounded the chairman of the Municipal Council, Mr. W. J. Keswick, an Englishman.

Compromise on Council membership and representation was reached in April 1941, by secret negotiation between British, American and Japanese officials and private citizens.[21]

[18] *Ibid.*, April 20, 1940, p. 251.
[19] *Ibid.*, January 4, 1941, p. 151.
[20] *Ibid.*, February 1, 1941, p. 291–3.
[21] *Ibid.*, April 5, 1941, p. 152; *New York Times*, April 18, 1941.

This informal procedure was made possible by the equally informal character of the old division of seats. The ratepayers ratified the plan on April 17. Under the new arrangement Council membership was raised from 14 to 16. The Chinese were reduced to four seats, the British to three; Americans and Japanese were raised to three each; Germans were allotted one seat, Swiss one, and Dutch one. In view of the extremely tense situation no election was held in 1941.

British Troops Withdrawn

The withdrawal of British troops from China in August 1940 raised a difficult issue of reallotment of defense sectors in the Settlement. The British and American members of the Shanghai Defense Committee favored dividing the British sectors between the American marines and the Japanese, the former to have the central downtown sector, the latter the western outside roads area. This plan was satisfactory to the Municipal Council but the Japanese naval commander opposed it. He wished to have both sectors manned by his forces.[22] As a compromise the downtown sector was allotted temporarily to the Volunteer Corps, an international force.

The French Concession

The French Concession was advantaged in the earlier months of the struggle by its character as a purely French-governed area. Its location also was favorable, the International Settlement forming a buffer between it and the Japanese in Hongkew. The fall of France placed the Concession at Japan's mercy, save as it might be aided by interested governments through their support of the International Settlement. Siccawei, a zone to the west of the Concession and adjoining the Western Extra-Settlement Roads Area, was

[22] *China Weekly Review,* August 24, 1940, p. 460–1.

policed by the French during the first three years of the Sino-Japanese controversy. In June 1940, the zone was turned over, on request, to the Japanese.[23] Concurrently the French authorities agreed to admit Japanese police into the Concession to search for terrorists.[24]

Pressure was employed by the Japanese from the time of the retreat of the Chinese army from Shanghai to obtain control of the Chinese courts in the two foreign areas. The resistance of both Governments to this demand was maintained effectively until the defeat of France. Transfer of the Chinese courts was regarded as tantamount to the recognition of political control since it was obvious that the interpretation of Chinese law and the execution of judgments would thereafter consult Japanese rather than Western interests, and that Japanese police would supervise Chinese judicial administration.

By an agreement of November 7, 1940, between the Chinese (Wang Ch'ing-wei) government at Nanking and the authorities of the Concession, the jurisdiction of the former over the Chinese courts was recognized; it was to become operative immediately.[25] New Chinese judges were appointed and accepted office. The agreement provided that the administration of the courts would continue in accordance with the Franco-Chinese convention of July 28, 1931.[26] Nominally this provision left to the French police the supervision of the enforcement of decisions and the execution of sentences. The National Government at Chungking excoriated the agreement.[27]

[23] *Ibid.*, July 6, 1940, p. 198.

[24] *Ibid.*, p. 200; gunmen fired on the French police director, apparently in retaliation for this unavoidable surrender. (*Ibid.*, August 31, 1940, p. 515.)

[25] *Ibid.*, November 16, 1940, p. 354–5.

[26] Text of agreement of 1931 in *Chinese Social and Political Science Review*, Public Documents Supplement, XV (1931), p. 466–74.

[27] A French consular judge who participated in negotiating the agreement was assassinated. (*New York Times*, December 17, 1940.)

Tientsin

The summer of 1939 brought hardship and apprehension to the residents of the British and French concessions at Tientsin. Nearly 5000 foreigners, including small garrison forces, and more than 70,000 Chinese lived in the British Concession (census of 1938), 1800 foreigners and 120,000 Chinese in the French. A challenge to the continued existence of the areas was issued on May 6, 1939, by the headquarters of the Japanese Army in North China.[28] The formal statement charged the Concession authorities with harboring agencies of the Kuomintang and the Communist International, and with protecting assassins of Japanese soldiers and Chinese officials. The general conclusion was drawn that the Concessions should be liquidated to make way for the "New Order."

The occasion for this broadside was the refusal of the British Concession authorities to hand over to the Japanese army four Chinese accused of murdering the Chinese manager of the Tientsin branch of the Federal Reserve Bank. Failing to prevail by threats, the army imposed a blockade of the British and French Concessions on June 14, 1939, which was not raised until June 20, 1940. In announcing the blockade the army commander declared that the issues involved were greater than the disposition of the four Chinese.[29] Great Britain was called upon to revise its China policy and to cease its support of Chiang K'ai-shek. This support was believed to be evidenced by the continued circulation of Chinese national currency in the Concessions and by the refusal to permit the Provisional Government at Peking to seize a considerable amount of silver belonging to the Bank of Communications, which was located in the Concession.

[28] *New York Times,* May 8, 1939.

[29] *Ibid.,* June 17, 1939; *China Weekly Review,* June 17, 1939, p. 77–8; Jones and Myers, *Documents,* I, p. 264–6.

The surrender of this silver and the acceptance of Federal Reserve notes were made conditions of raising the blockade. The fundamental issue was the economic control of North China.[30]

The Japanese placed squads of soldiers at entrances to the Concessions. Entrance and exit were not prohibited but British nationals passing the barriers were subject to search. The searching process was performed thoroughly; men and women in some instances were compelled to remove their clothing.[31] The admission of food was restricted, causing shortages of meat and vegetables. In the House of Commons Prime Minister Chamberlain referred to the "intolerable insults" to Britons at Tientsin. Ambassador Craigie at Tokyo was called upon to negotiate for a settlement. The Japanese negotiators, acting in theory on behalf of the Peking government, made such demands as, if satisfied, would have reduced the Concession government to a Japanese agency. These included delivery of terrorists and communists, cooperative questioning and searching of banks and other business concerns, strict control of opinion and movements unfavorable to the Provisional Government, and cooperation in the general control of the Concession.

The British declined to negotiate upon matters regarded as international rather than national issues. After a month's dilatory discussion they agreed to surrender the four Chinese to the Chinese courts, alleging that sufficient evidence of guilt was available to require such action. Ten months later, on June 20, 1940, the Japanese Foreign Office announced that certain other questions had been settled.[32] It was agreed, it stated, that Japanese police should "offer information and be present when action is taken by the British Municipal Council police against persons in whose criminal activities

[30] Taylor, George E., cited, p. 125–43.
[31] *China Weekly Review,* July 1, 1939, p. 129–30.
[32] *Contemporary Japan,* IX, 1940, p. 929–31.

the Japanese authorities are interested." This arrangement appeared to be far-reaching, enabling the Japanese gendarmerie to join with the British police in the supervision of publications and public meetings and dealings in arms and explosives.

The agreement also covered the disposal of the Chinese silver reserves and the currency issue. The silver was to be sealed jointly by the British and Japanese consuls-general and to be left in the vaults of the Bank of Communications in the British Concession until the British and Japanese Governments should make other arrangements. The sum of £100,000 was to be drawn from this reserve before seals were affixed to provide a fund for famine relief in North China. Regarding the currency question, the British agreed to "place no difficulty in the way of the use of Federal Reserve Bank currency" in the Concession.

The Japanese Foreign Office announced on the same date that a similar agreement had been reached with the French Government on the various issues as they related to the administration of the French Concession.

Kulangsu

The International Settlement at Amoy occupied an island only one and one half square miles in area. The small foreign community—normally about 250—and the 40,000 Chinese who composed its population elected a Municipal Council of eight men, among whom Chinese and Japanese members formed a majority.[33] Making use of allegations similar to those voiced at Shanghai and Tientsin, Japanese naval forces landed on the island on May 12, 1939.[34] The Japanese consul-general at Amoy presented five demands to the chairman of the Council:

[33] *China Year Book, 1939,* cited, p. 159.
[34] *China Weekly Review,* May 20, 1939, p. 370.

1. Strict control of anti-Japanese activities.
2. Election of Japanese nationals to the positions of chairman of the Council, chief secretary of the Council and police commissioner.
3. Grant of the suffrage and the right to Council membership to Formosan residents.
4. Appointment of Chinese ratepayers to three vacancies in the Council.
5. Cooperation between Japanese consular police and Council police against terrorists.

The Japanese marines ignored protests of the Council, searching the Settlement and arresting a considerable number of young Chinese whom they took to Amoy. Within a week a mixed contingent of American, British and French sailors and marines were landed on Kulangsu from naval vessels in the harbor. Japanese naval forces blockaded the little island, causing a shortage of food. The Council rejected the demands and the consular body at Amoy protested against the Japanese actions. After several months all four states withdrew their forces. Japanese representation on the Council and in the police force was increased.[35]

Hankow

A single Concession, that of France, remained at Hankow in 1938. The Japanese evacuated their Concession in 1937 and the Chinese applied the "scorched earth" policy to it upon the approach of the Japanese army and naval forces. Although French authority was not expelled by the latter, the Concession was placed under a food embargo and its water supply was cut off, ostensibly to compel surrender of "bad elements," i.e. anti-Japanese persons, Communists, and rich Chinese merchants.[36] Japanese searching parties entered the Concession at will. Chinese banks within the Concession did not escape Japanese levies upon their funds.

[35] *New York Times,* October 22, 1940.
[36] *China Weekly Review,* May 6, 1939, p. 310–1; May 13, 1939, p. 345–6.

IX

THE "NEW NATIONAL STRUCTURE" IN JAPAN

THE decade 1931–41 saw the creation of numerous administrative agencies in Japan necessitated by the war-time additions to governmental responsibilities.[1] That these changes produced a "new national structure" may be doubted. Rather it may be said that the basic structure remained and that the new agencies are supplementary to the older, fundamental organs. In the economic field the transformation was more far-reaching but there also it may hardly be regarded as productive of a new structure. Japan's political and economic system is peculiar to itself, though it contains elements drawn from others. It is logical, therefore, that it should reveal, under stress, developments relevant to its peculiarities. Official description of these developments as constituting a "new national structure" may portend further change, but this also, if it occurs, is likely to be not less but more in the Japanese tradition than that which characterized the constitutional movement of the Restoration period.[2]

Constitutional amendment is paradoxically difficult in Japan. Gift of the great Emperor Meiji, the constitution is second only to the dynasty in inviolability, although most of

[1] The best descriptions and analyses of recent administrative reorganization in Japan are given by Charles B. Fahs, in his *Government in Japan: Recent Trends in Its Scope and Operation,* cited, and Hugh Borton, *Japan Since 1931: Its Political and Social Developments,* cited; for a comprehensive discussion of economic conditions, with valuable references to administrative measures see *The Industrialization of Japan and Manchoukuo, 1930–1940,* edited by E. B. Schumpeter, cited.

[2] Cf. Chapter II.

its articles were copied from the Prussian and other German constitutions. It may be amended upon the initiative of the Emperor and approval of both Houses of the Diet. But it remains, as a document, unaltered after fifty years of application. Nothing less than revolution is likely to alter it. Thus the Diet, the two Houses, the Cabinet, the Privy Council, the courts, and the functions constitutionally prescribed for them, are beyond reach of extremist elements. The remarkable vitality of anti-oligarchical sentiment in the face of great odds suggests that constitutionalism has penetrated more deeply into Japanese political consciousness than even careful critics had believed.

On the other hand, much of Japan's fundamental law is statutory or in the form of imperial ordinances. The suffrage, the composition of the Houses of the Diet, and the qualifications, terms and emoluments of members are matters outside the constitution. Moreover, the ministers are not responsible to the Diet, which is severely limited even in discussion of executive proposals. By emergency ordinance the Diet's legislative and budgetary powers may be nullified. It should be noted, however, that the political danger involved in excessive use of executive powers has preserved for the Diet a larger influence than the terms of the constitution guarantee.

Increased Influence of the Supreme Command

Inevitably, in a period of war, the share of military organs in the shaping of national policy expands. The constitutional and legal position of these services in Japan,[3] combined with their inheritance of the feudal tradition of obedience to the soldier, provided a sure foundation for the usurpation of authority in a time of stress. Although there are liberals

[3] Quigley, H. S., *Japanese Government and Politics,* cited, Chapters VI, VII; Colegrove, Kenneth, *Militarism in Japan,* cited, *passim.*

among the high-ranking officers, the general trend of opinion is anti-parliamentary, anti-capitalist and anti-labor. Confidence in their superiority over civilian bureaucrats, politicians and businessmen distinguishes military men in Japan. Their efforts were exerted not only to control the course of the war but to centralize power and to emasculate the Diet and the political parties. The Army is more aggressive than the Navy but the latter's interest in maintaining the prerogatives of the Supreme Command attaches it firmly to the older service.

During the first five years of the controversy with China a younger, more violent element brought into question the discipline in both military services and the firmness of the Government, by attempts, through a series of *coups d'état,* to destroy the established order and compel the erection of a military dictatorship. Twice in 1931, again in 1932, and a fourth time in 1936, these thrusts were thwarted, either through prior discovery of plots or through police and military repression. Premier Inukai was assassinated in 1932, and in 1936 a number of the highest officials, including the Emperor's high adviser, Admiral Viscount Saito, were murdered, while others escaped only through the timely aid of informers. Certain of the senior officers, notably General Sadao Araki, whose chauvinistic speeches had inflamed the younger men to violence, must share responsibility for these rebellious acts.[4]

The Supreme Command could not, in its own interest, treat so grave an incident as that of February 26, 1936, as a mere outburst of patriotism. Death penalties were imposed on leaders of the revolt and there was no recurrence of large-scale violence. Rather than loss, however, there was a gain in the influence of the more reactionary officers. This was proved in 1937 when the Army refused to support the moderate General Ugaki for the premiership, though the Em-

[4] Young, A. Morgan, *Imperial Japan, 1926–1938,* cited, p. 127–30, 268–85.

peror had instructed him to form a government.[5] Although civilians were, as a rule, allowed to fill the post of premier, there was a steadily increasing tendency to entrust such civilian ministries as those of foreign affairs, education, justice and commerce to army or navy officers. An able propaganda office published lengthy memoranda for the Supreme Command, urging expansion of the armed forces, a vigorous pursuit of righteousness in Asia, popular welfare through territorial expansion, etc.

The allies of the military services against the Diet, the political parties and a large section of the business community, were the bureaucracy, the patriotic societies and the remainder of big business. This alignment of forces was with reference to a "new national structure" rather than to foreign policy. The House of Peers was sympathetic with oligarchical government but desired to preserve the Diet as an organ of discussion and criticism. The Privy Council also was highly conservative but its function of interpretation made it the guardian of the constitution. The Emperor's political views are not made public but his reputation is one of comparative liberalism. Until Prince Saionji died, in November 1940, he as *genro*, the last surviving elder statesman, exercised a diminishing restraint upon militarist usurpation.

The only serious checks upon this trend were those administered by the political parties through the House of Representatives and by the great business and industrial trusts such as Mitsui, Mitsubishi, Sumitomo and others. Politicians and businessmen had a valuable stake in keeping an independent place in the political and economic order. Their ingenuity in seeking ways and means of evading total eclipse was highly creditable; granted that they were defending their own interests, the objective of constitutionalism was none the less furthered by their tenacity and courage. Individuals in the lower House, such as the Minseito mem-

[5] *Ibid.*, p. 291–2.

ber T. Saito, the Seiyukai member K. Hamada, and the Independent Ozaki Yukio, who stoutly interpellated regarding the trend to military dictatorship, were taking their lives in their hands.[6] The elections demonstrated that the people still regarded the parties as their spokesmen against obscurantist government. In the 1937 election, held after an abrupt dissolution, General Hayashi, the Premier, called upon the voters to disown the parties and give him a personal majority. The results were a striking testimony of popular disapproval of such a proposition. The major parties—Minseito and Seiyukai—lost but 23 seats, 18 of which were won by the labor party which elected 36 members. A mere handful of government supporters was returned.[7] With the dissolution of the parties in 1940 the voters were faced with the problem of finding new means of expressing their sentiments at elections.

Legislative Trend Toward Totalitarianism

Not until 1940 was the "new national structure" advanced as governmental policy. Prior to that date the regular channels of legislation and imperial ordinance were employed to strengthen the country's administrative system and to deal with problems of special urgency. In 1938 a Cabinet Advisory Council was created, containing the representatives of the military services, the bureaucracy, the political parties and other interests, designed to assure continuity of policy. In the same year a Cabinet Planning Board of technically qualified persons was established, the most important of the war-time agencies. Whereas the Cabinet Advisory Council was a link with a variety of public interests, the Planning Board was an active participant in government, deciding between the claims of the various ministries, drafting bills and

[6] *Japan Weekly Chronicle,* May 14, 1936, p. 599; January 28, 1937, p. 100; February 25, 1937, p. 232–3.

[7] *Ibid.,* May 6, 1937, p. 545, 554.

ordinances, and operating to unify policy. In 1938 a Planning Council was added, under the chairmanship of the premier, to assist the ministries in the utilization of natural resources and in other economic matters.[8] The Planning Board kept its identity but was linked in operation with the Planning Council.

For more centralized administration, as distinct from advisory planning, the ministers of foreign affairs, war, the navy and finance, together with the premier, were accorded precedence by the institution of a five-minister conference. A Cabinet Information Bureau was created to centralize the functions of publicity bureaus in various ministries. For the conduct of military and naval operations an Imperial Headquarters, headed by the Emperor and actually directed by the chiefs of staff of the army and the navy, was established. This is the highest agency of the Supreme Command and is advised by imperial conferences. In September 1941, a new agency, the General Defense Headquarters, was added. Reputedly placed under the Emperor's direct command, this organ was to conduct the defense of Japan proper, Korea, Formosa and Karafuto (South Saghalien). It may be conjectured that its principal objectives were to inspire public confidence and to give recognition to a military faction comparable to that enjoyed by other factions dominant in the various Japanese armies in China. That it represented a change in the position of the Emperor seems highly improbable.[9] A China Administration Board independent of the Foreign Office and under the presidency of the premier, was created in 1938. Many other administrative agencies of more limited scope were provided to implement the extensive regulatory legislation of the emergency period. Of a perma-

[8] Fahs, cited, p. 65–6; Borton, cited, p. 57–9; *Tokyo Gazette,* May 1938, p. 48; Spinks, C. N., "Bureaucratic Japan," *Far Eastern Survey,* October 6, 1941, p. 219–25.

[9] *New York Times,* September 12, 13, 1941; *Far Eastern Survey,* September 22, 1941, p. 207.

nent nature a new Ministry of Welfare was added in January 1938.

The rapid extension of governmental control over private enterprise may best be appreciated by rapidly surveying the legislation of recent years. Conditions of depression caused the inauguration of regulatory legislation as early as 1931, when the Principal Industries Control Law was passed to encourage industrial rationalization and to require production quotas, price agreements, and cooperative purchase and sale of materials. An unsuccessful attempt to control rice prices was made in 1933. Steel and oil were brought under government control in 1934. In September 1937, the Munitions Industry Mobilization Law brought all industries essential in production of military materials under government control or operation.[10]

Most important among the new laws was the National General Mobilization Law enacted in March 1938. This law gave to the government authority, in case of emergency, to determine the utilization of all national resources, human and material, independently of the Diet.[11] A General Mobilization Commission of thirty members of the Diet and twenty officials and experts was created to advise the cabinet upon the issuance of ordinances for application of the law. Revised in 1941 and placed in full operation on August 11 of that year, the law suspended all parliamentary control over executive action in the wide field of its operation.[12] An example of the power it conferred was given when the Government established its control over all shipping and shipbuilding in August 1941.[13] Another action under the law was the nationalization of the electric power industry in 1938.

[10] Borton, cited, Chapter V; Fahs, cited, p. 24–36.

[11] Fahs, cited, p. 50–3; Borton, cited, p. 60–5; Fahs lists 26 ordinances issued under the law prior to November 30, 1939. The text of the National General Mobilization Law, promulgated April 1, 1939 and effective from May 5, 1939, is in *Japan Year Book, 1940–41,* p. 227.

[12] *New York Times,* February 4, 1941, August 12, 1941.

[13] *Ibid.,* August 20, 1941.

Public finance was the subject of extensive regulation. The national debt climbed from yen 10,578,000,000 in July 1937, to yen 30,000,000,000 in April 1941. During the same period authorized budget expenditures quintupled. Appropriations for carrying on the war in China up to January 1, 1942, amounted to yen 22,335,000,000, of which yen 19,459,900,000 was provided by borrowing, all of it in the home market. In order to assure absorption of the huge bond issues, which gradually became more difficult, the Government promulgated a number of ordinances regulative of private, corporate and bank funds. Most important of these were the Corporate Dividend and Financing Control Ordinance, the Capital Control Ordinance, the Corporation Accounting Control Ordinance, the Ordinance Fixing Salaries and Allowances for Corporate Staff Members and the Bank Fund Ordinance.[14] Taxes were increased under a Tax Reform Law which effected a wider distribution of the tax burden but also raised rates on the larger incomes and corporate profits.

The Government took control over the export of gold and effected a remarkable increase in the output of mined gold. This increase was not, however, sufficiently large to balance the excess of imports over exports in trade with foreign-currency countries. A new Foreign Exchange Control Law, passed in March 1933, allowed the Government to restrict or prohibit a variety of transactions related to the supply of exchange. Under the law the licensing of exchange contracts became more and more limited until in 1940 it almost entirely ceased for the importation of non-military materials. Under other legislation the Government was authorized to restrict or prohibit imports and exports and to determine the distribution and use of imports.[15]

[14] "Economic Conditions in Japan During 1940 and Early 1941," International Reference Service, Department of Commerce (U. S.), I, No. 33, June 1941, p. 6.

[15] Schumpeter, cited, p. 802–54.

The agrarian problem received attention in the Law for Agrarian Adjustment of April 2, 1938.[16] This law authorized cities, towns, villages and "other appropriate public organizations," to manage, protect or utilize farm land on behalf of farmers who were unable to manage their own or leased land. It further provided for protection of lessees against landowners and for arbitral or judicial settlement of disputes over tenancy. Under other laws debt readjustment associations were created and subsidized to rationalize farm debts, which totalled yen 6,000,000,000 in 1935. Small grants were made to the families of absent or dead soldiers. The Government took measures to assure an adequate supply of fertilizers. Rice and silk production received special consideration in a number of laws aimed at assuring stable prices to producers and consumers alike.[17]

The welfare and control of labor were the principal objective of the creation of the Ministry of Welfare. The extension of the health insurance provided in 1927 for factory and mine workers to rural laborers, small tradesmen and salaried persons was an important accomplishment.[18] The heavy drain of war expenditures prevented further progress along the lines of social betterment that had been laid down during the liberal decade of the 'twenties. It was small comfort to the overworked and underpaid industrial laborer to have his wages no more than keep pace with rising living costs. In many industries wages fell and unemployment resulted from shifts in production policy necessitated by the war. In 1940 average wage rates rose 9.2% over those of 1939 while average living costs increased 18.4%.[19] Yet it is not remarkable that under such conditions the attitude of labor should have been cooperative, that strikes should be infrequent and repressive police action unnecessary. Japanese la-

[16] *Tokyo Gazette,* Nos. 9–10, 1938, p. 5–9; No. 13, 1938, p. 53.
[17] Fahs, cited, p. 29–37.
[18] *Tokyo Gazette,* No. 14, 1938, p. 9–14; No. 23, 1939, p. 20–4.
[19] "Economic Conditions in Japan," cited, p. 4.

bor, ordinarily tolerant and law-abiding, exhibited the qualities that usually characterize men of its status in Western countries in similar circumstances.

The Government did not, of course, fail to use all agencies and methods available for the direction of public opinion along favorable lines.[20] Censorship of the press, the radio and education was tightened. Propaganda was carried on by the military services, business organizations and the political parties. Foreign newspapers of long and distinguished service—the *Japan Chronicle* (British), and the *Japan Advertiser* (American), were so hampered by censorship that they were forced to sell their plants to Japanese interests. All Protestant churches in Japan were obliged to unite in a single Japanese Christian Church under Japanese control and unsupported by foreign funds. Not the least interesting aspect of the program for control of opinion was the necessity of curbing the extreme chauvinism of the Black Dragon and other patriotic societies. To this end "thought control" was imposed in respect to matters of foreign as well as of domestic policy and ideology.[21]

Dissolution of Political Parties

An excellent argument can be made for the thesis that the developments described in preceding pages were similar to those observable in democratic states under conditions of depression and war. Events since the summer of 1940 reveal a more rapid trend toward a form of state socialism or totalitarianism. The abolition of political parties, attempts to organize a national society to replace them, moves toward limitation of the suffrage and further limitation of the Diet's small share in public affairs, and the establishment of corporative relations between Government and business are

[20] Borton, cited, p. 106–17.
[21] *New York Times,* July 14, 1941.

signs of the reversal of Japan's political orientation. Not constitutional democracy, but militarist-bureaucratic oligarchy overlaid with a veneer of paternalistic monarchy, is now the goal of the country's dominant elements.[22] No *führer* is likely to appear. The army and navy are Japan's fascist party. No military officer is strong enough to overcome the factionalism within the armed services. But even if he were there is no place in Japan for the *führer* principle. The Emperor is Japan's *führer*, symbol rather than bearer of power. While there is some evidence that the imperial office is becoming directly involved in administration, it appears to be more probable that the oligarchy in control is making more obvious use of it in the interest of national confidence and unity.

Pressure for the adjournment of party politics was felt early in the war. The parties were censured for corruption, for liaison with big business, for their aping of democratic practices. Before the Diet the ministers of war and the navy resented the efforts of the parties to curtail appropriations and to obtain explanations of cabinet policies. A "new party movement" was the first stroke toward elimination of the old parties. At the behest of Prince Konoye, then President of the House of Peers, Count Y. Arima called a conference late in 1935 to initiate such a movement. Arima was president of the central organ of the cooperative societies, which numbered 6,000,000 members.[23] At that time it was hoped that a number of Seiyukai and Minseito leaders would support the scheme. Prince Konoye subsequently came to the conclusion that a national society untrammeled by association with the old parties would be a fitter vehicle for uniting all elements of the population for the prosecution of the country's aims. The election of 1937, above referred to, showed

[22] Charles N. Spinks in the article cited above argues very interestingly that the Government has become "a dictatorship of the bureaucracy."

[23] *Japan Weekly Chronicle*, July 11, 1940, p. 59–60.

clearly the difficulty of reconciling national and party interests.[24]

Within the space of two months, July and August 1940, each of the political parties took action to bring about its own dissolution.[25] Possibly they were threatened with interdiction. In the case of the General Federation of Labor, dissolved in July 1940, such a threat was made.[26] It is more likely that, in the face of powerful elements urging "spiritual mobilization," the party leaders deemed it wise to fall into line, hoping to find an outlet for their activities in whatever new organization should be established.[27] Thus they emulated the self-denying tactics of the smaller clan leaders at the Restoration.[28] Whatever the explanation, the sudden disappearance of the only serious organized opposition to absolutist government, after nearly sixty years of intense activity, must be regarded as epochal.

Imperial Rule Assistance Association

Prince Konoye resigned from the presidency of the Privy Council in order to devote himself to the "renovation of the national political structure in the face of the extreme gravity of the world situation." [29] Shortly thereafter he was chosen Premier for the second time, whereupon he appointed a preparatory committee of 26 representatives of business, the Diet, the patriotic societies and other interests to plan a "new national structure." [30] In his address to this committee on August 28, 1940, he stated that he was motivated by the

[24] *Ibid.*, July 18, 1940, p. 72.

[25] *Ibid.*, July 4, 1940, p. 13; August 1, 1940, p. 136; August 22, 1940, p. 229.

[26] *Ibid.*, July 18, 1940, p. 72.

[27] Cabinet Information Bureau, "Reorganization of the Movement for Spiritual Mobilization," *Tokyo Gazette*, June 1940, p. 465–7.

[28] Quigley, H. S., *Japanese Government and Politics*, cited, Chapter II.

[29] *Tokyo Gazette*, August 1940, p. 45.

[30] Bisson, T. A., "Japan's 'New Structure,'" *Foreign Policy Reports*, April 15, 1941.

necessity for a strong internal organization to support the national military effort.[31] His desire was to have all phases of national life represented, and particularly that "the people should be enabled to take part, from the inside, in the establishing of the country's economic and cultural policies . . ." He expressed opposition to the formation of a new party, which would mean transforming a "part" into a "whole." He declared that

> In Japan it is the privilege of all His Majesty's subjects to assist the Throne, and that privilege cannot be monopolized by the power of either a single individual or a single party.

The preparatory commission drafted a plan for an Imperial Rule Assistance Association (Taisei-Yokusan-Kai, also translated National Service Association), which was inaugurated on October 12, 1940. To avoid a possible conflict of views the regulations provided that the premier should be *ex officio* the president of the Association. The National Headquarters of the Association was composed of a number of bureaus—at first five, later three—to administer policy, and a Central Cooperation Council.[32] The latter was a large body, representative of a wide variety of interests. It was intended to focus public opinion upon the Government, to apprize the Government of trends in public opinion, and to find means of stimulating enthusiastic support for governmental policy, particularly that related to the establishment of Japanese hegemony in Eastern Asia.

Local headquarters and cooperation councils were to be established in prefectures, cities, towns, villages and neighborhoods, i.e. groups of families. While all citizens were eligible to membership in the Association and expected to support it, the selection of members, as well as of officers,

[31] *Tokyo Gazette,* October 1940, p. 133–6.

[32] Cabinet Information Bureau, "National Movement for Assisting the Throne," *Tokyo Gazette,* November 1940, p. 177–92.

was placed in the hands of its President. Funds were to be obtained from government appropriations, membership fees and private contributions. The Diet appropriated yen 8,000,000 for support of the Association in the session of 1940–41.

Essentially the I.R.A.A. was a propaganda agency, an all-Japanese patriotic society, not in any sense a governmental structure. It was not the "new national structure" but a means of assisting the Government to bring one into existence. Among the items on the program of "renovation"—a term that suggests reform of something old rather than its complete replacement—are reform of the Diet and the civil service, and the creation of a hierarchy of economic and cultural councils. The latter bodies are to centralize in federations the various types of economic and cultural activity, under the direction of a National Economic Council and a National Cultural Council, which in turn are to be under the direction of the Government.[33]

The fundamental issue involved in the organization of the Association and the plans for further change is that of their bearing upon the position of the Diet. Prince Konoye moved cautiously, appointing a considerable number of former party members advisers and directors of the Association and finding places for a hundred members of the House of Representatives in the Diet Bureau.[34] Quite evidently the Government intended to use this Bureau to influence the House, but no constitutional or legal relationship was involved. The same observations applied to the interrelation of the House and the Cooperation Council. They applied also, in lesser degree, to relations between the organs of the Association and the House of Peers. That body, though highly conservative, is tenacious of its position and

[33] Ozaki, H., "The New National Structure," *Contemporary Japan*, IX, 1940, p. 1284–92.

[34] Takasugi, K., "The Diet Under the New Political Structure," *Contemporary Japan*, IX, 1940, p. 1398–410.

resistant to "renovation." Its parties have not been dissolved. Its prestige has not been undermined by corrupt practice and undignified conduct of business. The House of Peers did not oppose, rather it reserved judgment on the Association.

Reform of the House of Representatives was proposed by Prince Konoye. The proposals included reduction of membership, nomination of candidates by local "recommendation councils"—these might be the "cooperation councils"—limitation of the franchise to heads of families, and limitation of interpellations—the only means available for discussion of cabinet policy. He was unable to obtain consideration of such reforms in the 1940–41 session. Instead he was obliged to listen to criticism of the Association as unconstitutional, communistic and inadequate, to accept a cut in the appropriation proposed for the Association from yen 15,000,000 to yen 8,000,000, and to agree to an amendment of the Diet law extending the term of the present House of Representatives by one year. There is evidence of the reappearance of parties under the name of political societies.[35] In view of these developments the Army leaders, who were at first cool toward the Association, came to its rescue, urging young reservists to participate in its activities.

Toward a "New Economic Structure"

A Japanese writer states correctly that [36]

> . . . the method of economic control . . . has left the old economic structure intact—a liberalistic economic organization aimed at profit-making—and has attempted to force it to proceed in a designated direction by means of legislation or administrative measures.

35 Fujii, S., "The Cabinet, the Diet and the Taisei Yokusan Kai," *Contemporary Japan,* X, 1941, p. 487–97.

36 Minobe, Y., "The Principles of the New Economic Structure," *ibid.,* p. 179.

The Planning Board found in 1940 that this method of control "had fallen short of expectations." It concluded from its study of the problem that the failure to meet war-time requirements, while in part due "to inefficiency in the control technique of bureaucracy" was caused basically by "the defects of controlled economy itself."[37] It held that the regime of free enterprise and private profit must be reformed by the coordination of economic units in a national economy working for national ends under a comprehensive public plan. It rejected the method of nationalization of industry and proposed to retain private enterprise within a planned national economic structure.

The Board announced that ultimately a Supreme Economic Council supervising all industry and business would be necessary. Experience with a number of councils over separate divisions or categories of economic undertakings would precede its establishment. These councils were to be composed of leading industrialists recommended by concerns within a particular category and approved by the Government. They were to have the status of legal persons and authority to apportion production quotas, labor and materials, to determine methods and means of production, and to inspect plants and set standards of efficiency. Inefficient producers would be eliminated. In case of necessity the Government itself would operate individual units. Administrative reorganization necessary for supervision of the councils would be carried out. It is apparent that business influence was strongly felt in the drafting of this plan, which preserves a considerable degree of private enterprise. On the other hand its trend is clearly in the direction of totalitarianism. The proposed corporations resemble closely the *sindicato* of Fascist Italy and the federations of business and industrial concerns in Nazi Germany. There remains, how-

[37] *Tokyo Gazette,* February 1941, p. 310–16.

ever, the question whether or not the Japanese bureaucracy will obtain a control over the corporations corresponding to that of its Italian and German counterparts. In the light of history and in face of the growing crisis one may anticipate that it will.

X

JAPAN AND THE AXIS

JAPAN'S international situation after its withdrawal from the League of Nations, which became effective March 27, 1935, was one of isolation. Since the withdrawal signalized Japan's rejection of the League's statesmanly recommendations for settlement of the Manchurian controversy, it did not seem likely that any of the Members of the League would be willing to asperse the League's action by allying with Japan or entering into any entente that would signify approval of Japan's program of expansion. Germany, however, was unencumbered by pledges to the League from which it also had withdrawn on October 21, 1935, for reasons unconnected with Japan's withdrawal from membership. Both Germany and Japan were in need of friends, both were at odds in their policies with the democratic states and with the Soviet Union. Rapprochement between them was to be expected. The similarities in political ideology remarked upon in the previous chapter paralleled similarities in foreign policy.

Japanese statesmen did not regard Germany as a gilt-edged ally. Japan needed money and trade. Germany had no money and its economic ambition was autarky. Japan wished to avoid war with the United States and Great Britain. Germany's interest in Japan as an ally lay in the desire to immobilize as much as possible of the American and British fleets. Japanese *amour propre* was not salved by Führer Hitler's doctrine of Nordic superiority. And although the German Government sympathized with Japan's policy in Asia as a blow against the so-called "have" states, it had commercial and financial interests of its own people to conserve in that area. Germany ranked third in China's foreign trade in 1936. The export of German arms to China was considerable. Between 1934 and 1937 German bankers loaned $86,000,000 (Chinese) for railway-building in China.[1] The Chinese army was being trained and its strategy developed under a German military mission.

It was believed in Japan that an entente, or a revived alliance, with Great Britain was desirable and that only the United States stood in the way of a return to the cordial Anglo-Japanese relations of 1902–23. Foreign Minister Arita was applauded in the Diet when he referred to the desirability of improving relations with Great Britain.[2] The visit of Lord Rothermere to Japan in 1936 was taken as a favorable sign until he bluntly stated that British antagonism to Japanese policy was increasing.[3] It is probable that Japan's hesitancy in entering a full-fledged alliance with Germany was in part due to the wish to keep open the road to accommodation with Great Britain and that reconciliation with the United States was not deemed impossible.

Anti-Comintern Pact

Japan and Germany had a common interest in the restraint of communism. The decision of the Comintern (Communist International) in 1935 to form a "popular front" with less radical elements in any country was attended with a resolution to focus intensive subversive efforts upon Ger-

[1] Rosinger, L. K., "The Far East and the New Order in Europe," *Pacific Affairs,* XII, 1939, p. 357–69; Bloch, K., "German-Japanese Partnership in Eastern Asia," *Far Eastern Survey,* October 26, 1938, p. 242–3. Mr. Bloch believes that German commercial policy was based upon the expectation that the Chinese Government would be forced into cooperation with Japan, and that Germany, as Japan's best friend, would have entrée denied to others.

[2] *Japan Weekly Chronicle,* May 14, 1936, p. 604.

[3] *Oriental Economist,* October 1936, p. 618.

many and Japan.[4] Japanese commentators believed that the democracies were encouraging communism at home by their apparently acquiescent attitude toward this program, which also seemed to be progressing in China.[5] Unlike Metternich, who sought more than a century previously to choke out democratic nationalism by maintaining the *status quo,* German and Japanese statesmen aimed to crush revolution by destroying the *status quo.*

The Anti-Comintern Pact, signed at Berlin on November 25, 1936, was brief. The parties, expressing the desire to cooperate for defense against the disintegrating influence of communism, agreed to "keep each other informed" concerning activities of the Comintern, to confer upon measures of defense, to execute such measures cooperatively, and to invite other states to adhere to the Pact. The agreement was to run for five years, subject to modification before the end of the period.[6] The Japanese Foreign Office declared on the same date that the Pact was not directed at the Soviet Government and that no other agreement had been made with Germany.[7] A year later, on November 6, 1937, Italy signed a similar agreement with Germany and Japan.[8] Shortly thereafter Premier Konoye greeted an Italian good-will mission with these words: [9]

[4] Tomoyeda, T., "Germany and Japan," *Contemporary Japan,* V, 1936, p. 216–8.

[5] Kamikawa, H., "The Rome-Berlin-Tokyo Axis," *Contemporary Japan,* VII, 1938, p. 1–10.

[6] For text see Quigley and Blakeslee, cited, p. 304–5. The agreement was renewed, with a number of additional adherents, at a Nazi ceremony in Berlin on November 25, 1941, for a further period of five years.

[7] General W. G. Krivitsky, a former member of the German secret service, stated later that the Anti-Comintern Pact was a hoax and that Germany and Japan entered into a secret agreement to regulate between themselves all matters relating to the Soviet Union and China, to take no action in Europe or in the Pacific without consulting each other, and to exchange military missions. (*Saturday Evening Post,* April 29, 1939, p. 88; later published as *In Stalin's Secret Service,* New York. Harper, 1939.

[8] Quigley and Blakeslee, cited, p. 306–7; Tamagna, F. M., *Italy's Interests and Policies in the Far East,* New York, 1941.

[9] Chamberlin, W. H., "The Challenge to the Status Quo," *Contemporary Japan,* VII, 1938, p. 12.

I cannot but feel that at this present time, when the negative principle of maintenance of the *status quo,* built up after the last World War, has forfeited its function as a result of . . . conflicts and contradictions . . . , the responsibility for the creation of peace devolves on the three powers, Italy, Germany, and Japan.

The German Government exerted itself to restore peace in China. Its Ambassador, Dr. Trautmann, bore Japan's terms to the Chinese Government in January 1938. Germany did not, however, show partiality toward Japan for many months. In declining the invitation to the Brussels Conference it made no reference to Japan, excusing itself on the ground that it was not a co-contractant of the Nine-Power Treaty.[10] It continued to permit trade in arms with China and did not withdraw its military mission until May 1938. Recognition was accorded to "Manchoukuo" in the same month. The German Ambassador was withdrawn from Chungking in June 1938. Hitler's addresses contained few and brief references to Japan. The economic advantages of rapprochement were, however, tangible. The triangular arrangement for trade between Germany, Japan and "Manchoukuo," signed in April 1936, was renewed in 1937. The German firm of Otto Wolff loaned £2,000,000 to "Manchoukuo," to be received in various types of industrial equipment. German loans to China were discontinued and trade decreased, while it increased with Japan and "Manchoukuo." The close administrative regulation of foreign trade in Germany and Japan gave political color to these developments.[11]

The Anti-Comintern Pact was severely criticized in the Diet, where the view was expressed that it increased Japan's liabilities without conferring compensating advantages. It was realized in Japan that Great Britain and the United States viewed the Pact as a move against themselves. One newspaper advised the Government against making "red-

[10] Jones and Myers, *Documents,* I, p. 170–1.

[11] Bloch, Kurt, "German-Japanese Partnership," cited, p. 243–4.

hot enemies for the sake of lukewarm friends." [12] Germany's failure to terminate relations with General Chiang K'ai-shek upon the beginning of Sino-Japanese hostilities aroused bitter comment. The Japanese resented Germany's insistent efforts to bring about a settlement of the China "incident," including the pressure involved in a new Sino-German arms agreement signed in May 1939. Moderates in the Tokyo Government, led by Premier Hiranuma, opposed extremist pressure for a military alliance.[13] In the midst of the debate upon this issue came the unexpected announcement of a non-aggression treaty between Germany and the Soviet Union.[14]

Japan and the German-Soviet Pact

The *volte-face* of Germany brought a diplomatic protest from Tokyo and caused the resignation of Premier Hiranuma and his cabinet. A statement suggesting that a new alignment in Japan's foreign relations must be considered accompanied the resignation.[15] Various alternatives were before Japan. It might follow Germany into a pact with the U.S.S.R.; it might turn about and seek an understanding with the democracies; or it might seek to maintain the Anti-Comintern Pact while avoiding closer relations with Germany. The incredible happened when the first alternative was chosen.

Subsequently Germany's phenomenal military successes in Poland, the Netherlands and France swung the current of opinion toward outright alliance with Germany. This would open the way to an easy intimidation of French Indo-China and allow free rein to existing ambitions regarding the East

[12] *Christian Science Monitor,* April 2, 1938; *New York Times,* April 23, 1938.

[13] *New York Times,* August 12, 1939.

[14] Jones and Myers, *Documents,* II, p. 334–5.

[15] *Japan Weekly Chronicle,* August 31, 1939, p. 241–2.

Indies. These ambitions could not be realized if Germany were opposed to them since Germany, if victorious, would advance claims to the territories Japan coveted. Moreover, German rule in those areas would be as distasteful, if not more so, than British, French and Dutch, to the Japanese. Thus Japan was pulled back, not by reason or preference but by vaulting expansionism, into Germany's orbit.

During the summer of 1940 German propaganda was extremely active in Tokyo. The Japanese were urged to seize so favorable a moment. Fears of American naval strength were deprecated and the United States was portrayed as the principal obstacle to Japan's rise to world power.[16] Japanese military extremists gave free rein to denunciation of America.[17] Great Britain also was the subject of caustic criticism. A resolution signed by 126 members, introduced into the House of Representatives, called for strong measures to exterminate British influence in Eastern Asia.[18]

The Three-Power Pact

Prince Konoye succeeded Admiral Yonai as premier in July 1940. He appointed as foreign minister Yosuke Matsuoka, a graduate of the University of Oregon, whose reputation was higher as a railway executive, a fiery orator and skilled debater than as a prudent diplomat. He was one of the civilian bureaucracy dear to the extreme militarists because he was unrivalled at putting their sentiments into graphic English. His brief career as foreign minister was one of meteoric brilliance and equally meteoric collapse. In spite of the warning provided by Führer Hitler's sudden shift a year earlier, Mr. Matsuoka was led into a treaty with the Soviet Union which barred war with that country at

16 *New York Times,* July 10, 1940.
17 *Ibid.,* July 11, 1940.
18 *Ibid.,* August 9, 1940.

the most opportune moment that had presented itself in forty years.

The preamble to the treaty of alliance of September 27, 1940, between Germany, Italy and Japan states generously that the three Governments consider "it as a condition precedent to any lasting peace that all nations of the world be given each its own proper sphere." In the subsequent articles Japan recognizes Germany and Italy as leaders in the establishment of a new order in Europe. Germany and Italy recognize Japan's leadership in a new order in Greater East Asia (which is not defined). The three states agree to cooperate to accomplish these purposes and to assist each other by political, economic and military means when one is attacked "by a Power not at present involved in the European war or the Sino-Japanese conflict." They further agree to establish "joint technical commissions" to assist in executing these pledges and they affirm that the Pact's provisions "do not in any way affect the political status which exists at present as between each of the three Contracting Parties and Soviet Russia." [19]

Quite obviously the alliance was a warning to the United States. Mr. Matsuoka naively declared that it was not directed *against* the United States but rather *for* the United States, i.e. it was designed to keep America neutral for its own good.[20] Admiral N. Suetsugu expressed the wishful thinking of many Japanese when he denied that the treaty was merely a sphere-setting program and called it the enunciation of a "new world order," [21]

> . . . the outcome of mutual ideological antagonism between those Powers which seek to maintain the old political, economic and other structures, and those which are dissatisfied with the

[19] Appendix, p. 294.

[20] *Contemporary Japan,* IX, 1940, p. 1497; Griswold, A. W., "European Factors in Far Eastern Diplomacy," *Foreign Affairs,* XIX, 1941, p. 297–309.

[21] *Contemporary Japan,* IX, 1940, p. 1379–81.

injustice of the old order and are determined to bring about a fundamental reform. . . . Its overwhelming power and influence lie in the very fact that it was not signed for temporary gains or effects, but it was conceived rather with a definite conception of human life and of the world, and how men and nations should live therein.

Neutrality Pact with U.S.S.R.

Before the signing of the Three-Power Pact German efforts to establish relations of mutual tolerance between Japan and the Soviet Union were intensified. For many years Japan had spurned Soviet Russia's overtures for a non-aggression pact, although asserting that it had no territorial ambitions toward Siberia. Now under German urging the Japanese Government agreed to cease hostilities in the Nomonhan area, accepted a boundary demarcation between "Manchoukuo" and the Republic of Outer Mongolia which had previously been rejected, and made other concessions. The Soviet Union reciprocated by signing a new *modus vivendi* on fisheries and "Manchoukuo" paid, on January 4, 1940, the long-withheld final installment on the purchase price of the Chinese Eastern Railway. The newspapers ceased to insist upon the extension of Japan's "life-line" northward and turned their attentions to the South Seas.

Mr. Matsuoka's visit to Berlin in March 1941 was followed by a stay of some duration in Moscow. There he exchanged toasts and gifts with Stalin and, on April 13, signed a Neutrality Pact under the eyes of Major-General Eugen Ott, German Ambassador to Japan.[22] In it the two Governments undertook to maintain peaceful, friendly relations and to respect each other's territorial integrity; if either were attacked by a third state, the other would stand neutral. An accompanying "Frontier Declaration" pledged the Contract-

[22] Appendix, p. 296.

ing Parties to respect the territorial integrity of "Manchoukuo" and Outer Mongolia, which carried recognition of each other's protégés.

The Three-Power Pact was as valuable, politically and militarily, to Japan as the pledged word of Hitler was reliable. The Neutrality Pact was of no value up to June 22, 1941, when Hitler broke his word and attacked the Soviet Union. The Soviets merely had pledged not to do what they had no intention of doing. Japan's first incursion into French Indo-China preceded the making of the Neutrality Pact. The second followed Germany's attack upon the U.S.S.R. Neither action can be related to any change in the Union's relationship to Japan. After June 1941, the Pact was a millstone around Japan's over-extended neck, since it made attack upon Siberia impossible unless Japan was prepared to follow Hitler's example. The moral aspect of such action was less easily reasoned away when Great Britain and the United States undertook to support the Soviet Union. These consequences were not, apparently, anticipated by the crowds which welcomed Mr. Matsuoka home with *banzais* nor by the Privy Council, which voted unanimously for ratification in the presence of the Emperor.[23] The influx of German advisers increased until warnings were heard against the danger of Nazification.[24]

Outwardly at least, Japan's casting-off of isolation restored its self-assurance. The defeat of Chiang K'ai-shek was predicted more confidently. Press castigation of the United States was not discouraged. Premier Konoye dropped his usual calmness to say: [25]

> If the United States refuses to understand the real intentions of Japan, Germany, and Italy in concluding an alliance for positive cooperation in creating a new world order and persists

[23] *New York Times,* April 23, 25, 1941.
[24] *Ibid.,* May 10, 11, 1941.
[25] *Ibid.,* October 5, 1940.

in challenging these powers in the belief that the accord is a hostile action there will be no other course open to it than to go to war.

On the other hand the Foreign Office took pains to point out that Japan would construe the Three-Power Pact for itself, thus indicating that it did not intend to accept its partners' determination of the circumstances that would bring the Pact into operation.[26]

Exit Mr. Matsuoka

Hitler's invasion of the Soviet Union in June 1941, like his non-aggression treaty of August 1939, caught the Japanese unprepared. This was evident in the uncertainty admittedly felt by the Government as to the advisable policy to pursue in the presence of this sudden upsetting of the international balance of forces. Opinion was divided. There were those who counselled attack upon Siberia, others who advocated further advances in the South Seas; a third view was for turning away from the German alliance and seeking rapprochement with Britain and America. On July 17 the Konoye cabinet resigned. The Premier was commanded by the Emperor to form a new government. Mr. Matsuoka's name did not appear in the new cabinet, which was otherwise practically identical with its predecessor. With his passing the tone of official and press comment toward Britain and America softened. Japan rested on the precise terms of its treaties with Germany and the Soviet Union, waiting for the former to prove that where Napoleon had failed Hitler would succeed.

Japan and Siberia

An account of the military drive toward a "Greater East Asia" is given in the next chapter. It ended temporarily

[26] *Ibid.,* December 10, 1940.

when the United States and the United Kingdom warned against penetration into Thailand. These warnings were hardly more impressive than the assurances of the democracies of extensive assistance to the Soviet Union.[27] But Japan's sea-route to "Manchoukuo" and Siberia was less vulnerable than that to Thailand, and its military position in "Manchoukuo" and Korea was incomparably stronger than that in Indo-China. Moreover, the urgings of the German Government that Japan attack the Soviet Union were worthy of heed in view of Japan's dependence for ultimate success upon the victory of German arms. To cast the die for war with the Soviet Union was hazardous; to fail to do so meant absence from the peace table when Hitler should reach a settlement with Stalin. As for the Neutrality Pact, the rapprochement between the Soviet Union and the United States, involving probable aid to the Siberian armies, could be treated as an unfriendly act compromising Soviet neutrality.[28]

Heavy concentration of troops in "Manchoukuo" during the summer of 1941 appeared to augur a blow at Siberia when the opportune moment arrived.[29] The strong resistance of the Soviets in Europe and the continued maintenance of a powerful army plus a considerable number of submarines in eastern Siberia restrained the Japanese.

General Tojo Succeeds Konoye

As Moscow's fall appeared to be predictable, the expression of extremist sentiment in Japan foreshadowed a change of premiers. Colonel Mabuchi, chief of the army press section of Imperial Headquarters, and Captain Hiraide, chief of the

[27] See below, p. 274–6.
[28] *New York Times,* August 23, 1941.
[29] *Ibid.,* August 12, 1941; the estimated total had reached 25 divisions.

corresponding naval section, spoke publicly in vitriolic terms of an inevitable conflict with the United States. Although influential economic and business journals advocated caution and the *Oriental Economist* severely criticized the German program as a plan to dominate world economy, the opposing forces were too powerful for the moderates. The conversations of Admiral Nomura in Washington were tolerable to the more aggressive military leaders only so long as inactivity appeared to be advisable. Premier Konoye, while acceptable to the army, was not himself, in disposition, a warrior.

The Konoye cabinet resigned on October 16, 1941, and was succeeded by that of General Hideki Tojo, a member of the Kwantung army group and Minister of War under Konoye.[30] Tojo retained the war portfolio. Shigenori Togo, new foreign minister, had represented Japan at Berlin and Moscow and had been one of those whom Matsuoka had removed from active duty. Major-General T. Suzuki became a minister without portfolio. He had participated in the agitation and planning for the invasion of Manchuria in 1931. As a whole the cabinet was less distinguished than its predecessor and may be regarded as an obedient voice for the Supreme Command. It contained no businessmen but was composed entirely of military and naval officers and members of the civil bureaucracy.

Neither the Premier nor the Foreign Minister, in brief statements upon taking office, made reference to Japan's relations with the Axis. The continuance of this relationship was, however, implicit in such statements as that of General Tojo before officials of the Imperial Rule Assistance Association on October 30, 1941: [31]

At a time when the world is in an upheaval that seems to have no end, and when much of mankind is engaged in a most

[30] *Ibid.*, October 18, 1941.
[31] *Ibid.*, October 31, 1941.

ruthless struggle, the Japanese Government fully appreciates its role in history and is ready to shoulder the task of establishing the projected Greater East Asia Co-prosperity sphere on a basis of lofty ideals that will enable all nations to have their proper place in a movement designed to establish the solidarity of all races.

Japan's apparent but misguided effort to reach a *modus vivendi* with the United States is difficult to reconcile with its obligations under the pact with the Axis. Reconciliation was possible only upon the supposition that a secret understanding accompanied the pact whereby Japan was left completely free to determine the circumstances under which it would enter into war in the Pacific.[32] Japanese inaction when the German Government charged that the United States had broken the peace supports the probability of such an understanding. Japan was sufficiently justified in demanding such an understanding since its aid to Germany would be greater than Germany's aid to Japan. The Japanese, however, could not expect to win an empire without taking some risks. Their weight in the scales of war might be the deciding factor. And the longer they waited before taking the risk, the greater the risk became.

A word may be said regarding Germany's influence upon Japan's decision to take the risk. It is a mistake to hold that in this decision Japan was Hitler's tool. Japanese militarists had waited for "Der Tag" with a seething impatience belied by their well-schooled appearance of calm. They felt confident that they could rely upon public opinion in Japan. The division among the white nations and the alliance with the Germans seemed a heaven-sent opportunity. Nor were the Japanese intending to commit national *harakiri*. They believed in their cause and in their ability to win.

[32] Otto Tolischus stated definitely that this understanding existed. (*New York Times*, November 10, 1941.)

Japan's Strategic Position

The military power and geographical position of Japan combined to constitute that state an ally of imposing strength. Expansion of the navy was rapid after 1937. In 1938 its underage vessels included 10 battleships, 5 aircraft carriers, 26 cruisers, 79 destroyers and 41 submarines, totalling 738,060 tons.[33] At that date Japan had under construction or appropriated for 2 aircraft carriers, 2 cruisers, 6 destroyers and 3 submarines, totalling 50,000 tons. The overage tonnage of 13 cruisers, 26 destroyers and 16 submarines brought total combatant tonnage to approximately 900,000 tons. A five-year replenishment program was then in process of execution, which would add 3 battleships, 5 carriers, 7 cruisers, 43 destroyers and 8 submarines. One battleship of over 40,000 tons was launched in 1939, three in 1940. Two others were under construction in 1941. Three pocket-battleships of 12,000 to 15,000 tons each were launched and a fourth was under construction.[34] Two or three carriers and 11 destroyers were completed between 1937 and 1941. Sixteen submarines and numerous smaller craft were built during that period and several older cruisers and carriers were modernized and equipped with heavier guns. It is not, however, possible to give accurate figures on any navy at the present time.

Japan's air power was an unknown quantity, estimates concerning it varying between 3000 and 7000 planes of all types. The country's annual output was approximately 2500 units.[35] German experts and models were of great assistance in production. Western opinion was inclined to discount Japanese pilots as well as their planes. But there were reports that with German advice a "Model Zero" pursuit plane had

[33] Quigley and Blakeslee, cited, p. 322.

[34] *U. S. Naval Institute Proceedings,* LXVII, 1941, p. 732; *Jane's Fighting Ships,* London, 1941; Puleston, W. D., *The Armed Forces of the Pacific,* New Haven, 1941, Chapter V.

[35] *U. S. Naval Institute Proceedings,* LXVII, 1941, p. 880–3.

been developed that was superior to the Curtis P-40 planes which the Chinese had received from the United States.

The geographical situation of Japan was, in general, advantageous. Opponents must cross oceans to reach the theater of war. Japan proper was excellently guarded by island naval and air bases. The coast of China was in Japanese hands. Further out to sea lay the several groups of islands forming the Mandate,—the Mariana, Marshall and Caroline groups. These were not known to be fortified but they provided harbors and supply bases athwart the route between Hawaii and the Philippines. In Pacific waters still further south Japan held the Spratley Islands, lying between southeastern Indo-China and Palawan in the Philippines, and the Indo-Chinese bases. On Portuguese Timor, within 500 miles of Australia, a lease of ground and landing rights was obtained in 1939. In October 1941, an agreement with Portugal was signed making Dilli, capital of Portuguese Timor, the terminus of a Japanese commercial airline from Palao in the Mandate.[36] Although the French island groups in the Pacific—the Marquesas, Society and Tuamotu or Low Islands—declared allegiance to the Free French Movement of General Charles de Gaulle, they were unfortified and open to utilization by any naval force competent to outreach an opponent.

Japan could expect assistance from its ally Germany, principally through the necessity that might arise for the detachment of American naval units for service in the Atlantic. The sinking of the valiant Australian cruiser *Sydney* in East Asian waters in November 1941, by a German surface vessel, was an indication that more direct aid might be counted upon. German success against the Soviet Union might open new sources of oil and minerals to Japan. Of greatest importance, however, was the knowledge of *blitzkrieg* tactics which Japan might expect Germany to place at its disposal.

[36] *New York Times,* October 15, 1941; non-Portuguese Timor is a possession of the Netherlands.

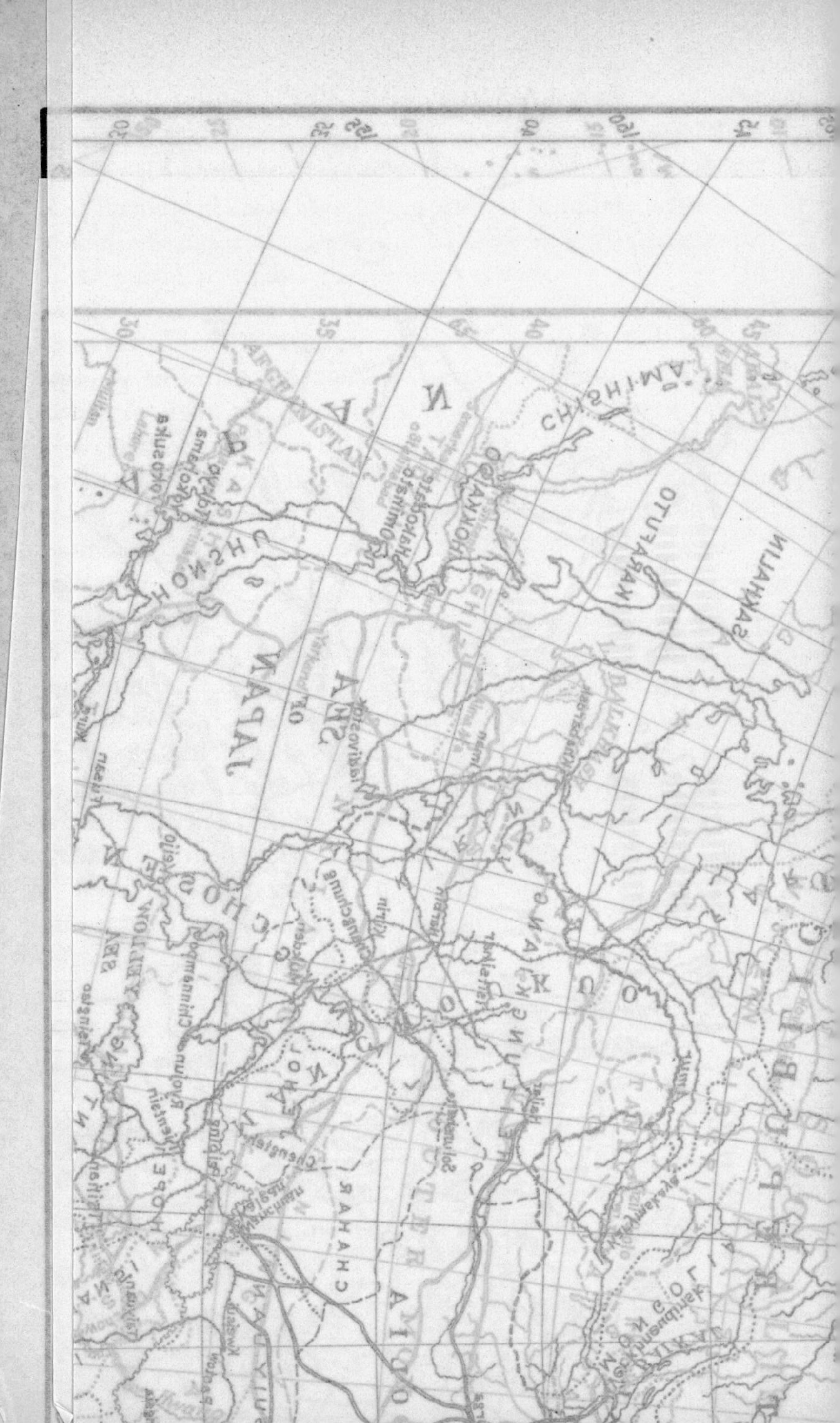

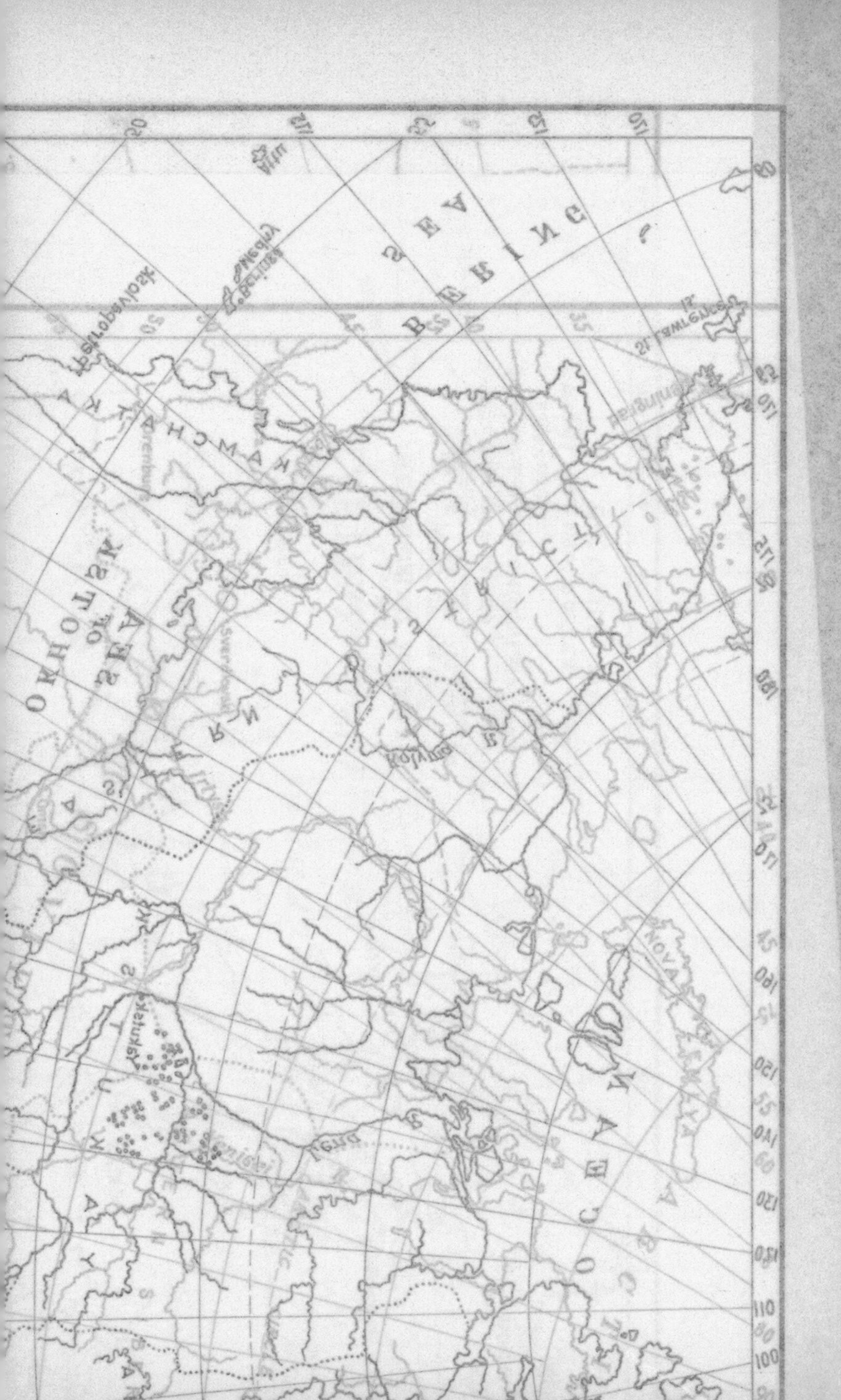

XI

"CO-PROSPERITY IN GREATER EAST ASIA"

THE appetite of imperialism grows with feeding. Areas overrun in "self-defense" must be "protected" by the acquisition of neighboring areas. Thus it has been with Japan. First the Liu Chiu Islands, then Korea and Formosa, then South Manchuria and South Saghalien, then all Manchuria and Inner Mongolia, then North China, then the military effort to conquer all China. The Japanese part in the intervention of 1918–21 in Eastern Siberia failed to add territory to Japan only because internal division, coupled with foreign disapprobation, compelled the Government to content itself with oil and other mineral concessions in North Saghalien. The enunciation, in 1940, of a program for establishing a sphere of "co-prosperity" in Greater East Asia lends credibility to the incredible "Tanaka Memorial." [1]

Prior to the invasion and occupation of the Netherlands under the German *blitzkrieg,* the Japanese Government notified the Netherlands Government, in April 1940, of its concern lest any change take place in the *status quo* of the Netherlands East Indies.[2] In May, when the Netherlands was under attack, the Japanese Government repeated its statement of concern and received assurances from the United Kingdom that it had no intention of intervening, from Germany that it was "not interested in the problem of the

[1] Published as a pamphlet by *The China Critic,* Shanghai, 1932.
[2] *Contemporary Japan,* IX, 1940, p. 778.

Netherlands East Indies."[3] Japan took occasion at that time to increase its efforts, through negotiation, to obtain from the Netherlands Government definite assurances that certain quantities of East Indies products would be exported to Japan.[4] In the midst of these negotiations Hachiro Arita, Foreign Minister, declared in a radio address that: [5]

> Japan is now engaged in the task of establishing a new order in East Asia . . . The countries of East Asia and the regions of the South Seas are geographically, historically, racially and economically very closely related to one another. They are destined to cooperate and minister to one another's needs for their common well-being and prosperity, and to promote peace and progress in their regions. The uniting of all these regions under a single sphere on the basis of common existence and insuring thereby the stability of that sphere is, I think, a natural conclusion . . . I desire to declare that the destiny of these regions—any development therein and any disposal thereof—is a matter of grave concern to Japan *in view of her mission and responsibility as the stabilizing force in East Asia.* (Author's italics)

With this pronunciamento Japan extended the application of its doctrine of a "new order" from "East Asia" to "Greater East Asia." Borrowing the classical Chinese epigram: "Within the four Seas all men are brothers," the Japanese Government asserted on August 1, 1940, that: [6]

> The basic aim of Japan's national policy lies in the firm establishment of world peace in accordance with the lofty spirit of *hakko ichiu* (the world as one family), in which the nation was founded, and in the construction, as the first step, of a new order in Greater East Asia, resting upon the solidarity of Japan, Manchoukuo and China.

The extent of "Greater East Asia" and the nature of the "new order" were not defined. The further developments suggested

[3] *Ibid.*, p. 778–9.
[4] *Ibid.*, August 1940, p. 1076.
[5] *Ibid.*, p. 1077–8.
[6] *Tokyo Gazette*, September 1940, p. 89.

by the clause "as the first step" were not outlined. Whether or not the "solidarity" envisaged for "Japan, Manchoukuo and China" would ultimately replace the "common prosperity" or "co-prosperity" of "Greater East Asia" waited upon events.

Treaty with Thailand

A treaty of friendship was entered into on June 12, 1940, between Japan and Thailand. It was not published but the Japanese Foreign Office announced that it provided for mutual respect for territorial integrity, the exchange of information and consultation upon matters of common interest, and a pledge of neutrality in the event of attack upon either by a third state.[7] Reference was made at this time to the unmistakable demonstration of friendship made by Thailand in abstaining from the final vote of the League Assembly in the Manchurian controversy.

Advance into Indo-China

Prior to the Japanese *démarche* respecting Indo-China, the occupation of the Paracels Islands in 1938 and of Hainan Island and the Spratley Islands early in 1939 by Japanese forces prompted inquiries by the French Ambassador at Tokyo. The French Government accepted an explanation that the occupation of Hainan was for temporary military purposes. Respecting the Spratley Islands, which Japan annexed on March 30, 1939, France formally protested but without effect. Japan based the annexation upon economic development of the Islands by Japanese interests since 1917.[8] Not until the publication of new maps in 1941 was the

[7] *Tokyo Gazette,* July 1940, p. 26. An agreement for the establishment of an air-service between Japan and Thailand was signed on January 27, 1939. (*Japan Year Book, 1940–1941,* p. 195.)

[8] *Japan Year Book, 1940–1941,* p. 181–2, see also Appendix, p. 308.

extent of the annexed area realized in foreign states. It was then found to include islets and coral reefs extending eastward from the Spratleys to Half Moon Shoal, 70 miles from Palawan in the Philippines. The Japanese named the entire group *Shinnan Gunto* (New Southern Islands).

The preoccupation of France with the German invasion was seized upon immediately by Japan as an opportunity to place in operation its plans for imperial expansion. Although the Japanese Foreign Office announced on June 20, 1940, that the French Government had stated that gasoline, trucks and many other types of commodities were prohibited transport to China through Indo-China, and that Japanese inspectors might be sent to verify the prohibition,[9] a Japanese squadron was sent to Haiphong on June 25.[10] At the same time a land force in the south China province of Kwangsi moved into position for invasion of Indo-China. Under the protection of these forces a large group of inspectors was stationed at Hanoi and Haiphong, and also in Kwangchowwan, Chinese territory under lease to France.[11]

For several months after that date, Japanese diplomatic and military moves were employed to obtain an agreement that would give Japan a foothold in northern Indo-China. The vigor of these actions was indicated when Secretary Hull took note of press reports that an ultimatum had been delivered, and reminded Japan of its earlier expression of concern for preservation of the *status quo*.[12] Negotiations were carried on at Hanoi with the colonial government and at Tokyo with the French ambassador. The Vichy Government, under German pressure, was compelled to enter into an agreement with Japan on September 22, 1940. The French Foreign Minister stated that "France made concessions to Japan be-

[9] *Tokyo Gazette,* July 1940, p. 30.

[10] *New York Times,* June 25, 1940.

[11] The Franco-Japanese entente of 1907 was in force when Japan's *démarche* began.

[12] Department of State, *Bulletin,* September 7, 1940, p. 196–7.

cause it was the only way to save what is to be saved in Indo-China."[13] He admitted that the agreement contained no guaranties that Japan would withdraw its troops at the end of the hostilities with China. The agreement was not published. The Japanese Government announced briefly that:[14]

> France agreed to afford in French Indo-China all such facilities of a military nature as are required by the Japanese army and navy for executing their campaign for the settlement of the China affair.

Thereupon Japanese armed forces entered Tongking from Kwangsi province in China and by sea through Hanoi. The border between Indo-China and China was closed to all traffic unlicensed by the occupying forces.[15] These forces garrisoned Haiphong and three air bases in Tongking. War materials and motor trucks in large quantities, en route to China, were confiscated. Parleys were urgently pressed in the interest of economic concessions involving the grant of priorities for the export to Japan of rice, coal, rubber, iron ore, tin and other resources.[16] From the Tongking air fields the bombing of Chinese sections of the Burma Road began in October 1940. Japanese forces were landed in larger numbers and

[13] *Japan Weekly Chronicle,* October 3, 1940, p. 411. However, Japan gave oral assurances that it would respect French rights and interests, "especially the territorial integrity of French Indo-China and the French sovereignty over all parts of the Union of Indo-China." (*Contemporary Japan,* IX, November 1940, p. 1492.) Mr. Early's unfortunate statement that the "Government of the United States wants to see . . . an application of the Monroe Doctrine in Europe and Asia similar to the interpretation and application for this hemisphere. . . . For example, in the case of French Indo-China, we think the disposition should be decided among the Asiatic countries" (Department of State, *Bulletin,* July 6, 1940, p. 12–13), had not been helpful to France.

[14] *Contemporary Japan,* IX, 1940, p. 1369.

[15] Roth, Andrew, *Japan Strikes South,* New York, 1941; this booklet gives a good appraisal of economic, political and military conditions in Indo-China prior to the Japanese advance.

[16] The Vichy government decreed in January 1941, that Indo-China should exercise autonomy in economic relations with other states.

pressure was exerted for an extension of Japan's sphere of control toward central Indo-China.

The concluding move in the first phase of Japan's advance into Indo-China was the signature, on May 7, 1941, of two agreements for economic collaboration.[17] The first, covering residence and navigation, provides for reciprocal rights in these fields and for admission of Japanese capital in the development of agriculture, mining and waterpower. The second, a commercial treaty, authorizes admission of Japanese products into Indo-China either free of duty or at minimum rates. It provides further for preferences to Japan in the exportation of rice, corn, minerals and other commodities and in the import of textiles and other Japanese products. Indo-China agreed also to admit Japanese concerns into its Federation of Importers and Exporters and to engage in periodic economic conferences with Japan.

Thailand and Indo-China

The friendly relations between Thailand and Japan enabled the former to revive its claims to territory in the southwestern part of Indo-China. These claims had such historical validity as could be based upon French seizures of Siamese land in 1867, 1893 and 1904.[18] Demands were voiced in Bangkok, and border incidents occurred after Japan succeeded in occupying Tongking. Thai forces crossed the frontier in November 1940, and took possession of a small section of the disputed area.[19] Fighting continued in Cambodia, causing the French minister at Bangkok to offer, on behalf of the Vichy Government, to negotiate for an adjustment of territorial claims.[20] Thereupon the Japanese Govern-

[17] *New York Times*, May 7, 1941.

[18] Christian, John L., "Thailand Renascent," *Pacific Affairs*, XIV, 1941, p. 186–7; Thompson, Virginia, *French Indo-China*, New York, 1937.

[19] *New York Times*, December 1, 1940.

[20] *Ibid.*, January 20, 1941.

ment offered to mediate between the disputants.[21] Obviously the Governor-General of Indo-China had no choice but to accept the proffered services.

Negotiations were begun at Tokyo in February 1941, after an armistice had been signed at Saigon aboard a Japanese cruiser.[22] Mr. Matsuoka opened the conference with a re-assertion of the benefits to be expected from his Government's plans for a "Greater East Asia." Japanese statesmen took pride in their role and expected it to yield advantages later, as opportunity was presented to move further southward. Apprehension was aroused throughout the Far East that such a move was already under way. The assembly of a considerable Japanese fleet in the Gulf of Siam to compel French acquiescence in the mediator's terms was the prime cause of this apprehension.

Early in March an agreement was reached under which France, with respect to Indo-China, ceded to Thailand the portion of the province of Laos lying west of the Mekong River and sections of northern and northeastern Cambodia amounting nearly to one third of that province.[23] The islands of Khong and Khone in the Mekong were declared to be under the sovereignty of Thailand though jointly administered by that state and France. Japan declared itself guarantor of the settlement and the three states exchanged notes to the effect that they would enter into agreements for especially close relations designed to maintain the peace of "Greater East Asia." France and Thailand, in separate notes requested of them by Japan, affirmed that they had "no intention of entering into any agreement or understanding with a third power or powers envisaging political, economic or military cooperation aimed either directly or indirectly against Japan."

[21] *Ibid.*, January 23, 1941.
[22] *Ibid.*, February 8, 1941.
[23] *Contemporary Japan*, X, 1941, p. 568–71; Jones and Myers, *Documents*, III, p. 294.

Japan and the Netherlands East Indies

Between 1913 and 1933 Japan's share of the imports of the Netherlands East Indies rose from 1% to 32%.[24] Dutch apprehension of this commercial boon to the impecunious natives induced a policy of restriction which benefited the Dutch and other Western exporters.[25] Although Japan's position remained favorable and was improved by a trade agreement in 1936, its trading interests believed themselves entitled to an open door swinging inward for their people and textiles, and outward for oil and other raw materials. Japanese imports of Indies products were, however, small—far smaller than were available to them.

Reference was made at the beginning of this chapter to evidences that Germany's control of the Netherlands gave Japan ground for hope that the Netherlands Indies might be included within its imagined "sphere of common prosperity." To accomplish this end appeared to be a more difficult problem than the occupation of Tongking. The government of the Indies received its directions from London, seat of the Netherlands Government in exile. The islands were under the shadow of Singapore and the United States expressed its belief that the *status quo* should not be disturbed, supporting this attitude by stationing the greater part of the fleet at Pearl Harbor.

Nevertheless the diplomacy of Japan was exerted strongly to obtain assurances of needed commodities from the Netherlands islands. This was Japan's own policy, not one urged upon it by Germany, though, for the war period, Germany would profit with Japan if the policy succeeded. American abrogation of the commercial treaty between the United

[24] Vandenbosch, Amry, "Netherlands India and Japan," *Pacific Affairs*, XIII, 1940, p. 257. For Japan's notice of termination of the arbitration treaty with the Netherlands see Appendix, p. 310.

[25] Quigley and Blakeslee, cited, p. 233–6.

States and Japan in January 1940 was a portent of dwindling oil supplies. Only in the Netherlands Indies were there adequate sources if the American oil market should be closed to Japan.[26] Shut off from such sources Japan must needs awake from the dream of a "Greater East Asia."

Ichizo Kobayashi, Minister of Commerce, was sent to Batavia in September 1940 to put pressure upon the government there for a "cooperative" attitude. He obtained no general concession but merely an agreement that the government would make oil available at the rate of 1,800,000 tons annually, for a period of six months. This oil was to be supplied by the Anglo-Dutch and American companies.[27] None of this oil was of high octane rating, suitable for immediate use in aeroplanes, since the United Kingdom previously had obtained a contract for the purchase of the Indies' entire export of that product.[28] In December Mr. Kobayashi was replaced as head of the Japanese mission by Kenkichi Yoshizawa, the unsuccessful pleader of Japan's cause at Geneva. He was met by a flat declaration of the Netherlands Government in exile that the Indies could not be incorporated into the "co-prosperity sphere." [29] To this the head of the Planning Board in Tokyo replied that Japan's objects were economic, not political, and that all Japan wanted was that the Indies should be part of a loose economic union, while remaining within the Netherlands empire.

No official statement was issued regarding Japan's specific

[26] Four fifths of Japan's normal import of oil—30,000,000 barrels—was received from the United States; less than 15% was obtained in Netherlands India. It is noteworthy that 55% of the oil extracted in the Indies is produced by British-Dutch companies, 33% by American companies. The total annual output in 1939 and 1940 was approximately 60,000,000 barrels. Japan's own sources in "Manchoukuo" and Formosa yield but 2,000,000 barrels annually, and 3,500,000 barrels are obtained from North Saghalien.

[27] *New York Times,* December 27, 1940; in barrels, approximately 14,000,000 annually.

[28] *Ibid.,* October 20, 1940. The Netherlands Indies government reserved priority rights of purchase for use in emergencies.

[29] *Ibid.,* February 4, 1941.

demands upon the Indies. In general they included larger quotas of oil, rubber and tin, concessions for the exploitation of resources by Japanese companies, and immigration quotas. These were considered by the Japanese to be reasonable in view of the privileges enjoyed by Western interests in the Indies. The colonial government stood firm, however. In May 1941, the oil contracts of the previous November were renewed.[30] Prolonged conversations culminated in June with a joint memorandum regretting that "economic negotiations . . . have unfortunately come to no satisfactory result." [31] The Japanese Government issued a candid statement covering the unsuccessful effort that had continued for twenty months.[32] In it occurred a paragraph appealing to the 60,000,000 natives:

> . . . the Netherlands Indies Government stressed that the basis of their policy lies in the progress, prosperity and emancipation of the inhabitants . . .
>
> It is needless to say that the progress, prosperity and emancipation of the inhabitants would be promoted . . . through the establishment of economic cooperation between Japan and the Netherlands Indies.

Japanese Occupation of Indo-China

Resumption of Japanese pressure upon French Indo-China followed closely upon German invasion of the Soviet Union. Apparently the decision to complete the emasculation of Indo-China was taken at an imperial conference on July 2, 1941.[33] Demands were made for military control of the whole colony in order to frustrate alleged British designs upon it. The Vichy Government presumed to see merit in this program since followers of General de Gaulle, leader of the Free French movement, were opposing the governor-general. It

[30] *Ibid.*, May 6, 1941.
[31] *Ibid.*, June 18, 1941.
[32] *Ibid.*, June 19, 1941.
[33] *Ibid.*, July 3, 1941.

asserted that Japan's new proposals were in accord with the earlier recognition by France of its leadership in the maintenance of peace in Eastern Asia.

Promptly Japanese warships and transports appeared off the southern coast and landings began. At bases in all strategic centers of the central and southern provinces many thousands of first-line troops were garrisoned. Cam Ranh, naval base 800 miles from Manila, Hong Kong, and Singapore, was occupied on July 29. Air bases were established along the borders of the colony. Air forces, tanks, artillery and complete equipment were landed. These actions, accomplished peaceably, were in accordance with a defense pact signed at Vichy.[34] This agreement termed the Franco-Japanese relationship one of military cooperation and referred to Japan's previous pledge, hereby renewed, to respect French sovereignty and the territorial integrity of Indo-China. However, when Japan moved 125,000 men into the colony instead of the 40,000 agreed upon at Vichy, the interpretation of this pledge became a political rather than a legal question. The Indo-Chinese government lost all authority to the Japanese though retained for the sake of appearances. French military forces were disbanded. The costs of occupation were paid from funds of the Bank of Indo-China. All export trade except that with Japan was prohibited and large tracts of cotton- and rubber-producing land were requisitioned.[35] Except in name Indo-China had become Japanese territory.

Renewed Pressure upon Thailand

Apprehension in Thailand that Japan's protective arm would be offered at an opportune moment to that state proved to be justified. Demands for military bases, and for priorities in the purchase of rubber, tin and rice were received

[34] *Ibid.,* July 24, 30, 1941; text in Appendix, p. 311.
[35] *Ibid.,* August 13, 1941.

from Tokyo in July 1941. Fortunately for Thailand its position at that time was far stronger than that of Indo-China, due to the presence of British re-enforcements in Singapore and northern Malaya. It was able to follow the profitable middle way, offering limited credits to Japan but relying upon Britain's strength to ward off undue intimacy. The recognition of "Manchoukuo" by Thailand on August 1, 1941, was an inexpensive gesture of friendship.[36] But the extensive movements of Thai troops into border stations fronting Indo-China contradicted Japanese assertions that Thailand was acquiescing in Japan's "co-prosperity" program. Thailand's policy was neutrality and independence, though its businessmen were glad to do extensive business with the Japanese provided that payments were made in gold at high prices.

The independent attitude of the Thai Government was galling to Japanese extremists, who attributed it to assurances allegedly given by Great Britain and the United States. These states were accused by the *Times-Advertiser,* organ of the Japanese Foreign Office, with conspiring to encircle southeastern Asia for purposes of aggression under cover of defending it against Japan.[37] Threats to break the cordon by Nazi methods were published. An attempt to assassinate Baron Hiranuma, minister without portfolio and intimate adviser of Premier Konoye, was explained as the act of an extremist, but appeared to express resentment toward him based upon suspicions that he was urging the Premier to act with caution.[38] Japanese nationals were repatriated from Singapore as British forces along the Thai border were strengthened. Additional Japanese troops were massed in southern and western Indo-China. Bribery and promises to raise the Thai people to an "independent" status among the

[36] *Ibid.,* August 2, 1941.
[37] *Ibid.,* August 8, 1941.
[38] *Ibid.,* August 15, 1941.

nations of the Far East were employed to undermine the Government and promote revolt against it. The Government stood firmly on its program of neutrality, relying upon British and American assurances of support if Japanese troops crossed the border.

Admiral N. Suetsugu, in a vigorous statement prepared for the Associated Press, expressed the views of the military extremists, views that were also widely held among the Japanese people.[39] These views were tragically mistaken as to the policy of the United States toward Japan, and as to the parallelism between American policy in Hispanic America and Japanese policy in Eastern Asia. It is incomprehensible that after a hundred years of friendly and profitable relations any Japanese of intelligence could see the attitude of the United States toward his country as one that endangered "the very existence of the Japanese Empire":

> Consciously or not, America seems inspired by the inhuman motive of holding us down in a subordinate position to herself and seeks to justify such a policy by the specious plea of defending the American ideal of peace and democracy . . .
>
> For this reason we conceived the prosperity sphere, which therefore is nothing but a child of Anglo-Saxon oppressive interference. The sphere is designed as a political and economic guaranty for independent existence of the Asiatic races, with the Japanese taking the leadership. It is passive, limitative, and defensive, and certainly not exclusive.

[39] *Ibid.,* November 24, 1941.

XII

AMERICAN LEADERSHIP IN RESISTANCE

ALONE among the greater states, the United States, for nearly a century, has made respect for the independence of China the keynote of its Far Eastern policy. Although it has accepted, even demanded, the same one-sided treaties that other states have won from China by war, it has regarded them as temporary, and it was the first to relinquish, in principle, treaty control of China's tariffs. On the other hand, it has insisted at all times upon equality of treatment in commercial relations. The doctrine of the "Open Door," so firmly and consistently enunciated, is the expression of American concern for freedom to trade. Its companion doctrine of regard for China's territorial and administrative integrity is corollary but essential to the "Open Door."

The United States, however, has coveted the good will of Japan and during the years of that state's novitiate in the international community it followed the same policy toward Japan as toward China. Only when Japan adopted the program of imperialism and began the process of partitioning China did America's policy come into collision with that of Japan. Increasing in degree since the first Sino-Japanese war, attended by periods of tension and relieved by more or less satisfactory compromises, America's antagonism to Japan's ever more ambitious moves brought it to the side of China in the present conflict. When the concern of the United States for free access to the Indies is added to its "stake" in China the motivation for a strong defensive program in the Pacific becomes clearer. It is doubtful, however, that this country would have given way even if Japan had limited its vision of a "new order" in East Asia to China. Nothing in American official statements or action since the invasion of Manchuria began in September 1931 justifies a notion that, in the long run, defeat would have been conceded without trial by combat. There has been no recession from the fundamental issue —an independent China.

Economic Interests

The trade of the United States with Asia in 1939 totaled $1,261,154,000; in 1940 it reached $1,600,093,000. In the latter year it was nearly twice as great as that with South America, only $160,500,000 short of that with other states of North America, and but $435,000,000 less than that with Europe, including the British Isles. Japan ranked first in both years, with totals of approximately $393,000,000 in 1939 and $386,000,000 in 1940. British Malaya was second with $159,000,000 in 1939 and $284,000,000 in 1940. Then followed the Netherlands Indies, with $128,000,000 in 1939 and $223,000,000 in 1940. China was fourth, with $117,500,000 in 1939 and $171,000,000 in 1940. British India was fifth, with $109,000,000 in 1939 and $170,600,000 in 1940.[1] The weight of these figures in any calculation of American interests in Eastern Asia must be obvious.

It is apparent that while American trade with Japan was one third of the Asiatic total in 1939 and one fourth in 1940, it was offset by the totals with other states of that area and was proportionately much smaller in 1940 than in 1939; this was due only slightly to decreased trade with Japan, mainly to increased trade with other areas. Included in American imports from southeastern Asia was the bulk of its imports of rubber and tin, essentials of both peace-time and

[1] Department of Commerce Release, February 6, 1941, p. 1–2.

defense industries. And the trend of American trade with Eastern Asia since 1900 has been rapidly upward.

Experience has demonstrated that American trade with areas previously absorbed into the Japanese empire has declined but that there has been a far more than compensating increase in trade with Japan. Since China and the other vast areas of Eastern Asia are not comparable with Formosa, Korea and Manchuria, this experience is of slight value. The assumption that as Japan's efforts to exploit raw materials and to develop markets for manufactured goods in China bear fruit the trade of other states with both Japan and China will decline would appear to be sound. The same assumption may be applied to the future of the trade with all of Eastern Asia that may fall under Japanese domination. But it is too early to go beyond assumptions at present. However, the United States is faced with the fact that as manufactured articles become more important, agricultural products less important, in its list of exports, the former amounting to 75.6%, the latter to 24.4% in 1936–38, its dependence upon freedom of admission to the markets of non-industrialized areas increases.

The losses suffered by American trade with China since 1931 have been smaller than might be assumed from the disturbance of the Chinese population.[2] Depression rather than hostilities was the cause of a marked decline in the trade from 1929 to 1933. In 1936 American trade with China was larger than that of any other country and in 1937 it showed an increase over 1936. It dropped nearly 50% in 1938 but recovered in 1939, and in 1940 it exceeded that of 1937. The absence of formal blockade, Japanese incapacity to supply the needs of areas under occupation, American credits to the Chinese Government, and other factors account for the con-

[2] Johnstone, W. C., *The United States and Japan's New Order*, New York, 1941, p. 169–70; Dietrich, E. B., *Far Eastern Trade of the United States*, New York, 1940.

tinuance of trade. American businessmen in China suffered most severely but the larger firms carried on by shifting to new lines of activity or to new locations.

American direct investments in Eastern Asia, exclusive of the Philippines, were, in 1930, approximately $310,000,000; portfolio holdings totalled about $550,000,000; the combined totals were $860,000,000.[3] This amount was 5½% of American foreign investment on that date. Somewhat less than half of it was in Japan, less than one fourth each in China and the Netherlands East Indies. Since 1930 there has been a general decline in portfolio investments but direct investments have remained close to the total of 1930, an indication that under conditions of depression direct holdings were relatively secure. In passing, the incentive to an extension of American influence or control over comparatively undeveloped areas is worthy of mention.[4] Indeed it seems clear that on the financial side the potential value of Eastern Asia rather than present holdings is the significant factor.

Cultural Interests

American missionaries were not long deterred by China's proscription of Roman Catholicism during the period 1724–1846, after two centuries of preaching, from following the merchants to Canton. Their study of the Chinese language made them indispensable to the diplomats and they had no difficulty in writing provisions for the toleration of Christianity into the early treaties. In 1846 an edict had restored the properties of all Christian missionaries. American missionaries increased in number until they exceeded those of any other nationality. Spread widely throughout China, they disseminated ideals of democracy as well as religious and

[3] Field, F. V., *Economic Handbook of the Pacific Area,* Garden City, 1934, p. 339, 353.

[4] Gayer, A. D., and Schmidt, C. T., cited, p. 23.

social doctrines that shook the decadent polity to its foundations. They have taken a correspondingly important part in rallying public opinion in the United States to support a firm program of resistance to Japan.[5] This propaganda may have been somewhat handicapped by the reaction of Americans to the attack of the Chinese nationalist movement upon the missionaries in the 1920's and the accompanying trend toward self-supporting and autonomous Christian institutions. But it contributed notably to the gradually stiffening resolution of the American Government.

Numerous missions were bombed by the Japanese and a number of colleges and schools were forced to close for a time or to move to safer locations. There was not, however, any general prohibition of missionary activities prior to December 7, 1941. The restraint upon freedom of expression within the occupied areas and the fear of arrest among the students depressed but did not devitalize the institutions administered by men of exceptional courage and finesse. Heroic work by missionaries in Nanking and other cities saved the lives of great numbers of refugees. Mission stations in the interior were not abandoned except upon the urgent advice of the Department of State.

American missionaries in Japan were a factor in restraining American opinion from unqualified condemnation of the Japanese people. So, for that matter, were the missionaries in China. The former were not apologists for aggression but asked that Japan's necessities and the political immaturity of its masses be recognized. The latter made an effort to keep the Christian elements of China and Japan in touch with one another. Christian internationalism may play an important part in the reconciliation of peoples.

How general American humanitarian interest in the Chinese may be is impossible to determine. Certainly it is

[5] Masland, J. W., "Missionary Influence upon American Far Eastern Policy," *Pacific Historical Review,* X, September 1941, p. 279–96.

not confined to the supporters of Christian missions. In part it may be an expression of sympathy for the "under dog." Admiration for Chinese art and artisanship may be an influence. Moral sentiment against war and the suffering of millions of simple peasants and coolies is no doubt the primary basis of the universal condemnation of Japan's vandalism. Insufficient in itself to sustain a vigorous opposition, this popular reaction provides a considerable supplement to economic and other motives.

Political Interests

Economic interests were also political interests when, as in Eastern Asia, they were the source of a considerable portion of the American national income and the essential elements in maintaining the standard of living. But there were additional reasons for the concern of the United States with Japan's attack upon the *status quo*. First in importance was the necessity of access to raw materials needed in the manufacture of arms and other types of military equipment. The United States produces no natural rubber, a negligible amount of tin, less than 10% of its consumption of manganese and about 60% of its tungsten.[6] Malaya, the Netherlands East Indies, India and China are the principal sources of these materials. Over a period of several years other sources can be developed and synthetic rubber can be produced on a commercial scale. But in the midst of wars that approached more closely day by day immediate necessities entered decisively into the defense program.

Strategic considerations were even more compelling than raw material limitations. The western shores of the United States, Hawaii and the Panama Canal are well guarded, but

[6] de Wilde, J. C., and Monson, George, "Defense Economy of the United States: An Inventory of Raw Materials," *Foreign Policy Reports*, November 15, 1940.

beyond Hawaii the only American naval base was at Manila, which had no facilities for dry-docking battleships, though it could handle cruisers and smaller vessels. Adequate fortification of Guam would take a longer period than seemed likely to be available. The use of Singapore was viewed as essential to effective naval action designed to protect American interests. In the hands of Japan Singapore would not only assure that country supplies of oil now obtained from California but would also enable Japan to close the port of Rangoon and the Burma Road, China's last important link with the outside world.

Protection of the Philippines will remain an obligation of this country until 1946. The Tydings-McDuffie Act looks beyond that date to international neutralization of the Islands.[7] Economic and humanitarian considerations opposed the use of this Oriental ward as a pawn. The unhappy fate of Korea would be a cynical reward for the Filipino effort to understand and apply republicanism.

Looking into the future, the program of opposition to Japan is seen by many Americans to be the means of preventing the welding of the Asiatic peoples into a vast military empire under the dominance of an immature political ideology. The "Yellow Peril" foreseen by Wilhelm II is now viewed as the menace of the colored races to white interests in Asia and indirectly, or perhaps directly, to the home territories of the white races. This forecast has too little regard for the resistance of the Chinese and Hindus to regimentation or to the differences of culture that would hinder collaboration for less difficult enterprises than world conquest. It is not, however, inconsistent with the grandiose conceptions of "cooperation" put forward by the Government of Japan.

A less tangible political interest is American concern for national prestige and for the spread of democracy, republi-

[7] Quigley and Blakeslee, cited, p. 224–8; Bisson, T. A., *American Policy in the Far East, 1931–1940*, New York, 1940, p. 43–54.

canism and federalism. The "Open Door" doctrine is something more than an insurance policy for commerce and for China's independence. It is a tradition of American foreign policy. To surrender it is to admit error or weakness, not an agreeable thing for a great state to do. This psychological "complex" is strengthened by a moral conviction that rights embodied in treaties must be maintained. Support for international law and order is logically related to this reliance upon treaty rights and broadens the base of America's moral position. It links the defense of right to the defense of rights.

A desire to assist the spread of democracy, in institutions modeled upon those of the United States, has animated public and private relations with China. The United States Government's gesture in returning half of the Boxer Indemnity for educational purposes was an expression of this interest which anticipates that friendly relations will be furthered by Chinese acceptance of American political ideas. The United States was first among the great states to recognize the Chinese Republic in 1913 and first to recognize the National Government in 1928. The American people believe firmly that the Chinese are basically democratic and hope to see the organization of China's provinces on the American federal pattern. The difficulties of this metamorphosis are but dimly appreciated.

Aid to Britain

It will be conceded that the American official position after the passage of the Lend-Lease Act in March 1941, if not before, was that the primary objective of foreign policy should be the defeat of Germany and its allies, and that this objective entailed the provision of all possible aid to Great Britain. The relation of this position to America's program in the Far East is, therefore, of particular interest.

British military power was dependent upon the oil, rubber,

tin, tungsten and other raw materials of southeast Asia, upon the revenues from trade and investment, and upon an open seaway for the transport of troops. Consequently, rather than diminishing the importance of American opposition to Japan, the concern for British success greatly increased it. British resources were strained severely to defend the United Kingdom and the Mediterranean. They were inadequate to the defense of more distant parts of the empire.

However, the combination of dangers in the Atlantic—one known: that without American naval aid the British supply lines might fail, the other unknown: Axis intentions toward the Western Hemisphere—operated as a brake upon American action in the Pacific. Public thinking, which was slow to respond to promptings from Washington and from private propaganda on the Far Eastern war, was more alert to the situation in the Atlantic. Anti-war sentiment was less opposed to unneutral moves which might be regarded as genuinely defensive than to the support of British imperial possessions, or even to the protection of American economic interests in Asia. Relatively few Americans believed that Japan would attack their territories east of the 180th meridian. How to maneuver industrial and military power to meet three dangers at critical moments was the problem of the American administration.

Economic Defense

Economic measures of defense took three forms: the application of moral and legal embargoes upon specified commodities among exports to Japan, the freezing of Japanese funds, and the extension of credits to the countries opposing Japan's policy. A moral embargo was first applied on July 1, 1938, in a letter from the Department of State to manufacturers or exporters of airplanes and their equipment.[8] It

[8] Jones and Myers, *Documents,* II, p. 725.

applied to Japan as one of the states engaged in bombing civilian populations and proved to be effective in terminating export of the banned articles. On December 20, 1939, a similar suggestion was sent to American oil companies respecting export of "plans, plants, manufacturing rights, or technical information required for the production of high quality aviation gasoline." [9]

Not until July 2, 1940, was it possible for the President, under an Act of Congress of that date, to prohibit the export of materials required for the national defense. He acted immediately to prohibit export, except under license, of munitions and a large number of commodities entering into their manufacture. More crippling to Japan was the President's order of July 26, 1940, requiring licenses for the export of petroleum products, tetraethyl lead and first quality iron and steel scrap.[10]

Unfortunately, the continuance of an open market for petroleum products in the Netherlands East Indies frustrated the President's order in relation to them. Japan pressed the weak government there to approve five-year contracts for 3,180,000 tons a year. By licensing shipments to Japan of all petroleum products except the highest octane gasoline the American Government enabled the Netherlands companies to limit their contract with Japan to 1,800,000 tons annually. While this arrangement may be viewed cynically as mere profit-seeking, its effect in restraining the extension of Japanese influence in the south Pacific was important.

The necessity felt by the American Government, contrary to its own desire, that Japan be supplied with these essentials of war, illuminates the relationship between embargoes and military action.[11] To prevent the supply of oil to Japan from California while permitting it from the Indies or elsewhere

[9] *Ibid.*, II, p. 727–8.
[10] *Ibid.*, II, p. 796–801.
[11] President Roosevelt's informally expressed explanation of this line of action is printed in Department of State, *Bulletin*, July 26, 1941, p. 72.

meant to surrender a sanction against Japanese policy. An embargo is a futile as well as an expensive gesture when other sources of supply are open. But to prevent supply meant war unless Japan surrendered its policy, since it depended for success upon continuous access to the wells. Until this country was prepared to resort to force, therefore, it would derive nothing beyond moral satisfaction from embargoes on petroleum. And as Japan might retaliate against an embargo on raw cotton or a boycott on raw silk by military action the possibility of war was latent in such moves as well.

In December 1940, the list of articles requiring licenses for export was greatly extended, to include iron ore, pig iron, ferro alloys and a large number of semi-finished and finished products of iron and steel.[12] The final step short of a comprehensive embargo was taken by the President on July 25, 1941. By it all Japanese assets in the United States were frozen.[13] "This measure," the White House stated, "in effect, brings all financial and import and export trade transactions in which Japanese interests are involved under the control of the Government." At the same time, "at the specific request of Generalissimo Chiang K'ai-shek," freezing control was extended to Chinese assets. But the administration of licensing over the latter was to be "conducted with a view to strengthening the foreign trade and exchange position of the Chinese Government."

Japanese assets in the United States at the date of the freezing order totalled $138,000,000. American assets in Japan were somewhat smaller – $110,000,000.[14] Retaliatory freezing of the latter occurred, as expected, with assurances that the decree would be enforced in proportion to the severity shown by the American administration. The Japanese

[12] Department of State, *Bulletin,* December 14, 1940, p. 529–31.

[13] *Ibid.,* July 26, 1941, p. 73.

[14] *New York Times,* July 26, 1941; in 1932 Japanese assets in the United States amounted to $1,700,000,000.

Government announced its intention to continue interest and amortization payments on its dollar bonds.[15]

Japanese trade felt the effects of the freezing orders immediately. The American Government withheld licenses for the export of oil for a brief period. Thereafter, under a presidential order of August 1, 1941, licenses were issuable only for such petroleum products as were unsuitable for use in aircraft or for processing into aircraft fuel; exportation of licensed oils was limited to average quantities received by importing countries in time of peace.[16] Actually the order prevented all export of oil to Japan, since that state had facilities for the processing of crude oil into aviation fuel. The effect of the blockade was felt throughout the whole expanse of Japanese commerce. Raw silk piled up in the warehouses, and cotton mills were closed down for lack of materials. Seventy-five per cent of its normal imports was shut off from Japan, creating a disastrous situation for a people so dependent upon foreign trade.

From 1931 to the end of 1941 the United States Government, through the Reconstruction Finance Corporation and the Export-Import Bank, provided credits to China amounting to U. S. $197,111,412.36.[17] Additional credits were in process of arrangement under the Lend-Lease Act. Allocations in chronological order were: $9,212,826.56 in 1931, for the purchase of wheat, $50,000,000 in 1933—reduced in operation to $17,165,385.80 and taken in the form of cotton, wheat and flour—$733,200.00 in 1937 for locomotives, $25,000,000 in 1938 for trucks, gasoline and other commodities, $95,000,000 in three agreements in 1940, and $50,000,000 in April 1941, as a stabilization fund to support the Chinese currency. It may be noted that the credits arranged in 1940 were granted

[15] *Ibid.*, July 28, 1941.

[16] *Ibid.*, August 2, 1941; this order did not mention Japan; it excepted certain areas from restriction.

[17] Figures obtained through the courtesy of Far Eastern Unit, Bureau of Foreign and Domestic Commerce, Department of Commerce.

against contracts for the delivery of certain strategic materials. The American government-owned Metal Reserves Company earmarked $60,000,000 for the purchase of Chinese minerals, making payments from this fund as the shipments were received, to the Export-Import Bank, thus reducing China's indebtedness to the Bank. Without these funds and additional amounts from the United Kingdom and the Soviet Union, China's economy and war effort might well have collapsed.

Military Defense

Japanese abrogation of the naval treaties of Washington (1922) and London (1930), with the exception of Part IV of the latter treaty (which stated the accepted rules of international law limiting submarine warfare against merchant vessels), became effective on December 31, 1936.[18] Japan was not a signatory of the naval treaty of 1936 and declined to give assurances that it would observe the qualitative limitations laid down in that treaty.[19] Consequently the American, British and French Governments exchanged notices of intention to escalate and to depart from the upper limits provided in the treaty for capital ships and their gun calibers. On June 30, 1938, the same three states, after consultation, signed a protocol amending the treaty. The figure of 35,000 tons as the limit for capital ships was replaced by 45,000; that of 16 inches for maximum gun calibers remained unaltered. In September and October 1939, all parties gave notice of suspension of the treaty of 1936.[20]

Released from all limitations, American naval expansion

[18] For a brief discussion of these treaties, see Quigley and Blakeslee, cited, p. 237–42; for the *procès-verbal* of November 6, 1936, relating to submarine warfare, see *American Journal of International Law,* XXXI, 1937, Supplement, p. 137–9. This was signed by Japan and adhered to by Germany.

[19] Jones and Myers, *Documents,* I, p. 483–4.

[20] *Ibid.,* II, p. 486–8, 739.

assumed gargantuan proportions. The first of the Congressional moves to build up the navy was the passage of the Vinson-Trammell Act of 1934. This law was supplemented in 1936 and the second Vinson-Trammell Act was passed in 1938.[21] This was followed in June 1940, by a third Act which provided for the addition of 167,000 tons of fighting ships to the 157,000 tons authorized by the earlier laws. These provisions were dwarfed by the authorizations of a fourth Act, passed under the stress of the *blitzkrieg* in July 1940. This Act, providing for what was known as the "two-ocean" navy, was designed to increase combatant tonnage by 1,325,000 tons or 70%. On February 1, 1941, the American navy was composed of 323 combatant vessels of 1,253,425 tons. On that date Congress had authorized the building of additional ships to bring the navy to a total of 3,500,000 tons, exclusive of auxiliary, non-combatant craft.[22] The building program contemplated the addition of 17 battleships (total 32), 12 aircraft carriers (total 18), 54 cruisers (total 91), 205 destroyers (total 364), and 79 submarines (total 185), raising the approximate total in all categories to some 700 combatant vessels.[23] These figures for categories were subject to modification. The great armada was to be completed in 1946. It would require an enlisted strength of 532,000 men.[24] The air force of the navy also was voted impressive increments. The Act of July 19, 1940, authorized a maximum number of 15,000 naval airplanes but left the President free to raise the limit if necessary. On June 30, 1941, the navy possessed 3,926 planes of all types.

The United States Navy was divided into three fleets in October 1940: the Pacific, Atlantic and Asiatic fleets. The

[21] For considerations affecting the passage of these bills, see Quigley and Blakeslee, cited, p. 245–9.

[22] Popper, D. H., "America's Naval Preparedness," *Foreign Policy Reports,* April 1, 1941, p. 15.

[23] Jones and Myers, *Documents,* III, p. 694.

[24] *New York Times,* April 16, 1941.

tripartite division existed previously but the Atlantic and Asiatic forces had been smaller and had not been termed fleets. The Pacific fleet was well known to be incomparably the strongest of the three.[25] Maintained in the Pacific during the greater part of the past decade, it was based on the Hawaiian Islands in May 1940. The Asiatic fleet, based at Manila, although the smallest of the fleets, was by no means inconsiderable. During 1941 the air forces attached to both fleets in the Pacific were greatly strengthened.

The states signatory to the naval limitation treaty of Washington (1922) were relieved also of limitations upon the fortification of Pacific bases by the abrogation of the treaty. In December 1938, a naval board headed by Rear Admiral A. J. Hepburn presented recommendations to Congress for extensive development of naval and air bases.[26] The Hepburn board strongly recommended that a major submarine and air base be established at Guam Island, which lies approximately 1350 miles from Tokyo but is itself surrounded by islands of the Japanese mandated territory. Congress failed to act upon this recommendation because of reluctance to antagonize Japan. Not until March 1941 was an appropriation ($4,700,000) made to initiate the improvement of Guam. In general, however, the recommendations were accepted and small appropriations were made which were supplemented appreciably in March 1941.[27]

Work upon the construction of submarine and air bases at Midway Island and Wake Island was commenced in 1939.[28] Midway, lying 1200 miles northwest of Honolulu, was the

[25] The transfer of major as well as minor units to the Atlantic was reported in the *New York Times* on April 30, 1941.

[26] *Report on Need of Additional Naval Bases to Defend the Coasts of the United States, Its Territories and Possessions. Letter of Secretary of Navy Transmitting Report* (H. Doc. No. 65, 76th Cong. 1st sess.).

[27] For the two authorization acts of 1941, see Jones and Myers, *Documents,* III, p. 706–8.

[28] *United States Naval Institute Proceedings,* LXVI, 1940, p. 1601; LXVII, 1941, p. 54–5.

focal point in the developing system of defense. Wake lies 1029 miles southwest of Midway. These two, with Guam, half-way between Wake and Manila, were essential links in America's supply-line between Hawaii and the Philippines. The three atolls were but ill-equipped stations on the pioneering route of Pan American Airways' Clippers prior to 1939.

A second field of development was the Alaska-Aleutian Islands area. The Aleutian chain of islands projects 1100 miles westward from the tip of the Alaskan peninsula. The many indentations along the chain provide a hundred harbors and anchorages along the shortest route between North America and Asia. From the bases it provides, a hostile naval expedition could be intercepted while still 2000 miles from Seattle. Air travel to Asiatic points by this route can be conducted in much shorter over-water flights than those of the central Pacific route.

Both the army and the navy were concerned with the development of Alaskan bases. Since the fall of 1939 army bases have been under construction at Anchorage and Fairbanks.[29] Air forces of several hundred planes were located there. Naval air bases at Sitka and Kodiak also were laid out in 1939. A third base of this type lies further westward on Unalaska Island. Dutch Harbor, on the same island, which was used as a naval base for surface vessels, received allocations of funds for enlarged facilities to accommodate all types of naval and air craft. The territorial waters and superjacent air spaces around Kiska and Unalaska Islands were reserved as defensive areas.[30]

The third line of island defenses and supply, lying south and southwest of Hawaii, was similarly strengthened. Johnston, Palmyra and Tutuila in Samoa, received the largest sums,

[29] Elliott, A. R., "U. S. Defense Outposts in the Pacific," *Foreign Policy Reports,* March 15, 1941.

[30] Jones and Myers, *Documents,* III, p. 708–9.

principally for aviation facilities.[31] Tutuila's equipment as a general naval base was enlarged and improved. Five islands hitherto hardly recognized as American territory—Jarvis, Baker, Howland, Canton and Enderbury—were colonized. Pearl Harbor, Oahu, Hawaiian Islands, although previously rated the strongest island naval base in the world, was brought to an even higher pitch of preparedness. Jointly guarded by the army and the navy, the Hawaiian Islands are the chief ocean rampart of the Pacific coast of North America and the main base of supplies for fleet operations in the western Pacific. The strong air force maintained there was provided with a new naval air station on Kaneohe Bay, Oahu, in February 1941. Auxiliary airports were constructed on the neighboring islands. A new drydock large enough to care for the largest battleships in the fleet was towed out and installed. Additional facilities for oil and ammunition storage, housing of troops and crews and hospitalization were built. An anti-aircraft regiment was added to the army's already considerable forces. Heavy bombing planes of the latest type were flown to Hawaii in April 1941.[32]

Reports of unexpectedly rapid progress on the extensive program of base-building[33] were accompanied by complaints from President Manuel Quezon that the Philippines were unprepared for war.[34] He referred to the lack of air-raid shelters and provision for civilian necessities under wartime conditions. The Philippines were, however, in a far better condition than ever before to repel an invader. American troops had been reinforced and provided with motorized equipment, and the Filipino army was larger and more thoroughly trained. Unification of the American regulars with the Filipino army was attained by the appointment of

[31] Naval stations on Palmyra and Johnston Islands were to be placed in commission on August 15, 1941. (*New York Times,* August 2, 1941.)

[32] *New York Times,* April 15, 1941.

[33] *Ibid.,* October 18, 1941.

[34] *Ibid.,* November 29, 1941.

Lieutenant General Douglas MacArthur to the command of all American army forces in the Far East. As military adviser to President Quezon and later as field marshal of the Philippine army, he had built up the native forces. The latter were estimated at the end of 1941 to have 130,000 men who had had a minimum of 6 months' training. To strengthen the air forces of the Islands was the American Government's main concern. Large bombing planes in unrevealed numbers were sent out, together with other types, and a naval air station was commissioned at Cavite.

Defense by Diplomacy

Diplomatic, as well as economic and military measures, have been employed by the United States to implement its Far Eastern policy. Diplomacy was extraordinarily patient and conciliatory up to July 26, 1939, when Secretary Hull notified Ambassador Horinouchi of the Government's desire that the commercial treaty of 1911 with Japan be terminated, in accordance with procedure prescribed by the treaty itself, at the end of six months.[35] To begin with, President Roosevelt issued no declaration of American neutrality under the joint resolution of Congress of May 1, 1937.[36] To have done so would have brought into operation restrictions of the Neutrality Act which would have worked disadvantageously to both Japan and China but with greater disadvantage to China. American merchant ships moved freely in Far Eastern waters, though warned by the Executive that munitions of war might be transported to China and Japan only at the shipowner's risk. Publicly-owned ships were forbidden to transport such materials.

Secretary of State Cordell Hull took every available opportunity to affirm the general bases of American foreign

[35] Jones and Myers, *Documents,* II, p. 244.

[36] United States Statutes at Large, Vol. 50, p. 121.

policy. His pronouncements were models of dignified statesmanship which had little effect upon the totalitarian powers. Their immediate value lay in the moral support they conveyed to China and other states under attack. Of more tangible consequence were Mr. Hull's protests against infringements of American treaty rights and interference with persons and property.

President Roosevelt's speech of October 5, 1937, in which he called war a "contagion," referred to "quarantine" as the community's method of checking an epidemic, and declared that "there must be positive efforts to preserve peace," was followed the next day by a statement from the Department of State that Japan had violated the Nine-Power Treaty and the Kellogg-Briand Pact.[37] But the effect of these vigorous affirmations was neutralized at the Brussels Conference, called on October 16, 1937, to consider the application of the Nine-Power Treaty. Mr. Norman Davis, leader of the American delegation, stated at the first session that [38]

> The Government of the United States is prepared to share in the common efforts to devise, within the scope of these treaty provisions and principles, a means of finding a pacific solution which will provide for terminating hostilities in the Far East and for restoring peace in that area.

A "pacific solution" was desirable but not anticipated. To speak of it when war was flagrant was unrealistic. But proposals of sanctions would have lacked popular support in the United States.

The sharp reaction of the American Government to the sinking of the American gunboat *Panay* in the Yangtze River by Japanese bombs might well have led to war had not the Japanese Government expressed regret, removed responsible

[37] Department of State, *Press Releases*, October 9, 1937, p. 275–85.

[38] *The Conference of Brussels*, Department of State Publication 1232, Conference Series 37, Washington, 1938, p. 27.

officers, and paid indemnities for losses of life and property.[39] A few days later, on December 18, 1937, Secretary Hull, in a letter to Senator Smathers, justified the presence of American naval vessels in China. They were there, he said, "with authorization by the Chinese Government" to assist "in the maintenance of order and security as affecting the lives, the property and the legitimate activities of American nationals." He made no specific reference to the fact that the *Panay* was escorting vessels of the Standard Oil Company. But this was unnecessary on legal grounds since war had not been declared nor recognized by any state. American reluctance to be drawn into hostilities was underlined when Mr. John M. Allison, third secretary of our embassy at Nanking, was slapped by a Japanese soldier while investigating reports of interference with American property. An apology and assurances that the offending soldier would be punished were accepted in satisfaction of this insult to a diplomatic officer.[40] Withdrawal of the 15th Infantry from Tientsin in March 1938 was a prudent action intended to lessen the probability of a local incident.

The anomaly of undeclared though unlimited warfare provided a legal basis for diplomatic efforts to protect foreigners and their property within the fighting zones. Such efforts could, however, do little more than compile a record of claims; the long list of bombings of mission properties proves that the protests, directed not only at protecting American interests but also at curbing inhumane treatment of the Chinese population, were unsuccessful. The Japanese command limited its concessions to the delimitation of zones of safety in certain instances and the payment of small "solatiums" for damages.

[39] Jones and Myers, *Documents,* I, p. 194–204; the Japanese Government paid $2,214,007.36 for damage to property, deaths, and injuries. Of this amount $1,287,942 represented losses to property of the Standard-Vacuum Oil Company.

[40] *Ibid.,* I, p. 212–3.

Diplomacy also had to deal singlehandedly with Japan's discriminatory measures against the trade of foreigners with Manchuria ("Manchoukuo"), North China, and in the Yangtze valley. In a lengthy note [41] dated October 6, 1938, the United States bluntly declared that "equality of opportunity or the Open Door has virtually ceased to exist in Manchuria notwithstanding the assurances of the Japanese Government that it would be maintained in that area." The note pointed to Japanese procedures in North China that appeared to portend the same consequences for American trade, mentioning exchange control, alteration of Chinese tariffs, the creation of monopolies and interference with American trade and shipping; to which Japan blandly replied that no discrimination was being practiced.[42] But Japan's interpretation was admittedly related to its proposed "new order" in East Asia which the American Government promptly declined to recognize. The comprehensive and well-argued statement of December 31, 1938, stood firmly on treaty rights.[43] While recognizing that changed conditions might justify modifications of international agreements, it insisted that "alterations can rightfully be made only by orderly processes of negotiation . . ." Japan's rejoinder was an intensified application of measures to which the United States was objecting.

That this country was approaching methods more forceful than diplomacy was indicated in the abrogation of the commercial treaty with Japan.[44] That did not take effect until January 26, 1940, and it had no immediate effect then since

[41] *Ibid.*, I, p. 237–42.

[42] *Ibid.*, I, p. 242–6.

[43] *Ibid.*, I, p. 246–51; this note referred to earlier negotiations on extraterritoriality but it was not until July 19, 1940, that Under Secretary Welles issued a statement that the American Government was maintaining unchanged its traditional and declared policy of negotiations for relinquishment of extraterritorial and all other special rights as conditions warranted. (*Ibid.*, III, p. 240–1.)

[44] *Ibid.*, II, p. 242.

trade was permitted to continue without restriction. The American Government took time to reappraise our situation in the light of Germany's prospect of success against France and Great Britain. In the meantime Ambassador Grew at Tokyo made an historic address on October 19, 1939, before the American-Japan Society in which he said that the American people were not ignorant of Japan's actions and underlying purposes and that their opposition to them was spreading and stiffening.[45]

Refusal to recognize the puppet government of Wang Ch'ing-wei at Nanking[46] was followed, after the fall of the Netherlands and France, by Secretary Hull's statements in support of the *status quo* in the Netherlands East Indies and French Indo-China. The Secretary declared that the United States "has not at any time or in any way approved the French concessions to Japan."[47] Secretary Hull also opposed the closure of the Burma Road by Great Britain in July 1940, terming it an "unwarranted interposition of obstacles to world trade."[48] These evidences of American tenacity did not deter Japan from entering into alliance with Germany and Italy. Japan's open affiliation with European fascism only stimulated Americans to more strenuous defensive efforts, aiding in the passage of the Lend-Lease Act. To impress the people of Japan with our firmness the Department of State advised Americans in the Far East to come home. The threat to Indonesia passed for the moment but apprehension remained.

Admiral Kichisaburo Nomura presented his credentials as Japanese Ambassador at Washington on February 14, 1941. He was a friend of President Roosevelt's who hoped to improve American understanding of Japan's position. Three weeks before his arrival the President had sent his Administra-

[45] *Ibid.*, II, p. 249–60.

[46] *Ibid.*, II, p. 301–2.

[47] *Ibid.*, II, p. 305–8; Department of State, *Bulletin*, September 28, 1940, p. 253.

[48] Department of State, *Bulletin*, July 20, 1940, p. 36.

tive Assistant, Lauchlin Currie, to Chungking to obtain a better understanding of China's position.[49] That China was to be aided under the Lend-Lease Act had been determined when Mr. Currie's mission was announced. Admiral Nomura's real task was to obtain for his Government a better understanding of America's position. In this he was aided by the able Kaname Wakasugi, former consul-general in New York. The Ambassador sought to obtain a neutrality pact similar to that under negotiation by Japan at Moscow.[50] This effort was unrealistic not only in the light of American policy toward China and Britain but also in relation to Japan's alliance with Germany and Italy. The United States could not be blind to the inconsistencies between Japan's declared policies and its actions. Although the latter left little ground for negotiation, the most intensive effort was exerted to discover a basis of peaceful settlement.

In August 1940, Sumner Welles, Under Secretary of State, had begun a series of conversations with the Soviet Ambassador, Constantine Oumansky, designed to open the way to mutually advantageous action. The reopening of the American consulate-general in Vladivostok was agreed upon.[51] Secretary Hull professed no surprise at the signing of the Soviet-Japanese neutrality pact, regarding it as "descriptive of a situation which has in effect existed between the two countries for some time past." [52] However, the significant contribution of the Welles-Oumansky conversations was the development of an atmosphere in which the United States could, with relative ease, offer economic assistance to the Soviet Union after the onset of the German invasion. The promise of priority for Soviet orders and of unlimited licenses for export of defense materials, made by Mr. Welles on

[49] *Ibid.*, January 25, 1941, p. 109.
[50] *New York Times*, June 6, 1941.
[51] *Ibid.*, November 30, 1940.
[52] Department of State, *Bulletin*, April 19, 1941, p. 472.

August 2, 1941, may be viewed in relation to Japan's East Asian policy as well as to the German "new order" for Europe.[53]

A serious crisis in American-Japanese relations was provoked by the agreement of Vichy to a sudden expansion of Japanese control in Indo-China. Mr. Welles, in a statement for the press,[54] declared that "there is no question of any threat to French Indo-China, unless it lies in the expansionist aims of the Japanese Government." He made it clear that American interests were being endangered:

> The turning over of bases for military operations and of territorial rights under pretext of "common defense" to a power whose territorial aspirations are apparent, here presents a situation which has a direct bearing upon the vital problem of American security.

While expressing sympathy for the French people, he concluded with words that carried a threat of action in self-defense:

> In its relations with the French Government at Vichy and with the local French authorities in French territories, the United States will be governed by the manifest effectiveness with which those authorities endeavor to protect these territories from domination and control by those powers which are seeking to extend their rule by force and conquest, or by the threat thereof.

American sentiment was aroused by the now obvious threat to areas from which certain indispensable materials were imported. The *New York Times* warned Japan that economic and military means were likely to be employed to halt further "aggressive action" in Siberia, Netherlands India or Indo-China.[55] The *Times* insisted that:

[53] *Ibid.*, August 9, 1941, p. 109.
[54] *Ibid.*, August 2, 1941, p. 87–8.
[55] *New York Times*, May 24, 1941.

Any action by Japan that threatens a legitimate American interest in the Far East should be met at once by efforts on our part to deal Japanese finance and industry and trade a deadly blow.

Japan proceeded with the occupation of Indo-China, whereupon President Roosevelt issued an order freezing Japanese assets in the United States. The United Kingdom's identical action on the following day (July 26, 1941) marked the close parallelism which had developed in Anglo-American diplomacy.[56] The Netherlands East Indies took the same course on July 28, thereby suspending the oil agreement which Japan had obtained after lengthy negotiations.[57] Although none of these actions was, of itself, terminative of trading relations, they were of consequence only if administered to that end. Consequently they must be viewed as definitely and dramatically concluding the program of toleration toward Japanese expansionism.

The joint declaration of President Roosevelt and Prime Minister Churchill of August 14, 1941, called "The Atlantic Charter," amounted to the establishment of an *entente cordiale* between their respective countries. Although Japan was not mentioned by name it was included by inference as one of the "other governments associated with" the "Hitlerite government of Germany" in "policies of military domination by conquest." [58] Concurrently both the United States and the United Kingdom warned Japan that any action threatening to Thailand's integrity or independence would be a matter of concern to them and that they were prepared to meet it with appropriate action.[59] Mr. Churchill put into words a situation already recognized when he stated in Parliament that if the United States should fail "to arrive

[56] *Ibid.*, July 26, 1941.
[57] *Ibid.*, July 29, 1941.
[58] Department of State, *Bulletin*, August 16, 1941, p. 125–6.
[59] *New York Times*, August 13, 1941.

at a fair and amicable settlement which will give Japan the utmost reassurance for her legitimate interests . . . we shall, of course, range ourselves unhesitatingly at the side of the United States." [60] America was to lead in resistance; Britain's role in the Pacific was secondary.

President Roosevelt did not apply the Neutrality Act of 1939 to the German-Soviet war, thereby leaving American shipping free to move to Vladivostok. The shipment of oil to that port stimulated controversy within the Japanese cabinet concerning measures that might be taken to oppose it. Representations against the shipment of high octane gasoline by the route to Vladivostok were made to the United States by the Japanese Government.[61] Objection was placed not upon legal grounds but upon those of prestige and of the danger involved to Far Eastern peace. Supposedly the injection of this issue into the extremely delicate situation prompted Premier Konoye to send a personal letter to President Roosevelt, the contents of which were not divulged. Apparently the Premier offered no important concessions but rather sought to impress upon the President Japan's determination to press forward with its program against any opposition. The dispatch of American military missions to Chungking and to Moscow at this time indicated a strengthening rather than a relaxation of American resolution.[62]

President Roosevelt, in his message to Congress on December 15, 1941, which he described as an "historical summary of the past policy of this country in relation to the Pacific area," stated that the United States, during negotiations with Japan, had "steadfastly advocated certain basic principles which should govern international relations": [63]

[60] *Ibid.*, August 25, 1941.
[61] *Ibid.*, August 28, 1941.
[62] Department of State, *Bulletin*, August 30, 1941, p. 166; September 6, 1941, p. 180.
[63] *Ibid.*, December 20, 1941, p. 533; see also Appendix, p. 300.

The principle of inviolability of territorial integrity and sovereignty of all nations.

The principle of non-interference in the internal affairs of other countries.

The principle of equality—including equality of commercial opportunity and treatment.

The principle of reliance upon international cooperation and conciliation for the prevention, and pacific settlement, of controversies.

The President revealed that the Japanese Government had proposed, early in August 1941, that he and the Premier of Japan should meet to discuss means of adjusting Japanese-American relations. He stated to the Congress that

I should have been happy to travel thousands of miles to meet the Premier of Japan for that purpose. But I felt it desirable, before so doing, to obtain some assurance that there could be some agreement on basic principles. This Government tried hard—but without success—to obtain such assurance from the Japanese Government.

In a document handed by the Secretary of State to the Japanese Ambassador on October 2, 1941, the effort referred to by the President was reviewed.[64] This document fully bears out the President's statement. It relates the President's reply of August 17, 1941, to the Japanese proposal, which is summed up in the assurance to Japan that "the Government of the United States, while desiring to proceed as rapidly as possible with consideration of arrangements for a meeting between the heads of state, felt it desirable, in order to assure that that meeting would accomplish the objectives in view, to clarify the interpretation of certain principles and the practical application thereof to concrete problems in the Pacific area." The principles referred to are those quoted above from the President's message to Congress. Hope that these

[64] Department of State, *Bulletin,* December 20, 1941, p. 537–40.

principles might prevail was entertained after receipt of a Japanese statement of August 28, 1941, and this hope was strengthened when, on September 6, 1941, Premier Konoye assured the American Ambassador that he subscribed fully to the four principles enunciated by the American Government.

However, the Japanese proposals of September 6, 1941, presented in Washington as a basis for discussions, were inconsistent with those principles. The proposals were not published but the document of October 2, 1941, now under review, makes it clear that they qualified Japan's general acceptance of the principles by justifying its military movements on the plea of self-defense. The American reaction to this plea was a denial not of "the inalienable right of self-defense" but of its applicability to the existing circumstances. The proposals of September 6 also diverged from the four principles in attempting to restrict their application "to the countries of the Southwest Pacific area (not the Pacific area as a whole)." They were inconsistent also in reiterating the desire of Japan to maintain troops in certain areas of China for an indeterminate period. The American Government, consequently, expressed its belief that "renewed consideration of these fundamental principles may be helpful in our effort to seek a meeting of minds in regard to the essential questions on which we seek agreement and thus lay a firm foundation for a meeting between the responsible heads of the two Governments."

General Tojo, who succeeded Prince Konoye as premier on October 17, 1941, had sent Saburo Kurusu on November 5 to assist Ambassador Nomura in the conduct of the conversations. He did not reach Washington until November 15. Japanese utterances during the interim continued truculent. Kurusu's mission was represented to be America's last chance to take advantage of Japan's preference for peace —on its own terms. Finance Minister Kaya Okinori cast diplomatic phrases to the winds, declaring that it was the aim of Japan to "force Britain and the United States to retreat from East Asia." [65] The "Throne Aid League," composed of 300 members of the lower house of the Diet, condemned the countries that had "drawn a ring of encirclement around Japan, both militarily and economically": [66]

> In the face of this situation the Japanese people have the grim determination to overcome the national crisis for the independence and honor of East Asia . . .

American moves during this ten-day period were equally indicative of an undeviating stand. The President made it known that he was considering removal of the marines from China. Secretary of the Navy Knox warned that continued Japanese expansionism would make a collision inevitable. Lend-lease aid of $1,000,000,000 was promised to the Soviet Union. And Congress amended the neutrality law to enable American cargo ships to enter war zones.

Conversations of Mr. Kurusu and Admiral Nomura with President Roosevelt, Secretary Hull and Under Secretary Welles were inaugurated on November 17. Before an extraordinary session of the Diet on that day Foreign Minister Togo reviewed the four years of war and reiterated well-worn declarations of high purpose. He thought it not impossible that peace with the United States might be preserved. But if it appeared that Japan's existence were menaced or its prestige compromised, Japan would face the crisis with firmness and resolution.[67] The conversations were secret but it was sufficiently evident as the days passed without announcement of conclusions that both parties were standing firmly upon the policies that have been elaborated in earlier chapters.

[65] *New York Times,* November 11, 1941.
[66] *Ibid.,* November 14, 1941.
[67] *Ibid.,* November 17, 1941.

On November 20, 1941, the Japanese Government submitted the following proposals:[68]

1. Both the Governments of Japan and the United States undertake not to make any armed advancement into any of the regions in the Southeastern Asia and the Southern Pacific area excepting the part of French Indo-China where the Japanese troops are stationed at present.

2. The Japanese Government undertakes to withdraw its troops now stationed in French Indo-China upon either the restoration of peace between Japan and China or the establishment of an equitable peace in the Pacific area.

In the meantime the Government of Japan declares that it is prepared to remove its troops now stationed on the southern part of French Indo-China to the northern part of the said territory upon the conclusion of the present arrangement which shall later be embodied in the final agreement.

3. The Governments of Japan and the United States shall cooperate with a view to securing the acquisition of those goods and commodities which the two countries need in Netherlands East Indies.

4. The Governments of Japan and the United States mutually undertake to restore their commercial relations to those prevailing prior to the freezing of the assets.

The Government of the United States shall supply Japan a required quantity of oil.

5. The Government of the United States undertakes to refrain from such measures and actions as will be prejudicial to the endeavors for the restoration of general peace between Japan and China.

It is at once apparent that these proposals, some of which have a specious appearance of moderation, actually asked the United States to entrust its policy to administration by Japan and to leave China to whatever fate the Japanese Government might decree.

[68] Department of State, *Bulletin,* December 20, 1941, p. 540.

Mr. Hull conferred from time to time, as the conversations proceeded, with the diplomatic representatives of the United Kingdom, Australia, China and the Netherlands. On November 26 he handed to Admiral Nomura a document entitled "An Outline of a Proposed Basis for Agreement between the United States and Japan," which was accompanied by an oral statement of fundamental principles:[69]

These principles include the principle of inviolability of territorial integrity and sovereignty of each and all nations; the principle of non-interference in the internal affairs of other countries; the principle of equality, including equality of commercial opportunity and treatment; and the principle of reliance upon international cooperation and conciliation for the prevention and pacific settlement of controversies and for improvement of international conditions by peaceful methods and processes.

Mr. Hull stated that his Government considered that "adoption of the Japanese proposals of November 20 would not be likely to contribute to the ultimate objectives of ensuring peace under law, order and justice in the Pacific area."

Section I of the "Outline" amplified, in the form of an agreement, the principles laid down in the oral statement. Section II suggested the following steps to be taken by the two Governments:

1. An endeavor to conclude a non-aggression agreement among the British Empire, China, Japan, the Netherlands, the Soviet Union, Thailand and the United States.

2. An endeavor to conclude among the same Governments, excepting the Soviet Union, an agreement to respect the territorial integrity of French Indo-China and to maintain an open door in trade with that state.

3. Withdrawal by Japan of all military, naval, air and police forces from China and from Indo-China.

4. Support of the National Government of China.

[69] Appendix, p. 300.

5. Surrender of extraterritoriality, settlements and concessions in China and rights under the Boxer Protocol; endeavor to influence other states to the same end.

6. Negotiation of a commercial treaty on liberal lines.

7. Removal of freezing restrictions and stabilization of the dollar-yen rate of exchange.

8. Non-application of any treaty so as to cause conflict with the terms of this agreement.

Clearly the United States was standing adamant against the Japanese "new order" but offering to aid in the reduction of foreign influence in China and the improvement of Japan's international economic position.

The Tojo cabinet took plenty of time for consideration of these proposals and asked that the conversations be continued for two weeks.[70] As information concerning them reached the Japanese press they were subjected to severe censure and declared to be utterly unacceptable. Meanwhile troops and mechanized equipment continued to pour into Indo-China. President Roosevelt, who kept in close touch with the conversations and participated in them on occasion, on December 2 asked the Japanese (through a memorandum addressed to the Secretary and Under Secretary of State and presented by Sumner Welles to the Japanese Ambassador) to explain why so large an army was being mobilized in Indo-China. Reports from the Far East at that moment indicated that an invasion of Thailand was about to begin. Premier Tojo belligerently declared on November 29 that British and American exploitation of Asiatic peoples must be "purged with a vengeance." His Government's reply to the President's question on December 5 was evasive.[71] Reinforcements did not exceed the numbers agreed upon with France, it stated, and

[70] The attack on Pearl Harbor was commenced before the two weeks were out.

[71] Department of State, *Bulletin,* December 20, 1941, p. 540; text of President's letter, *ibid.*, p. 464; on December 6 an official release of the Department of State set at 125,000 the number of Japanese troops in Indo-China.

they were needed to offset the threat of invasion allegedly created by heavy concentrations of Chinese troops on the Indo-Chinese border.

In a final gesture designed, in the words of the President, "to exhaust every conceivable effort for peace," President Roosevelt, on December 6, addressed a letter to Emperor Hirohito. After speaking of the long and prosperous era of peace between America and Japan, and of the desire of the American people that peace should be maintained, the President referred to the heavy concentrations of Japanese troops in Indo-China and of the consequent apprehension that attacks in one or more directions were in contemplation. Affirming that no other state was considering an attack upon Indo-China, he appealed to the Emperor to

> give thought in this definite emergency to ways of dispelling the dark clouds.

The President said further:

> I am confident that both of us, for the sake of the peoples not only of our own great countries, but for the sake of humanity in neighboring territories, have a sacred duty to restore traditional amity and prevent further death and destruction in the world.

The Emperor, so the Japanese Foreign Minister told the United States Ambassador on December 8, 7:00 A.M., Tokyo time (December 7, 5:00 P.M., E.S.T.), desired that the Japanese memorandum which had been delivered to the Secretary of State at 2:20 P.M. E.S.T. be regarded as his reply. The Emperor's message to the President, as quoted from the minister's oral statement, "trusts that the President is fully aware" of the Emperor's "earnest endeavors" for peace in the Pacific and in the world. President Roosevelt's comment on this communication was:[72]

[72] Department of State, *Bulletin*, December 20, 1941, p. 535.

Japan's real reply, however, made by Japan's war lords and evidently formulated many days before, took the form of the attack which had already been made without warning upon our territories at various points in the Pacific.

Attack on Pearl Harbor

At 7:50 A.M. Honolulu time (1:20 P.M. E.S.T.) on Sunday, December 7, 1941, the Japanese attacked Pearl Harbor from the air. The great Pacific war had begun. Ambassador Nomura and Mr. Kurusu chose a moment (E.S.T. 2:20 P.M.) shortly after bombs began to fall on Hawaiian barracks to present their Government's reply to Secretary Hull's note. This conjuncture of events provoked Mr. Hull to say that it was "now apparent to the whole world that Japan in its recent professions of a desire for peace has been infamously false and fraudulent." [73] The memorandum, in part already referred to above, was otherwise a general denunciation of American policy. Its argument carried the conclusion that:

> Obviously it is the intention of the American Government to conspire with Great Britain and other countries to obstruct Japan's efforts toward the establishment of peace through the creation of a new order in East Asia, and especially to preserve Anglo-American rights and interests by keeping Japan and China at war.

The memorandum concluded with a notification that "it is impossible to reach an agreement through further negotiations." As in 1894 and in 1904, Japan served notice, after the peace had been broken, that peaceful methods must be abandoned.

[73] *Ibid.*, December 13, 1941, p. 461; the Japanese memorandum is reprinted in Appendix, p. 317–24.

XIII

BRITAIN'S SECONDARY ROLE

BRITISH interests called for British leadership in resistance to Japan. They included the largest share in China's foreign trade (21.8% in 1936), and shipping (57% in 1936),[1] the largest investment in Chinese Government obligations and in British and foreign business and industrial establishments in China (£238,000,000 in 1931),[2] the leading position in the administration of the Chinese Customs Service, the colony of Hong Kong and the adjacent leased territory of Kowloon, and extensive claims to economic preference based upon spheres of interest. Beyond China they reached into the Netherlands East Indies and Thailand. With the unfolding of the scroll of Japanese ambition, not only India, Burma, Malaya and the East Indian and Central Pacific island possessions of Britain, but Australia and New Zealand appeared to be endangered. And their danger was shared by the British Isles and the Near Eastern and African colonies and the Commonwealth when the Germans and the Japanese joined forces to destroy the British Empire.

The United Kingdom, under the cabinets of Ramsay MacDonald, Stanley Baldwin and Neville Chamberlain, deliberately chose to play a conciliatory role from the beginning of the Sino-Japanese controversy in 1931. British policy appeared, if not to welcome, at least to tolerate the rise of Japan

[1] *China Year Book, 1939,* cited, p. 549, 612.

[2] Friedman, Irving S., *British Relations with China, 1931–1939,* New York, 1940, p. 9; the British journal, *Finance and Commerce* of Shanghai (Empire Trade Supplement, June 25, 1941), estimated British holdings of Chinese government bonds on June 1, 1941, at £16,000,000, one half in general loans, one half in railways.

as a stabilizing force against Chinese nationalism.[3] While it was opposed to the destruction of the Chinese state and contributed importantly to the maintenance of Chinese resistance, it was willing to bargain with Japan concerning interests in China. Unfortunately for the United Kingdom, the Japanese program was not so tolerant. By the time this fact had got home to Downing Street, the European menace was so urgent that British diplomacy in the Far East could not reassume its traditional authority. Britain's role became secondary to that of the United States.

Proposals of Anglo-Japanese Cooperation

The assistance of the British Economic Adviser, Sir Frederick Leith-Ross, to the Chinese Government in the establishment of a managed paper currency was hardly calculated to evoke a cooperative attitude toward Great Britain in Japan.[4] Yet in 1936 a plan of cooperation attributed to Sir Samuel Hoare, then First Lord of the Admiralty, was made public.[5] It contemplated British recognition of "Manchoukuo" and of extensive Japanese claims in North China, in return for Japan's reaffirmation of respect for the "Open Door," the territorial integrity of China and British rights and interests. It included provision for reciprocal trade arrangements, aid to Japan in matters of raw materials and immigration and limitation of naval building. This plan smacks of the old sphere-of-interest program. It was as inconsistent with the spirit of the Nine-Power treaty as with Japan's theory of a "new order." Although it did not represent the views of Anthony Eden, the Foreign Secretary, its prospects of partial success in 1937, which were ended by the outbreak of hostilities, caused apprehension in China.

[3] For British policy in the Manchurian issue see Quigley and Blakeslee, cited, Chapter IX; for a fuller account, Friedman, cited, Chapter II.

[4] Quigley and Blakeslee, cited, p. 194–6.

[5] Kamikawa, H., "An Anglo-Japanese Agreement," *Contemporary Japan,* V, 1936, p. 346–7.

British Efforts at Mediation

Throughout the years after Lukouchiao the British Government was consistently alert to opportunities for mediation between China and Japan. The first overtures were made within a week of the Lukouchiao incident. Since this incident followed a period of pressure for Chinese "cooperation" with Japan,[6] the British counsel could have no other effect than to aid Japan's effort. Again while the battle of Shanghai was at its height mediation was offered, again rejected by Japan. British "port merchants" and the leading British newspaper, the *North China Herald,* strongly urged the Chinese to capitulate during the disastrous autumn of 1938 that saw the fall of Canton and Hankow. The British Government, although finding no opportunity to mediate at that time, expressed, through Mr. Chamberlain, the cynical view that British capital would be needed by the Japanese for the reconstruction of China when the war ended.[7]

The United Kingdom's representatives at the Brussels Conference [8] were under instructions to defer to the position taken by the United States, which reduced the role of the conference to an attempt at conciliation. This type of action was implicit also in the action proceeding from the resolutions [9] of October 6, 1937, and February 2, 1938, passed by the Assembly and the Council, respectively, of the League of Nations, in which members were invited to consider "how far they could individually extend aid to China" but were also asked to "lose no opportunity of examining in consultation with similarly interested Powers, the feasibility of any further steps which may contribute to a just settlement." In a number of statements the British Foreign Office affirmed that it had in-

[6] Quigley and Blakeslee, cited, Chapter VIII.
[7] Friedman, cited, p. 160–7.
[8] Quigley and Blakeslee, cited, p. 119–22.
[9] Appendix, p. 325–30.

formed the Chinese and Japanese Governments of its readiness to lend good offices toward a settlement.[10]

Surrender of Customs Administration

Although the Chinese Maritime Customs Administration was, as its title implies, a Chinese Government service, the interest of foreign states in this service had been recognized in an agreement of 1858 entitled "Rules of Trade," entered into between China on the one hand, and separately, Great Britain, France and the United States on the other.[11] By the tenth rule of this agreement it was provided "that one uniform system shall be enforced at every port." Since British trade was far greater than that of any other country the "Rules of Trade" authorized the participation of a British subject in the service. Under this agreement the Chinese Government had regularly appointed a British subject as inspector-general, the highest officer in the service, and he had appointed numerous other British subjects and smaller numbers from other nationalities to the more responsible posts. In 1898 and again in 1908 Great Britain had obtained the pledge of China that the position of inspector-general should remain in British hands as long as British trade with China should be greater than that of any other country. Thus a position merely authorized by the original agreement had become a British prerogative by virtue of long-continued practice.

It would appear to follow from the fact that the original agreement was made with three foreign states rather than one, that any change in the status of the Customs service would require the consent of all three. This observation

[10] E.g., see *Finance and Commerce* (Shanghai), June 8, 1938, p. 454; also *Parliamentary Debates,* House of Commons, Vol. 338, cols. 2961–62.

[11] Mayers, W. F., *Treaties between the Empire of China and Foreign Powers,* 2d ed., Shanghai, 1897, p. 30.

applies with equal force to the right of China to be consulted. However, there is no evidence that either France or the United States objected to the *modus vivendi* outlined below. The protest of China was strongly worded but was ignored.[12]

Japan's occupation of North China ports was not accompanied by the taking over of the local Customs offices on behalf of the Provisional Government at Peking. With the fall of Shanghai, however, conversations were inaugurated at Tokyo between the Foreign Office and the British Ambassador. On May 3, 1938, the Japanese Government issued a statement that it had "notified His Majesty's Government in the United Kingdom of the temporary measures which they propose to take, during the hostilities, to regulate these matters" and that it had received assurances that the British Government would not object to them.[13] The salient provision was that all revenues collected within the area of Japanese occupation would be deposited in the Yokohama Specie Bank. Previously they had gone to the Hong Kong-Shanghai Bank. The general foreign interest in these funds was safeguarded by the provision that the amounts required to pay interest and principal charges on foreign loans would be regarded as a first charge on the revenues, after deduction of the costs of administering the service, and would be remitted to the Inspector-General.

This concession to Japanese military power was unavoidable under the circumstances. It proved to be a futile effort to protect the interests of foreign bondholders since the pledge to pay over the necessary funds was not kept. Moreover, although Sir Frederick Maze, the Inspector-General, retained his post, an appointee of the "Reformed Government" at Nanking, Li Chien-nan, was named to the position

[12] *Chinese Year Book, 1938–1939,* cited, p. 624; *China Weekly Review,* May 21, 1938, p. 341.

[13] Appendix, p. 331.

of Superintendent of Customs, and a new schedule of tariffs highly favorable to Japan was placed in operation.[14] *De facto* control thus passed to the puppet regime. Deprived of funds, the National Government at Chungking was compelled to reduce payments on bonds secured upon them early in 1939, continuing to pay only such part of the amounts falling due as the small proportion of customs receipts collected by it permitted.[15]

Resistance to Japan

Paralleling British moves to avoid open conflict with Japan by partially satisfying the latter's demands were protests against damage to commercial and other interests and injuries to British subjects. In the flagrant case of a bombing and machine-gun attack upon the automobile of the British Ambassador, on August 26, 1937, the British Government did not demand a monetary indemnity but asked for an apology, punishment of responsible officers and assurances against recurrence of attacks, basing its request not upon diplomatic immunities but upon those of non-combatants. It felt obliged to be content with a somewhat evasive and vague expression of regret.[16]

The British gunboat *Ladybird* and three other British patrol craft, as well as merchant ships, were fired upon by Japanese land and air forces on the Yangtze above Nanking on December 12, 1937, the date of the sinking of U. S. S.

[14] *China Weekly Review,* May 7, 1938, p. 284; May 14, 1938, p. 307; June 10, 1939, p. 37–8; *China Year Book, 1939,* p. 97–9.

[15] Japanese failure to pay over Customs funds was excused on the ground that the Chinese National Government had repudiated the arrangement and had refused to honor the British pledge that some £400,000 of Boxer Indemnity funds, which had been withheld, and $25,000,000 Mex. in accumulated Customs receipts, would be released to Japan. The new Superintendent discontinued remittances after the payment of approximately $1,000,000 Mex. in June 1938.

[16] *Japan Weekly Chronicle,* September 2, 1937, p. 317; *Contemporary Japan,* VI, 1937, p. 567–8.

Panay.[17] Although the Japanese Government apologized and promised amends without waiting for the British protest, the latter reminded Japan of previous incidents and assurances, and suggested that the problem of guarding against repetition of attacks might be discussed. The British protest succeeded in obtaining a Japanese pledge to accord the same respect to merchant shipping as to naval craft. But the contrast between the mild reproof and readiness to accept apologies and indemnities and the vigorous imperialism of the nineteenth century was not lost upon the Japanese.

Evidence is strong that British businessmen in China held to the hope that Chinese resistance would not be prolonged and that they were mainly concerned with obtaining an early conclusion of the fighting in order that foreign trade might be revived. Thus both in China and in London there was a spirit of defeatism respecting China's cause. However, this spirit did not extend to ideas of the future of British interests. The "Open Door" was firmly insisted upon, though its dependence upon an actually free China seemed not to be clearly realized. Only after many disappointments did British merchants accept the unpleasant reality that the eradication of their dominant position was only secondary to control of China in the policy of Japan.

A stronger note was sounded by Ambassador Craigie in a statement of his Government's position on January 14, 1939,[18] following a note of November 7 which paralleled American and French protests, of the same date, against the failure to open the Yangtze to foreign shipping other than Japanese.[19] Sir Robert Craigie's communication, somewhat inconsistent with Prime Minister Chamberlain's suggestion that British capital would profit by an early peace, expressed opposition, in diplomatic language, to Premier Konoye's recently an-

[17] *Contemporary Japan*, VII, 1938, p. 774–8.
[18] Jones and Myers, *Documents*, I, p. 252–4.
[19] None of these notes has been published.

nounced program for a tripartite bloc composed of Japan, China and "Manchoukuo." The United Kingdom, it stated, intended to adhere to the Nine-Power treaty:

> His Majesty's Government . . . cannot agree, as is suggested in Japan, that the Treaty is obsolete or that its provisions no longer meet the situation, except in so far as the situation has been altered by Japan in contravention of its terms.

The United Kingdom's position, like that of the United States, as laid down in its note of December 31, 1938, did not insist that "treaties are eternal." It required, however, that modification be obtained by negotiation between all the signatories and offered to consider "constructive suggestions" by Japan to that end. While pointing out that Prince Konoye's offer to consider abolition of extraterritoriality and foreign concessions in China would entail small sacrifice for Japan if it were to get control of China, Sir Robert referred to earlier negotiations on extraterritoriality and said:

> . . . His Majesty's Government have always been ready to resume negotiations at a suitable time and are prepared to discuss this and other similar questions with a fully independent Chinese Government when peace has been restored.

British Aid to China

With the fall of Shanghai, Canton became the principal port of entry for the National Government. The position of Hong Kong, a British colony off the mouth of the Pearl River, made it the warehouse for the port of Canton. Through it large supplies of war materials from several countries moved in increasing volume. Hong Kong prospered correspondingly until Canton surrendered to Japan on October 21, 1938. It also provided a neutral meeting-place for Chinese factional conferences. Although Japanese official statements strongly criticized Great Britain for aiding the Chinese cause, their

Government hesitated to challenge British commercial interests by attacking Canton until the Munich Conference in September 1938 gave it confidence. The capture of the southern metropolis, followed by the closure of the Pearl River, dammed the stream of military supplies to Free China, endangered the food-supply of Hong Kong, and threatened to destroy a highly profitable commerce.

Anxious to avoid any possibility of hostilities with Japan, the British Government was slow to heed Chinese requests and the urgings of liberal-minded people within the United Kingdom for financial aid. Closure of the Pearl River and Japanese rejection of protests against their acts and declared program appear to have influenced the British Export Credits Guarantee Department to provide a credit of £450,000 in December 1938 to the National Government of China for the purchase of British motor trucks and road-making machinery.[20] This move would assist in building the Yunnan-Burma highway, compensate interests in Burma for losses in Hong Kong, and assure an avenue of approach for trade and investment in Free China. The political significance of the loan lay in its testimony to something more than words in the developing parallelism of the United Kingdom and the United States.

British interest extended further to the consideration of assistance to the Chungking Government in building a railway, first from the border of Burma to Hsiangkwei, 300 miles to the east, and ultimately to Chungking via Kunming, a total distance of 1200 miles. The British and Chinese Corporation discussed with the Chinese Government early in 1939 the possibility of financing the project through a loan of £10,000,000. Although work was begun on preparation of a road-bed in February 1939, no announcement of a loan contract has been made public. Agreements in April 1939 and June 1941, by which the United Kingdom and China each

[20] *New York Times,* December 18, 1938.

ceded to the other small strips of land along the Yunnan-Burma border, appeared to be designed to facilitate the building of the railway.[21]

Another British financial gesture was the provision, in March 1939, of £5,000,000 to support the Chinese stabilization fund. The British Government guaranteed the two principal British Far Eastern banks against loss, the banks agreeing to provide the funds.[22] In the following month £3,000,000 was added to the credits advanced by the Export Credits agency, to be expended on machinery and munitions. Thereafter no British credits were forthcoming until December 1940, when £10,000,000 was made available, £5,000,000 for China's stabilization fund and the remainder for the purchase of materials within the sterling area. An agreement covering the stabilization fund was signed in Washington by British and Chinese representatives on April 26, 1941. The United Kingdom thus aligned itself firmly with the United States in furnishing financial aid to China.[23]

Recognition of Japanese Military Position

The long interim between the United Kingdom's loans of April 1939 and April 1941 was a period of humiliating acquiescence on the part of a nation faced with disaster at home and desperately anxious to avoid military attack upon its Far Eastern interests. Conscious of British unpreparedness, and desirous of closer relations with Germany, the Japanese Government did its utmost to stimulate anti-British feeling in China and in other ways to make existence there intolerable for British subjects. The treatment of British interests in Shanghai, Tientsin and other concessions

[21] *China Weekly Review,* May 13, 1939, p. 341; June 28, 1941, p. 121.
[22] Friedman, cited, p. 189.
[23] *New York Times,* December 11, 1940; Jones and Myers, *Documents,* III, p. 241–5.

is dealt with in an earlier chapter.[24] In the course of prolonged discussions at Tokyo regarding the issues raised at Tientsin, the Japanese sought assiduously to obtain British recognition of the "new order" in China. In this they failed, but they extorted from the hard-pressed British the following formula: [25]

> His Majesty's Government in the United Kingdom fully recognize the actual situation in China where hostilities on a large scale are in progress, and note that, as long as that state of affairs continues to exist, the Japanese forces in China have special requirements for the purpose of safeguarding their own security and maintaining public order in the regions under their control, and that they have to suppress or remove any such acts or causes as will obstruct them or benefit their enemy.
>
> His Majesty's Government have no intention of countenancing any acts or measures prejudicial to the attainment of the abovementioned objects by the Japanese forces and they will take this opportunity to confirm their policy in this respect by making it plain to the British authorities and the British nationals in China that they should refrain from such acts and measures.

The Craigie-Arita "agreement" threw a heavy weight of responsibility upon the United States in maintaining Western rights and Chinese morale. While, in terms, it was limited in application to regions under Japanese control, its broader significance lay in its revelation of Britain's impotence in the presence of European developments. It gave confidence to the Japanese and correspondingly depressed the hopes which British loans had raised in the Chinese. Actually, however, it was so vague as to be little more than a diplomatic formula, a clever evasion of specific commitments. Undoubtedly it contributed to the delay in Japan's adherence

[24] See Chapter VIII.

[25] *China Weekly Review*, July 29, 1939, p. 255–6; the statement was dated July 24, 1939; the *Asama Maru* incident, in which a British naval commander removed 21 Germans from a Japanese liner near the Japanese coast, occurred in January 1940, during the negotiations.

to the German-Italian axis. Whether or not Britain need have made the agreement is a pertinent question. That the British Government desired to make it cannot be assumed. Undoubtedly confidence was lacking that assistance in a firmer stand from other states was likely to be forthcoming.

Temporary Closure of the Burma Road

A year later British resistance fell to its lowest point with the closure of the Burma route into Yunnan at the behest of Japan. A few months prior to this action Great Britain had followed the American lead in refusing to accord recognition to the new government of Wang Ch'ing-wei.[26] But the collapse of France and the Japanese invasion of Indo-China, justifying anticipation of invasion at home and in Burma, caused the British Government to comply, after brief demur, to the Japanese demand of July 24, 1940, for closure of the Burma route, which had become the principal avenue of supply for Free China. Prime Minister Churchill announced on July 18 that:[27]

> The Government of Burma have agreed to suspend, for a period of three months, the transit to China of arms and ammunition, as well as . . . petrol, lorries and railways material. The categories of goods prohibited in Burma will be prohibited in Hong Kong.

Mr. Churchill's explanation, in which he pointed out that "His Majesty's Government . . . could [not] ignore the dominant fact that we are ourselves engaged in a life and

[26] *Chinese Year Book, 1940–1941,* cited, p. 268–9; Ambassador Craigie's speech in Tokyo on March 28, 1940, was unnecessarily cordial to Japan, awakening fear in China that his Government would recognize Wang; Britain contented itself with a "serious view" of the death of M. J. Cox, a journalist, while in custody of the Japanese police in Tokyo; the latter reported that Mr. Cox had committed suicide in fear of punishment as a spy. (*New York Times,* July 30, 31, 1940.)

[27] *Ibid.*, p. 276; Jones and Myers, *Documents,* III, p. 270–1.

death struggle," must be accepted as sincere. He declared that his Government wished to see "China's status and integrity preserved," and reiterated the pledge of January 14, 1939, respecting extraterritoriality, concessions and reciprocal treaties. His reference to Japan was an admirably concise phrasing of a fair deal for Japan:

> We wish to see Japan attain that state of prosperity which will insure to her population the welfare and economic security which every Japanese naturally desires. Towards attainment of the aims of both these nations, we are prepared to offer our collaboration and our contribution. But it must be clear that if they are to be attained, it must be by a process of peace and conciliation, and not by war or threat of war.

The United Kingdom again sought to mediate between the Chinese and Japanese during the period of closure.

When the three months expired, on October 18, 1940, the Burma Road was reopened in spite of Japan's further progress in reducing Indo-China to vassalage. In the meantime, however, the removal of British garrison forces from China appeared to weaken the common front of Western resistance to the "new order." The British War Office announced the decision to transfer the 1500 men remaining in China on August 9, 1940.[28] Actually the departure of the troops lessened restraints upon British action outside China, as the reopening of the Burma Road testified. Undoubtedly of greater importance to this action was the increasing evidence of American determination to resist a totalitarian "new order." The United Kingdom did not, however, reopen Hong Kong to embargoed trade, nor did it resist Japanese seizure of Liu Kung Island, summer station of the British navy off Weihaiwei.[29]

[28] *New York Times,* August 10, 1940; the *China Weekly Review* estimated 2000 as the strength of British garrison troops. (August 17, 1940, p. 415.)

[29] *New York Times,* October 9, 1940.

Effort to Maintain Peace in the Pacific

British policy was consistent in bending every effort toward avoidance of war with Japan, not for the Empire only but also for the United States. Mr. Churchill informed the Japanese Ambassador in February 1941, that his Government was thinking only of victory in Europe, that it desired to solve Far Eastern issues by pacific means, and that movements of troops, warcraft and planes to Asiatic positions were purely defensive.[30] British necessity for American materials of war and desire for American participation in the European struggle motivated diplomatic moves to restrain the United States from war in the Pacific. Collaboration in American economic measures against Japanese trade was, however, continued in the order of July 26, 1941, freezing Japanese assets in retaliation for the occupation of Indo-China. Foreign Secretary Eden also warned Japan that occupation of Thailand would be a matter of concern to his country, thereby paralleling a similar warning by Secretary Hull.[31] These warnings were attended by blunt avowals of the intention to meet any Japanese action with counter-action.

Mr. Churchill's statement in the House of Commons on August 24, 1941, that if American efforts toward peace should fail "we shall, of course, range ourselves unhesitatingly at the side of the United States" was applicable only to war at a distance from British territories. Obviously Britain would defend its own soil to the best of its ability, with or without allies. Mr. Churchill can hardly be supposed to have given the United States a blank check. His Government's views were bound to influence American decisions from day to day. However, the Prime Minister's unequivocal affirmation of

[30] *Ibid.,* February 26, 1941.
[31] *Ibid.,* August 7, 1941.

November 10, 1941, that if hostilities should break out between Japan and the United States, Britain would declare war "within the hour," left no room for doubt regarding British readiness to follow American leadership.

British Interests in Southeastern Asia

No consideration of British concern for imperial territory is called for here. It was taken for granted that sovereignty would be defended. It is clear, also, that the political status of French Indo-China, Thailand and the Netherlands East Indies, because of the proximity of these areas to British colonies and dominions, was of vital importance to the United Kingdom. Not only the danger of conquest but the stimulus to nationalist movements in India, Burma and Malaya had to be kept in mind. It is true that British commercial and financial interests were involved, as well as access to strategic materials. A brief survey will indicate however that the last-mentioned factor was of relatively small significance. Political and strategic aspects are dealt with in a later chapter.

British investment in and trade with French Indo-China were negligible, since French policy had produced a close integration between the colonv and the mother country.[32] Thailand, on the other hand. was "economically little more than a satellite of the British Empire." [33] The British held all but a small fraction of the little nation's foreign debt, which is small, and British direct investments in tin mines, teak forests and other enterprises exceeded all others. For the five years 1934–35 to 1938–39 Thailand's trade with the British Empire averaged 70.68% of its total foreign trade. All of the country's production of tin, which rose from 12,988 long tons in 1938 to 16,887 in 1939, has been shipped to Singa-

[32] *Far Eastern Survey,* August 14, 1940, p. 195–201.
[33] *Ibid.,* March 12, 1941, p. 46–7.

pore for smelting.[34] Although the rubber plantations are largely owned by Chinese, the product is distributed from Singapore. Rubber production in 1939 totalled 41,270 long tons.

Since 1932, when a revolution was followed by the establishment of a constitutional regime, Thailand's efforts have been devoted to freeing itself from external economic controls.[35] Although relations with Great Britain have been somewhat unfavorably affected by the nationalist movement, Thailand entered, in 1940, into a non-aggression pact with the United Kingdom. It is apparent that Thai nationalism should have operated to oppose such a degree of Japanese penetration as Indo-China had experienced. But Thailand's weakness prevented an independent policy and forced the country to cultivate the goodwill of both Britain and Japan. Thailand's historical claim to portions of northern Malaya offered an opportunity to Britain, as it did to Japan, to ingratiate itself with Bangkok.

British economic interests in the Netherlands East Indies were principally in the oil fields. Fifty-five per cent of oil production there was controlled by Anglo-Dutch companies. The rubber and tin of the Indies yielded rich returns to the distributors and smelters of Singapore and to British shippers but the British resources in Malaya were so great as to render it unnecessary to depend upon those of the Netherlands East Indies. Approximately 17% of the total exports from the Indies in 1938 was absorbed by British territories. The low purchasing power of the natives in the Indies has prevented the development of any considerable market for British goods.[36]

[34] United States Department of Commerce, *Economic Review of Foreign Countries, 1939 and Early 1940*, p. 351.

[35] *Far Eastern Survey*, October 23, 1940, p. 243–51.

[36] Emerson, R., "The Dutch East Indies Adrift," *Foreign Affairs*, XVIII, July 1940, p. 735–41.

The Position of Australia

Brief consideration, however inadequate, may suffice to indicate the relations of the three British Dominions in the Pacific area to the Far Eastern war. Of the three, Australia was the most seriously affected in its economic life and the most concerned with the problem of defense. Although prior to July 1937, there was anxiety in Australia over the aggressive program of Japan, this was counterbalanced by the desire for trade, Japan being Australia's second best customer and importing 85 to 95% of its raw wool from that state.[37] At the Imperial Conference in May 1937, the Australian Government advocated a non-aggression pact for the Pacific area, to include the United States and Japan.

The trade war of 1936, prompted by considerations of imperial preference and national defense, culminated at the end of that year in an agreement designed to restore normal conditions, though continuing limitations which the Japanese would have preferred to do away with entirely. The desired restoration was prevented by the development of Japan's program for self-sufficiency, induced by its necessity to conserve exchange for the purchase of war materials. The Japanese market for Australian iron improved but could not be utilized because of the Australian Government's embargo on the export of iron which it required for its own defense industries.[38] Taking the long view, the Australian Government permitted the continuance of Japanese imports in accordance with the agreement, and advocated lenient treatment of Japan as a matter of international policy.

When, in 1938, stevedores at Sydney, Melbourne and other

[37] Shepherd, Jack, *Australia's Interests and Policies in the Far East*, New York, 1940, p. 43, 60.

[38] Australian wool exports were rendered unavailable to Japan except by concession of the British Government, which had contracted for the entire exportable surplus; some wool was obtained in that way by Japan.

ports refused to load iron and scrap metal for shipment to Japan, the Government threatened legal action and broke the boycott, only to place an embargo on all export of iron on July 1 of that year. Australian policy in general paralleled that of the United Kingdom, exhibiting a conciliatory attitude which reflected political necessity rather than the moral sentiments of the people. In August 1940, when British prestige was suffering most severely from the hectoring of Japan, the Australian Government appointed its first minister to Japan, the distinguished jurist, Sir John Latham.[39] Japan appointed Tatsuo Kawai minister to Australia. One of Mr. Kawai's first public utterances was a denial of a prediction made earlier by A. W. Fadden, Acting Prime Minister of Australia, that British reverses in Europe would impel Japan to aggression in the south Pacific.[40]

Appointment of Sir Frederic Eggleston as minister to China in July 1941, was coincidental with a marked change in Australia's official attitude regarding Japan's policy. Australia followed the British lead in freezing Japanese assets. Cabinet ministers spoke out strongly. Mr. Hughes, naval minister, reproved Japan for talking of encirclement after seizing territories fifty times the area of Japan proper. "Australia," he said, "cannot look on these movements of Japan into other countries, threatening the foundations of the Empire and Australian interests in the Far East, and do nothing." [41] The Minister for External Affairs, Sir Frederic Stewart, was equally emphatic: [42]

> The Japanese must realize that the only encirclement they have to fear is the combination of those countries that feel their vital interests are threatened by Japanese aggression. The responsibility of raising such a combination would be Japan's alone.

[39] *New York Times,* August 19, 1940.
[40] *Ibid.,* April 29, 1941.
[41] *Ibid.,* August 9, 1941.
[42] *Ibid.,* August 11, 1941.

New Zealand's Position

Like Australia, New Zealand desired to expand its exports to Japan, which was a much larger market than China for New Zealand's wool and dairy products.[43] The coalition cabinet of 1931 was indifferent to the invasion of Manchuria, but in 1937 New Zealand had a Labor government which expressed itself strongly in favor of international sanctions at Geneva and in the Brussels Conference. Nevertheless official measures were taken, as in Australia, to induce stevedores to load scrap iron for Japan until, in October 1937, all export of scrap metal was placed under embargo. New Zealand took parallel action with Great Britain in freezing Japanese assets and abrogated its commercial treaty with Japan.[44] Prime Minister Peter Fraser, a Laborite, stated in Washington that New Zealand would cooperate fully with the United States if the latter became involved in war with Japan.[45]

The Position of Canada

"In a war in which Japan and the United States were the sole belligerents, the United States would have Canada's sympathies, but Ottawa would probably make an effort, at first, to remain neutral." [46]

Professor Lower's statement, which does not contemplate Canada's probable attitude toward an Anglo-American-Japanese war, is quoted only for its revelation of Canada's attitude of aloofness from a problem that so deeply concerns

[43] Milner, Ian F. G., *New Zealand's Interests and Policies in the Far East,* New York, 1940, p. 39; for the six years 1930–1935 inclusive, New Zealand's exports to Japan averaged in value £383,741, exports to China £25,152.

[44] *New York Times,* July 29, 1941.

[45] *Ibid.,* August 27, 1941.

[46] Lower, A. R. M., *Canada and the Far East — 1940,* Toronto, 1941, p. 109.

the United States. This attitude is not based upon moral considerations. Canadian sentiment probably has been as pro-Chinese as that of the people of the United States. But Canadian interests—"order, prosperity and peace" in the Western Pacific—did not, apparently, call for opposition to Japan. Nonetheless, Canada did not hesitate to range itself with the United States when war began.

Canada's trade with Eastern Asia averaged approximately 4½% of its total foreign trade between 1926 and 1935.[47] Wheat, flour, wood products, nickel and copper led among exports, which exceeded imports from 60 to 100% prior to the invasion of Manchuria but decreased in ratio of excess after 1932. Total trade with Japan was more than double that with China between 1929 and 1933.[48] Having risen rapidly after 1914 to $55,000,000 with Japan, and $27,200,000 with China in 1929, it fell during the depression to $14,200,000 (1933) with Japan and $9,300,000 with China. In 1928 the Canadian Government established a legation in Tokyo. It has no diplomatic or consular officers of its own in China.

Canada's involvement in the European war limited its capacity to export to the Far East. Metals were placed under license, which in practice meant a virtual embargo.[49] Lumber exports dropped nearly to zero for the same reason. Ottawa followed London in freezing Japanese assets in July 1941. Thereupon the Canadian Pacific Steamship Company closed its offices in Japan.[50]

Imperial Defense

The British navy grew from a total of 188 combatant vessels of 1,079,133 tons at the beginning of 1938 to a total

[47] Strange, Wm., *Canada, the Pacific and War,* Toronto, 1937, p. 156.
[48] *Ibid.,* p. 162.
[49] *Far Eastern Survey,* July 28, 1941, p. 162.
[50] *New York Times,* August 11, 1941.

of 368 vessels of unstated tonnage on February 1, 1941.[51] On the latter date the navy was composed of 16 battleships, eight aircraft carriers, 66 cruisers, 233 destroyers and 45 submarines. Seven battleships, four carriers and numbers of other types were then under construction. While it is impossible to state the geographical distribution of ships, it must be assumed that British strength in the Pacific was negligible in relation to that of Japan. Mr. Churchill stated on November 10, 1941, that the British then felt themselves strong enough to provide a powerful naval force of heavy ships if needed in the Indian and Pacific Oceans but not until the beginning of December 1941 was public notice given of the stationing of the battleship *Prince of Wales* and a considerable squadron of other vessels at Singapore.

At the outbreak of the war in 1939, the strength of the Canadian navy, including reserves, was about 3600 men and it had 13 ships of all kinds. On November 1, 1941, its mobilized strength was about 25,000 men, and it mustered 300 ships – including 13 destroyers, three armed merchant cruisers, a number of corvettes and minesweepers and a large fleet of smaller craft suitable for patrol and anti-submarine work. By March 1942, the strength of the Royal Canadian Navy was expected to be at least 27,000 men and more than 400 ships.[52]

In December 1940, Australia possessed six cruisers, four destroyers and a number of other ships; three destroyers, 12 motor torpedo-boats and 48 minesweepers of a new type were building or completing.[53] The fleet of the Netherlands East Indies, which could be counted upon to cooperate with

[51] Quigley and Blakeslee, cited, p. 321; Jones and Myers, *Documents,* III, p. 694; Mr. Churchill stated on December 10, after the sinking of the *Prince of Wales,* that Great Britain still had 20 battleships in commission.

[52] *Canada at War,* Director of Public Information, Ottawa, Canada, No. 8, November 1, 1941, p. 11.

[53] Green, J. F., "The British Dominions at War," *Foreign Policy Reports,* February 1, 1940; *The Statesman's Year-Book, 1941,* p. 358.

British forces, consisted of four cruisers, 12 destroyers, 18 submarines and some 50 torpedo boats in July 1941.

The principal reliance of the British for the defense of their interests in Eastern Asia and the Pacific was upon Singapore. That great naval base was opened on February 14, 1938. An immobile base may impede the attack of an enemy upon neighboring territory, but it cannot prevent eventual success of such attacks without an adequate defending fleet and air force. In fact its principal purpose is to afford the fleet facilities for dry-docking, restocking its lockers and larders and refueling. At no time since the base was opened has the United Kingdom been able to provide an adequate fleet.[54] The United States navy was the only possible source of such a fleet after the spring of 1940. Whether "possible" should become "actual" depended upon the strength that the navy could spare while meeting other responsibilities.

Not only was Singapore impotent in itself to guard British, Dutch and American territories, but unless it should prove capable of withstanding attack from a powerful enemy, it would, in the event of war, become a center of enemy operations against those territories. In order to prevent such an eventuality British troops were sent to Malaya during 1941 in large contingents. Australians and Hindus mingled with British regulars and native Malays. In February 1941, the strength of the defending forces, aside from native troops, was placed at 50,000 men. However, a considerable portion of these forces was moved to the Near East during the summer. The northern borders and the intervening coasts of Johore and Pahang were manned against invasion by land or sea. The defenses of neighboring Burma also were strengthened. The bases at Rangoon, Burma, and on Penang, Malaya, lie on the western flank of Thailand.

Hong Kong's proximity to China's mainland made the

[54] Dennett, Tyler, "Australia's Defense Problem," *Foreign Affairs,* XVIII, 1939, p. 116–26.

problem of defense there extremely difficult. The British Government determined, however, that it should be defended if attacked, and increased the number of gun batteries on the shores and hillsides of the island. Naval and air strength there was negligible. Kowloon, British leased territory on the adjacent mainland, could not, with total forces of a few thousand men, be held against an army. But Hong Kong was expected to hold out long enough to delay an attacker until the island could be relieved from Singapore or elsewhere. A Canadian infantry contingent joined its defenders in November 1941.

Port Darwin in northern Australia, 2500 miles southeast of Singapore, is a fortified naval and air base. Around the coast of Australia the harbors of Cooktown, Brisbane, Sydney, Melbourne, Adelaide and Perth maintain supplies of oil and coal for bunkering ships. Auckland and Wellington, New Zealand, also are bunkering stations. Surabaya, located about halfway between Singapore and Port Darwin, on the north coast of Java, is the best naval and air base in the Netherlands East Indies. It has drydocks for large cruisers and excellent facilities for repair of airplanes. A second Dutch base was situated on the island of Amboina between Celebes and New Guinea. A Dutch air force of some 500 bombers and pursuit planes, and an army more than 100,000 strong, about four fifths native, made the East Indies a useful ally.[55] Eastward from the Indies the South Pacific is virtually a British sea by reason of the many archipelagoes that lie there under the Union Jack. At Vancouver, British Columbia, there are strong shore batteries and an air base. At Prince Rupert, to the north, similar defenses exist, as well as a naval station. The Canadian Government has built a series of air bases from Edmonton, Alberta, to Alaska.

Airpower is inexpensive compared with seapower. Canada,

[55] Bisson, T. A., "The Netherlands Indies at War," *Foreign Policy Reports*, November 1, 1941.

Australia and New Zealand have specialized on the air arm in recent years. The position of Canada as administrator of the Empire Air Training Scheme assured that experience and an air force capable of important action in the Pacific would be available. Australia, which had but 132 airplanes in March 1939, planned, by purchase and home manufacture, to expand this force to 2000 planes, fully manned, by March 1943.[56] New Zealand, in May 1940, contemplated development of its air strength to 310 planes of all types.

[56] *Chicago Daily News,* July 2, 1940.

XIV

SOVIET RUSSIA'S DILEMMA

THE OBJECTIVES of the Soviet Union in Eastern Asia were to maintain the Siberian domain intact, to continue control over the Republic of Outer Mongolia, and to strengthen the economic hegemony which had been developed in Sinkiang. With China it carried on the normal relations resumed in 1924 except for a period of five years, 1927–32, during which the National Government was attempting to stamp out communism. In August 1937 it entered into a non-aggression pact with China which condemned aggression in general terms.[1] Support for the National Government of China through direct participation in the war with Japan by furnishing airplanes and pilots, credits, and advisers, and by sales of war materials was consistently maintained until the fall of 1941 when the Soviets were forced to reserve every means of defense for their own war effort. Soviet aid to China was more important than that of any other state up to that time.

Relations between Moscow and Japan were conducted on a friendly basis after the signature in 1925 of a "convention embodying basic rules."[2] The military clashes along the borders of "Manchoukuo," which began early in 1935 and recurred with increasing severity, did not interrupt diplomatic relations. The Soviets sought a non-aggression pact with Japan but failed to get it. The sale of the Chinese Eastern Railway to "Manchoukuo" in 1935 marked the abandonment by the Soviets of the Tsarist ambition to obtain a

[1] Quigley and Blakeslee, cited, p. 307–8.

[2] *American Journal of International Law,* XIX, 1925, Official Documents Supplement, p. 78–88; Quigley and Blakeslee, cited, p. 211–14.

warm-water port by dominating Manchuria. Soviet strategy aimed at assisting China to survive without becoming involved in Far Eastern hostilities, as the Soviet Government demonstrated in April 1941 by entering into a pact of neutrality with Japan (see p. 296).

Developments in Siberia

Not only Japan's known desire to include the riches of eastern Siberia in its "co-prosperity sphere," but also the necessities of regional autonomy in the economic development of so vast an area, explain the Soviet program of industrialism for Siberia.[3] Migration has been encouraged to considerable effect. An increase of four to five million inhabitants in all Siberia, 1,000,000 in the Far Eastern region, occurred between 1926 and 1939, bringing the Siberian population to more than 19,000,000.[4] Another major item of economic progress is seen in the rise in production of minerals—coal, oil, iron, copper, tin and others. Data on road- and railway-building are difficult to obtain but it is known that sections of a line from Lake Baikal to the mouth of the Amur (port of Sovietskaia Gavan) are in operation.[5] The new city of Konsomolsk on this route is connected by rail with Khabarovsk on the Trans-Siberian Railway. The latter is now double-tracked throughout its entire length. Air lines and telecommunications connect Moscow with Vladivostok.

Military measures cannot be documented with accuracy but available evidence indicates that they have been extensive. Along the borders with "Manchoukuo" have been built a series of concrete forts. In July 1941, the Soviets had in eastern Siberia some 26 divisions of infantry, 10 of cavalry,

[3] *Far Eastern Survey*, July 13, 1938, p. 157–63.

[4] *Ibid.*, January 3, 1940, p. 8.

[5] *Ibid.*, July 17, 1940, p. 181–2; a dispatch to the *New York Times* of April 25, 1941, stated the expectation that the entire line would be opened on November 1, 1941.

4 divisions of tank troops, 2000 aeroplanes and a naval force that included over 100 submarines and also torpedo-boats, gunboats and destroyers.[6] They could count also upon the trained army of Outer Mongolia. Soviet military policy treated the Far Eastern forces as autonomous in personnel, equipment and command, operating independently of those in Europe. To some extent their supply could be provided by industrial plants within Siberia. From Vladivostok, 650 miles by air from Tokyo, bombers might set fire to Japan's wood and paper cities and submarines attack its transports and cargo ships.

Border Hostilities

Commissions to demarcate a definitive boundary between "Manchoukuo," Outer Mongolia and Siberia were agreed upon in 1936 but failed to function. At the end of July 1938, near Changkufeng, on the "Manchoukuo" border with the Maritime Province of Siberia, severe fighting took place, continuing until August 11. It was then agreed at Moscow by Foreign Commissar Litvinov and Ambassador Shigemitsu that a commission would be appointed, consisting of two representatives from each party, the U.S.S.R. and Japan-"Manchoukuo," to redefine the boundary.[7] This agreement has not yet been implemented.

In the following year an even more serious outbreak occurred near Nomonhan on the Mongolian-"Manchoukuoan" border. From May 1939 until September the fighting continued, the Japanese losing 18,000 men killed or badly wounded. A truce was arranged which left the disputed area in Soviet possession. In December a border-delimitation commission convened at Chita, then moved to Harbin. Its con-

[6] *New York Times,* August 8, September 19, 1941.

[7] Bisson, T. A., "Soviet-Japanese Relations: 1931–1938," *Foreign Policy Reports,* February 1, 1939, p. 269–71; *Contemporary Japan,* VII, 1938, p. 387–93.

versations proved fruitless but negotiations between Foreign Commissar Molotov and Ambassador Togo at Moscow reached an agreement "in principle." [8] Not until October 16, 1941 was this agreement completed by a protocol signed at Harbin, which defined the border for a distance of 250 kilometers.[9]

Oil and Fisheries

Oil and coal concessions held under treaty provisions by Japanese companies in the Soviet half of Saghalien have been a cause of diplomatic controversy. The Soviet Government has charged that Russian workmen have been denied the stipulated rations of food, and that failure to increase production has kept royalties low. The Japanese have complained that Soviet procedure in locating wells adjacent to those which they have opened after expensive prospecting is unfair. They have protested also against interference with the hiring of workmen and the importation of certain articles used by Japanese families, and persecution by arrest and imprisonment of Japanese company officials.[10] Their explanation of low output, which ranged between 1,000,000 and 2,000,000 barrels a year prior to 1938, is found in the difficulties resulting from interference by Soviet officials.

Since 1936 the Soviets have declined to enter into a long-term fisheries agreement similar to the treaty of January 23, 1928, which expired in that year.[11] Within a 12-mile limit along the coast of Siberia Japanese are permitted to bid at auction for fishing lots and to lease the lots for which they are successful bidders. Since 1928 Soviet interest in the

[8] *Japan Year Book,* 1940–1941, p. 192–3.

[9] *New York Times,* November 3, 1941.

[10] Iwakura, Baron M., "The Focal Point of Japan-Soviet Relations," *Contemporary Japan,* VII, December 1938, p. 413–20; *Far Eastern Survey,* August 16, 1939, p. 206.

[11] *Far Eastern Survey,* March 27, 1940, p. 75–81; League of Nations, *Treaty Series,* vol. 80, p. 341.

fishing industry has increased, with the result that the percentage of lots obtainable by the Japanese has diminished, although the actual number has increased. Friction over exchange rates, leasing rates, standard catch and other matters have complicated the problem. The Japanese sought to obtain 12-year leases and to have the auctions discontinued. In 1936 a new convention was in process of ratification when the publication of the Anti-Comintern pact aroused such resentment at Moscow that it refused to ratify. Since that date the U.S.S.R. has discussed a new convention annually but nothing has resulted beyond annual extensions of arrangements existing in 1936. It is apparent that the Soviet Government wishes the Japanese fishing operations to continue, but on condition that the terms upon which they are conducted shall admit of no questioning of Russian sovereignty and no restraint upon the development of the national fisheries.[12]

Reaction to Japan's Attack upon China

The Soviet Union entered into a treaty of non-aggression with China on August 21, 1937, within a few weeks of the beginning of the war. Article I of the treaty, which condemns recourse to war for the solution of international controversies, may be viewed as the Soviet justification for assistance to China while maintaining a position of neutrality. Although it was denied that a secret agreement on military aid accompanied the treaty, such aid was given in a variety of forms. The Soviet Ambassador at Chungking stated the attitude of his Government on the occasion of a celebration of the 21st anniversary of the Bolshevik revolution:[13]

[12] In 1940 the Japanese paid nearly 9,000,000 rubles (3,000,000 yen), in rent and taxes on their lots and catch. (*Far Eastern Survey,* March 12, 1941, p. 41.)

[13] *China Weekly Review,* December 17, 1938, p. 83.

Soviet sympathies are wholly and permanently on the side of the oppressed people. Under the leadership of Generalissimo Chiang K'ai-shek, the great Chinese nation is now being united and has presented a united front to oppose the aggressor, and your struggle has won the wholehearted sympathies of the whole Soviet people.

The Soviet Union and New Zealand were the only members of the League Council to urge strong measures against Japan in 1938. Mr. Litvinov criticized the Council's report, which stated that sanctions under Article 16 of the Covenant were left to the discretion of individual members of the League. "My Government," he said, "would be happy to take coordinated measures but since other governments will not do so my Government is compelled to accept the report." [14] Again, in May 1939, Ivan Maisky stated to the Council, after the British and French representatives had declined to support Chinese proposals of economic sanctions, that [15]

> I would like to support the proposals put forward by the Chinese representative . . . China is the victim of brutal and unprovoked aggression and she is fighting hard and heroically for her independence. . .

The commercial accord signed by Sun Fo and A. I. Mikoyan in Moscow on June 16, 1939, provided for the exchange of Chinese raw materials for military supplies.[16] A second agreement was signed in July 1940.[17] Preceding and paralleling these broader conventions were four barter agreements, the first in October 1938 (250,000,000 rubles or approximately U. S. $50,000,000), the second in February 1939 (U. S. $50,000,000), the third in August 1939 (U. S. $150,000,000), and the fourth in December 1940 (U. S.

[14] *Japan Weekly Chronicle,* October 6, 1938, p. 393.
[15] *Chinese Year Book, 1940–1941,* p. 682.
[16] *Ibid.,* p. 693.
[17] *New York Times,* July 27, 1940.

$50,000,000), a total of U. S. $300,000,000.[18] Tungsten, antimony, tea and wool were the principal Chinese products desired by the U.S.S.R. In return China received planes, trucks, tanks, guns and bombs, transported along the Turkestan-Shensi and Vladivostok-Urga-Ninghsia land routes or by sea via Hanoi and Rangoon.

The rapprochement of the Soviet Union and Japan, culminating in the Neutrality Pact of April 13, 1941, appeared to undermine this program of assistance. However, Moscow declined to recognize Wang Ch'ing-wei's government at Nanking and announced that Soviet policy regarding China remained unaffected by Japan's recognition of that government.[19] Undoubtedly the arrangement of credits at Washington and London stiffened China's attitude toward communism within China as well as toward the Soviet dualistic program. Generalissimo Chiang's vigorous disposition of the claims of the Fourth Route Army in the autumn of 1940 was one indication of this new confidence. Dr. Wang Ch'ung-hui, China's Foreign Minister, apprehensive that the Soviet-Japanese neutrality pact involved the former's recognition of "Manchoukuo," issued a denial that such an action could have legal validity, and included a repudiation of Soviet assumptions of political influence over Outer Mongolia evidenced in the pact.[20] The Soviet Government, however, was not moved from its policy of friendship and assistance to China. It assured the latter of its desire to implement the barter agreements and gave proof of its attitude by sending munitions, planes and pilots.[21]

It is to be remembered that Soviet policy was in accord with the cooperative relations agreed upon early in 1937 between the National Government of China and the Chinese Communist organization which had its capital at Yenan,

[18] *Contemporary China,* May 25, 1941, p. 5.
[19] *New York Times,* December 6, 1940.
[20] *Ibid.,* April 18, 1941.
[21] *Ibid.,* April 18, July 8, August 6, 1941.

Shensi. So long as the Generalissimo did not turn his superior forces upon the troops of Mao Tse-tung, the Soviets were killing two birds with one stone. They were aiding to maintain resistance to Japan and thereby lessening the danger of attack upon Siberia. And they were helping to keep communism alive against the day when it might again assert itself in Chinese domestic affairs. Temporarily it was preferable to Moscow that Yenan should not grow too assertive. The stern measures of Chiang K'ai-shek against the Communist Fourth Army were, however, regarded as more severe than was necessary under existing circumstances. To the Chinese Communists aid from Soviet Russia to Chungking was welcome so long as their own necessities for war materials were not overlooked. To them Chungking was playing their game, not they Chungking's, the game of national salvation. They were aided, moreover, in getting representation in the Chungking Government by Stalin's support of Mao Tse-tung.[22]

It is difficult to view the expansion of Soviet influence in Sinkiang as other than a modern form of imperialism. Sinkiang's commercial orientation is toward central Asia rather than eastern China because of the superior facilities for transportation westward. The growth of trade was encouraged by the exemption of imports from Russia from customs duties under the Treaty of St. Petersburg of 1881. In 1931 the governor of Sinkiang, Chin Shu-jen, independently of the National Government, entered into a trade agreement with the Soviet Union by which Soviet institutions and nationals were accorded equality with those of China in respect to the payment of customs duties and other taxes.[23] This agreement, which was not approved at Nanking, then the capital, further provided for financial as-

[22] Snow, Edgar, "Will Stalin Sell Out China?", *Foreign Affairs,* XVIII, April 1940, p. 450–63.

[23] Weigh, K. S., "China, Soviet Russia, and Sinkiang," *China Weekly Review,* February 18, 1939, p. 364–7.

sistance to Chinese merchants and for technical experts and machinery for the development of communications, agriculture and industry. Since 1931 Soviet penetration has proceeded slowly but surely through manipulation of Governor Sheng Shih-tsai. The legal relationship of the huge province to China has not been altered but its *de facto* status grows continuously more like that of Outer Mongolia. Soviet inroads have been made easier by the complex racial composition of Sinkiang's 2,500,000 people and by the exploitation they have suffered at the hands of Chinese officials.[24]

If the Soviets are exacting a heavy price for their aid to China, the maintenance of supply along the Sinkiang-Kansu-Shensi route may become important in the struggle for survival. Lattimore attributes the failure of this route to play a larger part in supplying Chinese armies to political rather than physical obstacles. Kuomintang politicians were disinclined to expenditure of money and effort on the northwestern route. They preferred to receive Soviet war materials along routes that concealed their source. They desired also to involve the United Kingdom, France and the United States more deeply with Japan by emphasizing Chinese dependence upon the Indo-China and Burma routes. And they feared that larger Soviet supplies would be diverted in part to the Chinese Communists. While these considerations must be weighed it is logical to set against them the interest of Chungking in checking as effectively as possible the trend of Soviet policy toward absorption of Sinkiang.

Rapprochement with Japan

The Soviet Government saw in Japan's change of attitude after the former's pact of 1939 with the German Reich an excellent opportunity to further its major objectives, as above

[24] Lattimore, Owen, "China's Turkistan-Siberian Supply Road," *Pacific Affairs,* XIII, 1940, p. 393–412.

outlined, provided Japan did not demand cessation of aid to China.[25] It also appreciated that a Soviet-Japanese agreement for mutual self-denial would increase the importance of Soviet collaboration in the eyes of the United Kingdom and the United States. The Soviet Government at that time was suspicious of British and American motives, viewing their policies since the Bolshevik Revolution as an attempt to direct Japanese imperialism toward Manchuria, Mongolia, and Siberia and away from China proper and the South Pacific. Stalin alleged in 1939 that the democracies hoped to see the Soviets embroiled with Japan in order that they might "dictate conditions to the enfeebled belligerents." [26] Events brought both the United Kingdom and the United States to the Soviet's side. And time was gained for building up a better defensive position.

Soviet rather than Japanese initiative led up to the conclusion of the neutrality pact of April 1941. Chairman Molotov foresaw further improvement in Soviet-Japanese relations after the armistice at Nomonhan. The pressure being applied from Berlin for assistance with supplies and accommodation to Germany's program in the Balkans and the Near East increased after Japan joined the Axis. That the Soviet Government maintained an independent attitude was shown by its refusal to make the Axis a quadruple alliance. The neutrality pact [27] was a signal success for Soviet diplomacy. In return for a Japanese guaranty of neutrality and respect for Soviet and Outer Mongolian integrity it gave similar guaranties regarding Japan and "Manchoukuo." Its relations with China were unaffected by the pact.

A trade agreement followed in June 1941.[28] It provided

[25] Rosinger, L. K., "Soviet Far Eastern Policy," *Pacific Affairs,* XIII, 1940, p. 263–78; Asiaticus, "Soviet Relations with Japan," *ibid.,* XIV, 1941, p. 272–86.

[26] *Report on the Work of the Central Committee,* 1939.

[27] Appendix, p. 296.

[28] *New York Times,* June 13, 1941; *Far Eastern Survey,* June 30, 1941, p. 134–5.

for most-favored-nation treatment and exchange of commodities up to a maximum of Yen 30,000,000 for the first year. Negotiations had been proceeding for several months to improve commercial relations which had deteriorated since 1931 until in 1939 the total trade between the two countries had dropped to a value of Yen 672,000. In 1930 it was valued at Yen 66,000,000. Under the new agreement the Soviets were to receive raw silk, machinery, camphor, etc., in return for oil, metals and fertilizers.

The Soviets and the Democracies

Soviet policy ran parallel to that of the United States and the United Kingdom respecting aid to China. But the motives of the former were in contradiction to those of the democratic states: the one desiring to save China for communism, the others to prevent that development and assure the future for democracy and free economic enterprise. Not until the menace of Hitlerism compelled recognition of a common necessity for cooperative action was it possible for the governments to relegate their deeply rooted prejudices and conflicting interests to the background. It may be hoped that out of the common struggle against enemies opposed to the basic ideals professed alike by the democracies and the Soviet Union there will develop mutual confidence and tolerance.

XV

UNITED FRONT IN THE PACIFIC

On January 1, 1942, the governments of 26 countries signed at Washington the "Joint Declaration by United Nations"[1] in which each pledged itself "to employ its full resources, military or economic, against those members of the Tripartite Pact and its adherents with which such government is at war" and "to cooperate with the Governments signatory hereto and not to make a separate armistice or peace with the enemies." This alliance may be viewed as the culmination of a process of growing cooperation under the impact of events, a process which began, among certain Pacific states, several years earlier. It is the purpose of this chapter to trace, as well as may be with the limited evidence available, the evolution of an Anglo-American policy of collaboration, and of the association of the United States and Great Britain with China, the Netherlands East Indies and the Soviet Union in a common program of resistance.

The beginnings of a common military front between the United States and the British Commonwealth of Nations arose out of the Monroe Doctrine. In his Chautauqua address in August 1936, President Roosevelt declared that the United States would defend its "neighborhood" as well as itself against aggression.

Two years later he underlined this sentiment at Kingston, Ontario, when he gave Canadians the assurance that the United States would "not stand idly by if domination of Canadian soil is threatened by any other Empire." In 1938 also a joint commission was appointed to consider the costs

[1] Department of State, *Bulletin*, January 3, 1942, p. 3.

and political aspects of the building of a highway from the State of Washington to Alaska.[2] However, it was the creation by executive action, in August 1940, of the United States-Canadian Permanent Joint Board on Defense, that marked the close alignment which had developed.[3] This agreement provided that the Board would "commence immediate studies relating to sea, land and air problems. . ." The Board was appointed promptly and consisted of 11 members, six from the United States and five from Canada. Mayor Fiorello H. La Guardia of New York City and Colonel O. M. Biggar of Ottawa became co-chairmen of the Board. Seven members were officers of the respective armies, navies, and air forces of the two states, and the two secretaries represented the Department of State and the Department of External Affairs respectively. The Board announced on April 17, 1941, that plans were complete for the military and naval defense of the east and west coasts of both states. It continued to function in order to adapt plans to new developments.

In the "Hyde Park Declaration" of April 20, 1941, issued jointly by President Roosevelt and Prime Minister Mackenzie King after receiving the results of Board surveys, occurs this paragraph: [4]

> It was agreed as a general principle that in mobilizing the resources of this continent, each country should provide the other with the defense articles which it is best able to produce, and, above all, produce quickly, and that production programs should be coordinated to this end.

To implement the Hyde Park Declaration, the United States and Canadian Governments, upon the recommendation of the Joint Economic Committees, appointed a Joint Defense

[2] Lower, A. R. M., cited, p. 102; Maddox, W. P., "Canadian-American Defense Planning," *Foreign Policy Reports*, November 15, 1941.

[3] Jones and Myers, *Documents*, III, p. 160–1.

[4] *Ibid.*, p. 162.

Production Committee, the composition of which was made public on November 5, 1941.[5] Six high officials of each country made up the Committee, instructed to report from time to time to the President and Prime Minister, with recommendations assuring the most effective execution of the Hyde Park Declaration.

Whether or not these understandings were reached primarily with reference to defense against Germany, their implications for the Pacific were not overlooked in Japan. To Japanese editors the Defense Board portended a curvilinear front of the United States and the British Empire within which Japan would be encircled.[6] The Foreign Office accepted defense arrangements between contiguous states as logical, and attempted to show that they were analogous to Japan's program for a "new order" in Asia.[7]

Anglo-American Parallelism

Secretary Hull replied in the negative to three questions contained in a tabled Senate resolution of February 7, 1938.[8] These questions were asked to discover whether or not any alliance or other form of agreement existed between the United States and the United Kingdom. They were prompted by expressions in the latter country of an expectation of cooperation with it, based upon greatly enlarged appropriations for the American navy. In a letter of the same date from Representative Louis Ludlow to Secretary Hull, in which similar questions were asked, Winston Churchill, not then in office, was quoted as saying "that the United States can take care of the interests of Britain in China by sending its capital fleet across the Pacific with Britain in support." [9] Mr. Hull's

5 Department of State, *Bulletin,* November 8, 1941, p. 360–1.
6 *New York Times,* August 21, 1940.
7 *Ibid.,* August 22, 1940.
8 Jones and Myers, *Documents,* I, p. 495.
9 *Ibid.,* p. 496.

reply was a carefully worded statement of the traditional American policy. In part he said: [10]

For present purposes and in express reply to your question . . . the proposed program of naval building does not contemplate the use of any of the units in cooperation with any other nation in any part of the world. To be still more specific, I may say that the policy I announced last August is still being strictly observed, that is that this Government carefully avoids, on the one hand, extreme internationalism with its political entanglements, and, on the other hand, extreme isolation, with its tendency to cause other nations to believe that this nation is more or less afraid; *that while avoiding any alliances or entangling commitments, it is appropriate and advisable, when this and other countries have common interests and common objectives, for this Government to exchange information with governments of such other countries, to confer with those governments, and, where practicable, to proceed on parallel lines, but reserving always the fullest freedom of judgment and right of independence of action.* (Author's italics)

The extent of executive autonomy, under this procedure is sufficient, provided another state does not insist upon treaty pledges, to accomplish any purpose of foreign policy not in conflict with existing law. Dependence upon Congress for appropriations need not impede the executive in a program of parallelism since forces provided for national defense may be ordered into any area. The limitations of the American neutrality laws affected British policy in the Pacific to some extent and correspondingly hindered the trend toward Anglo-American cooperation there. As these limitations were repealed, one after another, that trend took more and more tangible form.

The transfer of 50 American destroyers to the United Kingdom under the executive agreement of September 2, 1940, reduced British necessity of denuding Pacific bases.

[10] *Ibid.*, p. 499.

Aid to the United Kingdom and the Dominions under the lend-lease appropriation acts approved by the President on March 27 and October 28, 1941, may also be mentioned here as convincing evidence of the alignment of the United States with the British cause.[11] Further aid in the form of naval patrols, the sending of troops to Iceland and the provision of convoys, though effected in the Atlantic, was important to the entire war effort of the British Commonwealth. Similarly the acquisition of naval and air bases on British colonies in the Atlantic enabled the United States more confidently to concentrate its grand fleet in the Pacific, while agreements for the exchange of American cotton for British rubber, and for the maintenance in the United States of a strategic reserve of Australian wool, assured American supplies of two vital necessities of national defense.[12]

Discussion of arrangements for joint use of bases in the Pacific followed the agreement of September 2, 1940, regarding Atlantic bases. Previously, on April 6, 1939, the United States and Great Britain had reached an agreement for a fifty-year condominium over Canton and Enderbury Islands, which lie on the southerly route from Hawaii to the western Pacific.[13] Both countries had claims to the Islands and had established a few settlers upon them. The agreement contained no reference to the provision of a naval base but authorized the construction and operation on Canton Island of an American airport, "which, in return for an agreed fee, shall provide facilities for British aircraft and British civil aviation companies equal to those enjoyed by United States aircraft and by American . . . companies." These islands, however, were included in the defense scheme of the two Governments.

American naval officers were agreed that the difficulty of

[11] Department of State, *Bulletin,* October 25, 1941, p. 311–4.
[12] Jones and Myers, *Documents,* I, p. 519–22; III, p. 739–42.
[13] *Ibid.,* I, p. 459–61.

effective patrol of the wide reaches of the Pacific would be greatly diminished if British and Netherlands bases were available for their use. This need was especially emphasized by men in the air arm of the service. Westward from Honolulu, Midway, Wake and Guam Islands, route of the Clippers, furnished well-spaced bases. Southward, Palmyra, Canton and the Samoan Islands were under development. But southwestward from Honolulu the only American territory in a vast expanse of sea was Johnston Island. But the Gilbert, Ellice, New Hebrides and Solomon groups, all British, were situated in those waters, easy stepping-stones to Manila for aeroplanes. Australia and New Zealand, further to the south, could provide 8 combined naval and air bases, with dockyards of varying capacity. Labuan in British Borneo, Penang and Singapore, second only to Pearl Harbor, completed the circuit of British bases, which was further strengthened by those of the friendly and allied Netherlands East Indies. Hong Kong lay to the north, between Manila and Japan's main islands, well-situated for a submarine base for attack upon Japan's supply line to the South China Sea.

Although no documents or official statements were issued covering arrangements, reciprocal or otherwise, for the use of bases in the Pacific, the information ascribed by reliable newspapers to authoritative sources indicated that early in November 1940, the United States, the United Kingdom and Australia reached an agreement in principle on a cooperative program.[14] The appointment at that time of Air Chief Marshal Sir Robert Brooke-Popham as commander-in-chief of all British land and air forces in Malaya, Burma and Hong Kong facilitated the work of planning the application of an agreement in anticipation of specific eventualities. Conversations to that end began in Manila in April 1941, between Sir Robert, Admiral Thomas C. Hart, commander of the Asiatic fleet of the United States, Major

[14] *New York Times,* November 8, 1940.

General Douglas MacArthur, military adviser to the Philippines and commander of American military forces in the Far East, High Commissioner Francis B. Sayre and other officials.[15] Mr. E. N. van Kleffens, Foreign Minister of the Netherlands, also took part in the discussion. A second conference of these officers, who were joined by Brigadier General John Magruder, head of an American military mission to Chungking, took place in October 1941.[16] Premier John Curtin of Australia stated shortly thereafter that negotiations had been completed for substantial cooperation in the Pacific between the United Kingdom, Australia, New Zealand, China, the Netherlands East Indies and the United States.[17]

The growing intimacy of British-American relations was marked in March, and again in August 1941, by visits of American naval detachments to ports of Australia and New Zealand.[18] Two cruisers and 5 destroyers visited Melbourne, Sydney and Brisbane while 2 cruisers and 4 destroyers put in at Auckland. Their complements paraded amid cheering crowds. Premier Fadden of Australia addressed the visitors as comrades who had given the hand of friendship in a time of trial. The wide scope of American naval patrolling was evidenced by these visits.

President Roosevelt's message to Congress regarding his conference at sea with Prime Minister Churchill spoke of the "national policy of American aid to the democracies which East and West are waging war against dictatorships" and stated that "the military and naval conversations at these meetings made clear gains in furthering the effectiveness of this aid." [19] New Zealand's readiness to grant the United States the use of its bases in the event of war with

[15] *Ibid.*, April 3, 1941.
[16] *Ibid.*, October 6, 8, 10, 1941.
[17] *Ibid.*, October 21, 1941.
[18] *Ibid.*, March 19, 20, 21, 26; August 6, 1941.
[19] Department of State, *Bulletin*, August 23, 1941, p. 147.

a statement of a Chinese spokesman on November 10, 1941.[26] He revealed that the British, American, Chinese and Netherlands Indies Governments had come to an understanding upon cooperative measures, military and other, in the event of a Japanese effort to cut the Burma Road.

Progress toward Chinese military cooperation was suggested by the visit of a Chinese military mission to Malaya in May 1941.[27] Chinese assistance, by a drive into Indo-China in the event of a Japanese attack upon Burma or Thailand, would relieve the pressure upon British forces in Burma or moving up from Malaya. And Chinese readiness to take advantage of any weakening of Japanese striking power within China would prevent the transfer of divisions to Indo-China. A British military mission visited Chungking concurrently with the Magruder mission. Generalissimo Chiang K'ai-shek assured the People's Political Council on November 17, 1941, that China, the United Kingdom and the United States had completed plans for united defense of their interests.[28] No evidence was offered, however, that a formal agreement had been signed.

President Roosevelt's order of November 14, 1941, for the departure of all American marines from China, was an unmistakable sign of the impasse in American-Japanese relations.[29] It may also be taken as additional evidence of Sino-American collaboration, since it removed the danger that the outbreak of hostilities would involve for so small a force. Before the month was out the 750 marines at Shanghai embarked for Manila. (Unfortunately the *President Harrison,* upon which the men posted at Tientsin and Peking were to sail, was delayed in departure and was captured by the Japanese. The Peking and Tientsin detachments, numbering 183 men, were made prisoners.) Departure of the

[26] *New York Times,* November 11, 1941.
[27] *Ibid.,* May 16, 1941.
[28] *Ibid.,* November 18, 1941.
[29] *Ibid.,* November 15, 1941.

marines from Shanghai did not bring an immediate demand by the Japanese commander there for police rights in the American defense sectors. The Shanghai Volunteer Corps added these sectors to those taken over by it in 1940 upon the withdrawal of British forces. Japanese representation in the regular police force was increased, in return for which the Japanese naval command agreed to the stationing of 250 regular police in Hongkew.[30]

The Netherlands East Indies

The dependence of the Netherlands East Indies upon Great Britain for protection has long been recognized. No formal agreement between the two was to be expected so long as the Indies remained a colony. It is apparent that the close relations existing between Great Britain and the Netherlands after the removal of the latter's government to London would be likely to bring about cooperation to safeguard an area so important economically and strategically to the British Empire. German occupation of the Netherlands did not alter the legal relationship between the British and Netherlands Governments since the former continued to accord the latter *de jure* recognition. Although the exiled Queen and her ministers could not exercise the same control as formerly at Batavia, they could count upon the loyalty of officials there so long as Netherlands policy did not move toward sacrificing colonial for national interests. Furthermore, the development of autonomy could not be rapid against the wishes of the British Government.

Quite apart from a political agreement, however, there was room and need for coordination of defensive arrangements between Singapore and Batavia. The same observation applies to the relations of Australia and New Zealand

[30] *Ibid.*, November 21, 28, 1941; for the treatment of earlier developments in Settlement administration, see Chapter VIII.

with the Indies. After the *blitzkrieg* in Holland the necessity for a rigid policy of neutrality which had prevented an earlier arrangement lost all meaning. Batavian officials were as eager as British for a plan of cooperative defense. They agreed also upon the importance of Manila in a defense scheme and upon the ultimate reliance of the Indies upon the American fleet if Japan should determine to include the colony within its "co-prosperity sphere."

No British or Anglo-American guaranty of the integrity of the Indies was made public. One must rely upon such evidence as the participation of Netherlands representatives in anti-Axis conversations at Manila and Singapore, and expressions of a semi-official character, for the belief that such guaranties had been given.[31] But whether given or not the fully recognized interest of Britain and America in the *status quo* was a sufficient guaranty that they would do all in their power to maintain it.

The Soviet Union

Prime Minister Churchill, in his searing broadcast of June 22, 1941, condemning the German invasion of the Soviet Union, made no direct reference to Japan. But any ally of Germany was included conditionally in the declaration that: "Any man or state who marches with Hitler is our foe."[32] Three weeks later, on July 12, Great Britain and the Soviets entered into an alliance against "Hitlerite Germany." The United States was less than a month behind Great Britain with an offer of economic assistance in the exchange of notes of August 2, 1941. The joint letter of President Roosevelt and Mr. Churchill to Joseph Stalin, on August 15, 1941, referring to Mr. Harry Hopkins' return

[31] Bisson, T. A., "The Netherlands Indies at War," *Foreign Policy Reports,* November 1, 1941, p. 206.

[32] Jones and Myers, *Documents,* III, p. 302.

from Moscow, stated that already supplies were being sent to the Soviet Union, and proposed a meeting in Moscow to plan a long-term program "for the future allocation of our joint resources." [33] Again one may read a caution to Japan in a single line: "The war goes on upon many fronts and before it is over there may be further fighting fronts that will be developed."

American aid to the Soviets expanded rapidly. Priority and unlimited licenses for export of materials needed for defense were authorized in early August.[34] Shortly afterward, at the President's direction, the Defense Supplies Corporation, a subsidiary of the Reconstruction Finance Corporation, contracted with the Russian-owned Amtorg Trading Corporation for the purchase of approximately $100,000,000 worth of manganese, chromite, asbestos and platinum. An advance credit of $50,000,000 was provided for. The Soviets agreed to expend the funds in the purchase of war materials in the United States.[35] In October 1941, $40,000,000 was advanced out of the Stabilization Fund against gold to be shipped within a specified period.[36] Finally, the Soviet Union was brought within the coverage of lend-lease aid. President Roosevelt promised on October 30 to provide $1,000,000,000 for the further acquisition of war supplies.[37]

The Soviet Government declared its adherence to the principles of the Roosevelt-Churchill Declaration at a meeting of the Inter-Allied Council in London on September 24, 1941.[38] At the same time it expressed its view of each nation's right "to the independence and territorial integrity of its country and its right to establish such a social order and to choose such a form of government as it deems opportune and

[33] *New York Times,* August 16, 1941.
[34] Department of State, *Bulletin,* August 9, 1941, p. 109.
[35] *New York Times,* September 18, 1941.
[36] *Ibid.,* October 21, 1941.
[37] *Ibid.,* November 7, 1941.
[38] Department of State, *Bulletin,* September 27, 1941, p. 233–4.

necessary for the better promotion of its economic and cultural prosperity." Premier Stalin, in an address on the anniversary of the Bolshevik revolution, gave his interpretation of the existing relationship with Great Britain and the United States:[39]

> And finally came the coalition of the U.S.S.R., Great Britain and the United States of America against the German-Fascist imperialists. It is a fact that Great Britain, the United States of America, and the Soviet have united into a single camp, having set themselves the aim of routing the Hitlerite imperialists and their invading armies.

[39] *New York Times,* November 7, 1941.

EPILOG

JAPAN struck at China ten years after a series of events, including the formation of the second financial consortium, the concessions to Japan in the Treaty of Versailles, and the Far Eastern arrangements of the Washington Conference, had made two things clear: (1) that European states had turned away from imperialism in China, and (2) that they would accord to Japan a degree of regional leadership consistent with the independence and integrity of China and the maintenance of treaty rights. Japan's second attack came after the inordinate success of the first, which no Western state had seriously interfered with. Rather than implementing the Nine-Power Treaty, which embodied a pledge to afford China an unembarrassed opportunity for self-reorganization, Japan took up arms to compel China to adapt its political and economic order to Japan's requirements. It is impossible for Japanese apologists to demonstrate that Western power politics was a menace to China either in 1931 or in 1937.

Was Japan endangered by a China heady with nationalist wine and resentful over a century of quasi-colonialism? One may safely answer "No" to this question. China was deeply involved in domestic difficulties that would require many years for solution. Western governments were concerned to assist in this process but were equally friendly toward a peaceably inclined Japan. There would be no logic in assuming that China, any more than Japan, would be encouraged to put on the mantle of a Far Eastern Caesar. Without access to Western resources it is doubtful that the Chinese could, for an indefinite period, develop the military power that might engender such pretensions. Moreover, the evolution of world organization, so callously checked by Japan's repudiation of the League Covenant, might have been expected to transform colonial and commercial policies and to open capital reservoirs on terms acceptable to all states.

It will be conceded that Japan's position in relation to China was unstable. One state could not continue to maintain political spheres there while others were relinquishing them without focussing upon itself such efforts for the restoration of sovereignty as the National Government could spare from its anti-Communist campaigns. Japan could, however, without loss of prestige, have aligned itself with other states in withdrawal from positions which were inconsistent with China's independence. Economic interests would have been freed in this way from political entanglements, and the confidence that such consideration for Chinese self-esteem brought into Sino-European relations would have been extended to Japan. Resultant improvement in trade with a gradually modernizing China would have substituted increased prosperity for the mountainous debt and privation which the war has imposed upon the Japanese people.

Did the Japanese army and navy throw their forces against China in order to assure their own predominance over increasingly influential elements favorable to civilian control of the state? Beyond doubt there was apprehension in the Supreme Command at the end of the comparatively liberal decade of the 'twenties. But the probability is great that broader considerations than the saving of its own prestige motivated the leadership of the armed services in precipitating war. The views advanced in preceding paragraphs were no more acceptable to these men than to their allies in industry and the bureaucracy. Beyond the issues therein canvassed, also, they raised the question of military security. They viewed this question as all other governments of powerful states view it, to be answered by freeing the state from dependence upon other states for military materials. Arguments on any ground fail, unhappily, before this universal axiom of statecraft.

Pride of race was the dynamo from which economic, political and strategic motives were galvanized for ordeal by battle. It is remarkable that so little attention is paid by analysts of the causes of war to psychological factors. Remarkable because every individual observes so frequently, in his dealings with other individuals, the overwhelming of reason by emotion. Shinto teaches a race-consciousness entirely lacking in humor, an ideological foundation for integral nationalism beside which Teutonism looks anaemic. No other explanation is satisfactory for the Japanese theory of "cooperation" or for the solemn accusation that Western nations have obstructed Japan's peaceful purposes. The Japanese believe that they are depreciated both in China and in the West. They mean to compel a change of attitude.

The resistance of the Chinese nation has won for it the respect which the Japanese have forfeited by their attack upon a poorly armed foe and their brutality in the conduct of warfare. The grand strategy of the National Government has been proved excellent. Chinese soldiers have fought bravely and intelligently. Behind Japanese lines in "occupied" areas they have shown a determination to reject defeat that would not have been expected of a "decadent" nation. With the most attenuated resources China's scientists and engineers have organized industry and transport, built roads and railroads, and developed agriculture. But of highest importance has been the morale of the unlettered masses. That civilization is not a matter of book-learning but rather the comprehension and application of ethical principles will be believed in the presence of their fortitude. No political party or faction should be permitted to deny them the reward they deserve, for when China is saved they will have saved it.

It is impossible even to guess at the capacity of Japan to continue to fight and to meet the added costs of war in the Pacific. The Japanese people appear to be resigned to unlimited privation. There is no apparent breach in their ranks. Undoubtedly the resources of China have been and will continue to be for some time important to Japan's war effort. The same may be said of those of Indo-China, Thailand and such other territories as may fall into Japanese hands. The ability of the country's scientific, industrial and political leaders to plan and execute measures for the prosecution of total war has been adequate. Add to these assets the advantage of geographical position which Japan enjoys and the sum is an impressive challenge even to the great states now arrayed against it. Alliance with Germany (and Italy) presents a combined power which will tax to the limit the resources and abilities of Japan's opponents.

Clearly, Premier Tojo and his colleagues in the Supreme Command did not launch Japan into war with the United States as the tools of Adolf Hitler. Their action was pursuant to the war upon China and their imperialist program in the South Pacific, which were the culmination of lines of policy that may be traced back to the later nineteenth century. Nazi German leaders are natural allies of Japan's latter-day *samurai,* whose political ideas and anti-democratic psychosis might well have been prototypes rather than copies of European totalitarianism. The Japanese, however, will have perceived that the Nazis, like themselves, are opportunists. Cleavage of the White front provides them with a long-anticipated opportunity to drive all White influence, be it British, Russian, American or German, out of Eastern Asia.

Americans may justly find comfort in the record of their relations with both China and Japan. They cannot fairly be charged with discrimination between the two states nor with the assertion of standards for Japanese policy that they do not demand of themselves. The confidence of the Chinese people is sufficient testimony to American consideration for their welfare. Unhappily the Japanese have resented American legislation affecting immigration and naturalization, yet they know that it applies to all Oriental peoples alike. American tariff policy has fallen comparatively lightly upon Japanese goods. In supporting China with loans and other forms of assistance the United States was maintaining a line of policy that combines concern for rights and interests with neighborly sentiments. In so doing it was guarding no preferential claims. If Japanese statesmen regarded American methods as ingratiating they were free to imitate them.

China has old scores to settle with both Great Britain and the Soviet Union. Not so Japan. Toward America's partners (if the Soviet Union may be regarded as a partner, which seems likely), Japan is patently an aggressor. What has been written of American aid to China applies to British and Russian aid as well. Against France, the Netherlands and Thailand Japan may not even allege a right of retaliation. No doubt it is naïve to remind General Tojo of the benefits derived over a period of twenty years from the Anglo-Japanese alliance. But Japanese statesmen should not expect to eat the cake of righteousness and have it too. Before an impartial tribunal their opponents would stand with cleaner hands than they.

In this indictment the "common people" of Japan are not included. One who has lived among them does not find them quarrelsome or vindictive. They are the victims of circumstance. Lacking in political experience and deprived of liberal leadership by a vigilant police, they tread submissively the traditional path of loyalty. While it may not be anticipated that they will revolt, it is important to realize that the Japanese policy of aggrandizement is not a people's movement. There is greater community of interest between the Japanese and Chinese peoples than either of them realizes. Is it beyond possibility that this common interest in peace and public welfare may find channels of communication? Can America and the British Commonwealth of Nations, the Soviet Union and the Netherlands, perhaps by elaboration of the Atlantic Charter with specific relation to Eastern Asia, further the opening of such channels? The Japanese people will not forsake their Emperor. But they may arrive at a new conception of the requirements of loyalty.

APPENDICES

I. STATEMENT BY PREMIER KONOYE, DECEMBER 22, 1938[1]

THE Japanese Government is resolved, as has been clearly set forth in its two previous statements issued this year, to carry on the military operations for the complete extermination of the anti-Japanese Kuomintang Government, and at the same time to proceed with the work of establishing a new order in East Asia together with those far-sighted Chinese who share in our ideals and aspirations.

The spirit of renaissance is now sweeping over all parts of China and enthusiasm for reconstruction is mounting ever higher. The Japanese Government desires to make public its basic policy for adjusting relations between Japan and China, in order that its intentions may be thoroughly understood both at home and abroad.

Japan, China and Manchoukuo will be united by the common aim of establishing the new order in East Asia and of realizing a relationship of neighborly amity, common defense against Communism and economic cooperation. For that purpose it is necessary first of all that China should cast aside all narrow and prejudiced views belonging to the past and do away with the folly of anti-Japanism and resentment regarding Manchoukuo. In other words, Japan frankly desires China to enter of her own will into complete diplomatic relations with Manchoukuo.

The existence of the Comintern influence in East Asia can not be tolerated. Japan therefore considers it an essential condition of the adjustment of the Sino-Japanese relations that there should be concluded an anti-Comintern agreement between the two

[1] Jones and Myers, *Documents,* II, cited, p. 299; *Tokyo Gazette,* February 1939, p. 24.

countries in consonance with the spirit of the anti-Comintern agreement between Japan, Germany and Italy. And, in order to insure the full accomplishment of her purpose, Japan demands, in view of the actual circumstances prevailing in China, that Japanese troops be stationed, as an anti-Communist measure, at specified points during the time the said agreement is in force, and also that the Inner Mongolian region be designated as a special anti-Communist area.

As regards economic relations between the two countries, Japan does not intend to exercise economic monopoly in China, nor does she intend to demand of China to limit the interests of those third Powers who grasp the meaning of the new East Asia and are willing to act accordingly. Japan only seeks to render effective the cooperation and collaboration between the two countries. That is to say, Japan demands that China, in accordance with the principle of equality between the two countries, should recognize the freedom of residence and trade on the part of Japanese subjects in the interior of China, with a view to promoting the economic interests of both peoples; and that, in the light of the historical and economic relations between the two nations, China should extend to Japan facilities for the development of China's natural resources, especially in the regions of North China and Inner Mongolia.

The above gives the general lines of what Japan demands of China.

If the true object of Japan in conducting the present vast military campaign be fully understood, it will be plain that what she seeks is neither territory nor indemnity for the costs of military operations. Japan demands only the minimum guaranty needed for the execution by China of her function as a participant in the establishment of the new order.

Japan not only respects the sovereignty of China, but she is prepared to give positive consideration to the questions of the abolition of extraterritoriality and of the rendition of concessions and settlements—matters which are necessary for the full independence of China.

II. STATEMENT BY GENERAL CHIANG K'AI-SHEK, DECEMBER 26, 1938[1]

Our campaign of armed resistance has now entered upon a new phase. As I have repeatedly pointed out, the fighting during the past 18 months may be called the first stage of resistance, and the second stage has just commenced and is going to be the final one. The morale of Chinese soldiers at various fronts both in the North and South is at its height, and this is indeed an unprecedentedly good symptom since the outbreak of the hostilities.

All our men in service are aware that the present war is fought because Japan wants to conquer China and China wants to save herself from extinction. To attain this end, efforts are being redoubled in military training. Likewise, the general public has fully realized that Japan's ultimate aim is to subjugate our country and that there will be no other way out, if we do not fight for existence. For this reason, the determination of both Chinese soldiers and civilians to fight to the end has been growing firmer and firmer despite hardships and sufferings. The growth of nationalism and the consolidation of national unity enhance our confidence in the ultimate victory.

Because of our firm determination and national solidarity, the enemy has been using the tactics of threats and inducements besides military action. Following the statement made by the Japanese Government on November 3,[2] a number of illogical and absurd utterances have successively been made by the Japanese Premier and Ministers of War, Navy and Foreign Affairs. These kaleidoscopic and paradoxical statements were apparently intended to hoodwink their own people and the world at large. What is more, these sugar-coated words were expected to produce intoxicating effects on the Chinese people. In the meanwhile, inspired public opinion in Japan has been clamoring support to these official views.

On December 22 Prince Konoye made another statement regarding Japan's policy of "rejuvenating China" and readjusting

[1] *China Year Book, 1939,* p. 422–6.

[2] Jones and Myers, *Documents,* I, p. 229.

the relations between China and Japan. This may be considered as the final attempt of the enemy to apply its policy of hypocrisy and completely disclosed to us the sinister scheme of our enemy.

Prince Konoye's statement was a mere repetition of what has been said before and, in fact, does not deserve a refutation. In short, all the utterances and actions thus far carried out by the Japanese were vague superficialities, but with deadly weapons behind them. In other words, their aim is to conquer China and to dominate East Asia and even the whole world.

The Japanese are experts in lie-telling and arguing. For instance, in the press interview given on December 24, closely following Prince Konoye's statement, a spokesman of the Japanese Government made a shrewd explanation of Japan's intentions. Such ridiculous and cunning tactics, I am afraid, may still command the confidence of a small section of people who are not aware of the sinister motive behind the smoke-screen. They may think that Japan's demands are not so harsh. It is therefore necessary to expose all the ambitions of Japan, so that they may serve as a warning to the Chinese nation as well as the whole world. What we should know now is the atrocities, madness and ignorance of the Japanese militarists and, what is more important, their ambition to conquer China. The following is an analysis of the Japanese official and private views regarding their intrigues in the Far East, with Prince Konoye's statement on December 22 as the basis:

1. Creation of a new order in East Asia has been the most favorite slogan of the Japanese. The new order in East Asia, as referred to by Mr. Arita, Japanese Foreign Minister, in his statement on December 19,[3] means political, economic and cultural cooperation between Japan, Manchoukuo and China, suppression of Communism, protection of Oriental culture, breaking down of economic walls, promotion of the status of China from a semi-colonial State to full statehood, and stabilization of the Far East. Prince Konoye, in a press interview of December 14, said that the end of the China incident does not only lie in military success but also in the rebirth of China and the creation of a new order in East Asia. The foundation of the new order will be laid after

[3] *Ibid.*, p. 232.

the rebirth of China and cooperation between Japan, Manchoukuo and China.

We must understand that the rebirth of China is taken by the Japanese to mean destruction of an independent China and creation of an enslaved China. The so-called new order is to be created after China has been reduced to a slave nation and linked up with made-in-Japan Manchoukuo. The aim of the Japanese is to control China militarily under the pretext of anti-Communism, to eliminate Chinese culture under the cloak of protection of Oriental culture and to expel European and American influences from the Far East under the pretext of breaking down economic walls. The formation of the "tripartite economic unit" or "economic bloc" is a tool to control the economic lifeline of China. In other words, creation of a new order in Asia means destruction of international order in the Far East, enslavement of China and domination of the Pacific and the whole world.

2. The so-called "East Asia Bloc," cooperation between Japan, China, Manchoukuo and the mutual and inseparable tie binding Japan, China and Manchoukuo, have been the favorite slogans of Japanese official and public quarters during the past few months. These slogans are even broader in sense than the "economic unit," or "economic bloc," that has been advocated before. Under the cloak of these slogans the Japanese attempted to devour the Northeastern provinces and the whole of China and make them an integral unit. Japanese magazines openly advocated that Japan, Manchoukuo and China under the "East Asia Bloc" should form a patriarchal system with Japan as the patriarch and Manchoukuo and China as his children. In other words, the former will be the governor and the latter the governed slaves. Is this not an idea of conquest? Is this not a plan to conquer China? Just a month ago Prince Konoye handed out leaflets which contained such a startling phrase as "establishment of a political, economic and cultural tie between Japan, Manchoukuo and China." This tie is nothing but a chain to fasten us and drag us into the hell beneath.

3. The so-called "economic unit" or "economic bloc" has been advocated in Japan for many years and is now being actively carried out. It is the most important point of the "East Asia Bloc"

and is sometimes called "economic assistance" or "economic cooperation." In the statement issued by the Japanese Government on November 4, it was called "economic tie." At the end of last November, the Japanese press reported that Japan, Manchoukuo and China would form an "economic unit." Mr. Arita in his statement on December 19 stated that Japan has decided to hold a conference to discuss measures for strengthening the economic set-up of Japan, Manchoukuo and China. In fact, the "economic bloc" has led to the establishment of the North and Central China Development Companies, Japan's tools for the economic exploitation of China. The Japanese Planning Board has, after Prince Konoye's statement, mapped out a comprehensive scheme for developing production in Japan, Manchoukuo and China. The formation of the "economic bloc" is not only intended to control China's customs and currency but also her production and trade in order to dominate the Far East. When this policy is pushed further, they will be able to control the livelihood of every Chinese citizen, thus gradually subjugating the Chinese race.

4. The recent establishment of the "Asia Development Board" marked the settlement of a long dispute among Japanese leaders over the creation of an organ to take charge of China affairs. A "China Affairs Bureau" was proposed some time ago, but it was later changed into the "Asia Development Board." As the "China Affairs Bureau" is already an insult to the Chinese, the establishment of the present "Asia Development Board" is apparently a greater insult to all the Asiatics. This is not only designed to dismember and conquer China, but also to threaten the whole of Asia. On the day previous to the inauguration of this Board, Prince Konoye declared that "Japan wants to form a new administrative organ to create a new order in East Asia, and to maintain contact with China, and this organ will decide on all policies toward China, and carry out the ultimate aim in the China Incident."

We should know that the "Asia Development Board" is the main organ that is entrusted with the task of carrying out all plans to conquer China. It may be regarded as the headquarters of all Japanese special service sections which have been responsible for all the crimes committed in this country. In the past, the Japanese were doing things in the dark, for they considered that the time was not opportune, but they have unmasked their sinister designs and carry out aggressive acts openly. The inauguration of the "Asia Development Board" should have made us fully understand Japan's designs in China and her ultimate aim in the so-called "China Incident." When we talk of a "protracted resistance campaign," they try to call it a "protracted reconstruction campaign." In plain words, the so-called "protracted reconstruction campaign" is a prolonged campaign for subjugating China.

A careful study of the statement made by Prince Konoye on December 22 will enable us to grasp the true significance of Japan's policy. In the first place, he again asserted the creation of a new order in East Asia through the cooperation of Japan, Manchoukuo and China. As this statement was intended for international consumption, the Japanese Premier had apparently exercised due care in choosing words and phrases that tend to conceal Japan's sinister aims. Therefore, on the surface the statement made no territorial claims nor demand for indemnities, and, what is more, it revealed that Japan is considering the relinquishment of her extraterritorial rights and retrocession of her concessions to China. Such sugar-coated words may, therefore, fool those people who are not aware of the true meaning of the so-called "new order," but to us, the motives behind their plans in China are as clear as daylight.

Secondly, the aim of the anti-Communist cooperation between China and Japan, suggested by Prince Konoye, is to station Japanese troops in North China and to demarcate Inner Mongolia as a Communist-suppression area. It is absurd to suggest that China, organized under the Three People's Principles, should fight Communism. It may be said that Japan's ultimate objective is to take advantage of the anti-Communism bugaboo in order to control the military, political, cultural and even diplomatic affairs of China.

The failure to realize this aim long before the outbreak of the hostilities has been the deep-rooted cause for Japan's hostile attitude toward this country. It was because we did not want to fall into the Japanese trap that we put up armed resistance against tremendous odds. If the proposal for anti-Communist cooperation were acceptable we would have accepted it long ago. In reality, the proposed anti-Communism cooperation is not aimed against the Comintern, nor against Soviet Russia, but against China. If this is really aimed against Soviet Russia, why was it that Japan yielded to the Soviet forces during the Changkufeng Incident? It is therefore apparent that anti-Communism is only a means to pull the wool over the eyes of the world and to fulfil their object of stationing troops in North China and Inner Mongolia. Had China agreed to the stationing of Japanese on Chinese soil, the present war of resistance would not have occurred at all. If China were really afraid of Japan and let the latter station troops in the North, she would have annexed the whole of North China and Inner Mongolia to Japan during the Tsinan Incident when Japanese forces attempted to block the advance of the National troops in their Northern Expedition.

Thirdly, the demand for the special privilege of developing North China and Inner Mongolia, made in Prince Konoye's statement, is in fact an attempt to dominate China economically and to control Chinese economic life. In addition, a claim was made for freedom of residence and trade for Japanese nationals in the interior. This reminds us of the Japanese special service sections and *ronin,* Japanese-sponsored drug traffic, white slavery, arms smuggling, manufacturing of traitors, and other atrocities that tend to undermine the morality of our people and the peace and order of this country.

The problem of the opening up of the interior to foreign nationals may be discussed after China has regained her administrative and territorial integrity, but China will not grant the request of Japan unless we are willing to abandon the right of maintaining peace and order and let the Japanese demoralize our people and absorb the economic blood of the nation. It may be recalled that in 1929 Mr. Arita, then Director of the East Asiatic Affairs Bureau, was instructed by Premier Tanaka to convey to Nanking Japan's request for the granting of the right of navigation to Japanese nationals in the Northeast, but this request was rejected because the past conduct of Japanese residents in China had created a very bad impression on us. If Japanese nationals were allowed to reside and do business in the interior,

I am afraid that the freedom of the Chinese people would soon disappear.

Fourthly, Prince Konoye, in his statement, further stated that Japan seeks only to render effective cooperation and collaboration between the two countries. Of course, it is only logical and proper that all nations should maintain cordial relations with each other, but the real motive behind Japan's overtures for "cooperation," "collaboration," and the "formation of an East Asia Bloc" is to undermine China's independence.

The points aforementioned, according to Prince Konoye, represent the "minimum demands of Japan." May we ask what else Japan is going to demand of China? These demands are many times harsher than the three-point program formulated by Mr. Hirota, former Japanese Foreign Minister. Since we had refused to accept Mr. Hirota's program before the outbreak of the hostilities, how can Japan expect us to accept the present terms, which are tantamount to capitulation?

Japan's ambitions are clearly indicated in Tanaka's Memorial to the Throne which stated that "to conquer the world, China must be first conquered." Prince Konoye, in a statement made on December 1 at the Privy Council, explaining the organization of the new Asia Development Board, said that "the Sino-Japanese conflict will be regarded as terminated when reconstruction work is under way with the cooperation of Japan, Manchoukuo and China."[4] The so-called "reconstruction work" may be taken to mean the work of conquering China, and it is clear to every one of us that Japan's aggression will not cease until China is completely conquered. Our friendly Powers ought to know that Japan's southward advance and continental policy are being carried out at the same time. In her program of conquering China is included the plan to destroy international order and to dominate East Asia by expelling foreign influence from this country.

Judging from Prince Konoye's statement, we can conclude that the real aim of Japan is to devour China and subjugate the Chinese race. The so-called cooperation between China and Japan is only a matter of formality. Territory and indemnity

[4] *Japan Weekly Chronicle,* December 8, 1938, p. 674.

are not wanted by Japan, simply because she is desirous of something more remunerative. In plain words, the "economic bloc" proposed by Japan is aimed to attain complete control over China's finances and economic resources, which is far better than an indemnity. Japan's demand for the stationing of troops in North China and Inner Mongolia and for freedom of residence and trade in the interior is apparently prompted by her desire to control Chinese territory and enslave the Chinese people. Japan conquered Korea under the pretext of "Japanese-Korean cooperation" and now she has coined new high-sounding terms, such as "East Asia Bloc." In other words, these terms are smoke-screens for annexing China and establishing a "Continental Empire of Japan." Japan is now all set for the execution of her program of conquest, but she still has to wait until China is fooled or beaten to her knees by force. Therefore, it would be a dream if we hope to seek peace by compromise with Japan.

In examining Japan's intrigues for the conquest of China, we are at a loss to know why Japan has completely lost her rational feelings. How can a nation with a population of only 70,000,000 expect to devour another with a long history of 5000 years, a population of 450,000,000 and a territory of 12,000,000 square kilometers? Is it possible for a revolutionized Government lightly to abandon the sacred mission of national salvation for which it has been working for years?

The enemy has repeatedly announced its ambition to establish political, economic and cultural relations between Japan, Manchoukuo and China. In other words, Japan's aim is to destroy the independent existence of the Chinese race through political, economic and cultural means. However, there is no independent culture in East Asia besides the Chinese culture, which has been holding a prominent position in Far Eastern civilization. China's political system, which is characterized by friendliness, kindness, filial piety, justice and good faith, has been the pillar of East Asia for more than five thousand years. The Three People's Principles expounded by Dr. Sun Yat-sen, founder of the Chinese Republic, are in reality doctrines of equality, peace and independence and a bulwark of permanent peace.

What kind of political system can Japan boast of? May we ask what kind of political system Japan is now practicing? Japan does not know herself well. She thinks that the world can be fooled. It is indeed a matter of profound regret that the fore-runners of the Meiji Restoration had made their efforts in vain; for the Empire is now dominated by a horde of militarists who know no law and order but the idea of conquest. In their eyes there is no China and even no world. If they are allowed to continue to hold sway, the fate of Japan is doomed. Although we are bitterly against Japanese militarists, we are still friends to the Japanese people, who are our neighbors, and feel sorry for them.

In conclusion, to Japan the present war is an act of violence that represents the collapse of morality; but to China it is a sacred struggle for international justice. Japanese militarists have run amuck regardless of human civilization and welfare. Nations which are responsible for the maintenance of the sanctity of international treaties are in duty bound to checkmate the aggressor, but they have thus far hesitated to take up the responsibility. Regardless of any sacrifice, China is now fighting alone for international justice. In the present war of resistance, we are not only fighting for our national independence, and complete realization of our revolutionary task, but also for the sanctity of international treaties and restoration of world order. The current war is a struggle between evil and good, right and wrong, might and right, law and disorder, and justice and violence. We believe justice will triumph. All the right-thinking peoples of the world will cooperate with us for the sake of justice. The final victory must be ours if we continue to struggle resolutely despite hardships and sufferings.

III. THE THREE-POWER PACT BETWEEN GERMANY, ITALY AND JAPAN, SIGNED AT BERLIN, SEPTEMBER 27, 1940[1]

In force September 27, 1940

[Translation]

The Governments of Germany, Italy and Japan consider it the prerequisite of a lasting peace that every nation in the world shall receive the space to which it is entitled. They have, therefore, decided to stand by and cooperate with one another in their efforts in Greater East Asia and the regions of Europe respectively. In doing this it is their prime purpose to establish and maintain a new order of things, calculated to promote the mutual prosperity and welfare of the peoples concerned.

It is, furthermore, the desire of the three Governments to extend cooperation to nations in other spheres of the world who are inclined to direct their efforts along lines similar to their own for the purpose of realizing their ultimate object, world peace.

Accordingly, the Governments of Germany, Italy and Japan have agreed as follows:

ARTICLE 1. Japan recognizes and respects the leadership of Germany and Italy in the establishment of a new order in Europe.

ARTICLE 2. Germany and Italy recognize and respect the leadership of Japan in the establishment of a new order in Greater East Asia.

ARTICLE 3. Germany, Italy and Japan agree to cooperate in their efforts on aforesaid lines. They further undertake to assist one another with all political, economic and military means if one of the three Contracting Powers is attacked by a Power at

[1] German Library of Information, *Facts in Review,* II, p. 486. The instrument has been officially called a treaty and a pact. German, Italian and Japanese texts exist in the *alternat,* but it is not stated which of them is controlling; the authorized English translation here given, which differs from other English translations in the grammatical construction of the preamble, is from the German text.

present not involved in the European War or in the Chinese-Japanese conflict.

ARTICLE 4. With the view to implementing the present pact, joint technical commissions, to be appointed by the respective Governments of Germany, Italy and Japan, will meet without delay.

ARTICLE 5. Germany, Italy and Japan affirm that the above agreement affects in no way the political status existing at present between each of the three Contracting Parties and Soviet Russia.

ARTICLE 6. The present pact shall become valid immediately upon signature and shall remain in force ten years from the date on which it becomes effective.

In due time, before the expiration of said term, the High Contracting Parties shall, at the request of any one of them, enter into negotiations for its renewal.

In recognition thereof, the undersigned, duly authorized by their respective governments, have signed this pact and have affixed their seals thereto.

DONE in triplicate at Berlin, the 27th day of September, 1940, in the eighteenth year of the Fascist era, corresponding to the 27th day of the ninth month of the fifteenth year of Showa.

[Here follow signatures.]

IV. NEUTRALITY PACT BETWEEN JAPAN AND THE UNION OF SOVIET SOCIALIST REPUBLICS, SIGNED AT MOSCOW, APRIL 13, 1941 [1]

The Presidium of the Supreme Soviet of the Union of Soviet Socialist Republics and His Majesty the Emperor of Japan, guided by a desire to strengthen peaceful and friendly relations between the two countries, decided to conclude a pact on neutrality, for the purpose of which they appointed as their representatives:

For the Presidium of the Supreme Soviet of the Union of Soviet Socialist Republics, Vyacheslav Molotov, Chairman of the Council of People's Commissars and People's Commissar for Foreign Affairs.

For His Majesty the Emperor of Japan, Yosuke Matsuoka, Minister of Foreign Affairs, Ju San Min, Cavalier of the Order of the Sacred Treasure, First Class; and Yoshitsugu Tatekawa, Ambassador Extraordinary and Plenipotentiary in the Union of Soviet Socialist Republics, Lieut. Gen., Ju San Min, Cavalier of the Order of the Rising Sun, First Class, and the Order of the Golden Kite, Fourth Class.

Who, after the exchange of their credentials, which were found in due and proper form, agreed on the following:

ARTICLE I. Both Contracting Parties undertake to maintain peaceful and friendly relations between them and mutually respect the territorial integrity and inviolability of the other Contracting Party.

ARTICLE II. Should one of the Contracting Parties become the object of hostilities on the part of one or several third Powers, the other Contracting Party will observe neutrality throughout the duration of the conflict.

[1] English version as released by Tass news agency, *New York Times,* April 14, 1941, p. 8. A French version, released through the Deutsches Nachrichtenbüro, Berlin, to France differs in phrasing. In that version, notably, Art. 2 reads:

"Art. 2.—Au cas où l'une des parties contractantes serait engagée dans une action militaire du fait d'une ou plusieurs autres puissances, l'autre partie contractante observerait une attitude de neutralité pendant toute la durée du conflit."

A third version, in English, corresponding in sense with the Tass version is given in *Tokyo Gazette,* IV, 1941, p. 487.

ARTICLE III. The present Pact comes into force from the day of its ratification by both Contracting Parties and remains valid for five years. In case neither of the Contracting Parties denounces the Pact one year before expiration of the term, it will be considered automatically prolonged for the next five years.

ARTICLE IV. The present Pact is subject to ratification as soon as possible. Instruments of ratification shall be exchanged in Tokyo also as soon as possible.

In confirmation whereof the above-named representatives signed the present Pact in two copies, drawn up in the Russian and Japanese languages, and affixed thereto their seals.

DONE in Moscow, April 13, 1941, which corresponds to the 13th day of the 4th month of the 16th year of Showa.

Signed by:

MOLOTOV,
YOSUKE MATSUOKA,
YOSHITSUGU TATEKAWA.

FRONTIER DECLARATION

In conformity with the spirit of the Neutrality Pact concluded April 13, 1941, between the Union of Soviet Socialist Republics and Japan, the Governments of the Union of Soviet Socialist Republics and Japan, in the interests of ensuring peaceful and friendly relations between the two countries, solemnly declare that the Union of Soviet Socialist Republics pledges to respect the territorial integrity and inviolability of Manchoukuo, and Japan pledges to respect the territorial integrity and inviolability of the Mongolian People's Republic.

Moscow, April 13, 1941.

Signed on behalf of the Government of the Union of Soviet Socialist Republics by:

MOLOTOV

On behalf of the Government of Japan by:

YOSUKE MATSUOKA,
YOSHITSUGU TATEKAWA.

V. SUMMARY OF PAST POLICY OF THE UNITED STATES IN THE PACIFIC. MESSAGE OF THE PRESIDENT TO THE CONGRESS, DECEMBER 15, 1941[1]

[Excerpt]

III

Pursuing this policy of conquest, Japan had first worked her way into and finally seized Manchuria. Next she had invaded China; and has sought for the past four and one-half years to subjugate her.

Passing through the China Sea close to the Philippine Islands, she then invaded and took possession of Indo-China. Today the Japanese are extending this conquest throughout Thailand—and seeking the occupation of Malaya and Burma. The Philippines, Borneo, Sumatra, Java come next on the Japanese timetable; and it is probable that further down the Japanese page, are the names of Australia, New Zealand, and all the other islands of the Pacific—including Hawaii and the great chain of the Aleutian Islands.

To the eastward of the Philippines, Japan violated the mandate under which she had received the custody of the Caroline, Marshall, and Mariana Islands after the World War, by fortifying them, and not only closing them to all commerce but her own but forbidding any foreigner even to visit them.

Japanese spokesmen, after their custom, cloaked these conquests with innocent-sounding names. They talked of the "New Order in Eastern Asia"; and then of the "co-prosperity sphere in Greater East Asia." What they really intended was the enslavement of every nation which they could bring within their power, and the enrichment—not of all Asia, not even of the common people of Japan—but of the warlords who had seized control

[1] House Doc. No. 458, 77th Cong., 1st sess.; Department of State, *Bulletin*, December 20, 1941, p. 529. The first two sections of the message review the earlier relations of the United States and the rise of the Hitler-Mussolini-Japanese policy of conquest.

of the Japanese State. Here too they were following the Nazi pattern.

By this course of aggression, Japan made it necessary for various countries, including our own, to keep in the Pacific in self-defense large armed forces and a vast amount of material which might otherwise have been used against Hitler. That, of course, is exactly what Hitler wanted them to do. The diversion thus created by Hitler's Japanese ally forced the peace-loving nations to establish and maintain a huge front in the Pacific.

IV

Throughout this course and program of Japanese aggression, the Government of the United States consistently endeavored to persuade the Government of Japan that Japan's best interests would lie in maintaining and cultivating friendly relations with the United States and with all other countries that believe in orderly and peaceful processes. Following the outbreak of hostilities between Japan and China in 1937, this Government made known to the Japanese Government and to the Chinese Government that whenever both those Governments considered it desirable we stood ready to exercise our good offices. During the following years of conflict that attitude on our part remained unchanged.

In October 1937, upon invitation by which the Belgian Government made itself the host, 19 countries which have interests in the Far East, including the United States, sent representatives to Brussels to consider the situation in the Far East in conformity with the Nine-Power Treaty and to endeavor to bring about an adjustment of the difficulties between Japan and China by peaceful means. Japan and Germany only of all the powers invited declined to attend. Japan was itself an original signatory of the treaty. China, one of the signatories, and the Soviet Union, not a signatory, attended. After the Conference opened, the countries in attendance made further attempts to persuade Japan to participate in the Conference. Japan again declined.

On November 24, 1937 the Conference adopted a declaration,

urging that "hostilities be suspended and resort be had to peaceful processes."

Japan scorned the Conference and ignored the recommendation.

It became clear that, unless this course of affairs in the Far East was halted, the Pacific area was doomed to experience the same horrors which have devastated Europe.

Therefore, in this year of 1941, in an endeavor to end this process by peaceful means while there seemed still to be a chance, the United States entered into discussions with Japan.

For nine months these conversations were carried on, for the purpose of arriving at some understanding acceptable to both countries.

Throughout all of these conversations, this Government took into account not only the legitimate interests of the United States but also those of Japan and other countries. When questions relating to the legitimate rights and interests of other countries came up, this Government kept in appropriate contact with the representatives of those countries.

In the course of these negotiations, the United States steadfastly advocated certain basic principles which should govern international relations. These were:

The principle of inviolability of territorial integrity and sovereignty of all nations.

The principle of non-interference in the internal affairs of other countries.

The principle of equality—including equality of commercial opportunity and treatment.

The principle of reliance upon international cooperation and conciliation for the prevention, and pacific settlement, of controversies.

The Japanese Government, it is true, repeatedly offered qualified statements of peaceful intention. But it became clear, as each proposal was explored, that Japan did not intend to modify in any way her greedy designs upon the whole Pacific world. Although she continually maintained that she was promoting only the peace and greater prosperity of East Asia, she continued her brutal assault upon the Chinese people.

Nor did Japan show any inclination to renounce her unholy alliance with Hitlerism.

In July of this year the Japanese Government connived with Hitler to force from the Vichy Government of France permission to place Japanese armed forces in southern Indo-China; and began sending her troops and equipment into that area.

The conversations between this Government and the Japanese Government were thereupon suspended.

But during the following month, at the urgent and insistent request of the Japanese Government, which again made emphatic profession of peaceful intent, the conversations were resumed.

At that time the Japanese Government made the suggestion that the responsible heads of the Japanese Government and of the Government of the United States meet personally to discuss means for bringing about an adjustment of relations between the two countries. I should have been happy to travel thousands of miles to meet the Premier of Japan for that purpose. But I felt it desirable, before so doing, to obtain some assurance that there could be some agreement on basic principles. This Government tried hard—but without success—to obtain such assurance from the Japanese Government.

The various proposals of the Japanese Government and the attitude taken by this Government are set forth in a document which the Secretary of State handed to the Japanese Ambassador on October 2, 1941 (see Annex 10).[2]

Thereafter, several formulas were offered and discussed. But the Japanese Government continued upon its course of war and conquest.

Finally, on November 20, 1941, the Japanese Government presented a new and narrow proposal (see Annex 11)[3] which called for supplying by the United States to Japan of as much oil as Japan might require, for suspension of freezing measures, and for discontinuance by the United States of aid to China. It con-

[2] Department of State, *Bulletin,* December 20, 1941, p. 537. cf. p. 220.
[3] See above, p. 223.

tained however no provision for abandonment by Japan of her war-like operations or aims.

Such a proposal obviously offered no basis for a peaceful settlement or even for a temporary adjustment. The American Government, in order to clarify the issues, presented to the Japanese Government on November 26, a clear-cut plan for a broad but simple settlement. (See Annex 12.)[4]

The outline of the proposed plan for agreement between the United States and Japan was divided into two parts:

In section one there was outlined a mutual declaration of policy containing affirmations that the national policies of the two countries were directed toward peace throughout the Pacific area, that the two countries had no territorial designs or aggressive intentions in that area, and that they would give active support to certain fundamental principles of peace upon which their relations with each other and all other nations would be based. There was provision for mutual pledges to support and apply in their economic relations with each other and with other nations and peoples liberal economic principles, which were enumerated, based upon the general principle of equality of commercial opportunity and treatment.

In section two there were outlined proposed steps to be taken by the two Governments. These steps envisaged a situation in which there would be no Japanese or other foreign armed forces in French Indo-China or in China. Mutual commitments were suggested along lines as follows: (a) to endeavor to conclude a multilateral non-aggression pact among the governments principally concerned in the Pacific area; (b) to endeavor to conclude among the principally interested governments an agreement to respect the territorial integrity of Indo-China and not to seek or accept preferential economic treatment therein; (c) not to support any government in China other than the National Government of the Republic of China with capital temporarily at Chungking; (d) to relinquish extraterritorial and related rights in China and to endeavor to obtain the agreement of other governments now possessing such rights to give up those rights;

[4] See Appendix, p. 312.

(e) to negotiate a trade agreement based upon reciprocal most-favored-nation treatment; (f) to remove freezing restrictions imposed by each country on the funds of the other; (g) to agree upon a plan for the stabilization of the dollar-yen rate; (h) to agree that no agreement which either had concluded with any third power or powers shall be interpreted by it in a way to conflict with the fundamental purpose of this agreement; and (i) to use their influence to cause other governments to adhere to the basic political and economic principles provided for in this suggested agreement.

In the midst of these conversations, we learned that new contingents of Japanese armed forces and new masses of equipment were moving into Indo-China. Toward the end of November these movements were intensified. During the first week of December new movements of Japanese forces made it clear that, under cover of the negotiations, attacks on unspecified objectives were being prepared.

I promptly asked the Japanese Government for a frank statement of the reasons for increasing its forces in Indo-China. (See Annex 13.)[5] I was given an evasive and specious reply (see Annex 14.)[6] Simultaneously, the Japanese operations went forward with increased tempo.

We did not know then, as we know now, that they had ordered and were even then carrying out their plan for a treacherous attack upon us.

I was determined, however, to exhaust every conceivable effort for peace. With this in mind, on the evening of December sixth last, I addressed a personal message to the Emperor of Japan. (See Annex 15.)[7]

To this Government's proposal of November twenty-sixth the Japanese Government made no reply until December seventh. On that day the Japanese Ambassador here and the Special Representative whom the Japanese Government had sent to the United States to assist in peaceful negotiations, delivered a lengthy document to our Secretary of State, one hour after the

[5] Department of State, *Bulletin,* December 20, 1941, p. 540.

[6] *Ibid.,* December 13, 1941, p. 464.

[7] *Ibid.*

Japanese had launched a vicious attack upon American territory and American citizens in the Pacific.

That document (see Annex 16)[8] was a few minutes after its receipt aptly characterized by the Secretary of State as follows:

"I must say that in all my conversations with you [the Japanese Ambassador] during the last nine months I have never uttered one word of untruth. This is borne out absolutely by the record. In all my fifty years of public service I have never seen a document that was more crowded with infamous falsehoods and distortions—infamous falsehoods and distortions on a scale so huge that I never imagined until today that any Government on this planet was capable of uttering them."

I concur emphatically in every word of that statement.

For the record of history, it is essential in reading this part of my Message always to bear in mind that the actual air and submarine attack in the Hawaiian Islands commenced on Sunday, December 7, at 1:20 P.M., Washington time—7:50 A.M., Honolulu time of same day—Monday, December 8, 3:20 A.M., Tokyo time.

To my message of December 6 (9 P.M. Washington time—December 7, 11 A.M., Tokyo time) to the Emperor of Japan, invoking his cooperation with me in further effort to preserve peace, there has finally come to me on December 10 (6:23 A.M., Washington time—December 10, 8:23 P.M., Tokyo time) a reply, conveyed in a telegraphic report by the American Ambassador at Tokyo dated December 8, 1 P.M. (December 7, 11 P.M., Washington time).

The Ambassador reported that at 7 o'clock on the morning of the eighth (December 7, 5 P.M., Washington time) the Japanese Minister for Foreign Affairs asked him to call at his official residence; that the Foreign Minister handed the Ambassador a memorandum dated December 8 (December 7, Washington time) the text of which had been transmitted to the Japanese Ambassador in Washington to be presented to the American Government (this was the memorandum which was delivered by the Japanese Ambassador to the Secretary of State at 2:20 P.M. on Sunday, December 7—Monday, December 8, 4:20 A.M., Tokyo time); that the Foreign Minister had been in touch with the

[8] Appendix, p. 312.

Emperor; and that the Emperor desired that the memorandum be regarded as the Emperor's reply to my message.

Further, the Ambassador reports, the Foreign Minister made an oral statement. Textually, the oral statement began, "His Majesty has expressed his gratefulness and appreciation for the cordial message of the President." The message further continued to the effect that, in regard to our inquiries on the subject of increase of Japanese forces in French Indo-China, His Majesty had commanded his Government to state its views to the American Government. The message concluded, textually, with the statement:

"Establishment of peace in the Pacific, and consequently of the world, has been the cherished desire of His Majesty for the realization of which he has hitherto made his Government to continue its earnest endeavors. His Majesty trusts that the President is fully aware of this fact."

Japan's real reply, however, made by Japan's warlords and evidently formulated many days before, took the form of the attack which had already been made without warning upon our territories at various points in the Pacific.

VI. JAPANESE ACTION RESPECTING STRATEGIC ISLANDS

1. Paracels Islands—Statement of the Foreign Office Spokesman regarding the Question of French Occupation of Sisha Islands, July 7, 1938[1]

On the 4th instant, the French Ambassador, Mr. Charles Arsène-Henry called on the Vice-Minister for Foreign Affairs, Mr. Kensuke Horinouchi, and verbally notified the latter that the Government of French Indo-China had appointed an administrator for the Sisha Islands (the Paracels Islands) and dispatched more than ten Annamese policemen there and established a light-house, buoys and wireless station, and had thereby effected a definite and complete occupation of the Islands by France. The French Ambassador also stated to the Vice-Minister that the Japanese nationals had for more than ten years been engaged in the collection of sea weeds and rock phosphate in the Islands but their interests would be respected.

With regard to the French verbal communication, the Foreign Office invited the French Ambassador to the office today and the Vice-Minister handed to Ambassador Arsène-Henry a *Note Verbale* which set forth clearly the views of the Japanese Government, and discussed the question at length with the Ambassador. The Vice-Minister called attention of the French Government to the possibility that the stationing of the Annamese policemen in the Islands was likely to give rise to some unexpected misunderstanding between them and the Japanese engaged in the work mentioned above, and expressed the hope that the said police force would be withdrawn.

2. Hainan Island

a. The Foreign Office Spokesman's Statement regarding the Occupation of Hainan Island, February 10, 1939[2]

[1] *Contemporary Japan,* VII, 1938, p. 386.
[2] *Ibid.,* VIII, 1939, p. 182.

1. Operation of Japanese forces on Hainan Island does not violate the Japanese-French agreement of 1907.[3]

2. At the time of the conclusion of the agreement China was virtually helpless under the rule of the Ching Dynasty, whose administrative power was almost paralyzed. The maintenance of peace and order was accordingly impossible. It was for the purpose of preventing unrest and disturbance in the contiguous regions and vicinities of their territories which might arise from such conditions of China that Japan and France entered into the agreement to support each other.

3. Since then the conditions in China have undergone a complete change. The unrest and disturbances have steadily decreased, and there has been an increasing danger of attack upon the regions already mentioned by China herself which has turned them into military bases for its large armies. It was indeed due to this that the present China Affair occurred.

4. With the extension of the fighting fronts, the zones of military operation have spread all over China. The major points of the operations have been tending to shift from the northern regions to the southern regions of China, and Hainan Island has thus become a very important base of Chinese military operations. The present Japanese operation on Hainan Island is for the purpose of exterminating Chinese military forces in the island, and is therefore an affair which has nothing to do with the question of assuring peace and security envisaged by the Japanese-French agreement.

5. The notes exchanged in 1897[4] between France and China regarding the non-cession of Hainan Island are simply a matter

[3] Agreement respecting the integrity of China, the equal treatment of commerce, the maintenance of order, etc., signed at Paris, June 10, 1907, 100 *British and Foreign State Papers,* p. 913.

[4] For the substance of the understanding see Reinach, Lucien de, *Recueil des traités conclus par la France en Extrême-Orient,* I, p. 369–70. In a conference on February 13, 1897, at Peking, Prince Kung of the Tsung-li Yamen categorically told A. Gerard, the French Minister, that China was not then nor ever disposed to consent under any form whatever to concessions that would excite the concern of France in their mutual interest of obviating any threat to the territorial *status quo* in the region of Hainan and the Kwangtung coast opposite it. The understanding was confirmed by a copy of the minutes of the conversation recorded by the Tsung-li Yamen.

concerning those two countries alone. They are therefore not binding upon Japan.

b. Statement of the Foreign Office regarding the Occupation of Hainan Island, February 13, 1939[5]

The French Ambassador, Mr. Charles Arsène-Henry, at 11 o'clock this morning called on the Foreign Minister, Mr. Hachiro Arita, at the Foreign Office to seek the Japanese Government's explanation regarding the object, duration and nature of the Japanese occupation of Hainan Island. Foreign Minister Arita assured the French Ambassador that Japan's occupation of Hainan Island has a military object to strengthen Japanese suspension of traffic against Chinese vessels off South China and thereby to accelerate the collapse of the Chiang K'ai-shek regime, while in its nature and duration Japan's occupation of the said island does not exceed military necessity. Foreign Minister Arita made it clear that Japan has no territorial designs on the island. The French Ambassador appreciated Foreign Minister Arita's explanation and left the Foreign Office after remaining with the latter for forty minutes.

3. Spratley Islands

a. The Foreign Office's Statement concerning the Administrative Jurisdiction over Shinnan Gunto (Spratley Islands), March 31, 1939[6]

Shinnan Gunto (or the Spratley Islands) are a group of small reefs lying in the South China Sea, off the coast of French Indo-China. These reefs had long been known as ownerless. However, in 1917 Japanese began, before the nationals of any other country, to embark upon the economic development of the reefs, which has continued ever since, by investing a considerable amount of capital and erecting various permanent establishments. The Japanese Government, officially recognizing the activities of these nationals, have on several occasions since sent warships to the reefs and been giving them various aids as oc-

[5] *Contemporary Japan,* VIII, 1939, p. 312.

casion demanded. But the absence of administrative jurisdiction over the reefs has caused not only inconveniences with regard to the protection and regulation of the lives, property and enterprises of the Japanese nationals there, but has been liable to give rise to unnecessary disputes with France. Accordingly, the Japanese Government, in order to eliminate such inconveniences and disadvantages, have decided to place the reefs under the jurisdiction of the Government-General of Taiwan, and having published the fact under date of March 30, 1939, the Vice-Minister for Foreign Affairs, Mr. Renzo Sawada, notified the French Ambassador in Tokyo, Mr. Charles Arsène-Henry, to this effect on March 31.

b. The Foreign Office Spokesman's Statement on the French Protest regarding the Same, April 7, 1939[6]

The French Ambassador, Mr. Arsène-Henry, called on Foreign Vice-Minister Sawada at the Foreign Office at noon on April 5 and, under instructions from his home Government, handed to him a note protesting against the Japanese Government's previous communication in connection with its decision to place the Shinnan Gunto under the jurisdiction of the Formosan Government-General.

The Foreign Vice-Minister told the French Ambassador that there is no room for consideration regarding the issue, which was decided on the basis of established policy, and that the Japanese Government would receive the note only as a matter of reference.

[6] *Ibid.*, p. 439, 440. The statement on the protest of France is a "Domei translation."

VII. JAPANESE–NETHERLANDS ARBITRATION TREATY – STATEMENT OF THE JAPANESE FOREIGN OFFICE SPOKESMAN, FEBRUARY 12, 1940[1]

1. The signed Protocol annexed to the treaty concluded between Japan and the Netherlands on April 19, 1933,[2] regarding judicial settlement, arbitration and conciliation, contained a provision stipulating that in case any change is made in Japan's legal position *vis-à-vis* the Permanent Court of International Justice as a consequence of Japan's withdrawal from the League of Nations, the two Contracting Parties should begin consultation for the purpose of examining whether or not it is necessary to revise the provisions of the said treaty which concern the Permanent Court of International Justice.

2. Japan's withdrawal from the League of Nations and the change in her relations with the Permanent Court of International Justice have caused her to consider it necessary to make some technical adjustments in the treaty. The Japanese Government have, therefore, requested the Netherlands Government to open conversations promptly with a view to revising the treaty, which has resulted in an agreement of views between the two Governments.

3. The Japanese Government have, under the provisions of Article 25 of the treaty, taken the steps which are necessary for terminating the validity of the treaty on August 11 of this year.

The sole purpose of the Japanese Government in terminating the treaty lies in their desire not to be further bound by it in case the conversations for the treaty revision do not reach a conclusion by the said date.

4. In view of these circumstances the Japanese Government are earnestly desirous of completing quickly the conversations on the treaty revision and concluding a new treaty before the invalidation of the abrogated treaty.

[1] *Contemporary Japan,* IX, 1940, p. 366; *Tokyo Gazette,* III, p. 402.
[2] League of Nations, *Treaty Series,* vol. 163, p. 351.

VIII. PROTOCOL BETWEEN JAPAN AND FRANCE REGARDING THE JOINT DEFENSE OF FRENCH INDO-CHINA, VICHY, JULY 29, 1941 [1]

[Translation]

The Imperial Japanese Government and the French Government,

Taking into consideration the present international situation;

Recognizing in consequence that should the security of French Indo-China be menaced, Japan would have reason to consider the general tranquillity in East Asia and its own security endangered;

Renewing on this occasion the engagements undertaken, on the part of Japan to respect the rights and interests of France in East Asia, in particular, the territorial integrity of French Indo-China, and the sovereign rights of France in all parts of the Union of Indo-China, and on the part of France to conclude in regard to Indo-China no agreement or understanding with a third power which envisages political, economic, or military cooperation of a character directly or indirectly opposed to Japan;

Have agreed upon the following dispositions:

1. The two Governments promise to cooperate in military matters for the defense of French Indo-China.

2. The measures to be taken for the purposes of the aforesaid cooperation shall constitute the object of special arrangements.

3. The foregoing dispositions shall remain in effect only so long as the circumstances motivating their adoption continue to exist.

In witness thereof the undersigned, duly authorized by their respective Governments, have signed the present protocol, which enters into effect from this day, and have affixed their seals thereto.

Executed in duplicate, in the Japanese and French languages, at Vichy, July 29 of the 16th year of Showa, corresponding to July 29, 1941.

SOTOMATSU KATO [SEAL]
F. DARLAN [SEAL]

[1] Department of State, *Bulletin,* October 11, 1941, p. 286.

IX. FINAL DOCUMENTS OF THE JAPANESE–UNITED STATES NEGOTIATIONS

1. United States Note to Japan, November 26, 1941, handed by the Secretary of State (Hull) to the Japanese Ambassador (Nomura)[1]

ORAL

Strictly confidential

NOVEMBER 26, 1941.

The representatives of the Government of the United States and of the Government of Japan have been carrying on during the past several months informal and exploratory conversations for the purpose of arriving at a settlement if possible of questions relating to the entire Pacific area based upon the principles of peace, law and order and fair dealing among nations. These principles include the principle of inviolability of territorial integrity and sovereignty of each and all nations; the principle of non-interference in the internal affairs of other countries; the principle of equality, including equality of commercial opportunity and treatment; and the principle of reliance upon international cooperation and conciliation for the prevention and pacific settlement of controversies and for improvement of international conditions by peaceful methods and processes.

It is believed that in our discussions some progress has been made in reference to the general principles which constitute the basis of a peaceful settlement covering the entire Pacific area. Recently the Japanese Ambassador has stated that the Japanese Government is desirous of continuing the conversations directed toward a comprehensive and peaceful settlement in the Pacific area; that it would be helpful toward creating an atmosphere favorable to the successful outcome of the conversations if a temporary *modus vivendi* could be agreed upon to be in effect while the conversations looking to a peaceful settlement in the

[1] House Doc. 458, 77th Cong., 1st sess., p. 107; Department of State, *Bulletin,* December 13, 1941, p. 461. This note consists of two parts, an oral statement and an outline of a proposed basis for agreement between the United States and Japan.

Pacific were continuing. On November 20 the Japanese Ambassador communicated to the Secretary of State proposals in regard to temporary measures to be taken respectively by the Government of Japan and by the Government of the United States, which measures are understood to have been designed to accomplish the purposes above indicated.

The Government of the United States most earnestly desires to contribute to the promotion and maintenance of peace and stability in the Pacific area, and to afford every opportunity for the continuance of discussions with the Japanese Government directed toward working out a broad-gauge program of peace throughout the Pacific area. The proposals which were presented by the Japanese Ambassador on November 20 contain some features which, in the opinion of this Government, conflict with the fundamental principles which form a part of the general settlement under consideration and to which each Government has declared that it is committed. The Government of the United States believes that the adoption of such proposals would not be likely to contribute to the ultimate objectives of ensuring peace under law, order and justice in the Pacific area, and it suggests that further effort be made to resolve our divergences of views in regard to the practical application of the fundamental principles already mentioned.

With this object in view the Government of the United States offers for the consideration of the Japanese Government a plan of a broad but simple settlement covering the entire Pacific area as one practical exemplification of a program which this Government envisages as something to be worked out during our further conversations.

The plan therein suggested represents an effort to bridge the gap between our draft of June 21, 1941 [2] and the Japanese draft of September 25 [2] by making a new approach to the essential problems underlying a comprehensive Pacific settlement. This plan contains provisions dealing with the practical application of the fundamental principles which we have agreed in our conversations constitute the only sound basis for worthwhile international relations. We hope that in this way progress toward reaching a

[2] Not printed.

meeting of minds between our two Governments may be expedited.

Strictly confidential, tentative and without commitment

NOVEMBER 26, 1941.

OUTLINE OF PROPOSED BASIS FOR AGREEMENT BETWEEN THE UNITED STATES AND JAPAN

Section I

Draft Mutual Declaration of Policy

The Government of the United States and the Government of Japan both being solicitous for the peace of the Pacific affirm that their national policies are directed toward lasting and extensive peace throughout the Pacific area, that they have no territorial designs in that area, that they have no intention of threatening other countries or of using military force aggressively against any neighboring nation, and that, accordingly, in their national policies they will actively support and give practical application to the following fundamental principles upon which their relations with each other and with all other governments are based:

(1) The principle of inviolability of territorial integrity and sovereignty of each and all nations.
(2) The principle of non-interference in the internal affairs of other countries.
(3) The principle of equality, including equality of commercial opportunity and treatment.
(4) The principle of reliance upon international cooperation and conciliation for the prevention and pacific settlement of controversies and for improvement of international conditions by peaceful methods and processes.

The Government of Japan and the Government of the United States have agreed that toward eliminating chronic political instability, preventing recurrent economic collapse, and providing a basis for peace, they will actively support and practically apply the following principles in their economic relations with each other and with other nations and peoples:

(1) The principle of non-discrimination in international commercial relations.

(2) The principle of international economic cooperation and abolition of extreme nationalism as expressed in excessive trade restrictions.

(3) The principle of non-discriminatory access by all nations to raw material supplies.

(4) The principle of full protection of the interests of consuming countries and populations as regards the operation of international commodity agreements.

(5) The principle of establishment of such institutions and arrangements of international finance as may lend aid to the essential enterprises and the continuous development of all countries and may permit payments through processes of trade consonant with the welfare of all countries.

Section II

Steps To Be Taken by the Government of the United States and by the Government of Japan

The Government of the United States and the Government of Japan propose to take steps as follows:

1. The Government of the United States and the Government of Japan will endeavor to conclude a multilateral non-aggression pact among the British Empire, China, Japan, the Netherlands, the Soviet Union, Thailand and the United States.

2. Both Governments will endeavor to conclude among the American, British, Chinese, Japanese, the Netherland and Thai Governments an agreement whereunder each of the Governments would pledge itself to respect the territorial integrity of French Indo-China and, in the event that there should develop a threat to the territorial integrity of Indo-China, to enter into immediate consultation with a view to taking such measures as may be deemed necessary and advisable to meet the threat in question. Such agreement would provide also that each of the Governments party to the agreement would not seek or accept preferential treatment in its trade or economic relations with Indo-China and

would use its influence to obtain for each of the signatories equality of treatment in trade and commerce with French Indo-China.

3. The Government of Japan will withdraw all military, naval, air and police forces from China and from Indo-China.

4. The Government of the United States and the Government of Japan will not support—militarily, politically, economically—any government or regime in China other than the National Government of the Republic of China with capital temporarily at Chungking.

5. Both Governments will give up all extraterritorial rights in China, including rights and interests in and with regard to international settlements and concessions, and rights under the Boxer Protocol of 1901.

Both Governments will endeavor to obtain the agreement of the British and other governments to give up extraterritorial rights in China, including rights in international settlements and in concessions and under the Boxer Protocol of 1901.

6. The Government of the United States and the Government of Japan will enter into negotiations for the conclusion between the United States and Japan of a trade agreement, based upon reciprocal most-favored-nation treatment and reduction of trade barriers by both countries, including an undertaking by the United States to bind raw silk on the free list.

7. The Government of the United States and the Government of Japan will, respectively, remove the freezing restrictions on Japanese funds in the United States and on American funds in Japan.

8. Both Governments will agree upon a plan for the stabilization of the dollar-yen rate, with the allocation of funds adequate for this purpose, half to be supplied by Japan and half by the United States.

9. Both Governments will agree that no agreement which either has concluded with any third power or powers shall be interpreted by it in such a way as to conflict with the fundamental purpose of this agreement, the establishment and preservation of peace throughout the Pacific area.

10. Both Governments will use their influence to cause other

governments to adhere to and to give practical application to the basic political and economic principles set forth in this agreement.

2. Memorandum of the Japanese Government, presented by the Japanese Ambassador (Nomura) to the Secretary of State (Hull), 2:20 p.m., E.S.T., December 7, 1941 [3]

The Department of State issued the following statement concerning the circumstances attending the delivery of this memorandum:

"At 1 P.M. December 7 the Japanese Ambassador asked for an appointment for the Japanese representatives to see the Secretary of State. The appointment was made for 1:45 P.M. The Japanese representatives arrived at the office of the Secretary of State at 2:05 P.M. They were received by the Secretary at 2:20 P.M.[4] The Japanese Ambassador handed to the Secretary of State what was understood to be a reply to the document handed to him by the Secretary of State on November 26.

"Secretary Hull carefully read the statement presented by the Japanese representatives and immediately turned to the Japanese Ambassador and with the greatest indignation said:

" 'I must say that in all my conversations with you [the Japanese Ambassador] during the last nine months I have never uttered one word of untruth. This is borne out absolutely by the record. In all my 50 years of public service I have never seen a document that was more crowded with infamous falsehoods and distortions—infamous falsehoods and distortions on a scale so huge that I never imagined until today that any Government on this planet was capable of uttering them.' "

MEMORANDUM

1. The Government of Japan, prompted by a genuine desire to come to an amicable understanding with the Government of

[3] Department of State, *Bulletin,* December 13, 1941, p. 466; House Doc. 458, 77th Congress, 1st. sess., p. 113.

[4] The attack on the Hawaiian Islands commenced December 7, at 1:20 P.M. Washington time, 7:50 A.M. Honolulu time, or one hour before the presentation of the memorandum.

the United States in order that the two countries by their joint efforts may secure the peace of the Pacific Area and thereby contribute toward the realization of world peace, has continued negotiations with the utmost sincerity since April last with the Government of the United States regarding the adjustment and advancement of Japanese-American relations and the stabilization of the Pacific Area.

The Japanese Government has the honor to state frankly its views concerning the claims the American Government has persistently maintained as well as the measures the United States and Great Britain have taken toward Japan during these eight months.

2. It is the immutable policy of the Japanese Government to insure the stability of East Asia and to promote world peace and thereby to enable all nations to find each its proper place in the world.

Ever since China Affair broke out owing to the failure on the part of China to comprehend Japan's true intentions, the Japanese Government has striven for the restoration of peace and it has consistently exerted its best efforts to prevent the extension of war-like disturbances. It was also to that end that in September last year Japan concluded the Tripartite Pact with Germany and Italy.

However, both the United States and Great Britain have resorted to every possible measure to assist the Chungking regime so as to obstruct the establishment of a general peace between Japan and China, interfering with Japan's constructive endeavors toward the stabilization of East Asia. Exerting pressure on the Netherlands East Indies, or menacing French Indo-China, they have attempted to frustrate Japan's aspiration to the ideal of common prosperity in cooperation with these regions. Furthermore, when Japan in accordance with its protocol with France took measures of joint defense of French Indo-China, both American and British Governments, wilfully misinterpreting it as a threat to their own possessions, and inducing the Netherlands Government to follow suit, they enforced the assets freezing order, thus severing economic relations with Japan. While manifesting thus an obviously hostile attitude, these countries have strengthened their military preparations perfecting an encirclement of Japan, and have brought about a situation which endangers the very existence of the Empire.

Nevertheless, to facilitate a speedy settlement, the Premier of Japan proposed, in August last, to meet the President of the United States for a discussion of important problems between the two countries covering the entire Pacific area. However, the American Government, while accepting in principle the Japanese proposal, insisted that the meeting should take place after an agreement of view had been reached on fundamental and essential questions.

3. Subsequently, on September 25 the Japanese Government submitted a proposal based on the formula proposed by the American Government, taking fully into consideration past American claims and also incorporating Japanese views. Repeated discussions proved of no avail in producing readily an agreement of view. The present cabinet, therefore, submitted a revised proposal, moderating still further the Japanese claims regarding the principal points of difficulty in the negotiation and endeavored strenuously to reach a settlement. But the American Government, adhering steadfastly to its original assertions, failed to display in the slightest degree a spirit of conciliation. The negotiation made no progress.

Therefore, the Japanese Government, with a view to doing its utmost for averting a crisis in Japanese-American relations, submitted on November 20 still another proposal in order to arrive at an equitable solution of the more essential and urgent questions which, simplifying its previous proposal, stipulated the following points:

(1) The Governments of Japan and the United States undertake not to dispatch armed forces into any of the regions, excepting French Indo-China, in the Southeastern Asia and the Southern Pacific area.

(2) Both Governments shall cooperate with the view to securing the acquisition in the Netherlands East Indies of those goods and commodities of which the two countries are in need.

(3) Both Governments mutually undertake to restore com-

mercial relations to those prevailing prior to the freezing of assets.

The Government of the United States shall supply Japan the required quantity of oil.

(4) The Government of the United States undertakes not to resort to measures and actions prejudicial to the endeavors for the restoration of general peace between Japan and China.

(5) The Japanese Government undertakes to withdraw troops now stationed in French Indo-China upon either the restoration of peace between Japan and China or the establishment of an equitable peace in the Pacific Area; and it is prepared to remove the Japanese troops in the southern part of French Indo-China to the northern part upon the conclusion of the present agreement.

As regards China, the Japanese Government, while expressing its readiness to accept the offer of the President of the United States to act as "introducer" of peace between Japan and China as was previously suggested, asked for an undertaking on the part of the United States to do nothing prejudicial to the restoration of Sino-Japanese peace when the two parties have commenced direct negotiations.

The American Government not only rejected the above-mentioned new proposal, but made known its intention to continue its aid to Chiang Kai-shek; and in spite of its suggestion mentioned above, withdrew the offer of the President to act as so-called "introducer" of peace between Japan and China, pleading that time was not yet ripe for it. Finally on November 26, in an attitude to impose upon the Japanese Government those principles it has persistently maintained, the American Government made a proposal totally ignoring Japanese claims, which is a source of profound regret to the Japanese Government.

4. From the beginning of the present negotiation the Japanese Government has always maintained an attitude of fairness and moderation, and did its best to reach a settlement, for which it made all possible concessions often in spite of great difficulties. As for the China question which constitutes an important subject of the negotiation, the Japanese Government showed a most conciliatory attitude. As for the principle of non-discrimination in international commerce, advocated by the American Government, the Japanese Government expressed its desire to see the said principle applied throughout the world, and declared that along with the actual practice of this principle in the world, the Japanese Government would endeavor to apply the same in the Pacific area including China, and made it clear that Japan had no intention of excluding from China economic activities of third powers pursued on an equitable basis. Furthermore, as regards the question of withdrawing troops from French Indo-China, the Japanese Government even volunteered, as mentioned above, to carry out an immediate evacuation of troops from Southern French Indo-China as a measure of easing the situation.

It is presumed that the spirit of conciliation exhibited to the utmost degree by the Japanese Government in all these matters is fully appreciated by the American Government.

On the other hand, the American Government, always holding fast to theories in disregard of realities, and refusing to yield an inch on its impractical principles, caused undue delay in the negotiation. It is difficult to understand this attitude of the American Government and the Japanese Government desires to call the attention of the American Government especially to the following points:

1. The American Government advocates in the name of world peace those principles favorable to it and urges upon the Japanese Government the acceptance thereof. The peace of the world may be brought about only by discovering a mutually acceptable formula through recognition of the reality of the situation and mutual appreciation of one another's position. An attitude such as ignores realities and imposes one's selfish views upon others will scarcely serve the purpose of facilitating the consummation of negotiations.

Of the various principles put forward by the American Government as a basis of the Japanese-American Agreement, there are some which the Japanese Government is ready to accept in principle, but in view of the world's actual condition it seems only a utopian ideal on the part of the American Government to attempt to force their immediate adoption.

Again, the proposal to conclude a multilateral non-aggression pact between Japan, United States, Great Britain, China, the Soviet Union, the Netherlands and Thailand, which is patterned after the old concept of collective security, is far removed from the realities of East Asia.

2. The American proposal contained a stipulation which states—"Both Governments will agree that no agreement, which either has concluded with any third power or powers, shall be interpreted by it in such a way as to conflict with the fundamental purpose of this agreement, the establishment and preservation of peace throughout the Pacific area." It is presumed that the above provision has been proposed with a view to restrain Japan from fulfilling its obligations under the Tripartite Pact when the United States participates in the war in Europe, and, as such, it cannot be accepted by the Japanese Government.

The American Government, obsessed with its own views and opinions, may be said to be scheming for the extension of the war. While it seeks, on the one hand, to secure its rear by stabilizing the Pacific Area, it is engaged, on the other hand, in aiding Great Britain and preparing to attack, in the name of self-defense, Germany and Italy, two powers that are striving to establish a new order in Europe. Such a policy is totally at variance with the many principles upon which the American Government proposes to found the stability of the Pacific Area through peaceful means.

3. Whereas the American Government, under the principles it rigidly upholds, objects to settle international issues through military pressure, it is exercising in conjunction with Great Britain and other nations pressure by economic power. Recourse to such pressure as a means of dealing with international relations should be condemned as it is at times more inhumane than military pressure.

4. It is impossible not to reach the conclusion that the American Government desires to maintain and strengthen, in coalition with Great Britain and other powers, its dominant position it has hitherto occupied not only in China but in other areas of East

Asia. It is a fact of history that the countries of East Asia for the past hundred years or more have been compelled to observe the *status quo* under the Anglo-American policy of imperialistic exploitation and to sacrifice themselves to the prosperity of the two nations. The Japanese Government cannot tolerate the perpetuation of such a situation since it directly runs counter to Japan's fundamental policy to enable all nations to enjoy each its proper place in the world.

The stipulation proposed by the American Government relative to French Indo-China is a good exemplification of the above-mentioned American policy. Thus the six countries,—Japan, the United States, Great Britain, the Netherlands, China, and Thailand,—excepting France, should undertake among themselves to respect the territorial integrity and sovereignty of French Indo-China and equality of treatment in trade and commerce would be tantamount to placing that territory under the joint guaranty of the Governments of those six countries. Apart from the fact that such a proposal totally ignores the position of France, it is unacceptable to the Japanese Government in that such an arrangement cannot but be considered as an extension to French Indo-China of a system similar to the Nine-Power Treaty structure which is the chief factor responsible for the present predicament of East Asia.

5. All the items demanded of Japan by the American Government regarding China such as wholesale evacuation of troops or unconditional application of the principle of non-discrimination in international commerce ignored the actual conditions of China, and are calculated to destroy Japan's position as the stabilizing factor of East Asia. The attitude of the American Government in demanding Japan not to support militarily, politically or economically any regime other than the regime at Chungking, disregarding thereby the existence of the Nanking Government, shatters the very basis of the present negotiation. This demand of the American Government falling, as it does, in line with its above-mentioned refusal to cease from aiding the Chungking regime, demonstrates clearly the intention of the American Government to obstruct the restoration of normal relations between Japan and China and the return of peace to East Asia.

5. In brief, the American proposal contains certain acceptable items such as those concerning commerce, including the conclusion of a trade agreement, mutual removal of the freezing restrictions, and stabilization of yen and dollar exchange, or the abolition of extraterritorial rights in China. On the other hand, however, the proposal in question ignores Japan's sacrifices in the four years of the China Affair, menaces the Empire's existence itself and disparages its honor and prestige. Therefore, viewed in its entirety, the Japanese Government regrets that it cannot accept the proposal as a basis of negotiation.

6. The Japanese Government, in its desire for an early conclusion of the negotiation, proposed simultaneously with the conclusion of the Japanese-American negotiation, agreements to be signed with Great Britain and other interested countries. The proposal was accepted by the American Government. However, since the American Government has made the proposal of November 26 as a result of frequent consultation with Great Britain, Australia, the Netherlands and Chungking, and presumably by catering to the wishes of the Chungking regime in the questions of China, it must be concluded that all these countries are at one with the United States in ignoring Japan's position.

7. Obviously it is the intention of the American Government to conspire with Great Britain and other countries to obstruct Japan's efforts toward the establishment of peace through the creation of a new order in East Asia, and especially to preserve Anglo-American rights and interests by keeping Japan and China at war. This intention has been revealed clearly during the course of the present negotiation. Thus, the earnest hope of the Japanese Government to adjust Japanese-American relations and to preserve and promote the peace of the Pacific through cooperation with the American Government has finally been lost.

The Japanese Government regrets to have to notify hereby the American Government that in view of the attitude of the American Government it cannot but consider that it is impossible to reach an agreement through further negotiations.

DECEMBER 7, 1941.

X. ACTION TAKEN BY THE LEAGUE OF NATIONS

1. Resolution of the Assembly of the League of Nations adopted October 6, 1937 [1]

The Assembly,

Adopts as its own the reports submitted to it by its [Far East] Advisory Committee [2] on the subject of the conflict between China and Japan (documents A.78, A.79, and A.80, 1937. VII);

Approves the proposals contained in the second of the said reports (document A.80, 1937. VII) and requests its President to take the necessary action with regard to the proposed meeting of the Members of the League which are parties to the Nine-Power Treaty signed at Washington on February 6, 1922;

Expresses its moral support for China, and recommends that Members of the League should refrain from taking any action which might have the effect of weakening China's power of resistance and thus of increasing her difficulties in the present conflict, and should also consider how far they can individually extend aid to China;

Decides to adjourn its present session and to authorize the President to summon a further meeting if the Advisory Committee so requests.

[1] *Resolutions adopted by the Assembly during its Eighteenth Ordinary Session, September 13th to October 6th, 1937* (League of Nations, *Official Journal, Special Supplement* No. 168 (1937)), p. 34; Jones and Myers, *Documents,* I, p. 161

[2] The reports are printed in the League of Nations, *Official Journal, Special Supplement* No. 177 (1937), p. 37–44, and in substance in *Documents,* I, p. 158–61.

The Far East Advisory Committee consisted of representatives of the following Governments: Australia, Belgium, United Kingdom, Bolivia, Canada, China, Colombia, Czechoslovakia, Ecuador, France, Hungary, Iran, Latvia, Netherlands, New Zealand, Peru, Poland, Portugal, Rumania, Sweden, Switzerland, Union of Soviet Socialist Republics and the United States of America.

2. Resolution of the Council of the League of Nations adopted February 2, 1938 [3]

The Council,

Having taken into consideration the situation in the Far East:

Notes with regret that hostilities in China continue and have been intensified since the last meeting of the Council;

Deplores this deterioration in the situation the more in view of the efforts and achievements of the National Government of China in her political and economic reconstruction;

Recalls that the Assembly, by its resolution of October 6, 1937, has expressed its moral support for China and has recommended that Members of the League should refrain from taking any action which might have the effect of weakening China's power of resistance and thus of increasing her difficulties in the present conflict, and should also consider how far they can individually extend aid to China;

Calls the most serious attention of the Members of the League to the terms of the above-mentioned resolution;

Is confident that those States represented on the Council for whom the situation is of special interest, will lose no opportunity of examining, in consultation with other similarly interested powers, the feasibility of any further steps which may contribute to a just settlement of the conflict in the Far East.

3. Resolution of the Council of the League of Nations adopted May 14, 1938 [4]

The Council,

Having heard the statement by the representative of China on the situation in the Far East and on the needs of the national defense of China:

I

Earnestly urges Members of the League to do their utmost to give effect to the recommendations contained in previous resolu-

[3] League of Nations, *Official Journal,* XIX, 1938, p. 120.
[4] *Ibid.,* p. 378.

tions of the Assembly and Council in this matter, and to take into serious and sympathetic consideration requests they may receive from the Chinese Government in conformity with the said resolutions;

Expresses its sympathy with China in her heroic struggle for the maintenance of her independence and territorial integrity, threatened by the Japanese invasion, and in the suffering which is thereby inflicted on her people.

II

Recalls that the use of toxic gases is a method of war condemned by international law, which cannot fail, should resort be had to it, to meet with the reprobation of the civilized world; and requests the Governments of States who may be in a position to do so to communicate to the League any information that they may obtain on the subject.

4. Invitation from the President of the Council of the League of Nations to the Government of Japan, September 19, 1938 [5]

The Council, having before it a formal request from the Chinese Government for the application to the Sino-Japanese dispute of the provisions of Article 17 of the Covenant relating to disputes between a Member of the League of Nations and a non-member State, has the honor to address to the Imperial Government the invitation provided for by the first sentence of the said Article 17, on the understanding that, if the invitation is accepted, Japan will have, as regards the dealing with the dispute under Article 17, the same rights as a Member of the League of Nations. The Council would be glad to be informed of the reply of the Imperial Government as soon as possible.

[5] *Ibid.*, p. 865.

5. Reply Telegram, dated September 22, 1938, from the Japanese Government to the Secretary General of the League of Nations (Avenol)[6]

Tokyo, September 22, 1938

I hasten to acknowledge receipt of your telegram of September 19, 1938, transmitting the invitation, provided for by the first sentence of Article 17 of the Covenant, which has been addressed to the Imperial Government by the Council of the League of Nations. The Imperial Government is firmly convinced that means such as those laid down in the Covenant cannot provide a just and adequate solution of the present conflict between Japan and China, and its attitude in this connection has been clearly stated on many occasions. I have therefore the honor to inform you that, for this reason, the Imperial Government regrets its inability to accept the Council's invitation.

K. Ugaki, *Japanese Minister for Foreign Affairs.*

6. Statement of the Japanese Foreign Office Spokesman concerning the Application of Article 16 of the League of Nations Covenant, October 3, 1938[7]

The Japanese Government, having always taken the stand that the China Affair cannot be expected to reach a just and adequate settlement by procedures envisaged by the Covenant of the League of Nations, had previously declined to accept the invitation of the League Council based on paragraph 1 Article 17 of the Covenant. On the thirtieth of last month, however, the Council adopted a report that the League Members may individually apply Article 16 to Japan by virtue of paragraph 3 Article 17. By thus invoking paragraph 3 Article 17 the League of Nations recognizes the existence of a state of war between Japan and China, which is inconsistent with the attitude of its Member-States, which, with regard to the question of respect for their interests in China, profess that no state of war exists between the

[6] *Ibid.*, p. 988.
[7] *Contemporary Japan*, VII, 1938, p. 582.

two countries. The Japanese Government attach great importance to this point. Moreover, should there be any country resorting to measures of sanction against Japan in accordance with the decision of the League Council, our Government would be ready to adopt counter-measures.

For the sake of world peace, Japan, after her withdrawal from the League, has continued to cooperate with that body in social and technical fields. However, the League's organs even in these spheres have, since the outbreak of the present affair, gone beyond their proper duties and assumed a greatly deplorable attitude of indulging in political discussions and of slandering at every turn the actions of Japan in China. Now the adoption by the Council of the report concerning sanctions against Japan has made clear the irreconcilability between the positions of Japan and the League, as a result of which Japan cannot but find it difficult to maintain the policy of cooperation she has hitherto pursued toward the League.

The Japanese Government regret the decision which the League Council, misled by intrigues of certain powers, has reached; and they hope that its Member-States, studying carefully the significance and practicability of the report adopted by the Council, will give a full consideration to its possible consequences.

7. Resolution of the Council of the League of Nations adopted January 20, 1939 [8]

The Council,

Referring to its report adopted on September 30, 1938, relating to the appeal of the Chinese Government;

Recalling the resolutions adopted by the Assembly on October 6, 1937, and by the Council on February 2 and on May 14, 1938;

Recalling in particular the terms of the Assembly resolution of October 6, 1937, which expresses its moral support for China, and recommends that Members of the League should refrain from taking any action which might have the effect of weakening

[8] League of Nations, *Official Journal,* XX, 1939, p. 99.

China's power of resistance and thus of increasing her difficulties in the present conflict, and should also consider how far they can individually extend aid to China; and the terms of the resolution of February 2nd, 1938, which expresses the Council's confidence that those States represented on the Council for whom the situation is of special interest will lose no opportunity of examining, in consultation with other similarly interested powers, the feasibility of any further steps which may contribute to a just settlement of the conflict in the Far East;

Having heard the statement of the Chinese representative in regard to the present situation in the Far East, in which he rejected the claim of Japan to establish a new order in the Far East and outlined certain proposals of the Chinese Government;

Taking note of the fact that a number of States have been taking individual action in aiding China:

Invites the Members of the League, particularly those directly concerned in the Far East, to examine, in consultation, should this appear appropriate, with other similarly interested powers, the proposals made in the statement of the representative of China before the Council on January 17, 1939,[9] for the taking of effective measures, especially measures of aid to China.

[9] *Ibid.*, p. 73–8.

XI. STATEMENT OF THE JAPANESE GOVERNMENT REGARDING THE CHINESE MARITIME CUSTOMS QUESTION, MAY 3, 1938[1]

This paper exists in two forms, the other being the communiqué given out in China by the Japanese authorities and credited with being an "agreement."[2] The form issued in Tokyo, where it immediately met the eye of the British Embassy, is believed more likely to record the exact scope of the conclusions. Significant passages contained only in the communiqué circulated in China are annotated to the Tokyo text.

Unofficial conversations have been taking place since February last between the British Ambassador, Sir Robert Craigie, and the Vice-Minister of Foreign Affairs, Mr. Kensuke Horinouchi, regarding the service of foreign obligations secured on the Chinese Maritime Customs revenue and other relevant matters. As a result of this exchange of views, the Japanese Government has notified His Majesty's Government in the United Kingdom of the temporary measures which it proposes to take, during the period of hostilities, to regulate these matters and it has received in reply the assurance that the British Government will, for its part, offer no objection to the application of these measures for the period mentioned.[3]

According to these arrangements, which will be subject to reconsideration in the event of a radical change occurring in economic conditions, all revenues collected by the Customs at each port within the areas under Japanese occupation are to be deposited with the Yokohama Specie Bank. From the revenues thus deposited, foreign loan quotas will be remitted to the Inspector-General of Customs in order to meet in full the service

[1] *Contemporary Japan,* VII, 1938, p. 193.

[2] *Chinese Year Book, 1938–1939,* p. 624.

[3] Here follows this paragraph in the edition for China:

"It is further understood that the Governments of the United States and France do not propose to raise any objection to the temporary application of these arrangements, which will be subject to reconsideration in the event of a radical change occurring in economic conditions."

The next paragraph began with the words in the first sentence: "all revenues collected . . ."

of the foreign loans and indemnities secured on the Customs revenue. The service of such foreign loans and indemnities will be treated as the first charge on the revenue, after deducting the maintenance expenses of the Customs Administration and certain customary payments and grants. Foreign loan quotas for each port will be determined monthly in proportion to the share of that port in the total gross collections for all ports during the preceding month.

Arrangements will also be made for the payment to the Japanese Government of the arrears of the Japanese portion of the Boxer Indemnity held at the Hong Kong and Shanghai Bank since last September, for the meeting of future payments in respect of the Japanese portion of the Boxer Indemnity and the Japanese share of the Reorganization Loan of 1913, for the repayment of the overdraft incurred by the Inspector-General since January in relation to the Shanghai share of the foreign loan which has been accumulating in the Hong Kong and Shanghai Bank, at Shanghai, and for the transfer to the Yokohama Specie Bank of the balance of the Customs accounts with the Hong Kong and Shanghai Bank in each port under Japanese occupation and its utilization for the future service of foreign obligations.[4]

[4] The following paragraph was added in the edition for China:

"The arrangements, having regard to the military situation in the Far East, appear to the British Government to offer the best guaranty obtainable for safeguarding the interests of the holders of China's foreign obligations secured on the Customs Revenues and, by this, assist in maintaining China's credit."

BIBLIOGRAPHY

BOOKS, ARTICLES AND SPECIAL STUDIES

Ahlers, John, "Empire of the Mitsuis," *China Weekly Review,* April 20, 1940, p. 253–4

——"The House of Mitsui Reorganizes," *ibid.,* April 13, 1940, p. 222–3

——*Japan Closing the Open Door in China,* Shanghai, 1939

——"The Mitsuis in Politics," *China Weekly Review,* April 27, 1940, p. 291–2

Allen, G. C., *Japanese Industry: Its Recent Development and Present Condition,* New York, 1940

Alley, Rewi, "The Chinese Industrial Cooperatives," Chungking Pamphlets, No. 4, 1940

American Information Committee, "Japan's Cultural Aggression in China," Shanghai, April 3, 1940

——"Japan's Puppets on the Chinese Stage," Shanghai, January 18, 1940

Asiaticus, "Soviet Relations with Japan," *Pacific Affairs,* XIV, 1941, p. 272–86

Barnes, Joseph (ed.), *Empire in the East,* New York, 1934

Barnett, Robert W., "China's Industrial Cooperatives on Trial," *Far Eastern Survey,* February 28, 1940, p. 51–6

——*Economic Shanghai: Hostage to Politics,* New York, 1941

Bisson, Thomas A., *American Policy in the Far East, 1931–1940,* New York, 1940

——"China's National Front," *Foreign Policy Reports,* XVII, No. 9, July 15, 1941, p. 109–10

——"The Communist Movement in China," *ibid.,* IX, No. 4, April 26, 1933

——"Japan's New Structure," *ibid.,* XVII, No. 3, April 15, 1941

——"The Netherlands Indies at War," *ibid.,* XVII, No. 16, November 1, 1941

Bisson, Thomas A., "Soviet-Japanese Relations: 1931–1938," *ibid.*, XIV, No. 22, February 1, 1939

Blakeslee, George H., "The Japanese Monroe Doctrine," *Foreign Affairs,* XI, p. 671–81

Bloch, Kurt, "Far Eastern War Inflation," *Pacific Affairs,* XIII, p. 320–43

——— "German-Japanese Partnership in Eastern Asia," *Far Eastern Survey,* October 26, 1938, p. 242–3

Borton, Hugh, *Japan Since 1931: Its Political and Social Developments,* New York, 1941

Bukharin, N., "Imperialism and Communism," *Foreign Affairs,* XIV, p. 563–77

Canada. Director of Public Information, Ottawa, *Canada at War,* No. 8, November 1, 1941

Carlson, Evans F., *The Chinese Army: Its Organization and Military Efficiency,* New York, 1940

——— *Twin Stars of China,* New York, 1940

Carnegie Endowment for International Peace, Division of International Law, *Treaties and Agreements with and Concerning China, 1919–1929,* Washington, 1929

Chamberlin, William H., "The Challenge to the Status Quo," *Contemporary Japan,* VII, 1938, p. 12

Chen, Han-seng, *Landlord and Peasant in China,* New York, 1936

Chiang, K'ai-shek and Mei-ling, *Sian, a Coup d'État,* Shanghai, 1938

China's Leaders and Their Policies, China United Press, 1935

"Chinese Higher Education," *China Institute Bulletin,* October 1939 (New York)

Christian, John L., "Thailand Renascent," *Pacific Affairs,* XIV, 1941, p. 186–7

Colegrove, Kenneth W., "Labor Parties in Japan," *American Political Science Review,* XXIII, May 1929, p. 329–63

——— Kenneth W., *Militarism in Japan,* Boston, 1936

Condliffe, John B., *China Today: Economic,* Boston, 1932

Conference on the Limitation of Armament, Washington, Government Printing Office, 1922

Conolly, Violet, *Soviet Economic Policy in the East,* London, 1933

Council of International Affairs, "Highways in China," Nanking, November 21, 1936

Cressey, George B., *China's Geographic Foundations,* New York, 1934

Crocker, W. R., *The Japanese Population Problem,* New York, 1931

Dennett, Tyler, "Australia's Defense Problem," *Foreign Affairs,* XVIII, 1939, p. 116–26 de Wilde, John C., and Monson, George, "Defense Economy of the United States: An Inventory of Raw Materials," *Foreign Policy Reports,* XVI, No. 17, November 15, 1940

Dietrich, Ethel B., "Closing Doors Against Japan," *Far Eastern Survey,* August 10, 1935, p. 181–6

——— *Far Eastern Trade of the United States,* New York, 1940

Elliott, A. Randle, "U. S. Defense Outposts in the Pacific," *Foreign Policy Reports,* XVII, No. 1, March 15, 1941

Emerson, Rupert, "The Dutch East Indies Adrift," *Foreign Affairs,* XVIII, 1940, p. 735–41

Fahs, C. B., *Government in Japan: Recent Trends in Its Scope and Operation,* New York, 1941

Farjenel, F., *Through the Chinese Revolution,* New York, 1916

Farley, Miriam S., "Japan's Unsolved Tenancy Problem," *Far Eastern Survey,* July 7, 1937, p. 155

Fenwick, Charles G., "War without a Declaration," *American Journal of International Law,* XXXI, p. 694–6

Field, Frederick V., *American Participation in the China Consortiums,* Chicago, 1931

——— "Battle of the Bankers," in Barnes, Joseph (ed.), *Empire in the East,* p. 151–2, 167

——— *Economic Handbook of the Pacific Area,* Garden City, 1934

Fisher, G. M., "The Landlord-Peasant Struggle in Japan," *Far Eastern Survey,* September 1, 1937, p. 201–6

Freyn, Hubert, *Chinese Education in the War,* Chungking, Council of International Affairs, 1940, Political and Economic Studies No. 9

Friedman, Irving S., *British Relations with China, 1931–1939,* New York, 1940

Fujii, S., "The Cabinet, the Diet and the Taisei Yokusan Kai," *Contemporary Japan,* X, 1941, p. 487–97

——— *The Essentials of Japanese Constitutional Law,* Tokyo, 1940

Gayer, A. D., and Schmidt, C. T., *American Economic Foreign Policy,* New York, 1939

Green, James F., "The British Dominions at War," *Foreign Policy Reports,* XV, No. 22, February 1, 1940

Griswold, A. Whitney, "European Factors in Far Eastern Diplomacy," *Foreign Affairs,* XIX, 1941, p. 297–309

——— *The Far Eastern Policy of the United States,* New York, 1938

Hanson, Haldore, *"Humane Endeavor," The Story of the China War,* New York, 1939

Hanson, Haldore, "The People Behind the Chinese Guerrillas," *Pacific Affairs,* XI, 1938, p. 285–98

Hauser, Ernest O., *Shanghai: City for Sale,* New York, 1940

Holcombe, Arthur N., *The Chinese Revolution,* Cambridge, Mass., 1930

Holland, W. L., "The Plight of Japanese Agriculture," *Far Eastern Survey,* January 1, 1936, p. 1–5

Honjo, Eijiro, *The Social and Economic History of Japan,* Kyoto, 1935

Hsü, Leonard S., "Rural Reconstruction in China," *Pacific Affairs,* X, September 1937, p. 249–65

Hsü, Shuhsi, *How the Far Eastern War Was Begun,* Shanghai, 1938

——— *Japan and Shanghai,* Shanghai, 1938

——— *Japan and the Third Powers,* Shanghai, 1938

Hubbard, G. E., *Eastern Industrialization and Its Effect on the West,* London, 1935

Hyde, Charles Cheney, *International Law, Chiefly as Interpreted and Applied by the United States,* 2 vols., Boston, 1922

Ichihashi, Y., *The Washington Conference and After,* Stanford University, 1928

Isaacs, Harold, *The Tragedy of the Chinese Revolution,* London, 1938

Ishii, R., *Population Pressure and Economic Life in Japan,* London, 1937

Ishii, Viscount Kikujiro, "The Permanent Bases of Japanese Foreign Policy," *Foreign Affairs,* XI, p. 220–9

Iwakura, Baron M., "The Focal Point of Japan-Soviet Relations," *Contemporary Japan,* VII, 1938, p. 413–20

Japan. Cabinet Information Bureau, "National Movement for Assisting the Throne," *Tokyo Gazette,* November 1940, p. 177–92

Japan. Cabinet Information Bureau, "Reorganization of the Movement for Spiritual Mobilization," *Tokyo Gazette,* June 1940, p. 465–7

Japan's War in China, II (*China Weekly Review*), 1938

Jane's Fighting Ships, London, 1941

Johnstone, William C., *The Shanghai Problem,* Stanford University, 1937

——— *The United States and Japan's New Order,* New York, 1941

Jones, S. Shepard and Myers, Denys P., *Documents on American Foreign Relations,* 3 vols., Boston, 1939, 1940 and 1941

Kamikawa, H., "An Anglo-Japanese Agreement," *Contemporary Japan,* V, 1936, p. 346–7

——— "The Rome-Berlin-Tokyo Axis," *Contemporary Japan,* VII, 1938, p. 1–10

Krivitsky, General W. G., *In Stalin's Secret Service,* New York, 1939

La Fargue, T. E., *China and the World War,* Stanford University, 1937

Lattimore, Owen, "China's Turkistan-Siberian Supply Road," *Pacific Affairs,* XIII, 1940, p. 393–412

—— "Sinkiang," in *China Year Book, 1939,* p. 463–5

League of Nations. First Report of the Subcommittee of the Far East Advisory Committee, adopted by the League of Nations Assembly, October 6, 1937. Geneva, Doc. A. 78. 1937. VII. in *Official Journal, Special Supplement* No. 177 (1937), p. 37

League of Nations. Reply dated February 23, 1932 from the Japanese Government to the Appeal of the President of the Council dated February 16, 1932, Official Journal, XIII, 1932, p. 384

League of Nations. Resolutions adopted by the Assembly during its Eighteenth Ordinary Session, September 13th to October 6th, 1937. (*Official Journal, Special Supplement* No. 168, 1937)

Lieu, D. K., "The Sino-Japanese Currency War," *Pacific Affairs,* XII, 1939, p. 413–26

Lin, P. S., "Aide Defends Peace Drive," *China Weekly Review,* October 21, 1939, p. 285

Linebarger, Paul M. A., *The China of Chiang K'ai-shek,* Boston, 1941

—— *Government in Republican China,* New York and London, 1938

Lockwood, William W., "America's Stake in the Far East, II: Investments," *Far Eastern Survey,* August 12, 1936, p. 176–85

—— "Japanese Silk and the American Market," *ibid.,* February 12, 1936, p. 31–6

Lowe, Chuan-Hua, *Facing Labor Issues in China,* Shanghai, 1934

—— *Japan's Economic Offensive in China,* London, 1939

Lower, A. R. M., *Canada and the Far East—1940,* Toronto, 1941

MacMurray, John V. A., "Problems of Foreign Capital in China," *Foreign Affairs,* III, 1925, p. 411–22

—— (ed.), *Treaties with and concerning China,* 1894–1919, 2 vols., New York, 1921

Macnair, Harley F., *China in Revolution,* Chicago, 1931

Maddox, William P., "Canadian-American Defense Planning," *Foreign Policy Reports,* XVII, No. 17, November 15, 1941

Malraux, André, *Man's Fate,* New York, 1934

Masland, J. W., "Missionary Influence upon American Far Eastern Policy," *Pacific Historical Review,* X, September 1941, p. 279–96

Mayers, W. F., *Treaties between the Empire of China and Foreign Powers,* 2d ed., Shanghai, 1897

Michael, F., "The Significance of Puppet Governments," *Pacific Affairs,* XII, 1939, p. 400–12

Milner, Ian F. G., *New Zealand's Interests and Policies in the Far East,* New York, 1940

Minobe, Y., "The Principles of the New Economic Structure," *Contemporary Japan,* X, 1941, p. 179

Miyaoka, Tsunejiro, "The Foreign Policy of Japan," *International Conciliation,* No. 307, February 1935

National Munitions Control Board. Second Annual Report for the year ending November 30, 1937 (H. Doc. No. 465, 75th Cong., 3d sess.), Washington, 1938

—— *Third Annual Report for the year ending November 30, 1938* (H. Doc. No. 92, 76th Cong., 1st sess.), Washington, 1939

Nearing, Scott, and Freeman, J., *Dollar Diplomacy: A Study in American Imperialism,* New York, 1925

Norem, Ralph A., *Kiaochow Leased Territory,* University of California, Berkeley, 1936

Norins, M. R., "Agrarian Democracy in Northwest China," *Pacific Affairs,* XIII, 1940, p. 413–22

Norman, E. H., *Japan's Emergence as a Modern State,* New York, 1940

Oliver, Frank, *Special Undeclared War,* London, 1939

Orchard, J. E., "The Japanese Dilemma" in Barnes, Joseph (ed.), *Empire in the East,* New York, 1934, p. 39–83

—— "Japan's Economic Invasion of China," *Foreign Affairs,* XVIII, p. 464–76

Ozaki, H., "The New National Structure," *Contemporary Japan,* IX, 1940, p. 1284–92

Pollard, Robert T., *China's Foreign Relations, 1917–1931,* New York, 1933

Popper, David H., "America's Naval Preparedness," *Foreign Policy Reports,* XVII, No. 2, April 1, 1941

Porter, Catherine, "Mineral Deficiency versus Self-Sufficiency in Japan," *Far Eastern Survey,* January 15, 1936, p. 9–14

Puleston, W. D., *The Armed Forces of the Pacific,* New Haven, 1941

Quigley, Harold S., "Free China," New York, *International Conciliation,* No. 359, April 1940

—— *Japanese Government and Politics,* New York, 1932

Quigley, Harold S., and Blakeslee, George H., *The Far East: An International Survey,* Boston, 1938

Radek, Karl, "The Bases of Soviet Foreign Policy," *Foreign Affairs,* XII, p. 193–206

Reinach, Lucien de, *Recueil des traités conclus par la France en Extrême Orient,* 2 vols., Paris, E. Leroux, 1902–7

Reischauer, R. K., *Japan: Government-Politics,* New York, 1939

Remer, C. F., *Foreign Investments in China,* New York, 1933

The Reorganization of Education in China, League of Nations' Institute of Intellectual Cooperation, Paris, 1932

Report on Need of Additional Naval Bases to Defend the Coasts of the United States, Its Territories and Possessions. Letter of Secretary of the Navy Transmitting Report (H. Doc. No. 65, 76th Cong., 1st sess.) [Admiral Hepburn Board report.]

Rosinger, Lawrence K., "The Far East and the New Order in Europe," *Pacific Affairs,* XII, 1939, p. 357–69

——— "Politics and Strategy of China's Mobile War," *Pacific Affairs,* XII, 1939, p. 263–77

——— "Soviet Far Eastern Policy," *Pacific Affairs,* XIII, 1940, p. 263–78

Roth, Andrew, *Japan Strikes South,* New York, 1941

Russell, O. D., *The House of Mitsui,* Boston, 1939

Schumpeter, Elizabeth B., ed., *The Industrialization of Japan and Manchukuo, 1930–1940,* New York, 1940

Shepherd, Jack, *Australia's Interests and Policies in the Far East,* New York, 1940

Smythe, Dr. Lewis S. C., *War Damage in the Nanking Area,* Nanking (Nanking International Relief Committee), 1938

Snow, Edgar, "China's Fighting Generalissimo," *Foreign Affairs,* XVI, 1938, p. 612–25

——— *Red Star Over China,* New York, 1938

——— "Soviet Society in Northwest China," *Pacific Affairs,* X, 1937, p. 266–75

——— "Will Stalin Sell Out China?", *Foreign Affairs,* XVIII, 1940, p. 450–63

Spinks, Charles N., "Bureaucratic Japan," *Far Eastern Survey,* October, 6, 1941, p. 219–25

Strange, William, *Canada, the Pacific and War,* Toronto, 1937

Strong, Anna Louise, "The Kuomintang-Communist Crisis in China," *Amerasia,* V, 1941, p. 11–23

Takasugi, K., "The Diet Under the New Political Structure," *Contemporary Japan,* IX, 1940, p. 1398–410

Tamagna, F. M., *Italy's Interests and Policies in the Far East,* New York, 1941

Tanaka Memorial, Shanghai, *The China Critic,* 1932

Tannin, O., and Yohan, E., *Militarism and Fascism in Japan,* London, 1934

Taylor, George E., "The Reconstruction Movement in China," *Problems of the Pacific,* New York, 1936

——— *The Struggle for North China,* New York, 1940

Thompson, Virginia, *French Indo-China,* New York, 1937

Timperley, H. J., *What War Means: the Japanese Terror in China,* London, 1938

Tomoyeda, T., "Germany and Japan," *Contemporary Japan,* V, 1936, p. 216–8

Tong, H. K., *Chiang K'ai-shek, Soldier and Statesman,* Shanghai, 1937

Trotsky, Leon, *Problems of the Chinese Revolution,* London, 1932

U. S. Department of Commerce, "Economic Conditions in Japan During 1940 and early 1941," Washington, International Reference Service, I, No. 33, June 1941, p. 6

——— *Economic Review of Foreign Countries, 1939 and Early 1940,* Washington, 1941

——— "Expansion of Japan's Foreign Trade and Industry," Trade Information Bulletin No. 836, Washington, 1937

U. S. Department of State, *The Conference of Brussels, November 3–24, 1937 . . .* Washington, 1938, Publication 1232

U. S. Tariff Commission, *Recent Developments in the Foreign Trade of Japan,* Report No. 105, Second Series, Washington, 1936

Utley, Freda, *China at War,* Shanghai, 1939

——— *Japan's Feet of Clay,* New York, 1937

Uyeda, T., *The Recent Development of Japanese Foreign Trade,* Tokyo, 1936

Vandenbosch, Amry, "Netherlands India and Japan," *Pacific Affairs,* XIII, 1940, p. 253–62

Wales, Nym, "China's New Line of Industrial Defense," *Pacific Affairs,* XII, p. 286

Wallace, B. B., "Fallacies of Economic Nationalism," in *Peace or War,* ed. by Harold S. Quigley, Minneapolis, University of Minnesota, Day and Hour Series, Nos. 17–18, June 1937

Wang Ch'ing-wei, *China and the Nations,* New York, 1927

Wang, Shih-fu, "Naval Strategy in the Sino-Japanese War," *U. S. Naval Institute Proceedings,* LXVII, 1941, p. 991–8

Weale, Putnam, *Why China Sees Red,* New York, 1925

Weigh, K. S., China, Soviet Russia and Sinkiang," *China Weekly Review,* February 18, 1939, p. 364–7

Willoughby, W. W., *China at the Conference,* Baltimore, 1922

——— *Foreign Rights and Interests in China,* Baltimore, 1920, 2 vols.

——— *Japan's Case Examined,* Baltimore, 1940

——— *The Sino-Japanese Controversy and the League of Nations,* Baltimore, 1935

Woo, T. C., *The Kuomintang and the Future of the Chinese Revolution,* London, 1928

Woodhead, H. G., "Sino-Japanese Hostilities: A Frank British Opinion," *Contemporary Japan,* VI, 1937, p. 411–12

Woolsey, Lester H., "Peaceful War in China," *American Journal of International Law,* XXXII, p. 314–9

Wu, Leonard T. K., "Merchant Capital and Usury Capital in Rural China," *Far Eastern Survey,* March 25, 1936

——— "Rural Bankruptcy in China," *Far Eastern Survey,* October 8, 1936

Yakhontoff, V. A., *Russia and the Soviet Union in the Far East,* New York, 1931, London, 1932

Young, A. Morgan, *Imperial Japan, 1926–1938,* New York, 1938

NEWSPAPERS, PERIODICALS AND REFERENCE WORKS

American Journal of International Law, XIX, 1925, Official Documents Supplement; XXXI, 1937, Supplement

British and Foreign State Papers, London, vol. 100, p. 913

Chicago Daily News, Jul. 2, 1940

China Institute Bulletin, Oct. 1939

China Weekly Review, Aug. 14, Sept. 11, 18, Oct. 23, Nov. 27, 1937; Apr. 2, May 7, 14, 21, Oct. 22, Dec. 17, 24, 1938; Jan. 7, Feb. 25, Mar. 4, 25, Apr. 8, 15, May 6, 13, 20, Jun. 10, 17, Jul. 1, 29, Oct. 14, 21, Nov. 25, Dec. 2, 23, 1939; Feb. 24, Mar. 9, Apr. 6, 20, Jul. 6, 20, Aug. 17, 24, 31, Dec. 11, 1940; Jan. 4, Feb. 1, Apr. 5, Jun. 28, 1941

China Year Book (Shanghai), 1913, 1914, 1921, 1923, 1924, 1925, 1926, 1931–32, 1934, 1936, 1938, 1939

Chinese Social and Political Science Review, Public Documents Supplement, XV, 1931, p. 466–74

Chinese Year Book (Shanghai), 1935–36, 1937, 1938–39, 1940–41

Christian Science Monitor, Apr. 2, 1938

Contemporary China, May 25, 1941

Contemporary Japan, II, 1933–34, p. 765; IV, 1936, p. 638–9; V, 1937, p. 567–8, 710–11; VI, 1937, p. 351–3, 563; VII, 1938, p. 386, 582, 744–8; VIII, 1939, p. 182, 435; IX, 1940, p. 366, 778–9, 929–31, 1076–8, 1369, 1379–81; X, 1941, p. 131–8, 568–71

Far Eastern Survey, Apr. 6, May 18, Jun. 1, Jul. 13, Nov. 9, 1938; Jan. 19, Mar. 29, May 24, Jun. 21, 1939; Jan. 3, 17, Mar. 27, Apr. 24, Jul. 3, 17, 28, Aug. 8, 14, Sept. 18, 25, Oct. 23, 1940; Mar. 12, Jun. 30, Sept. 22, 1941

Finance and Commerce (Shanghai), Jun. 8, 1938, p. 454

German Library of Information (New York), *Facts in Review,* II, p. 486

Great Britain. *Parliamentary Debates,* House of Commons, vol. 338, cols. 2961–62

Institute of International Education, *Bulletin* No. 1, 14th series, Jan. 9, 1933

Japan Weekly Chronicle, May 14, 1936, Jan. 28, Feb. 25, May 6, Aug. 19, Sept. 2, 11, Oct. 21, 1937; Oct. 6, Dec. 8, 1938; Aug. 1, 22, 31, Jul. 4, 11, 18, Nov. 16, 1939; Oct. 3, 1940; Apr. 10, 1941

Japan Year Book, 1939–1940, 1940–1941

League of Nations, *Official Journal,* XIII, 1932, p. 384; XIX, 1938, p. 120, 378, 865, 988; XX, 1939, p. 73–8, 99

—— *Official Journal, Special Supplements* No. 168, 1937; No. 177, 1937

—— *Treaty Series,* vol. 80, p. 341; vol. 163, p. 351

New York Times, 1941, Jan. 20, 21, 23, Feb. 4, 8, 26, Mar. 19, 20, 21, 26, Apr. 3, 15, 16, 18, 25, 29, May 6, 7, 10, 11, 16, 24, 26, Jun. 4, 6, 13, 18, 19, Jul. 3, 8, 14, 24, 26, 29, 30, Aug. 2, 6, 7, 8, 9, 11, 12, 13, 15, 18–23, 25, 27, 28, Sept. 12, 13, 18, Oct. 6, 8, 10, 21, Nov. 3, 7, 10, 11, 14, 15, 17, 18, 21, 24, 28, 29, Dec. 2

Oriental Economist, Oct. 1936

People's Tribune, Aug., Nov. 1938; Feb. 1939

Saturday Evening Post, Apr. 29, 1939

The Statesman's Year-Book, 1941

Teachers College Record (New York), Mar. 1933

Tokyo Gazette, Nos. 9–10, 13, 14, 18, 23, 1938; No. 19, Jan. 1939; III, No. 12–IV, No. 6, Jun.-Dec. 1940; IV, No. 8, Feb. 1941, No. 12, Jun. 1941

U. S. S. R., *Report on Work of Central Committee,* 1939

U. S. Department of Commerce, Release, Feb. 6, 1941

United States, Department of State, *Bulletin,* 1939, III, No. 56, Jul. 20, No. 63, Sept. 7, No. 66, Sept. 28, No. 77, Dec. 14; 1941, IV, No. 83, Jan. 25, No. 95, Apr. 19, V, No. 109, Jul. 26, No. 110, Aug. 2, No. 111, Aug. 9, No. 112, Aug. 16, No. 113, Aug. 23, No. 114, Aug. 30, No. 117, Sept. 20, No. 118, Sept. 27, No. 120, Oct. 11, No. 122, Oct. 25, No. 124, Nov. 8, No. 129, Dec. 13, No. 130, Dec. 20; 1942, VI, No. 132, Jan. 3, 1942

—— *Press Releases,* Oct. 9, 1937, p. 275–85

U. S. Naval Institute Proceedings, LXVI, 1940, p. 1601; LXVII, 1941, p. 54–5, 732, 880–3

United States Statutes at Large, vol. 50, p. 121

INDEX

A

Agrarian problem in China, 10, 13, 100
Aircraft companies, U. S., investments in China, 41
Alaska-Aleutian Islands, air and naval bases, 209
Alaska, highway from U. S., 263–4
Allison, John M., 213
Amau statement (1934), 52, 54, 56, 58
Amboina, naval base of, 250
Amoy:
 bombardment of, 79
 International Settlement, 44, 147
Amtorg Trading Corporation, 275
Anchorage, army base, 209
Anglo-Japanese alliance, 281
Anti-Comintern Pact, 53, 167–70, 283
Anti-Communism:
 cooperation between Chinese groups and Japan, 289–90
 purpose of Japanese support of, 290
Araki, General Sadao, 151
Arima, Count Y., 159
Arita, Hachiro:
 "agreement" with Sir Robert Craigie on Japanese rights, Jul. 24, 1939, 238
 Anglo-Japanese relations, desire to improve, 167
 Anti-Comintern Pact, explanation of Japan's entrance into, 53
 Hainan Island occupation, statement to French Ambassador, 308
 "new order" in China, statement on, 114
 "New Order in East Asia":
  definition of, 286, 288
  radio address on, 182
Arnstein, Daniel, 271
Arsène-Henry, Charles, French Ambassador to Tokyo, 306, 308–9
Asia, trade of U. S. with, 1939, 195
"Asia Development Board," 288, 291
"Asia for Asiatics," 193
Assembly of League of Nations. *See* League of Nations.
"The Atlantic Charter":
 signature of, 218
 U.S.S.R. adherence to, Sept. 24, 1941, 275
Australia:
 air forces, 250
 appointment of Minister to Japan, 245
 attitude toward Japan, 244–5
 Darwin, Port, naval base of, 250
 defenses of, 250
 iron, embargo on export of, 244–5
 Japanese assets, freezing of, 245
 naval and air bases, 268
 naval strength, 1940, 248–9
 raw wool exports to Japan, 244–5
 relation to Far Eastern war, 244
 Sydney, sinking by German raider, 180
 trade with Japan, 244–5
 use of bases by U. S., agreement in principle, 268
Axis powers:
 Three-Power Pact. *See that title.*
 Western Hemisphere program, 202

B

Bhutan, British influence in, 33
Biggar, Col. O. M., 264
Blockade of British and French concessions at Tientsin, 145
Blücher (Galens), Genl., 3, 12, 46
Border governments, 106
Borodin, Michael, 3, 12, 46
Boxer indemnity, Japanese portion of, 332
Boxer protocol, 1901, rights under, 316

British Empire (*see also* Great Britain *and* United Kingdom):
  imperial defense, 247
British Exports Credits Guarantee Department, 236
British India, trade with U. S., 1939 and 1940, 195
British Malaya, trade with U. S., 1939 and 1940, 195
Brooke-Popham, Sir Robert:
  conversations with Adml. Thos. C. Hart and Major Genl. Douglas MacArthur, Apr. and Oct. 1941, 268–9
Brussels Conference (1937):
  American policy regarding, 299–300
  Japanese refusal to attend, 53
  statement by Norman Davis, American delegate, 212
Burma:
  British influence in, 33
  defenses of, 249
Burma Road:
  bombing by Japan, 78, 186
  closure by Great Britain for three months, 239–40
    protest by U. S., 215
    reopening, Oct. 18, 1940, 240
  description of, 103
  effect of Japan's closure, 200
  traffic over, 271
  truck repairs by American technicians, 271
  understanding between U. S., Great Britain, China and Netherlands East Indies if road cut by Japan, 272
  U. S. protest on closure by Great Britain, 215

C

Cambodia, 187
Canada:
  air bases, 250
  Chinese trade, 247
  commission on highway from U. S. to Alaska, 263–4
  cooperation with U. S. in war, 246–7
  diplomatic relations with Japan, 247
  embargoes on export of lumber and metals, 247
  Empire Air Training Scheme, 250
  freezing of Japan's assets, July 1941, 247
  Japanese trade, 247
  Joint Defense Production Committee, 265
  Joint Economic Committees, with U. S., 264–5
  naval strength, 1939 and 1942, 248
  Permanent Joint Board on Defense, U. S., 264
  pledge of Pres. Roosevelt on defense, Aug. 18, 1938, Kingston, Ontario, 263
  position in relation to Far Eastern war, 246
  trade with Eastern Asia, 247
Canadian Pacific Steamship Co., 247
Canton and Enderbury Islands, 210, 267
Canton, surrender of, 76, 235
Caroline Islands, 180
Central China Promotion Company, 124, 127
Central China, stalemate in, 77
Central Salt Administration, 37
Chahar, invasion by Japan, 69
Chamberlain, Neville:
  views on Sino-Japanese war, 230
Chang Chun, General, 54, 87
Changsha, Chinese victory at, 77
Ch'en Li-fu, 95
Ch'en Tu-Hsin, 12
Chiang K'ai-shek:
  analysis of Japanese intrigues, 286
  biography of, 92
  Communist Fourth Army, repression of, 259
  compromise with Communists, 16, 93
  governorship of Szechwan, 87
  inauguration of New Life Movement, 6
  New Fourth Army, order to disband, 112
  position in government, 88
  role in national revolution, 3

Chiang K'ai-shek—*Continued*
statement on Japanese policy toward China, Dec. 26, 1938, 285–93
united defense plans, Nov. 17, 1941, statement to People's Political Council, 272
Chiang K'ai-shek, Madam, 94
Ch'ih Feng-ch'eng, General, 76
China:
agrarian problem, 10, 13, 100
American missionary activities in, 197–9
anti-Japanism, 60
army, modernization of, 5
assets in U. S., freezing of, 204
border governments, 106
Burma Road:
closure by Great Britain for three months, 239–40
reopening of, Oct. 18, 1940, 240
traffic over, 271
capital of Westerns powers in, 55
Central Salt Administration, 37
Central, stalemate in, 77
Chinese Maritime Customs Service. *See that title.*
Chungking, transfer of capital to, 73, 86
commerce, development of, 7
Communist organization (*see also under* Communism *and* Chinese Communist organization):
aid from Soviet Russia, 259
"cooperation" with Japan, 58
cooperatives, 101
currency, 94, 96, 229
customs administration. *See* Chinese Maritime Customs Service.
democratic institutions in education of, 201
economic relations with Japan, 284
education, 6, 104, 201
Eighth Route Army, 70, 108
farm problem, 9, 13, 100
foreign residential areas, 33, 44, 134–48
"Free China," activities and status, 85–113
Great Britain:
aid from, 235–7
credits from, 236–7
good offices for settlement offered, 230–1
government obligations, Chinese, held by, 228
investments, 228
loans, 236–8
military mission, 272
trade, 228
withdrawal of troops, 143
guerrillas, 106
industry, 7, 101
inflation, 98
international relations, with great powers, 32, 48
investments, foreign, in, 36, 40, 197, 228
Kuomintang. *See that title.*
labor:
conscription of, 6
growth of unions, 11
land distribution, 9
landlordism, 8
leases by foreign powers, 32
Malaya, military mission to, 272
Manchu dynasty, 2, 33
manpower, importance of, to United Nations, 270
missionaries, foreign, 45, 198–9
Mongolia, Outer:
repudiation of Soviet political influence in, 258
morale of people, 279
national debt, 99
National Economic Council, 5
national existence, struggle for, 63
National Government:
establishment of, 3
structure, 88
Nationalist leaders, 93
naval activities in war, 79
naval activities of Japan on coast of, 79
New Life Movement, 6
occupied area (*see also under* Japan):
economic conditions in, 124
economic controls in operation by Japan, 126

China—*Continued*
education under Japanese control, 131
government by Japan, 115
Japan's "new order" in, 114–33
local government, 123
peace overtures by Japan. *See under* Peace.
peasants, 8, 10, 46
People's Economic Reconstruction Movement, 6
People's Political Council, 90
political disorder, 62
Principle of the People's Livelihood, 14
proletarianism in, 11
public finance, 4, 94, 96
reform measures, 5, 14
Reorganization Loan of 1913, Japanese share of, 332
resistance program against Japanese aggression, 95
resources, natural, 8, 99
revolution of 1911–12, 2
Roman Catholicism, proscription of, 1724–1846, 197
schools and colleges, missionary, 198–9
bombing of, by Japan, 198
Sinkiang, relation to, 259–60
Soviet protectorates in, 48
spheres of influence, foreign, 33
Stabilization Board, 98
Stabilization Fund, agreement, Apr. 26, 1941, 237
students, attitude of, 105
Sun Yat-sen. *See that title.*
tariffs, treaty control of, 34, 194
trade, foreign, 8, 228
traffic management over Burma Road, 271
transportation, 5, 102
treaty limitations, 34, 44
"Twenty-One Demands," 42, 58, 105
U.S.S.R.:
barter agreements, Oct. 1938, Feb., Aug. 1939, Dec. 1940, 257–8
commercial accords, June 16, 1939 and July 1940, 257
non-aggression treaty, Aug. 21, 1937, 256–7
United Nations membership, 270
United States:
airplanes, delivery by, 271
credits, 205–6
delivery of war materials, difficulties of, 271
indebtedness to, 206
independence of Chinese Republic, basic policy, 194–5
investments of, 197
lend-lease aid, 205, 216, 271
loans, 37, 98
military mission headed by Brig. Genl. John Magruder, 271
recognition of Republic and of National Government by, 201
trade with, 1939 and 1940, 195–6
war with Japan. *See under* Japan: China.
Western power politics, 277
China Affairs Board, 123, 288
Chinese Communist organization:
admittance to Kuomintang, 11
areas controlled by, 13, 16, 108
beginnings, 12
conflict with Chiang K'ai-shek, 93
Eighth Route Army, 70, 108–11
expulsion from Kuomintang, 6, 46
Fourth Army, 111, 259
relation to U.S.S.R., 47, 258–9
Soviet supplies to, 260
Chinese Eastern Railway:
final installment paid by "Manchoukuo," 173
sale to "Manchoukuo" by U.S.S.R., 252
Chinese Maritime Customs Service:
British administration of, 33, 228
customs receipts, 232–3
foreign loans, service on, 331–2
Japanese regulations in North China ports, 232–3
Japanese tariff schedules, operation of, 233
National Government, deprivation of funds by puppet government, 233
"Reformed Government" at Nan-

Chinese Maritime Customs Service —*Continued*
king appointee as Superintendent of Customs, 232–3
"Rules of Trade," 1858, 231
Superintendent of Customs, 232–3
surrender of control by Great Britain to Japan, 231
Chou En-lai, 95
Christian missionaries in Far East, 197–9
Chu Teh, 12, 94
Chungking:
bombing of, 78
transfer of Chinese capital to, 73, 86
Churchill, Prime Minister Winston:
"The Atlantic Charter," Aug. 14, 1941, 218
Burma Road, announcement on closure of, 239–40
declaration of war against Japan, statement of Nov. 10, 1941, 241–2
defense of Indian and Pacific Oceans, statement of Nov. 10, 1941, 248
pledge to U. S. on cooperation in Far East, Aug. 24, 1941, 219, 241
statement on Japan, 240
statement to Japanese Ambassador, Feb. 1941, 241
Civilian populations, bombing of, 203
Comintern (*see also* Communism):
Japanese opposition to, 283
Commercial equality, 300
Communism:
Anti-Comintern Pact, 53, 167–70
in China (*see also* Chinese Communist organization):
Chiang's fight against, 93
controlled areas, 13, 16, 108
expulsion of Party from Kuomintang, 6, 46
growth of movement, 12, 47
Kuomintang opposition, 110
in Japan, underground movement, 25
Japanese demand for Chinese collaboration against, 81
Japanese fears of growth in China, 52
Concessions:
effects of hostilities on residents in, 73, 136
foreign nationals, treatment by Japan, 134–48
Conciliation of disputes, 300
Consortium:
second financial, 37, 49
Chinese attitude toward, 39, 57
Cooperatives, Chinese, 101
Co-Prosperity Sphere in Greater East Asia. *See* "New Order in Greater East Asia."
Council of League of Nations. *See* League of Nations.
Court of International Justice, the Permanent, 310
Craigie-Arita "agreement," July 24, 1939, 238
Craigie, Sir Robert:
"agreement" on Japanese rights, July 24, 1939, 238
conversations with Japan on Chinese maritime customs, 331
statement of Jan. 14, 1939 on British policy, 234–5
Cultural interests of U. S. in Far East, 197–9
Currency:
Chinese, 94, 96, 229
Japanse controls in occupied China, 129
Currie, Lauchlin, mission to Chungking, 216
Curtin, John, Premier of Australia:
cooperation of United Kingdom, Australia, New Zealand, China, Netherlands East Indies and United States in Pacific, 269
Customs Service. *See* Chinese Maritime Customs Service.

D

Dalai Lama, enthronement in 1940, 85
Darlan, François, 311
Darwin, Port, naval base of, 250
Davis, Norman, 212
Defense Supplies Corporation, 275

Department of State. *See* United States, State, Department of.
Destroyers, American, transfer to United Kingdom, 266
"Dollar diplomacy," 35
Drug traffic, Japanese-sponsored, 290
Dutch East Indies. *See* Netherlands East Indies.
Dutch Harbor, naval base, 209

E

"East Asia Bloc," 287, 292
East Asiatic Affairs Bureau, 290
Eastern Asia:
  American investments in, 197
  potential value of, to U. S., 197
Economic relations, fundamental principles of, 315
Eden, Anthony, 229
Education:
  Chinese, 6, 104
  Japanese program in occupied China, 131
Eggleston, Sir Frederic, 245
Eighth Route Army, 70, 108
Ellice Islands, 268
Enderbury Island, 267
Export-Import Bank, 206
Extraterritoriality:
  abolition of, 235
  efforts to abolish, 44
  privileges under, 34

F

Fadden, A. W., 245
Fairbanks, army base, 209
Far East Advisory Committee, membership, 325, n. 2
Federation of Autonomous Governments of Mongolian Provinces, 122
Fengt'ai, 66
Finance, Chinese, 4, 94, 96
Fisheries, 255
Formosa:
  jurisdiction over Spratley Islands, 309
  seizure by Japan, 34, 181
Four-Power Consortium, 37
Fourth Route Army, 111, 258
France:
  China, notes exchanged in 1897 on non-cession of Hainan Island, 307
  Chinese Maritime Customs Administration, relation to, 231–3
  concessions in China, 33, 134, 143, 145, 147–8
  Indo-China:
    agreement with Japan, Sept. 22, 1940, 184, 217
    cession to Thailand of Laos and Cambodia, 187
    defense pact with Japan, Jul. 29, 1941, 191
  Japan:
    agreement (1907), 80
    agreement, Sept. 22, 1940, on Indo-China, 184, 217
    Hainan, seizure of, 80, 183–4, 306–8
    protocol on joint defense of Indo-China, Jul. 29, 1941, 311
    Spratley Islands, seizure of, 80, 308–9
  Paracels Islands, occupation of, 306
  Siam, seizures of land in, 186
Fraser, Peter, Prime Minister of New Zealand, 246, 269–70
"Free China," activities and status, 85–113
Free French Movement:
  islands in Pacific, allegiance of, 180
French Indo-China. *See* Indo-China.
Fukien, 34 n.

G

Galens (Blücher), General, 3, 12, 46
Gases, toxic, 327
Gasoline, octane, 203
Gaulle, Genl. Charles de:
  French islands in Pacific, control of, 180
genro, 20
German-Soviet war:
  U. S. neutrality act, non-application of, 219
Germany:
  alliance with Italy and Japan, Sept. 27, 1940, 172–3

Germany—*Continued*
efforts to restore peace in China, 81, 169
non-aggression treaty with U.S.S.R., Aug. 23, 1939, 170
sphere of influence in China, 33
Japanese succession to rights in Shantung, 43
relations with China, 169
Three-Power Pact. *See that title.*
U.S.S.R., invasion of, Jun. 22, 1941, 175
Wang Ch'ing-wei regime, recognition of, 122
Gilbert Islands, 268
Great Britain:
American neutrality laws, effect of, 266
British businessmen in China, attitude toward war, 234
Burma Road:
Churchill announcement, Jul. 18, 1940, 239
closure of, 239–40
reopening of, 240
Canton and Enderbury Islands, condominium with U. S. over, 267
China:
aid to, 235–7
Burma Road, closure of, 239–40
reopening of, Oct. 18, 1940, 240
credits to, 236–7
defeatism among British respecting, 234
extraterritoriality, abolition of, 235, 240
financial aid to, 235–7
garrison forces, removal of, 240
good offices for settlement offered, 230–1
interests in cities and concessions, 237–9
investments in, 36, 41, 228
loans, 98, 236–8
mediation efforts, 240
military mission to, 272
plan of cooperation with Japan made public, 229
relations with, 228–51
Shanghai International Settlement, position in, 134
spheres of influence in, 33
stabilization fund, support of, 236
trade with, 228
trucks and road-making machinery, purchase of, 236
withdrawal of troops, 143
Chinese Maritime Customs Administration surrendered to Japanese control, 231
Craigie-Arita "agreement," Jul. 24, 1939, 238
defense in Far East, inadequacy of, 202
defense of Indian and Pacific Oceans, statement of Prime Minister Churchill on, 248
Far Eastern interests, 228
Far Eastern policy, 228–51
financial policy toward China, 235–7
gasoline, high octane, contract with Netherlands East Indies, 189
investments in China, 228
Japan:
accusations against British policy, 322–4
"agreement" on rights in treatment of British nationals, Jul. 24, 1939, 238
attack on British vessels, 74, 233
British Ambassador, attack on, 233
British gunboats damaged, 74, 233
British subjects in China, injury of, 233
cooperation, proposals for, 229
customs control in China, statement of May 3, 1938, 232–3
freezing of assets, 241
good offices for settlement offered by British, 230–1
hostilities, desire to avoid, 236
humiliations of British nationals, 237
mediation efforts, 230–3, 240
merchant ships damaged by, 233
"Open Door" in China asked for, 229

Germany—*Continued*
policy of toleration, in war with China, 228–33
prestige lost, 229
proposal for settlement of war with China, 229–33, 240
protests on damages to British interests, 233–5
retaliation for occupation of Indo-China, 241
statement of Sir Robert Craigie on policy, Jan. 14, 1939, 234–5
Tientsin concession, 145
treatment of British interests in China by, 237
Yangtze River, protest on stoppage of foreign shipping, 234–5
Ladybird, damage to, 74, 233
lend-lease aid from U. S., 267
Malaya, defense of, 249
"Manchoukuo," proposed recognition of, 229
mediation efforts to end Sino-Japanese conflict, 230, 240
military power in Far East, 201–2
naval armament, Feb. 1941, 247–8
navy, growth of, 247–8
Netherlands East Indies, contract for high octane gasoline, 189
North China, recognition of Japanese rights in, 229
parallel policy with U. S., 265
peace in Pacific, efforts to maintain, 230, 241
policy in the Pacific area, 228–51
recognition, refusal of, to Wang Ch'ing-wei govt., 239
Singapore, naval base of, 249
Sino-Japanese controversy, conciliatory role in, 228–33
Tibet, influence in, 33, 85
trade with China, 228
troops withdrawn from China, 143
united front with U. S., 263–70
United States:
air and naval bases leased in British colonies in Caribbean, 267
bases in Pacific, cooperative program for use of, 267–8
collaboration in restriction of Japanese trade, 241
conversations between Sir Robert Brooke-Popham, Adml. Hart and Major Genl. MacArthur, Apr. and Oct. 1941, 268–9
convoying of vessels, 267
lend-lease aid, 267
naval patrols, 267
pledge of cooperation, Aug. 24, 1941, 241
statement of Prime Minister Churchill, Nov. 10, 1941, on declaration of war against Japan, 241–2
Greater East Asia, co-prosperity sphere of Japan in. *See* "New Order in Greater East Asia."
Grew, Joseph C., 215
Guam, 208–9, 268
Guerrilla warfare, 106

H

Hainan Island, Japanese seizure of (1939), 80, 183, 306–8
Half Moon Shoal, 184
Hamada, K., 153
Hamaguchi, O., 21
Han Fu-chu, Governor of Shantung, 75, 79
Hankow:
fall of, 75
French concession at, 148
temporary seat of Chinese Govt., 73
Hart, Adml. Thomas C., 268
Hawaiian Islands:
defense of, 199–200
naval bases and air stations on, 210
Hay, Secretary, 34
Hayashi, General, 153
Hepburn, Rear Adml. A. J.:
naval board recommendations to Congress on naval and air bases, 208
Congressional attitude on, 208
Hiraide, Captain, 176–7
Hiranuma, Premier, 170, 192
Hirohito, Emperor:
message of Pres. Roosevelt, Dec. 6, 1941, 304

Hirohito, Emperor—*Continued*
reply in form of memorandum of Dec. 7, 1941, 304–5, 317–24
Hirota, Koki:
statements on —
Chinese cooperation with Japan, 59
communism in China, 53
Hoare, Sir Samuel, 229
Hong Kong:
British interests in, 33, 228
closure to embargoed trade, 240
defense of, 249–50
food supply, 236
Hong Kong-Shanghai Bank, 232
Hopei-Chahar Political Council, 115
Hopkins, Harry, 274
Horinouchi, Kensuke, 306, 331
Howland Island, 210
Hsin Min Hui (New People's Association), 117, 132
Hukuang railway, American interest in, 37
Hull, Cordell:
American foreign policy pronouncements, 211–12
consultation with ABCD powers, 224
reply to Rep. Ludlow in re American policy in the Pacific, 265–6
Smathers, Sen., letter of Dec. 18, 1937, 213
statements on —
Japanese memorandum of Dec. 7, 1941, 227, 304, 317
naval building in relation to Far Eastern policy, 265–6
Hu Shih, 95
"Hyde Park Declaration," Apr. 20, 1941, 264

I

Imperial Rule Assistance Association, 160, 177
Indo-China:
British interests in, 242
defense pact between France and Japan, Jul. 29, 1941, 191, 311
economic collaboration agreements, May 7, 1941, 186
export trade, prohibition of, except with Japan, 191
funds in Bank of, 191
Japan:
air bases, establishment by, 185, 191
concessions to, 215
U. S. disapproval, statement of Secy. Welles, 217
economic concessions to, 185–6
government negotiations with, 184–6
invasion by, 183, 185, 190
Japanese offer to withdraw troops, 223, 319–20
requisition of cotton plantations by, 191
requisition of rubber plantations by, 191
Japanese announcement on agreement with France, 185
Japanese proposals in note to U. S., Nov. 20, 1941, 223
occupation costs of Japanese defense, 191
raw materials source for Japan, 186
Thailand:
cession of Laos and Cambodia to, 187
invasion by, 186
Japanese mediation offer, 186–7
relations with, 186
territorial claims of, 186–7
Inner Mongolia. *See* Mongolia, Inner.
Inter-Allied Council, 275
International relations, fundamental principles of, 220, 315
Investments, foreign, in China, 36, 40–2, 55, 197, 228
Ishii, Viscount, 43, 52, 55, 59
Italy:
alliance with Germany and Japan, Sept. 27, 1940, 172–3
Anti-Comintern Pact, 168
Three-Power Pact. *See that title.*

J

Japan:
agrarian problem, 22, 157
aircraft production, 179–80
German assistance in, 179

Japan—*Continued*
airpower, quantity of, 179
alliance with Germany and Italy, Sept. 27, 1940, 172–3
American missionary activities in, 198–9
Amoy, demands on, 147
arbitration treaty with Netherlands, Feb. 12, 1940, statement by Foreign Office spokesman, 310
area of occupation in China, 86
"Asia Development Board," 288–9
assets frozen by Great Britain and U. S., 241
attitude toward Western capital in China, 55
Axis relations:
Anti-Comintern Pact, 53, 167
blitzkrieg tactics, 180
Boxer indemnity, payments of, 332
China:
demand of nationals' right of navigation in interior of China, 290
demands for trade and residence, 284
drug traffic, 290
extraterritoriality, abolition of, Japanese promises, 284
intrigues for conquest of, 292–3
occupied area. *See below* "New Order" in occupied China.
sovereignty, respect for, 284
war with:
beginnings of 1937 conflict, 65
bombing attacks, 78
efforts of Genl. Sung Cheh-yuan to reach settlement, 68
invasion of territory, 66
Japanese statements on war aims, 56
military campaign, 68–81
naval activities, 79
Tangku truce (1933), 51
China Affairs Board, 123
"China Affairs Bureau," 288
Chinese Maritime Customs, statement on, May 3, 1938, two forms published, 331–2
Chinese Reorganization Loan of 1913, share of, 332
common people of, 281
communism:
Anti-Comintern Pact, 53, 167–70
fears of Chinese, 52
underground movement, 25
"cooperation," theory of, 279
"cooperation" with China, 58
cooperation with Great Britain, proposals for, 229
"co-prosperity in Greater East Asia." *See* "New Order in Greater East Asia."
cotton mills, closing of, 205
currency, efforts against Chinese, 97
customs administration in China, statement of May 3, 1938, 232–3
doctrine of divine origin, 30
"East Asia Bloc," 287
economic conditions, 26
economic measures by U. S. against, 202–6
economic nationalism, 278
economic relations with occupied China, 124–31, 287
embargoes, legal and moral, by U. S., against, 202–6
Emperor Hirohito:
message of Pres. Roosevelt, Dec. 6, 1941, 304
reply in form of memorandum of Dec. 7, 1941, 304–5, 317–24
feudal system, 17
fleet stationed in Gulf of Siam, 187
France, protocol on joint defense of Indo-China, Jul. 29, 1941, 311
genro, 20, 152
geographical position, advantages of, 179–80, 280
German aid in aircraft production, 179
German influence on relations with U. S., 178
German-Soviet Pact, relation to, 170
Germany's invasion of U.S.S.R., effect on, 175
government:
Army influence, increase of, 150, 278

Japan—*Continued*
constitution, 19, 149
Diet, 19, 150
"new national structure," 149–65
Restoration period, 18–21
Great Britain:
accusation of economic warfare by, 322–4
freezing of assets, 241
gunboats damaged, 233
Hainan Island, occupation of, 80, 306–8
Hankow, action against French concession at, 148
imperial conference, Jul. 2, 1941, 190
imperialist program in South Pacific, 280
Imperial Rule Assistance Association, 160
Indo-China. *See that title.*
industrialization, 21, 23
intervention of 1918–21 in Eastern Siberia, 181
investments in China, 36, 40–1
Japanese Planning Board, 288
kodo, 29–30
Konoye cabinet, resignation of, 175, 177
labor, 21, 23, 25, 157
landlordism, 22
League of Nations, withdrawal from, 166, 310
"Manchoukuo." *See that title.*
mandated islands in Pacific, 180
mediation offer in Thailand-Indo-China controversy, 186–7
memorandum of Dec. 7, 1941 in reply to American proposals of Nov. 26, 317–24
statement of Secy. of State Hull on, 227, 304, 317
militarism, 17, 293
military power of, 179
Mitsui, 17
Mongolia, Inner, invasion of, 68
Mongolian People's Republic, pledge to respect territory of, 297
munitions of war, importation of from U. S., 211
national existence, 63
nationalism, 29
naval activities on China coast, 79
naval strength, 179
naval treaties of 1922 and 1930, abrogation of, 206
Netherlands:
arbitration treaty, Feb. 12, 1940, statement of Foreign Office spokesman, 310
treaty of judicial settlement, arbitration and conciliation, Apr. 19, 1933, 310
Netherlands East Indies. *See that title.*
"new economic structure," 163
"new national structure," 149–65
"New Order in Greater East Asia." *See that title.*
"New Order" in occupied China:
aim of "reconstruction work" in, statement of Chiang K'ai-shek, 291
banking and currency, 129
China Affairs Board, establishment of, 123
economic program, 124
joint declaration by Japan, Manchoukuo and Wang regime, Nov. 30, 1940, 122
local government, 123
Provisional Government, Peking (1937), 115
New People's Association, 117
Political Council of North China, 117
"Reformed Government of the Chinese Republic" (1938), 118
"Reorganized National Government of China":
establishment at Nanking, Mar. 30, 1940, 117, 120
recognition by certain governments, 122
structure, 120
treaty with Japan (1940), 121
Wang Ch'ing-wei, role of, 119
United Council of China (1938), 118
North and Central China Development Companies, 124, 127, 288

Japan—*Continued*
North China:
customs control of, 232
Paracels (Sisha) Islands, statement on French occupation of, 306
peace overtures to China:
Dec. 1938, statement by Premier Konoye, 82
statement by Chiang K'ai-shek, 83
Jan. 1938, through German Ambassador, 81, 169
declaration of Premier Konoye, 82
policy of government, 318
political parties:
dissolution of, 158
Minseito, 21, 153
Seiyukai, 21, 153
population pressure, 23
premiers:
Hamaguchi, 21
Hayashi, 153
Hiranuma, 170
Inukai, 21, 151
Konoye, 82, 159–60, 168, 171, 174–7, 283–4
Tanaka, 21
Tojo, 280
Yonai, 171
proletarianism in, 24
propaganda measures, 158
public finance, regulation of, 156
raw materials, supply of, 28–9
raw silk trade, stoppage of, 205
Restoration period, 17
samurai, 17
seizure of Korea, Formosa and Pescadores Islands, 34
Shanghai International Settlement, reorganization of, 138
Shantung, succession to German rights in, 43, 46
Shinnan Gunto, 308
shogunate, 18
Spratley Islands, Foreign Office statements concerning, 308–9
steel scrap, licenses required for U. S. export to, 203
strategic position in Pacific, 179
suffrage, 19
tariff policy, 27
Thailand:
attitude toward, 193
treaty of friendship, 183
Three-Power Pact. *See that title.*
Tientsin, blockade of, 145
Timor, Portuguese, landing rights on, for airline, 180
totalitarianism, trend toward, 153, 280
trade, foreign, 26
tripartite bloc of China, "Manchoukuo" and, 235
"Twenty-One Demands," 42, 58, 105
U.S.S.R.:
"convention embodying basic rules," 1925, 252
frontier declaration with Japan respecting "Manchoukuo," Apr. 13, 1941, 173, 297
Neutrality Pact, Apr. 13, 1941, 173, 258, 261
oil and coal concessions in North Saghalien, 255
protocol, Oct. 16, 1941, boundary with "Manchoukuo," 255
rapprochement with, 260
trade agreement, June 1941, 261, 296
war with, prospects of, 176
U. S. *See* United States: Japan.
war effort, effect on people, 278, 280
white influence in Eastern Asia, desire to eradicate, 280
world organization, repudiation of, 278
Zaibatsu, influence of, 20
Japanese Planning Board, 288
Jarvis Island, 210
Joffe, Alexander, 12
Johnston Island, 209, 268
Juichin, 13

K

Karakhan, M., 46
Kawai, Tatsuo, 245

Kellogg-Briand Pact, violation of, by Japan, 212
Keswick, W. J., 142
Khone, 187
Khong, 187
Kiaochow, 33, 44
Kleffens, E. N. van, 269
Kobayashi, Ichizo, 189
Kodiak, naval base, 209
Kodo, 29–30
Konoye, Prince Fumimaro, 82, 159–60, 168, 171, 174–7, 283–4
Korea, 34, 176, 181, 292
Kowloon:
  British position in, 33, 228
  defense of, 250
Krivitsky, Genl. W. G., statement on Anti-Comintern Pact, 168
Kulangsu, 147
Kung, H. H., 94
Kuomintang (National Party):
  admission of Communists, 46
  Communist friction, 110
  emergency congress, April 1938, 82
  expulsion of Communists, 46
  relation to Govt. of China, 88
  reorganization of, 3
  resolution of censure upon Communists, 55
  structure of, 88
Kurusu, Saburo, mission to U. S., 221–7
Kwangchowwan, French naval base at, 33
Kwangsi, French influence in, 33
Kwangtung, French influence in, 33
Kweichow, French influence in, 33

L

Labor:
  in China, 6, 11
  in Japan, 21, 23, 25
Labuan, British Borneo, 268
La Guardia, Fiorello H., 264
Land distribution in China, 9, 14
Land Regulations of Shanghai International Settlement, 138
Lansing-Ishii Agreement of 1917, 43, 59
Lansing, Robert, U. S. Secy. of State, 39, 43, 59
Latham, Sir John, 245
Lattimore, Owen, 260
League of Nations:
  China, aid to, 326, 330
  Covenant, 65, 328
  Japanese cooperation in social and technical fields, termination of, 329
  Japanese withdrawal from, 166, 310
  "moral support" for China, 325–6, 329
  Sino-Japanese conflict, action taken on:
    Assembly resolution, Oct. 6, 1937, 325
    Council resolutions, Feb. 2 and May 14, 1938, Jan. 20, 1939, 326, 329
    invitation to Japan by Pres. of Council, 327
      reply telegram, 328
    statement of Japanese Foreign Office on Art. 16 of Covenant, 328
Leases in China by foreign powers, 33
Leith-Ross, Sir Frederick, 229
Lend-lease aid to:
  China, 205, 216, 271
  Great Britain, 267
  U.S.S.R., 275
Li Ta-chao, 12
Litvinov, Maxim:
  statement in League Council on application of sanctions against Japan, 257
Liu Chiu Islands, 181
Liu, Dr. Herman, assassination of, 137
Liu Hsiang, General, 87
Liu Kung Island, seizure of, by Japan, 240
Loans to China, 37, 98, 236–8
Low Islands, 180
Lower, A. R. M., 246
Ludlow, Louis, 265
Lukouchiao, 51, 61, 66–8, 230
Lung Yün, General, 87

"New Order in Greater East Asia" —*Continued*
economic union for Netherlands Indies, proposal of, 189
Japanese statements on, 52, 114
Japan's basic aim of *hakko ichiu,* statement on, 182
Matsuoka statement on, 187
Netherlands East Indies:
importance of, 188–9
refusal of incorporation in, 189–90
program, enunciation of, 181
recognition by Japan of German and Italian leadership, 294
recognition of Japan's leadership by Axis partners, 294
solidarity of Japan, "Manchoukuo" and China, 183
U. S. policy regarding, 298–9
statement of Adml. Suetsugu on, 193
New People's Association, 117
New Zealand:
air strength, 250
cooperation with U. S. in war with Japan, promise of, 246
defenses of, 250
Japan:
attitude toward, in 1938, 257
commercial treaty, abrogation of, 246
Labor govt., policy of, 246
naval and air bases, 268
position in relation to Far Eastern war, 246
scrap metal, embargo on, 246
Nine-Power Treaty (1922):
Japan's attitude toward, 323
violation of, by Japan, 212
Nishihara, Mr., 36
Nomonhan, armistice of, 261
Nomura, Adml. Kichisaburo:
credentials, presentation of, 215
negotiations for understanding, 216
neutrality pact with U. S., proposed by, 216
Non-interference in internal affairs of nations, 300
North and Central China Development Companies, 124, 127, 288
North China:
American protest to Japan on trade restrictions in, 214
British recognition of Japanese rights in, 229, 232
customs administration, Japanese control of, 232
political control by Japan, 68
North China Herald:
Chinese capitulation to Japan urged by, 230

O

Occupied China. *See under* Japan.
Oil, 188–9, 203, 218, 243, 255
Okinori, Kaya, 222
"Open Door" in China:
American insistence upon, 194
corollary to territorial integrity, 194
equality of treatment in commercial relations, 194
trade, freedom of, 194
tradition of American foreign policy, 34–5, 201
Oriental Economist, 177
Ott, Major Genl. Eugen, 173
Outline of Proposed Basis for Agreement between U. S. and Japan, 224–5

P

Pacific:
growth of intimacy in British-American relations, 269–70
U. S. policy in, message of Pres., Dec. 15, 1941, excerpt, 298–305
Pacific bases, fortification of, 208–11
Pact of Paris, 65
Pai Ch'ung-hsi, General, 94
Pakhoi, occupation of, 77
Palmyra Island, 268
Pan American Airways, 41, 209
Panama Canal, defense of, 199
Panay, U.S.S., 74, 234
indemnity paid by Japan, 213
sinking of, reaction to, 212–13
Paracels Islands, 183, 306
Paris Peace Conference (1919), 43

Peace:
British attempts at mediation, 230
overtures by Japan to China:
Dec. 1938, statement by Premier Konoye, 82
statement by Chiang K'ai-shek, 83
Jan. 1938, through German Ambassador, 81
declaration of Premier Konoye, 82
Pearl Harbor:
attack on, Dec. 7, 1941, 227, 304
naval base, 210
Pearl River, closure of, 236
Penang, British base, 268
People's Economic Reconstruction Movement, 6
People's Political Council, 90, 272
Pescadores Islands, seizure by Japan, 34
Petroleum and products, 188–9, 203, 218, 243, 255
Philippines:
air forces in, 211
American obligations toward, 200
army, Filipino, 210–11
defense facilities, 210
neutralization of, 200
Tydings-McDuffie Act, 200
U. S. army regulars in, 210
Prince of Wales, H.M.S., 248
Principle of the People's Livelihood, 14
Principles, fundamental, 314–5
Proletarianism:
in China, 11
in Japan, 24
Provisional Govt. of the Chinese Republic (1937), 115

Q

Quezon, Pres. Manuel, 210

R

Raw materials:
Chinese, 99
Japanese, 29
Reconstruction Finance Corporation, 275
"Reformed Govt." of the Chinese Republic (1938), 118, 232
Reorganization Loan, 37, 57, 332
"Reorganized National Govt.," Nanking (1940), 117–22
Restoration period in Japan, 18–21
Ronin, 290
Roosevelt, Pres. Franklin D.:
"The Atlantic Charter," Aug. 14, 1941, 218
Canadian defense pledge, Aug. 18, 1938, Kingston, Ontario, 263
Chautauqua, address, Aug. 1936, defense of "neighborhood," 263
"Hyde Park Declaration," Apr. 20, 1941, issued jointly with Prime Minister Mackenzie King, 264
Indo-China, memorandum of Dec. 2, 1941 on mobilization of Japanese troops in, 225
Japanese assets, order for freezing, Jul. 25, 1941, 204, 218
message to Congress on Far East policy, Dec. 15, 1941, 219, 298–305
principles of international relations, 220
message to Emperor Hirohito, Dec. 6, 1941, and reply message, 304–5
memorandum reply, 317–24
petroleum and scrap metal to Japan, order requiring licenses for export of, 203
Premier Konoye, statement on invitation to meet, 220
speech of Oct. 5, 1937, 212
Stalin, letter to, Aug. 15, 1941, 274–5
Rothermere, Lord, 167
Rubber, synthetic, 199
Russia (*see also* Union of Soviet Socialist Republics):
sphere of influence in China, 34

S

Saghalien, 181, 255
Saionji, Prince, 152
Saito, Adml. Viscount, 151
Saito, T., 153

Salt Administration, Central, of China, 37
Samoan Islands, 268
samurai, 17
San Min Chu I, 117
Sayre, Francis B., 269
Seiyukai, 21
Shanghai, battle of, 70
Shanghai International Settlement:
  American marines, departure of, 273
  character of, 134
  effects of hostilities on residents, 73, 136–8
  Japanese representation in police force, 273
  Municipal Council:
    agreement to revise police control, 140
    representation in, 142
  reorganization of govt., Japanese demands for, 138
Shanghai Volunteer Corps, 273
Shansi, invasion by Japan, 69
Shantung:
  German influence in, 33
  Japanese succession to rights in, 43, 46
Shinnan Gunto (Spratley Islands), 184, 308
Shinto teachings, 279
Shogunate, 18
Siam. *See* Thailand.
Siberia:
  defense measures, 253–4
  intervention of Japan, 1918–21, in Eastern, 181
  Japanese troop concentration against, 176
  mineral production, 253
  population increase, 253
  railway building, 253
  road-building, 253
Siberia, Maritime Province of, Russian control of, 34
Siems-Carey Company, 39
Sikkim, 33
Silk, proposed binding on free list, 316
Singapore, naval base of, 249
  use of, by Japan, 200
Sinkiang:
  population, 260
  relation to China, 259–60
  Soviet influence in, 48, 252, 259–60
  trade agreement with Soviet Union, 1931, 259
Sinkiang-Kansu-Shensi route, 260
Sino-Japanese Economic Council, 124
Sisha Islands, 306
Sitka, naval base, 209
Smathers, Sen., letter to Secy. Hull, Dec. 18, 1937, 213
Society Islands, French, 180
Solomon Islands, 268
Soong, T. V., 4, 94
South America, U. S. trade with, in 1939 and 1940, 195
South Manchuria, 34
Southeastern Asia, British interests in, 242–3
Sovereignty of nations, 300
Soviet Russia. *See* Union of Soviet Socialist Republics.
Soviets, Chinese, 13
Spratley Islands, Japanese seizure of, 80, 180, 183, 308
Stabilization Fund, agreement, Apr. 26, 1941, 237
Stalin, Josef:
  allegation that democracies welcomed Soviet-Japan war, 261
  coalition with Great Britain and U. S. defined, 276
  joint letter from Pres. Roosevelt and Prime Minister Churchill, Aug. 15, 1941, 274–5
Standard Oil Co., 213
State, Department of. *See* United States, State, Department of.
Stewart, Sir Frederic, 245
Suetsugu, Adml. N., 172–3, 193
Sumitomo, 20, 152
Sun Fo, 94
Sung Cheh-yuan, General, 68
Sun Yat-sen, Dr.:
  Chiang K'ai-shek, 92
  collaboration with Russian Communists, 12
  leadership of National Party, 89
  Principle of the People's Livelihood, 14

Sun Yat-sen, Dr.—*Continued*
San Min Chu I, 117
views, 111
Wang Ch'ing-wei, 119
Sun Yat-sen, Madam, 10
Suzuki, 20

T

T'ai Chih-t'ao, 95
Taiwan, Government-General, jurisdiction of Spratley Islands, 309
Tanaka, General, 21, 291
"Tanaka Memorial," 181
Tangku truce (1933), 51, 67
Tariff:
Chinese, treaty control of, 34, 194
Japanese policy, 27
Tatsukichi, Minobe, 30
Tenno, 30
Territorial integrity, 300
Thailand:
American assurances, 193
British interests in, 242–3
British warning to Japan on invasion of, 241
government of, 243
Great Britain, attitude toward, 192
Indo-China, relations with, 186–7
Japan:
credits to, 192
demands for military bases, 191
guaranty of settlement with Indo-China, 187
mediation offer in dispute with Indo-China, 186–7
penetration into, 176
recognition of "Manchoukuo," Aug. 1, 1941, 192
revolt against government promoted by, 193
treaty of friendship, 183
League Assembly, vote, abstention, in Sino-Japanese dispute, 183
"Manchoukuo," recognition of, 192
neutrality and independence, policy of, 192–3
non-aggression pact with United Kingdom, 1940, 243
rubber production, 243
territorial claims against Indo-China, 186–7
tin mines, 242
trade with British Empire, 242–3
treaty of friendship with Japan, June 12, 1940, 183
provisions of, 183
U. S., attitude toward, 192
Third International, 45–7, 52
The Three People's Principles, definition of, 292
Three-Power Pact:
American efforts to counteract, 215
Japanese interpretation, 171
Japanese refusal to modify position in regard to, 322
operation of, Japanese statement on possible, 175
technical commissions under, 295
text, 294–5
U. S., relation to, 294–5
value to Japan, 174–5
warning to U. S., 172
"Throne Aid League," 222
Tibet, 33, 85
Tientsin, concessions at:
American infantry withdrawal, Mar. 1938, 213
blockade by Japanese army, 145
British interests in, 238
Japanese negotiations with British and French, 146
Timor, Portuguese, 180
Togo, Shigenori, Foreign Minister, 177–8
Tojo, Genl. Hideki:
cabinet of, 177
Premier of Japan, Oct. 17, 1941, 177, 221
statement of Nov. 29, 1941 on British and American "exploitation" of Asiatic peoples, 225
war policy in relation to Germany, 280
Tokugawa, 18
Trade. *See individual countries.*
Trans-Siberian Railway, 253
Trautmann, Dr. Oscar, 81, 83, 169
Treaties, agreements, conventions, etc.:
Anti-Comintern Pact, Nov. 25, 1936, 53, 167–70, 283

Treaties, agreements, conventions, etc. —*Continued*
China, agreement of 1858 on "Rules of trade" for Chinese Maritime Customs Administration, 231–3
China, treaty limitations of, 34
China-France, Jun. 10, 1907, integrity, commerce, order, 307, n. 3
China-France, Jul. 28, 1931, convention, 144
China-Germany, May 1939, arms agreement, 170
China-Japan, May 5, 1932, armistice agreement, 71
China-Russia, 1881, St. Petersburg, 259
China-U.S.S.R., Aug. 21, 1937, non-aggression treaty, 252, 256–7
China-U.S.S.R., Oct. 1938, Feb., Aug. 1939, Dec. 1940, barter agreements, 257–8
China-U.S.S.R., Jun. 16, 1939 and July 1940, commercial accords, 257
France-China, Jun. 10, 1907, integrity, commerce, order, 307, n. 3
France-China, Jul. 28, 1931, convention, 144
France-Japan, 1907, entente, 80
France-Japan, Sept. 22, 1940, on Indo-China, 184
France-Japan, May 7, 1941, agreements for economic collaboration, 186
France-Japan, Jul. 29, 1941, joint defense of Indo-China, 191, 311
France-Thailand, Mar. 1941, on Indo-China and peace of "Greater East Asia," 187
French Concession, Nov. 7, 1940, agreement with Wang Ch'ing-wei regime, 144
Germany-China, May 1939, arms agreement, 170
Germany-Japan-Italy, Sept. 27, 1940 (Three-Power Pact), 171, 294–5
Germany, Japan and "Manchoukuo," Apr. 1936, renewal 1937, trade agreement, 169
Germany-U.S.S.R., Aug. 23, 1939, non-aggression, 170
Great Britain-U.S.S.R., Jul. 12, 1941, alliance, 274
Indo-China, Jul. 29, 1941, protocol between France and Japan on joint defense, 311
Japan-China, May 5, 1932, armistice agreement, 71
Japan-France, Sept. 22, 1940, on Indo-China, 184
Japan-France, May 7, 1941, agreements for economic collaboration, 186
Japan-France, Jul. 29, 1941, protocol on joint defense of Indo-China, 191, 311
Japan-Netherlands, Apr. 19, 1933, judicial settlement, arbitration and conciliation, 310
Japan-Netherlands, 1936, trade agreement, 188
Japan-U.S.S.R., 1925, "convention embodying basic rules," 252
Japan-U.S.S.R., Jan. 23, 1928, fisheries agreement, 255
Japan-U.S.S.R., Apr. 13, 1941, frontier declaration, 297
Japan-U.S.S.R., Apr. 13, 1941, Neutrality Pact, 173, 258, 261
Japan-U. S., 1911, commercial, termination of, 211, 214–5
Lansing-Ishii Agreement of 1917, 43
"Manchoukuo," Apr. 13, 1941, frontier declaration between Japan and U.S.S.R., 297
Netherlands-Japan, Apr. 19, 1933, judicial settlement, arbitration and conciliation, 310
Netherlands-Japan, 1936, trade agreement, 188
Neutrality Pact between Japan and U.S.S.R., Apr. 13, 1941, 173
Nine-Power Treaty, 36, 43
violation of, by Japan, 212
"Reorganized National Govt. of China" and Japan, Nov. 30, 1940, 121
Russia-China, 1881, St. Petersburg, 259

Treaties, agreements, conventions, etc. —*Continued*
- Thailand-Japan, Jun. 12, 1940, treaty of friendship, 183
- Thailand-United Kingdom, 1940, non-aggression pact, 243
- Three-Power Pact, Sept. 27, 1940, between Germany, Italy and Japan, 171, 294–5
- U.S.S.R.-China, Aug. 21, 1937, non-aggression treaty, 252, 256–7
- U.S.S.R.-China, Oct. 1938, Feb., Aug. 1939, Dec. 1940, barter agreements, 257–8
- U.S.S.R.-China, Jun. 16, 1939 and July 1940, commercial accords, 257
- U.S.S.R.-Germany, Aug. 23, 1939, non-aggression, 170
- U.S.S.R.-Great Britain, Jul. 12, 1941, alliance, 274
- U.S.S.R.-Japan, 1925, "convention embodying basic rules," 252
- U.S.S.R.-Japan, Jan. 23, 1928, fisheries agreement, 255
- U.S.S.R.-Japan, Apr. 13, 1941, frontier declaration, 297
- U.S.S.R.-Japan, Apr. 13, 1941, Neutrality Pact, 173, 258, 261
- United Kingdom-Thailand, 1940, non-aggression pact, 243
- U.S.-Japan, Jul. 26, 1911, commercial, termination of. 211, 214–5
- Versailles, Treaty of, 46

Tsingtao, temporary exemption from Japanese blockade, 79

Tuamotu Islands, 180

Tungminghui, 119

Tutuila, naval base, 210

"Twenty-One Demands" by Japan, 42, 58, 105

Tydings-McDuffie Act, 200

U

Ugaki, General, 123, 151, 328

Unalaska Island, 209

Union of Soviet Socialist Republics:
- alliance with Great Britain, Jul. 12, 1941, 274
- "Atlantic Charter," declaration of adherence to, Sept. 24, 1941, 275
- Axis relationship, 261
- boundary demarcation with "Manchoukuo" and Outer Mongolia, 254
- China:
  - barter agreements, Oct. 1938, Feb., Aug. 1939, Dec. 1940, 257–8
  - commercial accords, Jun. 16, 1939 and July 1940, 257
  - military supplies, 252, 257
  - non-aggression treaty, Aug. 21, 1937, 252, 256–7
  - policy toward, 46, 257–60, 262
  - Soviet protectorates in, 48
- democratic states, attitude toward, 261
- Far Eastern defense forces, 253–4
- fisheries agreement with Japan, 255–6
- frontier declaration with Japan respecting "Manchoukuo," 297
- Germany:
  - invasion by, 175
  - treaty, Aug. 23, 1939, non-aggression, 170
- Great Britain:
  - alliance, Jul. 12, 1941, 274
- Japan:
  - approval of proposed League sanctions against, 257
  - border hostilities with, 254
  - "convention embodying basic rules," 1925, 252
  - fisheries agreement, Jan. 23, 1928, 255–6
    - annual extensions, 256
  - League Covenant, attitude toward application of Art. 16, 257
  - negotiations on border hostilities in "Manchoukuo," 254–5
  - Neutrality Pact, Apr. 13, 1941, 173–4, 258, 261
  - oil and coal concessions in North Saghalien, 255
  - protocol, Oct. 16, 1941, boundary between U.S.S.R. and "Manchoukuo," 255

Union of Soviet Socialist Republics —*Continued*
rapprochement, 260–2
relations with, June 1941, 174
trade agreement, June 1941, 261, 296
Mongolian People's Republic, pledge to respect territory of, 297
neutrality pact with Japan, Apr. 13, 1941, 253
non-aggression treaty with Germany, Aug. 23, 1939, 170
objectives in Eastern Asia, 252
Outer Mongolia, influence in, 48, 85, 252
Siberia, developments in, 253
Sino-Japanese conflict, attitude toward, 256–60
Three-Power Pact, relation to, 295
United States:
conversations between Secy. Welles and Ambassador Oumansky, 216–7
economic assistance offer, Aug. 2, 1941, exchange of notes, 274
export of war materials, 275
Hopkins, Harry, mission to Moscow, 274–5
lend-lease aid of $1,000,000,000, 222
Stalin's interpretation of relations with, 276
warm-water port, 253
United Council of China (1938), 118
United Front in Pacific, 263–76
United Kingdom (*see also* Great Britain):
American destroyers, transfer of, 266
Japanese assets, freezing of, Jul. 26, 1941, 218
Japanese notification on Chinese maritime customs, 331–2
non-aggression pact with Thailand, 243
United Nations:
Joint Declaration by 26 countries, Jan. 1, 1942, 263
members, 270
United States:
American leadership in resistance to Japanese policies, 194–227
Anglo-American parallelism in policy, 265–70
anti-war sentiment, 202
army bases in Pacific area, 209–11
Asiatic fleet, 208
Atlantic fleet, 208
Atlantic situation, attitude toward, 202
Australia:
visits of American naval detachments to, 269
British Commonwealth of Nations, united front with, 263–70
Brussels Conference, participation in, 299–300
Canada:
defense articles, manufacture of, 264
"Hyde Park Declaration," Apr. 20, 1941, 264
Joint Defense Production Committee, 265
Joint Economic Committees, 264–5
Permanent Joint Board on Defense, 264
Canton and Enderbury Islands, condominium with Great Britain over, 267
China:
American admiration of art and and craftsmanship, 199
American missionary activities in, 197–9
arms shipments to, 271
assets in U. S., freezing of, at request of Chiang K'ai-shek, 204
credits, 205–6
cultural interests in, 197–9
democratic institutions sponsored by Americans, 201
economic interests in, 195–7
independence of, respect for, 194–5
investments in, 36, 40–2
lend-lease aid to, 205, 216, 271
loans to:
May 1941, 98
policy of Wilson administration, 37
private, 37

United States—*Continued*
marines, evacuation of, Nov. 14, 1941, 272
military mission to, 271
minerals, purchase of, 206
"Open Door" policy, 34, 194, 201
policy toward, 194–227
political interests in, 199–201
protection of American interests in, 213–4
recognition of Republic in 1913 and National Govt. in 1928, 201
silver purchasing policy, 10
stabilization fund to support currency, 205
strategic materials, in exchange for credits, 205–6
Tientsin, American infantry withdrawal from, 213
trade decrease since 1931, 196–7
Chinese Maritime Customs Administration, relation to, 231–3
consultations with United Kingdom, Australia, China and Netherlands, 224
cultural interests in Far East, 197–9
Eastern Asia, investments in, 197
economic interests in Asia, protection of, attitude of people on, 202
economic relations, fundamental principles of, 315
embargoes to Japan and military action, 203
Far Eastern policy:
diplomatic defense of, 211–27
foreign policy in Mar. 1941, 201
message of the Pres. to Congress, Dec. 15, 1941, summary, 298–305
principles of, 194–227
French Indo-China:
assets of Japan, freezing of, 218
Japanese occupation of, protest on, 215, 217
sentiment of American people, 217–8
Great Britain:
air and naval bases in British colonies in Caribbean, 267
bases in Pacific, cooperative program for use of, 268
conversations between Sir Robert Brooke-Popham, Adml. Hart and Major Genl. MacArthur, Apr. and Oct. 1941, 268–9
convoying of vessels with supplies for, 267
joint use of bases in Pacific, 267
lend-lease aid, 267
naval patrols, 267
parallel policy in Pacific, question to Secy. Hull on commitments, 265–6
relation of America's program in Far East to aid to, 201–2
Japan:
Act of Jul. 2, 1940 prohibiting export of articles of national defense to, 203
American assets in, 197
freezing of, 204
American immigration policy, 280
American policy in Pacific, summary, message of Pres., Dec. 15, 1941, excerpt, 298–305
antagonism to imperialism, 194–5
armed forces, withdrawal of, from China and Indo-China, proposed in "Outline," 224
assets, freezing of, 204–5, 218
value of, 204
attitude expressed by Adml. Suetsugu, Nov. 24, 1941, 193
blockade, effect of, 205
Boxer Protocol rights to be relinquished, proposed in "Outline," 225
commercial treaty of 1911, termination of, 211, 214–5
commercial treaty on liberal lines, proposed in "Outline," 225
concessions and settlements in China, to be given up as proposed in "Outline," 225
consultations with Great Britain, Australia and the Netherlands on proposals of Nov. 26, to, 324

United States—*Continued*
conversations for peaceful settlement, 222–7, 300–5, 312–4, 319
denunciation of "impractical principles" by, 321–4
diplomatic defense against, 211–27
diplomatic officer at Nanking, slapping of, by Japanese, 213
dollar-yen rate, stabilization of, proposed in "Outline," 225
draft proposals of Jun. 21, 1941, 313
draft proposals of Sept. 25, 1941, 313, 319
economic defense against, 202–6
embargoes, legal and moral against, 202–6
extraterritoriality, surrender of, proposed in "Outline," 225
four principles as basis of negotiations, 220
Japanese acceptance of, 221
freezing restrictions, removal of, proposed in "Outline," 225
French Indo-China, agreement to respect territorial integrity, proposed in "Outline," 224
good offices proffered in conflict with China, 299
goodwill policy, 194
investments in, 197
invitation to Pres. Roosevelt to meet Premier Konoye, 220, 301, 319
reply of Pres. Roosevelt, Aug. 17, 1941, 220
iron scrap from U. S., subject to license, 203
Konoye's assurance of acceptance of four principles, Sept. 6, 1941, 221
letter from Dept. of State, Jul. 1, 1938, on embargo of airplanes and their equipment to, 202
licenses for shipments of certain commodities, 203–4
memorandum of Dec. 2, 1941 on mobilization of Japanese troops in Indo-China, 225
Japanese reply, Dec. 5, 1941, 225
memorandum of Japanese Ambassador, Nov. 26, 1941, termination of negotiations, 227
memorandum of Japanese Ambassador, Dec. 7, 1941, 317–24
statement of Secy. of State Hull on, 227, 304, 317
message to Emperor Hirohito by Pres. Roosevelt, Dec. 6, 1941, and reply, Dec. 10, 303–5
metals for export to, licenses for shipment of, 204
military defense against, 206–11
modus vivendi, efforts to reach, 178
moral embargoes on exports to, 202–6
National Govt. of China, support of, proposed in "Outline," 224
negotiations for settlement in Pacific, 178, 220–7, 300–5, 312–24
neutrality law, non-application to war with China, 211
"New Order," opposition to, 225
non-aggression agreement, proposed in "Outline," 224
non-application of any treaty in conflict with "Outline," 225
note of Oct. 2, 1941 to Japanese Ambassador, 220–1
note of Nov. 26, 1941 to Japanese Ambassador, 312–7
oil export, curtailment of, 203–5
oil shipments to Vladivostok, protest on, 219
opposition to interference with raw materials export, 199
oral statement of fundamental principles made to Ambassador Nomura, Nov. 26, 1941, 224
"Outline of Proposed Basis for Agreement between U. S. and Japan":
policy, draft mutual declaration of, 314–5

United States—*Continued*
steps to be taken by Governments, 315–7
summary of, 224–5
Panay, U.S.S., sinking of, by Japanese bombs, 74, 212–3, 234
plan of agreement proposed by U. S. Govt., Nov. 26, 1941, 302–3
policy of good will toward, 194
Pres. Roosevelt's letter to Emperor Hirohito, Dec. 6, 1941, 226
comment on reply to, 226–7
Emperor's reply in memorandum of Dec. 7, 1941, 226
press campaign against U. S., 176–7
proposals of Sept. 6, 1941, 221
proposals of Nov. 20, 1941, 223, 301–2, 313, 319
raw material limitation on American trade, 199
rejection of American proposals, 317–24
Shanghai International Settlement, reply to Japanese request for reorganization, 139
silk, 204
statement of Aug. 28, 1941 by, 221
statement of Dec. 31, 1938 on trade restrictions in Manchuria ("Manchoukuo"), 214
statement of Premier Konoye on relations with U. S., Oct. 5, 1940, 174
steel scrap, embargo on, 203
steps proposed for Pacific settlement:
Boxer protocol of 1901, rights under, to be given up, 316
dollar-yen rate, stabilization of, 316, 324
extraterritorial rights in China, relinquishment of, 316, 324
freezing restrictions on funds, in both countries, removal of, 316, 324
French Indo-China, territorial integrity, respect for, and non-discrimination in trade relations, 315, 323
international settlements and concessions, to be given up, 316
Japanese withdrawal of all forces from China, 316, 323
National Govt. of the Republic of China, Chungking, to be only one recognized, 316, 323
non-aggression pact among British Empire, China, Japan, Netherlands, Soviet Union, Thailand and U. S., 315, 322
non-discrimination in treaty relations, 316, 322
principles, basic political and economic, adherence to and application of, 316–7
silk, binding of raw, on free list, 316
trade agreement with reciprocal most-favored-nation treatment, 316, 324
strategic considerations in policy toward, 199–201
trade control established under freezing of assets, 204
trade in 1939, 1940, 195
treaty rights, infringement of, 212
Lend-Lease Act, Mar. 1941:
aid to—
China, 205, 216, 271
Great Britain, 201, 267
U.S.S.R., 211, 275
manufactured articles, 196
marines, evacuation of, from China, Nov. 14, 1941, 272
capture of *President Harrison* by Japan with contingents from Tientsin and Peking, 272
military mission to Chungking, 219
military mission to Moscow, 219
missionary activities in Far East, 197–9
naval armament, treaties on:
consultation with signatories, 206

United States—*Continued*
escalation clause, 206
Japanese abrogation of 1922 and 1930, 206
suspension of treaty of 1936, 206
Navy:
airplanes, 207
capital ships, tonnage of, 206
expansion of, 206–11
fleets, 207
strength of, 207
neutrality law:
cargo ships to enter war zones, 222
non-application to Far Eastern war, 271
New Zealand:
use of naval bases in case of war offered by Prime Minister Fraser, 269–70
visits of American naval detachments to, 269
"Open Door" in Manchuria, end of, Oct. 6, 1938, note of protest, 214
Pacific bases, British, use of, agreement in principle, 268
Pacific fleet, 208
Pacific situation, attitude toward, 202
Pearl Harbor attack by Japan, 227
political interests in Far East, 199–201
principles, fundamental, in international relations, 300, 314
Roosevelt-Churchill joint declaration, Aug. 14, 1941, 218
rubber imports, 195
State, Department of:
statement on delivery of Japanese memorandum of Dec. 7, 1941, 317
Three-Power Pact. *See that title.*
tin imports, 195
trade with—
Asia, 1939 and 1940, 195
British India, 1939 and 1940, 195
British Malaya, 1939 and 1940, 195
China, 1939 and 1940, 195
Japan, 1939 and 1940, 195
Manchuria, 196
Netherlands East Indies, 1939 and 1940, 195
South America, 1939 and 1940, 195
treaties, modification by negotiation, 235
U.S.S.R.:
conversations between Secy. Welles and Ambassador Oumansky, 216–7
credits to, 275
economic assistance offer, Aug. 2, 1941, exchange of notes, 274
lend-lease aid to, 211, 275
manganese, chromite, asbestos and platinum, purchase of, from, 275
oil shipments to Vladivostok, 219
objection of Japan to, 219
rapprochement with, 176
Stalin's interpretation of coalition with Great Britain and U. S., 276
Welles-Oumansky conversations, Aug. 1940, 216–7
United States-Canadian Permanent Joint Board on Defense, 264
U. S. Maritime Commission:
British shipping services to Pacific taken over by, 270

V

Vancouver, air base of, 250
Versailles, Treaty of, 46, 105
Vichy Government. *See* France.
Vinson-Trammell Acts, 207
Vladivostok:
American consulate-general reopened at, 216
oil shipments to, by U. S., 219

W

Wakasugi, Kaname, 216
Wake Island, 208–9, 268
Wang Ch'ing-wei:
attempts to reach settlement with Japan, 84

Wang Ch'ing-wei—*Continued*
  government at Nanking:
    agreement with French concession, Nov. 7, 1940, 144
    joint declaration with Japan and "Manchoukuo," Nov. 30, 1940, 122
    recognition of:
      British refusal, 239
      Jul. 1, 1941, by Germany, Italy, Spain, Rumania, "Slovakia" and "Croatia," 122
      Soviet refusal, 258
      U. S. refusal, 215
  Reorganized Govt. in occupied China, role in, 119
  undertaking by Chiang K'ai-shek to settle "Manchoukuo" question, statement on, 82
Wang Ch'ung-hui, 94, 258
Wanping, 66
War, definition of, 65
War, psychological factors in causes of, 279
Washington Conference on Limitation of Naval Armament, 42–4
Weihaiwei, 33, 44
Welles, Sumner:
  conversations with Soviet Ambassador, 216–7
  press conference statement on occupation of French Indo-China by Japan, 217
Western Extra-Settlement Roads, 137, 141
White slavery, 290
Wilson, Pres., policy toward loans to China, 37
Wong, W. H., 95
Wu Pei-fu, General, 118

Y

Yamagata, Marshal, 20
Yangtze River basin:
  British influence in, 33
  evacuation of civilians, 71
Yangtze River, shipping on, 234–5
Yasuda, 20
"Yellow Peril," 200
Yoshizawa, Kenkichi, 189
Yuan Shih-k'ai, General, 38, 57
Yukio, Ozaki, 153
Yunnan, French influence in, 33

Z

Zaibatsu, 20